Representing 'Race'

Representing 'Race'

Racisms, Ethnicities and Media

John Downing and Charles Husband

SAGE Publications
London ● Thousand Oaks ● New Delhi

SAGE Publications Ltd
1 Oliver's Yard
55 City Road
London EC1Y 1SP

SAGE Publications Inc.
2455 Teller Road
Thousand Oaks, California 91320

SAGE Publications India Pvt Ltd
B-42, Panchsheel Enclave
Post Box 4109
New Delhi 110 017

British Library Cataloguing in Publication data

A catalogue record for this book is available
from the British Library

ISBN 0-7619-6911-X
ISBN 0-7619-6912-8 (pbk)

Library of Congress Control Number available

Typeset by C&M Digitals (P) Ltd., Chennai, India
Printed in Great Britain by Athenaeum Press, Gateshead

To Barbara Husband, my essential colleague
and co-author of my life.
[CH]

To Ash Corea, *the fire and the rose*, and to the necessary
spirit, courage and commitment of the next generation
of media-makers.
[JD]

Contents

Acknowledgements   viii

Preface   ix

1   'Race' and Ethnicity: Definitions and Issues   1

2   Research on Racism, Ethnicity and Media   25

3   Racism and the Media of the Extremist Right   60

4   Violence, 'Race' and Media: Comparative Perspectives   86

5   The Distinctive Challenge of Indigeneity   122

6   Media Monitoring and Codes of Practice   145

7   Pressurizing the Media Industry:
Achievements and Limitations   160

8   Communities of Practice and the
Cultures of Media Production   194

9   The Multi-Ethnic Public Sphere and
Differentiated Citizenship   175

References   219

Index   239

Acknowledgements

In writing a text like this you are inevitably aware of all the very many contributions, concrete and intentional as well as elusive and serendipitous, that very many colleagues and friends have made to its production. It is always invidious to single out some for explicit mention whilst failing to similarly identify others. However, in this case there are two colleagues and friends whose support and input unequivocally demands recognition.

In writing Chapter 5, *The Distinctive Challenge of Indigeneity*, Dr Lia Markelin, who was the Doctoral Research Fellow on the University of Bradford Ethnicity and Social Policy Research Unit's Sami Media Project, has been a source of specific advice and invaluable generic support. Lia's personal and scholarly skills were central to the success of that project and the insights generated through it have been central to the production of this chapter and her continued friendship and support is invaluable. Additionally, both Lia and I would wish to record our thanks to the very many persons in Sami media and political life whose generosity, openness and commitment made that research both possible and so rewarding.

Equally, in writing Chapter 6, *Media Monitoring and Codes of Practice*, I am deeply indebted to my colleague and friend Yunis Alam. This chapter draws directly upon our work 'Codes of Practice and Media Performance: a Systems Approach', which was an element of a larger EU funded project entitled *Tuning in to Diversity*. Not everyone is fortunate enough to have a Yunis in their life. For his sharp-edged, untrammelled and creative stimulation, I remain perpetually grateful. His warmth, humour and humanity are an ever present antidote to some of the persistent irritations of contemporary academic life.

As a representative of the elusive and serendipitous support I have enjoyed and savored I would like to acknowledge my gratitude to the staff group and many students of the *European Doctoral Programme on Migration, Diversity and Identities*, of which I have had the privilege of being Director for the past four years. This demonstration of the viability and rewards of interdisciplinary international collaboration has been in equal parts hugely demanding and profoundly enriching. Something of the style and ambitions of this Programme are invested in this text.

And, of course, 'J.D.' – lifelong friend, sounding board and too infrequent collaborator.

Charles Husband

My deep thanks indeed, first and foremost, to the many, many people of colour who over my life have thought it worthwhile to try to make me wiser on these issues; at their head the Right Reverend Dr Sir Wilfred and Lady Ina Wood. I hope that my contribution to this book echoes at least some of their efforts. Listing them all by name would fill a *real* Book of Life. Gratitude as well to my former students, and faculty and staff friends at the University of Texas, and before that at Hunter College (New York), at Greenwich University (London) – and now in the College of Mass Communication and Media Arts at Southern Illinois University, Carbondale.

I must log my tremendous appreciation of Julia Hall at Sage, editor *extraordinaire*, whose fierce commitment to this project weathered its lengthy production, and of her ever-supportive colleague Jamilah Ahmed. Fabienne Pedroletti ferreted out a dismayingly large stock of oversights, but if Barbara Steele had not, unpaid, thrashed the manuscript into shape first, Sage would rightly have returned it to its senders. As for Charlie Husband, if you don't like perspicacity, wit, self-mockery and a consuming passion for practicable roads to social justice – stay away from him.

John Downing

Preface

The political and ethical correlates of research in this sphere

We have been struck for well over thirty years now, in both the USA and the UK, and via research evidence from still other nations, by the continuing failures on the part of mainstream media, globally, to fulfill their potential to inform, enlighten, question, imagine and explain in this often troubled and dangerous field of ethnic diversity in the contemporary world. These potentials could be and urgently need to be realized in entertainment as well as news, in sports coverage as well as popular music, in computer games as well as trade magazines and textbooks. But, mostly, this does not happen, or only in badly tarnished forms.

Published research on this subject grew very substantially indeed over the 1990s, a sharp difference from the 1970s and 1980s when the topic drew remarkably little scholarly attention from sociologists, anthropologists, political scientists or even media analysts. After a long gap following the very early work of Robert Park (1970 [1922]) on the USA's immigrant press,[1] British researchers[2] were among the first in the field, but by even as late as 1990 it was still difficult to fill a short shelf with book-length publications on the topic from all countries combined. The bulk of what has become available since, stretching over a number of shelves, has come from the USA, but there is a continuing contribution from Britain, together with a rise in research from other nations such as the Netherlands, France, Australia and Canada.[3] There is also a particularly welcome growth in work from scholars of color.[4]

Why this sudden interest, especially in the USA? A necessary element in the equation is no doubt the expansion of communication technologies and the corresponding growth of media studies,[5] but to provide a sufficient explanation we need to look further.

Migration, as a major and ongoing international phenomenon, forced public attention to ethnicity and 'race' in general from the 1970s onwards. In Western Europe it took a generation for the reality to percolate that migrant workers and their families had arrived to stay. In the USA, 1965's immigration law changes and continuing economic expansion jointly stimulated the arrival of new Asian and Latin American migrant workers, unprecedented in number since the massive industrialization of 1880–1920. They in turn were pivotal to sustained economic growth thereafter.[6]

Subsequently, links between media representation of African, Asian, Latin American and Middle Eastern nations and of their emigrants within metropolitan countries, summoned the attention of some more globally focused scholars.[7] So did media discourses in the 1990s, glibly projecting 'ethnicity' as the cause of brutal civil wars in Bosnia, Rwanda and Chechnya.[8]

Other factors made themselves felt as well. However, much as governments, corporate leaders and majority populations persist in trying to sweep them under the rug, the unresolved issues of institutional racism and the pervasive tenacity of racist discourses consistently attract the attention of some of the more alert and responsive among academic researchers. Ever since the 1950s civil rights confrontations, aspects of 'race' relations, however distortedly, have been common in the US national news. Intermittent urban explosions acted via their media coverage – to quote Dr Martin Luther King – as 'the voice of the unheard.'

Examples come from the USA and beyond. As well as the tumults such as those in Los Angeles following the Rodney King assault verdict in April 1992, and the four days of rioting against police violence in Cincinnati, Ohio, in 2001, these include the 32 British cities in which violent street protests took place in 1981, the 1990 explosion of migrant workers' rage in Vaulx-en-Velin, France, and the Asian riots in Bradford, England, in 2001. The repeated success of neo-Nazi and authoritarian populist movements in Europe, local pogroms against migrant workers and Roma communities (e.g. eastern Germany and the Czech Republic during the 1990s, southern Spain in 2000), issues raised by refugee migration, the question of indigenous peoples' demands brought to the surface by the Zapatista movement in Mexico and by Aboriginal and Maori movements in Canada, Australia and New Zealand, the victory for majority rule in South Africa, the two *intifadas* against the Israeli government's illegal occupation of Palestinian soil, all featured from time to time across the world's media.

However, it would be Pollyanna-like to assume that the sources of academic interest in media coverage of 'race' and ethnicity were solely intellectual alertness and responsiveness to these expressions of injustice and protest. Intellectual alertness does not automatically include any commitment at all to working for 'racial' and ethnic equity. State- and corporate-sponsored research have indeed often been designed precisely to enable the sting of protest to be drawn, but in no way to attack the roots of racism. Ethnicity may simply offer a tempting array of the diverse and exotic to academics hunting for something fresh to focus on for their dissertations and research grant proposals. Such 'research opportunities' may seem almost inexhaustible within the so-called 'gorgeous mosaic' of most metropolitan nations.

We only need observe how sadly feminist research has sometimes lost its original impetus through getting enmeshed in the dead ends of academic culture, to see how easily research on ethnic and 'racial' issues, including their media representation, may go down exactly the same dismal path. Therefore research on this subject that merely seeks to feed a career or fill pages is much more likely – if it has any impact at all – to contribute to perpetuating racism and ethnic discrimination than to help overcome them. Our position is, unequivocally, that the prime motive in framing research on 'race' and/or ethnicity needs to be to contribute to a just and thus – indeed *only* thus – peaceful and stimulating society. Our aim should be to critique media failures and outrages tellingly, not sloppily, and to help reframe media practice.

We do not propose these principles as an excuse for rhetorically virtuous but clumsy research design. We do not imagine for a second that there is a single shining path to good media coverage that basic principle alone will uncover, nor do we suppose that good media coverage, however it might be defined, will rapidly *by itself* unlock the door to 'racial' justice: structures of privilege do not just melt on exposure to light. Nor can we escape the fact that a number of those whose research work is used to underpin policies hostile to communities of color have claimed that they are setting the scene for a truly non-racist society, that they are actually the only non-racists or anti-racists in the field.[9] The painless claim to be non-racist or even anti-racist guarantees neither solid research nor the absence of racism, whether in intent or effect.

To sum up so far: for over a decade now, media representations of political upsurges and social conflicts have sparked substantial research interest in media, racism and ethnicity. In and of itself that does not render the results insightful, the objectives laudable, or the methods adequate. Neither academic nor government sponsorship, nor goodwill, offer any such guarantee.

We plan to propose and partially illustrate significant and often under-explored directions for research in this centrally important sphere. Our best reward for writing this book will be to find it rapidly overtaken by committed and searching scholarship, aimed at fomenting an exciting and imaginative media revolution that engages citizens of every background.

Notes

1 Park's research was funded by the US government following the USA's 1917 entry into World War I because of anxiety concerning the national loyalties of the many new European migrant worker communities which had formed over the previous thirty years.

2 Cf. Hartmann, Husband and Clark, 1974; Hartmann and Husband, 1974; Husband, 1975; Critcher et al., 1977; Hall et al., 1978; Downing, 1980.

3 In developing this manuscript we have for some time used the 'working title' *Representing 'Race'*, and now that it is complete we feel that this title, with the sub-title, very accurately indicates the focus of our work. We are aware that there is a prior text by Robert Ferguson (1998) with the same title. The existence of such texts confirms to us the importance and ongoing topicality of this issue and we hope that those authors who have preceded this text will understand our wish to keep this title.

4 E.g. Daniel Bernardi, Venise Berry, Jacqueline Bobo, Arlene Dávila, Oscar Gandy, Herman Gray, Ed Gnerrero, Darrell Hamamoto, Darnell Hunt, Jacquelyn Kilpatrick, Robert Lee, Lisa Lowe, Robin Means Coleman, Chon Noriega, Charles Ramírez-Berg, América Rodríguez, Otta Santa Ana, Beretta Smith-Shomade, Linda Steet, Angharad Valdivia, Craig Watkins.

5 It may be that the difference between the earlier expression of research interest in media and 'race' in Britain than in the USA had its source partly in academic fashions. That is, the dominant assumption in the US academy throughout the 60s and 70s was that media had little or no social impact, as per Joseph Klapper's influential *The Effects of Mass Communication* (1960). Conversely in Britain, the two most active centers for media and cultural research (the Centre for Mass Communication Research at Leicester University and the Centre for Contemporary Cultural Studies at Birmingham University), whatever their differences in approach, were populated by people mostly skeptical of American empiricist sociology and broadly committed to an anti-racist agenda. Meanwhile the upsurge in racist sentiment and action catalyzed by speeches from 1968 onwards by a British Conservative Party politician, Enoch Powell, speeches given tremendous media coverage in part because of Powell's own detailed knowledge of journalistic routines, helped to focus attention on these issues (Smithies and Fiddick, 1969; Reeves, 1983).

6 Similar labor migration waves were evident in Saudi Arabia and the Gulf States, in India, China, Australia, Brazil, Mexico, Egypt, Nigeria, South Africa and many other places, but media studies as an academic specialization was only widely developed outside the USA and Britain in Australia, Canada, Mexico and Brazil, and in the two latter nations the refusal to acknowledge the force of 'racial' and ethnic divisions was only beginning to be challenged during the 1990s (Araújo, 2000; Fernández and Paxman, 2000).

7 E.g. Johnson (1980), Said (1980/1997), Dorfman (1983), Shaheen (1984).

8 Cf. Allen and Seaton (1999). Oddly, the decades-long repression in Guatemala, where anti-Maya racism really was a major dimension, never made the headlines in the same way.

9 Cf. Charles Murray and Herrnstein, *The Bell Curve*; Dinesh D'Souza; Thomas Sowell; Thernstrom and Thernstrom.

1 'Race' and Ethnicity: Definitions and Issues

Recognizing difference has become a central concern of contemporary societies. The processes of globalization, and the national restructuring and international realignment of economies, are destabilizing nation states. Nation building is a fraught, contemporary process in the twenty-six countries of the ex-Soviet Union and ex-Yugoslavia (Brubaker, 1996). Extra-national economic arrangements, whether in the case of the European Union, the ASEAN states or the North American Free Trade Association have sensitized citizens of member states in relation to the integrity of their political sovereignty and the viability of their national cultures. Global flows of economic migrants and asylum seekers (Castles and Miller, 1993) have added to the demographic diversity of countries in every continent. And, the politicization of gender, sexual preference, age and disability has provided not only a further mechanism for making identities salient and contested, it has also created niche markets that are targeted and exploited by commercial enterprises. Identities are not simply non-problematic motors of stable interaction; rather, they are the highly charged frameworks through which contemporary life is actively negotiated.[1]

In this book we will be charting the dynamics of two modes of identity construction, 'race' and ethnicity, and exploring their interaction with the mass media. Racism is a poisonous ideology and a destructive practice. It is predominantly anathematized by states, politicians and populations as a stain on civilized society. And yet, it is also virtually endemic. The discourses which vilify racism are more than amply countered by the many other discourses through which racism is made invisible, normative and even virtuous. Consequently, one of the ambitions of this chapter is to explicitly explore the historical bases and current manifestations of racism.

If racism is a formally unacceptable means of defining and constituting collective identities, then we may also conclude that ethnicity is currently a ubiquitous and valued form of group formation. In developed Western societies multi-culturalism has emerged as a necessary political negotiation of ethnic diversity in nation states. Throughout the world collectivities of people meld their shared interests and claim their common rights through the language of ethnicity (Torres et al., 1999, Shapiro and

Kymlicka, 1997). International legal instruments recognize the legitimacy of ethnic identities.

It is troubling, therefore, that racism and ethnicity so easily interact in the day-to-day practices of identity formation. The politics of ethnicity become vulnerable to the discourses of racism, and the ideology of 'race' can be effectively disguised and embedded in the language of ethnicity. Consequently, it is important that we are all able to develop a competence in distinguishing one from the other.

'Race'

The power of 'race' as a way of comprehending human diversity lies essentially in our ease with categorization. Cognitive psychology is fascinated by the human capacity to bring meaning to the world. Faced with the 'blooming, buzzing, confusion' of the physical world we learn to process stimuli and, amongst other things, to reduce continuous dimensions into bi-polar categories, for example, 'length' or 'brightness', to distinct categories defined by bi-polar extremes: long–short, dark–light. This conceptual original sin enables us to process data but at some cost to our perceptual precision. If categorization can introduce degrees of distortion into the neutral dimensions of the physical world, how much more significant then may be the distortions of perception generated when the social categories we employ are additionally suffused with accretions of feeling and moral worth. Social psychology, by exploring identity formation and inter-group perception, has gone a long way to revealing just how powerful the affective and ego-enhancing dynamics of social categorization are. (Capozza and Brown, 2000).

'Race' as a constructed social category derives its power partially from the social psychological dynamics of social-categorization *per se*, but also from the powerful taken-for-granted legitimacy which race categories have acquired in their historical formulation. One crucial element in the success of race as an ideology has been this taken-for-granted reasonableness of employing racial categories. 'Race' has become a social fact: a self-evident characteristic of human identity and character.

Consequently, it is therefore essential to register explicitly the non-scientific basis of race as a social category. In the words of Banton and Harwood:

> As a way of categorising people, race is based upon a delusion because popular ideas about racial classification lack scientific validity and are moulded by political pressures rather than by the evidence from biology. (1975: 8)

The arbitrary and perverse formulation of racial categories is underscored by Mason (1986) who, in reviewing historical constructions of racial categories, notes the very wide range that has existed in defining the number and type of races. The idea of 'race' has been extensively studied and any understanding of the contemporary meaning and usage of race requires an understanding of its historical emergence and development. Race categories and the meanings attached to them are not static. Both the substantive content of racial stereotypes and the ideas which legitimate them vary over time.

One example from 1860 may usefully illustrate the point, as a traveler records his experience of a different people:

> But I am haunted by the human chimpanzees I saw along that hundred miles of horrible country. I don't believe they are our fault. I believe there are not only many more of them than of old, but that they are happier, better, more comfortably fed and lodged under our rule than they ever were. But to see white chimpanzees is dreadful; if they were black, one would not feel it so much, but their skins, except where tanned by exposure, are as white as ours. (cited in Curtis, 1968: 84)

Hopefully, we can agree that this is a gloriously unambiguous piece of racist observation and it contains classic elements of 'race' thinking, namely a positioning of the self as superior, an accounting of the relationship between self and 'the other', and an explicit reference to color as a key marker of difference. However, the fact that this statement was from Charles Kingsley, distinguished English author, writing to his wife about his visit to Ireland, also usefully reminds us that racism is not necessarily about color. Nor, despite the assertions of some, is racism a unique perversion of white Europeans. Weimer's (1996) account of Japanese racism is but one indicative instance of the adaptability of race thinking to different histories and cultures. And Kingsley's rabid anti-Irish sentiment, infused with the conventional language of the day, wherein the Celtic 'blood' of the Irish and the Saxon 'blood' of the English determined their contrasting character would be unlikely to be employed in contemporary English society. Anti-Irish sentiment has not vanished, but its mode of expression and theorization has changed. Race imagery and race theory have a degree of autonomy, one from the other, and both are capable of change; at different rates, at different times and for different reasons.

Before moving on to note how structures of racial discourse can and have changed over time, it is useful to reflect upon the basic consequences of employing race as real in our thinking. Jacques Barzun, in a book first published in 1937, succinctly laid down the core characteristics of race thinking:

> In short, race-thinking is a habit. It is not confined to the anthropologists and ethnologists, the historians and publicists who make up systems or preach discrimination; race-thinking occurs whenever someone, in a

casual or considered remark, implies the truth of any of the following propositions:

1. That mankind is divided into unchanging natural types, recognizable by physical features, which are transmitted 'through the blood' and that permit distinctions to be made between 'pure' and 'mixed' races.
2. That the mental and moral behaviour of human beings can be related to physical structure, and that knowledge of the structure or of the racial label which denotes it provides a satisfactory account of the behaviour.
3. That individual personality, ideas and capacities, as well as national culture, politics, and morals, are the products of social entities variously termed race, nation, class, family, whose causative force is clear without further definition or inquiry into the connection between the group and the spiritual 'product'.

These three types of race-thinking naturally merge into one another. Few writers limit themselves to any one type and mankind at large uses all three with equal readiness according to the occasion. The formal rejection of the fallacy in one guise does not protect against its other guises. (1965 [1937]): 12–14)

What Barzun offers us in his description of race thinking is a graphic account of the mental economy of employing 'race' as a descriptive and explanatory concept. Great sweeps of human variation can be reduced to one supposedly stable property of an individual; their 'race'. Awesomely complex social relations can be 'explained' by deploying the potent theory of race. Clearly, one reason for the resilience of race thinking is its utility. Barzun's discussion of race thinking underscores a critical insight that must be carried through the subsequent analyses in this text; namely, that *racism starts with the use of race categories.* Yet another way of emphasizing this same principle is to be found in the concept of *racialization*, which Omi and Winant define as: 'the extension of racial meaning to a previous racially unclassified relationships, social practice or group … it is an ideological process, an historically specific one' (1986: 64).

In coming to grips with this concept of racialization it is important to have a sense of the origin and reproduction of the 'racial meanings' that are at the core of the process. This is not some ad hoc pragmatic linguistic strategy which draws upon a definite body of thought that happens to be present in the collective discourse. As the quote above notes, racialization is a historically specific ideological process. Racial meanings have been evolved through specific historical circumstances of human relations and are currently embellished and deployed within particular socio-economic circumstances. Something of the dynamic and emergent nature of racial meanings is encapsulated in Winant's (1994) discussion of racial formation as a hegemonic process. In this frame 'race', along with other comparable concepts such as gender and class, is most definitely seen as being constructed in a contested struggle for power in a society shaped by stable social differentiation and inequality. Thus:

> Such concepts [as race] are essentially metaphors for institutionalized social relationships that combine processes of exploitation and domination, on the one hand, with processes of subjection and representation, that is, with struggles over meaning and identity, on the other. (1994: 113)

Illuminating the processes which are integral to such struggles over meaning and identity is a core ambition of this book. As the chapters successively expand this process, the complexity of racialization will be cumulatively revealed, and the necessity of a sophisticated interdisciplinary understanding of the phenomenon will be underscored.

In identifying the role of the media in the hegemonic racialization of social relations the news media are self-evidently an appropriate place from which to start. For it is precisely in the definition of the situation offered by news media that a racialization of events may be transmitted more or less uncritically to audiences (Hartmann and Husband, 1974; van Dijk, 1991, 1993). Employing 'race' as real, whether in news media or entertainment, is to participate in racialization: it is a reproduction of 'race' thinking.

One of the challenges to media analysis is to sustain an appropriate sophistication in tracking the penetration of race thinking into media institutions and media products. This process is facilitated by the extensive literature which has explored the nature of racism and its expression in institutional and communicative processes. It is possible to approach an exploration of racism through a systematic analysis of the race categories in circulation and the stereotypical attributes attached to members of each 'race'. This process reveals the content of 'race' thinking and any perusal of the research literature will reveal that the stereotypes associated with members of specific 'races' are quite capable of change over time. If the cognitive function of race thinking is to generate plausible accounts of reality that reflect positively on the identity of those employing it, then racial stereotypes must have plausibility. They must be able to account for the observed world.

The elements employed in constructing a racialized world view have no need to meet the requirements of formal logic: they must merely be psychologically coherent. Thus, the array of elements that constitute the substantive content of racial stereotypes can operate with a degree of relative independence one from the other. This is facilitated by the selective deployment of different elements at different times. Thus, immigrants may simultaneously be 'taking our jobs' and 'living off state social support'. Essed (1991) and Wetherall and Potter (1992) have illustrated the wonderful casuistry of racist thought in everyday speech and thought. Additionally, the psycho-logic of racist thought is shaped by self-interest sustained through the selective perception of each individual. Ego-involved judgement is very frequently egocentric, partial and not subject to critical reflection. The psychological literature on stereotyping persuasively suggests that inter-group cognition is inherently biased (Brown, 1995). Consequently, any attempt to map the elements of racist stereotypes in media content must be subtle and open to the complexity of the phenomenon. (This will be developed elsewhere in our discussion of content and discourse analyses.)

A successful exposure of the elements of racial stereotyping within the media will necessarily only accomplish one key task in illuminating the nature of racism. The attributions made to others through racial stereotyping have their effect because they are credible, not because they are true. The legitimacy of these attributions is found in the ideology of race itself: in the system of beliefs which underpin the existence and mode of reproduction of 'race'. Thus, ideas regarding the inferiority of the Black African have persisted for centuries, but the arguments which have legitimated these beliefs have changed over time. As Jordan (1969) so powerfully illustrated, in the seventeenth and eighteenth centuries belief in African inferiority was supported by a particularly creative piece of Christian exegesis. The African's lowly station was a consequence of God's judgement.

In a world where Christianity had a ubiquity and an acceptance it no longer enjoys in Europe, this provided a powerful legitimacy for race thinking. However, the continuation of these racial stereotypes survived the shifting credence given to Christian epistemology. With the nineteenth-century ascendancy of the physical sciences as an explanatory system that had palpably revolutionized the known world, so too the 'realities' of race became amenable to scientific justification. Thus, social Darwinism provided a new, and credible, theorization of the established 'social facts' of racial variation. And throughout the latter half of the twentieth century science continued to provide a flow of information to the lay public, derived from academic production, that has helped to sustain the acceptability of race. From Eysenck's (1971) *'Race', Intelligence and Education*, through to *The Bell Curve*, (see Fraser, 1995) the race and intelligence debate has continued to reify both race and intelligence. Belief in the biological determination of human characteristics remains widespread and normalizes the claims of race thinking.[2]

For those who would track the epistemological underpinnings of contemporary racism, the selective abuse of the quiet certitudes of the biological sciences are but one of the explanatory systems that must be monitored. We have seen in the last two decades a new culturalist determinism. Drawing upon the ideas of the selfish gene and its variants, sociobiology has provided a mechanism for asserting the 'naturalness' of in-group preference. Linked to a strong assertion of the non-negotiability of in-group cultures and their power to reproduce collective identities, there is now a sophisticated hybrid theorization of race: 'the New Racism' (Barker, 1981). The rigidity and inevitability of racial boundaries and the reproduction of the characteristics of distinct races is now capable of being theorized through an apparently cultural determinism.

The metamorphosis of race thinking into systems of argument that have a paradigmatic quality has been extensively commented upon. In the USA distinctions have been made between *symbolic racism* (McConahy, 1986) and *enlightened racism* (Jhally and Lewis, 1992). Symbolic racism has been characterized as being built around a general animosity of White Americans toward African Americans. This is complemented by a resistance to Black political demands and an assertion that racial discrimination is a thing of the past. This belief in the demise of racial discrimination is also found in enlightened racism where it provides the assumptive framework to protect the liberal self-image and support for equal rights, whilst at the same time blaming minority ethnic Americans for failing to prosper in democratic America. This blaming the victim rationale had a fulsome previous life in relation to the 'culture of poverty' (Valentine, 1968). It had the great virtue of allowing for the recognition of extensive inequalities between categories of people whilst deflecting any responsibility for this reality. Useful extended accounts of the varieties of race ideology and their articulation with the practices and products of the mass media have been provided by Ferguson (1999) and Gandy (1998).

For our purposes here the simultaneous existence of different epistemologies of 'race' renders the observable realities of racism complex, and often subtly multi-layered. A good illustration of this reality is to be found in the concept of *discursive de-racialization*. Reeves defines this as: 'persons speak purposely to their audience about racial matters, while avoiding the overt deployment of racial descriptions, evaluations and prescriptions' (1983: 4). For example, in the British context the word 'immigrant' has a long history of having a racialized significance (Hartmann and Husband, 1974). And the variant, 'illegal immigrant', very strongly conveys a routinized sense of alien threat in which 'the other' is seen as culturally threatening. 'Race' inhabits a ubiquitous connotative presence within the British political debate around immigration (Philo and Beattie, 1999).

At its simplest, discursive de-racialization points to the poly-semic creativity of human communication. In the pragmatics of language use meanings can be embedded in linked signifiers that allow for the exchange of shared meanings in the absence of an explicit denotative lexicon. Visual codes and iconography can similarly provide the means of cosmetically erasing explicit racist imagery, whilst still effectively transmitting racist messages.[3] (The issue of representation will be developed further in the next chapter.)

The lesson here is that the task of tracing the racial content of mass media production is not necessarily a simple process. The explicit expression of racist sentiment to be found in some instances of talk radio, and in the propaganda of some state media, is not by any means the norm. Consequently, the expanding techniques of deconstruction have proved a necessary but contentious tool of media analysis. As we will elaborate more fully in Chapter 2, the simple logics of early media content analysis have been necessarily superceded by post-colonial analyses and a variety of approaches to discourse analysis.

Unfortunately, the more subtle (or abstruse) the method of analysis, the more readily are the arguments drawn from it dismissed by those who regard the pursuit of racist discourse as a neurotic activity of 'politically correct' extreme malcontents.[4] As human rights movements on a global scale have made explicit racism more universally condemned, so too have racist discourses become more sophisticated. Not only has the strident directness of racist politics been significantly moderated in many contexts by the use of discursive alternatives, but the subtle framing of the racist assertion has shown its potential for legitimating the utterance of xenophobic and discriminatory arguments. Thus, in the British context, Margaret Thatcher's invocation of the 'genuine fears' of the majority population that their culture might be 'swamped' provided a homely reasonableness to the anti-immigrant politics of her regime. It linked the neo-Conservative concerns with nation and tradition to the naturalness of in-group preference. Socio-biology and evolutionary psychology have provided supportive respectability to such notions of self-interest rooted in 'human nature' (Gordon and Klug, 1986; Husband, 1994). Set against the benchmark of Nazi rhetoric or the more contemporary extremism of the language of attack in Serbia or Rwanda, this type of discourse seems comparatively innocuous, that is except to those who are the target of its venom. Hence any academic revelation of the lineaments of contemporary racist discourse requires a degree of political sophistication from those who are the intended audience for these findings. Unfortunately, the political sensitivities found in contemporary societies are routinely xenophobic and unimaginative in their approach to ethnic diversity.

Consequently, any attempt to unmask the racist content of the mass media is political. It necessarily begins from a series of assertions that are not routinely consistent with the dominant political values, and particularly the practice, of most nation states.

- It starts from an assertion that 'races' are a social construction.
- It asserts the common worth of all human beings.
- It rejects a necessary linkage of racism with an extremist (neo-Nazi or KKK) minority – racism may be inherent in the taken-for-granted common sense of everyday life.
- It underscores the way racial myths of a country's origin and uniqueness are often at the heart of its self-understanding.

- It does not presume a need to reveal the presence of intent in order to identify a communication as racist.
- It asserts that everyone, including the victims of racism, are capable of racism.

Revealing racism within the discourses of the mass media is a provocative activity.

Mass Media as Institutions: an Initial Foray

Whilst a knowledge of the variety of manifestations of racism may facilitate an examination of racism within the output of the mass media, this would not exhaust the research task. Race thinking also has a behavioral expression in racial discrimination. As institutions, the mass media provide an organizational framework within which individuals interact in the context of set roles and established power hierarchies. Consequently, the mass media provide a venue within which individuals' life opportunities may be constrained by the practical expression of racial ideologies in the form of racial discrimination. The existence of racial discrimination amongst the workforce of the mass media industries has been an historical reality and is a continuing issue (Husband, 1994a; Cottle, 1997; Gandy, 1998).

Again, any attempt to reveal the current prevalence of racial discrimination within the media industries requires a foundational understanding of the nature of racial discrimination *per se*. It is appropriate to identify two approaches to understanding racial discrimination and to indicate the particular practical and political correlates of each. One account has its roots in social psychology and focuses upon the dynamics of *prejudice*, whilst the other is based in organizational analysis and addresses *institutional racism*.

Going back to Gordon Allport's extraordinarily perceptive *The Nature of Prejudice* (1954), there is a long and continuous vein of research within social psychology which has addressed the individual psychological dynamics of out-group hostility and discrimination (Brown, 1995). In Allport's words: 'Ethnic prejudice is an antipathy based upon a faulty and inflexible generalisation. It may be felt or expressed. It may be directed toward a group as a whole, or toward an individual because he is a member of that group' (Allport, 1954: 10). In essence, this is presented as an irrational hostility supported by strongly held stereotypes. It is a form of self-sustaining cognitive strategy:

- Because we avoid those we dislike and are consequently unlikely to disprove our stereotypes.
- We sustain our stereotypes through selective perception.

- When we are forced to admit that someone does not fit the stereotype we do not correct the stereotype. Rather, in Allport's words, we 'fence them off'. They are the exceptions that prove the rule.

When prejudices are widely shared, as part of a common culture, they can be very resilient and difficult to eradicate. Such prejudices become racist when race thinking and racial ideologies are drawn upon to provide the content of the stereotype and to legitimate the reasonableness of the hostility. The psychological dynamic at the heart of accounts of prejudice whether neo-Freudian (Adorno et al., 1950; Young-Bruehl, 1996) or based on contemporary social identity theory (Capozza and Brown, 2000), results in prejudice being seen as essentially the property of an individual. Consequently, both in its origin in the social sciences and in the ways that it has been co-opted by policy-makers, prejudice has proved to be a very conservative conceptual tool.

Where discrimination is explained as a product of prejudice then it can be seen as a more or less human foible: an individual pathology which must be expected in some proportion of all societies. Such an account provides the apparently rational basis for the 'rotten apple theory' of discrimination. The argument runs that since all institutions recruit from the general population they will have their inevitable share of rotten apples. Such a psychological account of prejudice all too easily leaves the basis of discrimination resting upon the flawed nature of individuals. It distracts attention from those political processes that seek to promote and exploit hatred of the stranger. It focuses attention away from those ideologies and institutional structures which facilitate or promote discrimination. Thus, the rhetoric of prejudice provides an account of discrimination that is highly consistent with a belief in the essential equity and openness of society which characterizes Western European social democracies. Accounting for discrimination in terms of individual prejudice leaves the essential integrity of the social order, and its institutions, intact and unchallenged.[5]

Looking at discrimination through the prism of institutional discrimination produces a very different analytical dynamic. This approach does not say that individually prejudiced people do not exist. Indeed they do, and their malevolent presence can be disruptive within any organization; their purposeful malice can be a daily assault upon their unfortunate victims. However, the essence of institutional discrimination is to demonstrate the unpalatable truth that even 'nice' people can be racist. Through adopting a systems approach to the operation of an organization, the strategy of revealing institutional discrimination seeks to demonstrate how the routine and mundane activities of an organization can reproduce inequality. A major British inquiry into institutional racism within the Metropolitan Police Service in London defined *institutional racism* as:

> The collective failure of an organisation to provide an appropriate and professional service to people because of their colour, culture or ethnic origin. It can be seen or detected in processes, attitudes and behaviour which amount to discrimination through unwitting prejudice, ignorance, thoughtlessness and racist stereotyping which disadvantage minority ethnic people. (Stephen Lawrence Report, 1999)

Thus, in institutional discrimination the focus is upon the routine practices of the organization and their normalization within the workplace culture. Institutional racism begins to enter into an organization when the institutional routines reflect the interests of only one dominant group. Importantly, these discriminatory routines remain undetected and unchallenged because of consensual racism. Thus, institutional racism can be represented as:

$$\text{Institutional Racism} = \begin{array}{c} \text{routine institutional practices} \\ \text{and structures} \\ + \\ \text{made unproblematic by routine} \\ \text{unreflecting race thinking} \end{array}$$

Access into media professions, processes of retention and promotion, and the forces determining the dominant workplace culture are research targets in pursuing this perspective regarding the functioning of the media in multi-ethnic societies. Locating the presence of race thinking and racial ideologies is crucial to the identification of institutional racism. There are many other levers of discrimination, including gender, age, sexual orientation and religious affiliation. The interaction of these identities and their attendant ideologies and practices further complicates our understanding of the nature of racisms. Ideologies of oppression feed into and off each other and generate more power than a single factor could summon up (Guillaumin, 1995; Back and Solomos, 2000).

Racial dynamics cannot be assumed. There is a strong debate around the casual and inappropriate invocation of the language of institutional racism (see for example, Miles, 1989) and it remains an ever-present requirement to demonstrate the dynamic interaction of racial ideologies and institutional practices. As Williams (1985) pointed out in an early article that explicitly addressed the contribution of Carmichael and Hamilton (1967) to the analysis of institutional racism, not all forms of racial discrimination are supported by racial discourse, and racial discourse is not inevitably accompanied by racial discrimination. If we follow Winant's approach of seeing racial formation as being a hegemonic process, then we must expect to map the complexity of discourses and practices that in combination give continuing vitality to racism in the contemporary world. Thus, for example, matters become complicated when we acknowledge that racially discriminatory processes may be legitimated by non-racial ideologies. For example, professional identities and ideologies normalize the way things are. Socialization into a profession is intended to ensure that those inhabiting it will accept the existing values and structures as normal. Thus, for example, professional 'communities of practice' (Lesser et al., 2000) make all staff familiar with hierarchies of power.[6] Whether in the newsroom, or in making 'good' film, there are people with authority, there are proper procedures for getting things done, accepted criteria of excellence, and shared routines for cooling conflict without confronting these power structures. As we shall see in Chapter 6, the urge and requirement 'to be professional' is one of the routes into unthinking ethnocentrism and racial discrimination.

'Race' then, whilst being biologically and genetically irrelevant, is a social fact. Though a scientifically spurious way of differentiating between human beings, it is real enough in its consequences. As a social construct race is dynamic and adaptive to its environment. The stereotypical content of racial attributions is palpably capable of altering in order to retain a credible reflection of changing social relations. The systems of thought that provide the framing legitimacy for these beliefs have also a demonstrable capacity to change, and to operate synchronously through eclectic usage. Mapping race thinking and the permeations of racism within the mass media is not a task to be accomplished, it is a task to be sustained.

Ethnicity

If we accept the general consensus that racism is a social evil and a politically divisive ideology we should perhaps also assert that ethnicity, as a means of categorizing human beings, has widespread credibility and positive affirmation. From 'ethnic' food to 'ethnic' fashion the idea of ethnicity has been employed as a positive phenomenon in contemporary life. More importantly, as post-colonial nation states have defined their distinctive identities, ethnicity has been frequently invoked as a primordial basis for nation building. And, within established political formations, ethnic diversity has been increasingly politicized as human rights movements have, over the last four decades, fed into the dynamics of the politics of identity. In the contemporary world ethnicity is not merely one of a plethora of available means of self-categorization and group formation: it is one of *the* most salient systems of categorization in contemporary usage.[7]

If we posit a framework in which racism is 'bad' and ethnicity is 'good', then a number of challenges for the agendas of this text immediately emerge. One obvious, though not necessarily easily resolvable, conundrum lies in the presumption that it is easy, or even relatively easy, to distinguish between politically illegitimate expressions of racist xenophobia and politically acceptable assertions of ethnic pride. We have already seen through our discussion of racism why the polysemic possibilities of race discourses may make this so. We shall shortly begin, through an examination of ethnicity, to understand why its characteristic nature also contributes to ambiguity. We may safely anticipate our ultimate conclusion to this challenge; namely, that there is no political, aesthetic or moral calculus which can readily provide definitive resolutions of this question. Research into the interaction of ethnicity and the media must aspire to a sophistication that transcends a head count of the number of ethnic participants in a dialogue.

A further observation necessarily arises from the juxtaposition of 'bad' racism and 'good' ethnicity. This has its roots in the frequent popular, and academic, association of ethnicity with a minority subordinate status. As we shall shortly see, this is a dangerous, though oft-repeated fallacy. However, the point to be made here builds upon a political elaboration of this flawed perspective. Namely, there is an easy transposition of minority ethnic status into inevitable victimhood. Within this paradigm historical realities are catalyzed by inchoate sentiments of majority guilt into a tumbling chaos of facts, righteous empathy and, paradoxically, continuing fear of the minority ethnic community. When discussions of ethnicity are infused by this paradigm a new human hierarchy is frequently implicitly constructed wherein the minority ethnic person is inherently good and the majority ethnic person is tainted by collective evil. There are, of course, echoes of Rousseauesque 'noble savagery' in this. However, the emotional infantilism that is at the heart of this 'righteous guilt/glorious victim' dyad should not be confused with the very considerable, and diverse, scholarly inquiries into the historical formations through which racism was shaped and thrived, and the related attempts to track its contemporary expression.

Related to this activity has been the parallel process of revealing the past and contemporary voices of those who have been oppressed and exploited through specific racial formations. Post-colonial analyses generated by authors such as Said (1985), Bhabha (1994) and Spivak and Harasym (1990) have revealed how complexly related the discourses of the oppressor and the oppressed can be. A point strongly reiterated by Gilroy (2000) in his critique of the penetration of majority race thinking into the discourse of some segments of the Black community. A powerful question emerges from this cumulative body of scholarship; namely, where are you standing when you wish to interrogate contemporary ethnic relations? The possibility of objective analysis is always haunted by the seemingly inevitable presence of a distinctly personal existential frame of reference. Thus, for example, Young (1990) has provocatively argued that much 'history' is profoundly Eurocentric and Bonnett (2000) poses the question of how the White anti-racists shall transcend their whiteness.

Auto-critiques of past, or indeed current, exploitative ethnic relations with other peoples and communities are by no means unnecessary or irrelevant for members of contemporary ethnic communities who enjoy positions of relative dominance and privilege. It is, indeed, a necessary foundation for engaging in contemporary political and cultural analysis. However, honest self-criticism should not be confused with Pollyannaish naïvety. Membership of a minority ethnic community is no guarantee of either individual or collective virtue. Promoting ethnic rights and ethnic community autonomy is not necessarily the same as increasing the sum of human freedoms, or extending the domain of the public good. Ethnicity is a social construction that is readily and routinely politicized. As such, it may provide a system of values, practices and institutions that would be widely regarded as positive. It may also provide an engine for the repression of individual freedoms and malicious assaults upon the integrity and viability of other peoples. The phrase 'ethnic cleansing' is testimony to this truth.

As we shall see in Chapter 9, 'good' ethnicity is difficult to take for granted for the further reason that has its roots in the nature of ethnicity itself. Ethnicity is both a property of self-identification, a route to self-affirmation, *and* a collective phenomenon grounded in the interaction and political mobilization of the group: the ethnic group. There is always the possibility of a conflict, certainly a tension, between the social psychological benefits of ethnic self-identification and the costs to personal liberties of the social and political means of sustaining and reproducing the collective viability of the group. If Freud in his *Civilisation and Its Discontents* (1930) saw the possibility of social cohesion requiring the necessary restraint of the individual's autonomous *Id*, so it is possible to speculate that the psychological benefits of identity formation and positive self-regard that an individual finds through membership of an ethnic group are bought at a cost of subjugating themselves to the discipline of that group. Group membership has to be earned and the positive affirmation to be had from other group members requires a demonstrable adherence to group norms. We may ascribe group identities to others and label them, but on the whole, admission to a valued group has to be earned. Anticipating the discussion that is to follow, we may note that group rights, achieved and expressed through ethnic identification, may be in conflict with the processes of claiming and asserting individual rights.[8]

This discussion is intended to provide a preliminary sensitization to some of the dilemmas raised by ethnicity as we briefly examine routes to an understanding of it provided by the social sciences. Ethnicity is not a stable property of an individual, implanted, like some microchip at birth. It is a continuous process of identity construction in which individuals participate collectively in defining and valorizing a group identity. One very simple definition of ethnicity is 'cultures in contact'. This reminds us that a fundamental basis of ethnic group formation is an active negotiation of in-group and out-group identities. We become aware of our ethnicity when we interact with members of a different culture. But this awareness of difference must be based upon relatively stable markers of in-group and out-group ethnic identity. Inter-group social comparison essentially takes place in relation to relatively few important key variables (Turner et al., 1987). Thus, for example, language provides a wonderfully flexible means of declaring in-group affiliation. Not just 'national' languages, but modes of inflection, argot and transitory 'in-words' readily expose the outsider. Rather like the processes of defining national identity, ethnicity is tied up with an ability to recognize 'those like us' and exclude 'those not like us' from inclusion in our identity group. Eriksen has suggested that:

> Ethnicity occurs when cultural differences are made relevant through interaction. This concerns what is socially relevant, not which cultural differences are 'actually there'. In an article on ethnic relations in Thailand, Michael Moerma (1965) has shown that many of his inform-ants mention cultural particulars which they presume are characteristic of themselves but which they in fact share with neighbouring peoples. Indeed, a variety of criteria can be used as markers of cultural difference in inter-ethnic situations – phenotype (appearance or 'race'), language, religion or even clothes. If any such marker is socially recog-nised as an indicator of an ethnic contrast, it matters little if the 'objec-tive cultural differences' are negligible. (1995: 251)

Two points in Eriksen's definition of ethnicity are worthy of emphasis. The first is his reference to the fact that 'a variety of criteria can be used as markers of cultural difference in inter-ethnic situations'. The role of such markers is to locate the *boundary* between the in-group and the out-group. In making this observation Eriksen is benefiting from the earlier contribution of Barth (1969) who helpfully criticized earlier anthropology's fascination with the artefacts and practices of ethnic communities. He stressed the importance of examining the mechanisms whereby commu-nities create and maintain the boundaries between them. He has helped us to make a distinction between the apparently static cultural content of ethnic communities, that 'ain't they quaint' fascination with the 'cultural stuff' of other ethnic communities that we can still find in popular trave-logues in print and on television (Steet, 2000), and the dynamic social processes of sustaining ethnic identities. In this latter process, it is the construction of social boundaries and their policing that are the core focus of our interest.

We have already noted above how language frequently serves as a boundary marker of ethnic identity. It is a complex signalling system within which any of a wide range of elements may be chosen as a critical criterial attribute. This allows for change which will expose the 'cultural tourist' or interloper as their sources of information date. Its flexibility also allows for a subtle denial of recognition or, if preferred, a robust rejection of the poseur.

The fact that a variety of markers may be used to define these boundaries is central to our understanding of ethnicity (see Wallman, 1986). A complementary *range* of markers helps to minimize the risk that a genuine member of an ethnic group may have their claim to membership denied because they fail on *one* marker. They also ensure that no outsider can claim membership of the ethnic group because they satisfy one of the criteria. And, crucially, multiple criteria build flexibility into ethnic boundary maintenance. New criteria can be introduced and established whilst others can be allowed to lapse without causing a catastrophically radical redefinition of the boundary. Each marker is a contingent part of an interactive whole.

The second point to highlight from Eriksen's statement is his observation that 'it matters little if the "objective cultural differences" are negligible'. As with other forms of social constructionist enterprise, whether nationhood (Balakrishnan, 1996) or gender (Burkitt, 1999), the absence of veridical truth has never been a match for shared conviction. The integrity and viability of ethnic boundary maintenance are derived not only from the effective daily deployment of the boundary markers, a utility proven by their efficacy, but also these boundary markers are themselves frequently embedded in a valued collective history. Ethnic communities may be engaged in a process of negotiating their identity on a day-to-day basis, but they do so with a strong sense of continuity with a shared history. This history is likely to contain potent origin myths which identify the ancient roots of contemporary people. Specific events in this history are likely to be given iconic status as moments which exemplify the enduring qualities and values of the group. And this history will offer a cumulative process of conflict and resistance in relation to significant ethnic out-groups. This construction of a shared history provides a coherent body of belief which serves to legitimate contemporary claims to a common identity. Thus, for example, indigenous peoples are likely to give a central role to their long association with a specific territory, whilst globally migrant diasporic communities may well find their historical connection through historically located cultural markers. The nature of the strategic deployment of a consensual shared history yet again underlines the specificity of ethnic self-definition and political mobilization. (See for example, Cunningham and Sinclair, 2000.)

It is this historical embedding of contemporary values and beliefs which *inter alia* so frustrates the easy external reading of an ethnic culture. Identifying the more obvious boundary markers of language, dress and diet may in some circumstances be relatively easy. Identifying other subtle codes of identity may prove much more taxing. But comprehending how to weight the performative expression of these markers, in the absence of this historical sensibility, may be deeply confusing.

If, along with Eriksen (1995: 244) we can agree that 'ethnicity is relational and processual: it is not a "thing", but an aspect of a social process', then we may build upon this insight by identifying in further detail the elements of this process. Wallman (1986) importantly distinguished between ethnicity as 'consciousness of kind' and the organizational and 'infrastructural bases of ethnicity.' Ethnicity as consciousness of kind directly refers us to the social-psychological mechanisms that provide the motor for each individual's engagement with their ontological self. As with the logistics of prejudice discussed above, this approach reminds us of the active agency of the human being. The modern concern with authenticity (Taylor, 1991), with being 'true to oneself', provides an ego-involved dynamic to the claim that someone has an ethnic identity. Social constructionism (Burr, 1995) and social identity theory (Capozza and Brown, 2000) provide accounts of the psychology of identity. In essence, if in the social sciences there is a well-rehearsed contempt for psychological reductionism, then Wallman's qualifying message is that in order to comprehend ethnicity we must articulate a psychological account of identity formation with a social and political analysis of ethnic group construction. The essence of the analytic sin of psychological reductionism lies in accounting for social phenomena in purely psychological terms. A classic instance would be to explain everything from aggression to altruism in terms of instincts. However, the potential and not infrequent abuse of psychological insights is not a legitimate basis for rejecting the contribution of psychological theory to an interdisciplinary understanding of ethnicity.

Proponents of social constructionism, psycho-dynamic theory and social identity theory would all stand forward to provide that input. Clearly, there is no inherent incompatibility with interrogating the dynamics of individual identity whilst simultaneously locating that individual in a social environment. But crucially, an understanding of contemporary social psychology would lead to an acknowledgement that social psychological dynamics are a present and potent element of ethnic relations. At its simplest this psychology would provide insight into the fact that ethnicity is not a merely over-learned artifact of socialization. The criterial attributes of in-group and out-group boundary maintenance are not merely 'noted' as in some social actuarial accounting. Inter-group dynamics, experienced as individual social comparison of self with others, have a capacity to amplify and exaggerate the salience of boundary markers (see Turner, 1987). If nothing else, this social psychology would demand a degree of sophistication in reception studies of the ethnic content of the mass media. If it were not for the potency of these psychological dynamics there would be no meaningful difference between content analyses and reception studies. It is the ego-involvement of individuals in social judgements that provides the basis for selective perception and selective exposure. Amongst other things, this means that the hegemonic processes of racial formation argued by Winant (1994) are not mere triumphs of indoctrination through cohorent and sustained propaganda. When it comes to judgements of our in-groups against critical outgroups, we are *psychologically* disposed to be willing participants in perceptual bias and cognitive distortion. But psychology alone could not provide an account of the content of these partisan perceptions. A socio-political analysis grounded in a keen historical sensitivity would be needed to explain on what dimensions we make partisan distinctions between self and others.

The social psychology of ethnicity as consciousness of kind additionally opens up our preparedness for the complexity of ethnic identities. From the early days of George Herbert Mead (1934) there has been acceptance that we all have multiple social roles and consequently multiple facets to our identity. The multifaceted nature of human identities is entirely consistent with one further aspect of ethnicity, namely that it has been described as being *situational* (Wallman, 1986). All that is meant by this statement is that we do not routinely proceed through our day perceiving everything through the self-conscious prism of our ethnicity. Similarly, we do not sustain a permanent self-conscious reflexivity in relation to our age, class, gender or the size of our ears. All of these may be made temporarily salient by the particular circumstances of the moment. Consequently, we cannot assume that because we know someone's ethnicity we have insight into how they are reading a particular situation. Their ethnic sensibilities may or may not be engaged. Or their ethnic sensibility may be salient but essentially subordinated by another contingent identity cluster.

For not only is ethnicity situational, it is also frequently understood to be *hybrid*. Hybridity is one of the most recurrent concepts employed in contemporary discussions of ethnicity and it is not without its ambiguities in use (Young, 1995). Hybridity is a further acknowledgement of the complex multi-faceted nature of human identity, and particularly of the fact that different identities are uniquely melded together within individual biographies. Thus, ethnicity is not routinely experienced, or expressed, as a single self-sufficient vehicle of identity (Werbner and Modood, 1997). The writings of black feminists, for example, critiqued the whiteness, and middle-class locus, of feminist politics (Grewal et al., 1988; Mohanty et al., 1991; Bhavnani and Phoenix, 1994). The title of hooks' (1981) book *Ain't I A Woman* powerfully asserted the possibility of being whole as an African American and a woman.

A further contemporary vogue concept, *diaspora*, offers an additional edge to our understanding of ethnic hybridity. Echoing our earlier discussion of the ubiquitous realities of present and past migrations in shaping the ethnic demography of the contemporary world, the concept of diaspora locates individuals within their temporal and spatial history. Past and current migrations have provided individuals with networks of kin and friends spread across the globe. But they are not spread at random, rather as a lasting reflection of earlier patterns of migration. This history additionally informs the contemporary understanding of this diasporic reality (Gilroy, 1993; Radhakrishnan, 1996; Werbner, 2002). This shared history and contemporary consciousness feed the linguistic and cultural mapping of ethnic communities over the globe that in its turn provides the geo-linguistic territories identified by Sinclair et al. (1996) as shaping contemporary media flows.

More recently Cunningham and Sinclair have provided a valuable cautionary critique of the concept of diaspora and its use and misuse. They note that: '(A) sense of cultural adaptiveness, innovation and hybridity (which), along with the notions of dispersal and unassimilated difference, is at the heart of the concept of diaspora ...' (2000: 16). They complement this emphasis upon a dynamic of cultural adaptiveness and continually creative hybridity as characteristic of the diasporic experience with an explicit warning of essentializing conceptions of culture that can be deployed in some accounts of diaspora. There is a clear danger of invoking some notion of an historically continuous cultural core as providing the foundational essence that has defined a diasporic identity across time and territory. When the diversity *within* diasporic communities is recognized and illuminated through the language of hybridity, then the dynamic processes within diasporic communities are more readily rendered visible. Importantly, throughout their text Cunningham and Sinclair provide evidence of the need to explicitly *historicize* the distinctive nature of specific diasporas. Clearly, a postmodern celebration of the diasporic *zeitgeist* is no substitute for a careful and detailed analysis of specific diasporic processes and contemporary realities.

Additionally, an adequate comprehension of such ethnic identities and their attendant media flows requires that we return to the other complementary dimension of Wallman's account of ethnicity: ethnicity as infrastructural. It is all very well having a clear and strong consciousness of kind, but how shall this identity be expressed in lived engagement with the environment? Where shall the culinary raw materials of an 'ethnic' cuisine be obtained? Where shall the artistic and cultural expression of an ethnic community be reproduced? How should the collective worship of a community be sustained? These realities cannot be conjured by a summation of ethnic feeling: there must be commercial, political, social and religious organizational structures that can convert demand into provision. It is the absence of such institutional infrastructures which renders recent refugees so vulnerable. It is the extensive presence of such ethnic infrastructures that is routinely present in the ethnic community as characterized by academic ethnographic research and by a genre of migrant literature. A political economy of the media that addresses the institutional dynamics of ethnic representation is a necessary adjunct to any study of the ethnic specificities of media content (Husband, 1996).[9]

Before concluding this section it is important to make explicit the linkages between these two aspects of ethnicity, for whilst they are conceptually distinguishable they are inevitably the multiply-linked double helix of contemporary ethnic politics. The different phenomena invoked by a research focus upon ethnicity as 'consciousness of kind', and by a concentration on the infrastructural dynamics of ethnicity, logically draw differentially upon different disciplinary insights. We must remain self-consciously aware of how specific research questions attract particular theoretical paradigms and tend to pre-empt the choice of research method. Consequently, we must question the adequacy of the method for the research question. We must look beyond the pragmatic focus of the specific research project. And we must seek an inter-disciplinary sophistication in learning how to appropriately articulate different research inputs into a coherent and legitimate synthesis. A recent significant shift within the academic analysis of ethnicity has been towards a postmodern theorization of identities as fragile, shifting, multiple and transitory (Rattansi and Westwood, 1994). This 'postmodern turn' has challenged the certainty and unambiguous power of 'the great narratives', including those of class, sex and nationality. This approach has emphasized the fluidity and complexity of identities. It is entirely sympathetic to ideas of the situationally contingent nature of ethnicity. In making space and time themselves problematic, postmodernism has provided a language, and analytic style, that comfortably addresses notions of spatiality and diaspora in relation to ethnic identities. Hybridity from this perspective is entirely expected and endlessly nuanced. It is the essence of postmodern ethnicity. And within this analytic paradigm globalization is an ever-present chimera; part engine of indetermancy and part the consequence of postmodern consciousness. The global is the logical, and even necessary, adjunct of de-centered identities.

Not surprisingly this paradigm has generated very many ethnographic accounts of contemporary ethnic identities. Regrettably, in their argument and in their negotiation through policy debates, some proponents of these studies render the possibility of meaningful collective ethnic identities impossible. It seemed for a time in the 1990s that for some, to speak of ethnic communities in academic discourse was an invitation to be charged with a crass reification of categories. We would argue that a critical and nuanced awareness of the complexity of ethnic identity construction does not require a jettisoning of the basic concepts of 'identity', 'imagined community' or 'diaspora'. A radical postmodernist rejection of extensively used concepts because they are *reputedly* irredeemably contaminated by essentializing connotations is both Draconian and unhelpful. The field of socio-linguistics has extensively revealed the inherent problematics of language use, and the social sciences have no unique inoculation against the ambiguous pragmatics of language in use. Caution in the use of concepts and an acute attention to the insights that arise through the contested use of key concepts would seem to be a more fruitful strategy for collaborative research, rather than an endless cycle of generating 'uncontaminated' neologisms.

In the multi-disciplinary field of mass communication research insights may be derived from research undertaken from within different academic paradigms. However, the fusion of disparate research outputs into a coherent meta-analysis is not a simple summation of the parts. In developing our approach to exploring the relationships of ethnicity and the media we would wish to propose that a degree of mutual respect for different research methods and research agendas would be a deeply rewarding stance. In this field, for example, we may wish to see postmodernism as a necessary corrective to the simplification and arrogant explanatory claims of earlier grand theory. We may also note that it is a paradigm which, in its structure and use, reflects the apparent indeterminacy and flux of our times. In terms of the sociology of knowledge we could reasonably see postmodernism as a creature of its times.

There is, in fact, an ironic juxtaposition of the celebration of indeterminacy and flux found in a range of postmodern contributions to the analysis of ethnicity and the utterly opposed politics of *essentialism* to be found within the existential realities of the contemporary politics of identity (of which much more in later chapters). Essentialism is the antithesis in practice of the imaginary identity relations of postmodern theory. As Meekosha observed:

> The interconnection of race, sexuality and gender provokes a politics of identity often resulting in opposition between and inside different minorities and within feminist politics. These dimensions of 'difference' have generated overwhelming issues for practitioners in the 1990s ... The surfacing of essentialist politics – claiming that solidarity with the identity group transcends all other competing claims to loyalty – simplifies complex layers of interacting oppressions into crude dichotomies or polarities: black/white, gay/straight, male/female, disability/ablebodiedness. The politics of difference, diversity and identity have given a new edge to demands for equality and social justice. (1993: 172)

The implications of Meekosha's statement for our analysis of ethnicity and the media are far-reaching. For while one positive aspect of postmodernist analysis has been to stress the complexity and situational contingency of individual identity, simultaneously we must be alert to the radical boundary policing that may be found in contemporary inter-ethnic politics. This is a tension, a paradox, that would not distress social psychologists following the later developments of Henri Tajfel's (1982) discussion of the shift from inter-personal to inter-group dynamics.

Simply stated, as two people interact as individuals they express, and engage with, unique aspects of each other. Some appreciation of each other's unique holistic identity is built into the assumptive framework of the interaction. However, when the same two individuals lock horns as members of opposed groups they then proceed to interact on the basis of reciprocal group stereotypes. Individuality is lost as group criterial attributes are invoked to define the interaction.

Thus, in any analysis of ethnicity in relation to the media, this potential shift from the individual to the group is a social, psychological and political reality that would be ignored at our peril. As we shall see below, the hybrid realities of individual indigenous identities are not always paralleled in the exclusionary politics of essentialist definitions of identity (Langton, 1993). Amongst other things, this dynamic explicitly raises questions of who shall speak for whom. Particularly, where access to scarce ethnically-linked resources is an issue, then regulating access to a minority ethnic identity has a real economic edge.

Such essentialist politics also force us back to an engagement with the infrastructural bases of ethnic identity. Whilst the literature on ethnicity and the media is replete with studies of the representation of ethnic identities, considerably less sustained attention has been given to the political economy of minority ethnic participation within the media industries, and to the economic and institutional determinants of ethnic representation. The distinctive benefits of a political economy of the media are well established (Mosco, 1996). Given the transposition of the demographics of ethnic diversity into the commercial imperatives of economically viable media audiences, the relevance of such an approach to ethnicity and the media is not hard to discern. Diasporic communities become globalized audiences (Cunningham and Sinclair, 2000; Sinclair et al., 1996) and minority ethnic media become infrastructural prerequisites of a viable multi-ethnic public sphere (Husband, 1994a).

In sum, all adequate accounts of ethnicity necessarily require a sophisticated articulation of different modes of analysis. The extant literature on ethnicity and the media bears witness to the great diversity of research methods that have been employed, and of the range of micro or macro foci that have been selected. Part of the task of sustaining a legitimate and coherent analysis of this field lies in sustaining a critical reflexivity about the methods employed at any time, their suitability to the research task, and the means whereby the subsequent findings may be linked to a greater integrative analysis.

Conclusion

This chapter has had a relatively simple purpose: it has aspired to introduce the reader to a critical understanding of some of the key concepts and research issues which will underpin later arguments in this book. In unpacking some of the conceptual issues surrounding the realities and politics of 'race', emphasis has been placed upon the historical grounding of the commonly held understanding of this concept. Past patterns of material relations between current majority and minority ethnic communities are argued to have continuing relevance for today's ethnic relations. Equally, the different historical experiences of nation-building must be factored in to any understanding of contemporary ideologies of 'race'. We have explicitly cautioned against reducing all manifestations of racism to individual psychopathology. Indeed, in discussing the phenomenon of institutional racism we have hopefully shown how malicious intention is not essential to the viability of racially discriminatory practices. In the last chapter, and elsewhere, we explore the relevance of an understanding of institutional racism for planning systemic strategies to challenge discrimination within the media industries.

The discussion of ethnicity provides an essential introduction to understanding the multi-layered complexities of ethnicity. We regard a multi-disciplinary approach to analysing the relationships between ethnicity and the media as essential. A social psychological insight into the subjective existential nature of ethnicity as a facet of personal identity is necessary to examining the partisan engagement of audiences, and professionals, with ethnicity in the media. Equally, an understanding of the structural location of ethnicity as infrastructural resources within a particular society feeds an appreciation of a political economy of minority ethnic media, and of power relations within media industries. These two facets of ethnicity become echoed in later discussions of the role of communities of practice in the determination of media production.

In both the analysis of 'race' and racism, and of ethnicity, we have emphasized how as 'taken for granted' ways of accounting for personal identity and social relations both of these concepts actively interact with other powerful ideologies. Gender, class, age, nationality, sexual preference and other powerful social constructions interlock in multiple and complex ways with 'race' and ethnicity. This makes the task of analysis perpetually challenging. The chapters that follow, whilst adding detail to this complexity, will hopefully cumulatively assist in building a critical repertoire that can address this challenge.

Notes

1 In all the arguments that follow we are acutely aware of the complexity and contingency of our experience of identity. From different theoretical perspectives the dynamic character and 'hybrid' complexity of contemporary identities has been frequently explored. (Appadurai, 1996; Werbner and Modood, 1997; Abrams and Hogg, 1999) 'Race' and ethnicity do not exist as hermetically sealed social categories, or personal repertoires.

2 In any contemporary understanding of the formation and expression of 'race' in a particular society or context an historical understanding of its antecedents and metamorphosis is essential. The roots of the creditability of contemporary racism are to be found in the sedimented beliefs that have been laid down as nations and peoples made sense of their behavior in relation to the dominant ideas of their time. Thus, an historical account provides insight into the roots and their continuing relevance. Jordan's (1969) account of the parallel, and different, emergent attitudes to color under slavery in America and the Caribbean is an exemplary study. As, in the context of Australia, Hughes, 1987; and Reynold, 1999, 2001, have done for the Australian construction of its understanding of the Aboriginal presence. That the key elements in these historical accounts are capable of transformation in order to address changed circumstances is central to their continuing power. For this reason the historical analysis of the writing of history is itself a valuable activity when seeking to understand contemporary 'race' relations (see, for example, Griffiths, 1996; Schwarz, 1996).

3 Discursive de-racialization does not require advanced skills in linguistic manipulation. As Essed (1991) and Wetherell and Potter (1992) have illustrated, our normal everyday speech contains a full range of routine discursive strategies that enable us to be euphemistic and embed 'indelicate' messages in anodyne conversation.

4 In contemporary Britain the charge of being 'politically correct' is employed in order to place persons challenging racism/sexism/disablism in the wrong. They are, in effect, being accused of being neurotically fixated with discrimination and having a rigid, and self-aggrandizing, moral agenda. Reciprocally, the accusation quietly asserts that the complainant is 'political' whilst the behavior being objected to is everyday, routine; normal.

5 In Britain in the 1970s and 1980's, there was a vogue for 'Race Awareness Training'; otherwise known as R.A.T. Frequently influenced by Katz (1978) *White Awareness: Handbook for Anti-Racism Training*, these race awareness training courses put 'normally prejudiced people in touch with themselves and their prejudices. Typically, individuals went alone from their workplace to the course. Hence there was no shared learning or self-critique from colleagues in a common community of practice. They returned to their workplace as isolates, where routinely no measures were in place to monitor their changed practice. (For critiques see Gurnah, 1989; Sivanandan, 1981.)

6 In Chapter 8 you will find an extensive discussion of the concept of communities of practice in relation to the processes of media production.

7 Whilst being happy to assert the contemporary political salience of ethnicity in the contemporary world, we would again reiterate our earlier concern to emphasize the complexity found in both the construction and routine existential negotiation of ethnicity. One of the potential consequences of the politicization of ethnicity is an attempt to narrow and limit this complexity: to essentialize the shared definition of ethnicity around a few key defining elements.

8 Kymlicka among others has been concerned to explore the potential repressive power of ethnic group cultural mores in constraining the individual rights of their members. This leads to a possible tension between defending the group rights of ethnic communities in sustaining their collective heritage, and the individual rights of group members in negotiating their personal autonomy (see, for example, Kymlicka, 1995; 2001).

9 Something of the complex interaction of social psychological, economic and political forces present in ethnic identity formation in the context of contemporary globalizing transformations in social relations is to be found in Appadurai. (1996)

2 Research on Racism, Ethnicity and Media

Our purpose in this chapter is distinctly ambitious for the space at our disposal. It is nothing less than to characterize and critically evaluate published arguments concerning the roles of media in articulating, underpinning or subverting racism, and in sustaining, developing or dissolving ethnic cultural identities. As we stated in our Preface, the mediation of racism via mass media of all kinds is not the only source of its devastating impact, but it also operates in a molecular and penetrative fashion throughout the capillaries and pores of today's world, as – in varying forms – it has done through five centuries since the onset of European colonial expansion. Likewise, the endless routines of media flows put daily flesh on ethnic identifications of oneself and one's visualized community, as with others. Thus this chapter's exercise is vital but could also easily become a strange amalgam of the Last Judgement and the Oscars. Or a crazed bibliographic gallop.

We plan to spare our readers these unappetizing experiences. Our discussion will necessarily be indicative, particularly as we seek to illustrate not only from the USA and Britain but from other nations as well. In the bulk of the chapter we will assess the basic conceptual frames and methods which have been used in this area of media research. That may seem much less tasty than picking revelations (and idiocies) from the literature, but it is primary, as we shall show. For how our questions are asked powerfully affects the answers we get – the 'facts' we think our research has established. And behind the questions, willy-nilly, lurk the concepts.

Our task for the remainder of the chapter, then, is to assess the tools used in this research, namely the typical concepts deployed in it. How have they guided investigation? How productive have they been? Where have they fallen short? We will also address from time to time the media of minority-ethnic groups as well as mainstream majority-ethnic media, though the former have received only a fraction of the attention of the latter.

The Dominance of Textual Research

Either in qualitative or quantitative modes, research has overwhelmingly focused on text[1]/content. This is hardly surprising, for several reasons.

First and foremost the communication process is symbolic, and deciphering it inevitably has pride of place. Second, researchers can access media content much more simply than either (a) the production process and the corporate nexus behind most of it, or (b) how users interpret and act upon the text. Third, though a bad reason, people only too often assume that making meaning is straightforward and only goes awry occasionally, so that extrapolating from the text backwards to its producers, and/or forward to its users, is pretty well hazard-free.[2]

The methods which have been applied to textual analysis range from the heavily quantitative to the strictly qualitative. The classic example of the former is 'content analysis'[3] and of the latter 'symptomatic readings,' performed with or without the aid of one or more conceptual approaches, such as ideological critique, feminism, semiotics and psychoanalytic theory. Symptomatic readings are more or less exclusively qualitative, whereas content analysis normally offers a discussion to make sense of the statistics it has generated, and this discussion frequently draws upon a qualitative grab-bag of theory, other research data and taken-for-granted notions.

We will turn in a moment to a discussion of these methods of analysis. After that we will examine the prime concepts that have been deployed in the analysis of 'racial' and 'ethnic' media content: image, stereotype, framing, ideology, representation, discourse, text. It is often the case that specific studies address particular media technologies (digital platforms, print) or particular genres (news, sitcoms), and in either case there are facets peculiar to those dimensions which significantly mould the more general processes that these concepts endeavor to capture. Nonetheless, it makes sense to focus initially on the wider concepts because of their broader power to define the issues.

The issues, we repeat, are not simply academic concept-juggling. Cuban refugees to the USA, mostly White, were defined in the 1980s and 1990s as fleeing dictatorship and incidental extreme poverty, whereas Haitians and Salvadorans were defined simply as 'economic' refugees with zero attention to the brutal regimes that terrorized their lives throughout the 1980s and into the earlier 1990s. The former were welcomed, even fêted, given special welfare payments to aid their transition; the latter were refused entry, and those who evaded controls were subject to immigration police raids and summary deportation, often to face violent reprisals on their return. Cuban rafters were heroes, Haitian boat people were a nuisance. These cynical US government definitions were diffused widely through the media, were only challenged by marginal groups, and had the most direct impact on all three nationalities. The concept of an 'economic' refugee was pivotal.

Our example draws on a government's deployment of a concept and subsequently on its media diffusion, rather than on a concept applied purely in media research, but we shall see below that the selection and use of particular concepts in studies of media content equally have very practical consequences. We turn first to methods of textual analysis, their implications and effects.

Content Analysis and the Symptomatic Reading

Content analysis has long been the standard method of textual analysis among US social scientists doing media research, and symptomatic reading the approach favored by humanistic scholarship, especially in cinema studies and more latterly in cultural studies of television and popular music as well. The terms represent phases as well as schools, with the pre-eminence of content analysis in the 1950s through the 1970s increasingly under assault from deconstructionist, post-colonialist and other postmodernist approaches from the 1980s onwards. We share substantial reservations, which we will develop below, concerning the merits of both sides in this dispute.

Content analysis in practice (e.g., Berelson, 1971; Krippendorff, 1980) meant dividing up various plausible sub-components of an issue featuring in the text or texts to be studied, labeling them as categories, and then studying the media in question over a set period or periods of time to count how many times the issue and its sub-components turned up. This way it became possible to establish certain contours of coverage of a given subject, whether ethnicity or anything else: for example, did some media outlets frequently cover stories related to people of color, did others typically render them invisible, were there spikes and lulls in their media coverage?

In this way also the leitmotifs of coverage became more visible, such as the frequency with which people of color were associated in the media with immigrant or refugee status, violence, crime, disease, unemployment, welfare abuse, as opposed to being covered as everyday citizens of all sorts and conditions. It became possible to check personal impressions of frequent coverage, or of coverage in a particular fashion, against systematic study of the media in question. Statistically random sampling of media appeared to offer a measurable estimate that research did accurately represent their content, and certainly reduced to a manageable size the huge volume of data that textual analysis generates.

An example of how this approach could be used productively is the study by Entman and Rojecki (2000: 162–81) of images in US television commercials containing Black and White characters. By means of rigorously counting frequencies in over 1600 ads, it was possible to establish important patterns of representation, including the substantial favoring of Black models with lighter skin-hues. Hartmann and Husband (1974) established the prioritization of the category 'immigrant' in British news media when covering issues regarding people or communities of color.

However, there were also drawbacks associated with this methodology, drawbacks triumphantly pilloried by humanist and postmodernist critics. Principal among them was its frequent failure to acknowledge the multiple ways in which language is used, including irony, parody, sarcasm, rhetorical over- and under-statement, phrases carrying a particular symbolic charge at a given moment in time or laden with historical associations, bureaucratic obfuscation, political double-speak, and so on. The practice of discursive de-racialization touched upon in Chapter 1 offers a very clear example of the problems created by refusing to acknowledge these aspects of constructing meaning in human communication. The categories which researchers established typically assumed language was always lucid and operated on a single level, and that these categories could neatly distinguish between one sub-component and the next. Second, if say the unit of analysis were newspaper stories but these addressed several sub-components of the issue, how would one decide to assign the story to one category over another?

Third, there was a problem in the classical 'content analysis' approach's typical inability to take into account the specificities of genre, whether the lead paragraph in print journalism, the drive for dramatic pictures in TV journalism, or the character of the action-adventure or Western movie. A fourth problem was the neglect of the narrative dimension. This was significant both for news media and for dramatic series on TV, in that random sampling of content which would often miss a pivotal story, or chop out the beginning or the end or even the middle, so that the importance of narrative sequence, build-up, and build-down, would risk being entirely lost.

The symptomatic reading, when conducted by a careful and seasoned analyst, can produce finely tuned and illuminating results. An example would be Ramírez-Berg's discussion of the treatment of 'race' and indigenous communities in Golden Age Mexican cinema (Ramírez-Berg, 1993). He disentangles a series of nuances involved and thereby identifies just how, despite its signal artistic achievements in that era, Mexican cinema helped reproduce and prolong the refusal to engage with the problem of 'race' characteristic of mainstream Mexican culture, at least until the Zapatista movement began to challenge hegemonic codes. Similarly Watkins (1998) traces the interrelation between hip-hop music and recent Black American cinema with a series of symptomatic readings of texts from both genres that illuminate the continuing undertow of cultural resistance against racial exclusion in the USA.

Yet high octane postmodernists have gone much much further, disputing the possibility of any stable and consensual definitions or evaluations. Meaning was individual, no one view had any basis for acceptability or plausibility over any other, all positions were personally and emotionally invested. Advocates of such arguments went far beyond anything propounded or actuated by Foucault or Derrida, despite citing them with quasi-religious devotion. The end result was one in which the inelegance of the clumsy pun and the tortured aphoristic throw-away line became the supreme rhetorical signal of contemporary relevance.[4] We were back, oddly enough, though in a totally different vehicle, to the spurious solidity so attractive to the empiricist content analysts. Being in synch with 'post-modernity' perhaps felt as reassuring in its own way as 'hard' data.

In our view, however, the content analysis approach still has a limited validity. A purely intuitive 'symptomatic' textual reading may be in the extreme entirely solipsistic, the self-indulgent fantasy of but a single reader. The reading may be buttressed with historical scholarship, with intricate theory, with glittering inter-textual allusions, but in the end be solely the artifact of its author. The anti-positivist critique, whether decon-structionist, postmodernist or post-colonial, manages to shoot large holes in traditional content analysis but has no answer of its own to the demand for replicability or reliability.

The answer, for us, is to design appropriate combinations of both approaches, appropriate in the sense of their being fitted to questions they can answer, not to questions beyond their scope. At the risk of self-aggrandizement, we would illustrate this by reference to two studies. One of us and another research colleague (Hartmann and Husband, 1974) both categorized and enumerated media content but in the same study, for example, also investigated qualitatively the historical tenacity of certain racist images. The other study (Downing, 1975) counted the infrequency with which Black people were allowed to speak on British television in relation to issues directly concerning them collectively, versus the nor-malcy of their absence or of White individuals purporting to speak for them. Yet it interpreted these statistics in the context of racist repression in Britain and of anti-apartheid and anti-colonial struggles in Africa.

One realm in which this methodological issue has immediate relevance is in the process of media monitoring for racist and anti-racist content. We discuss this activity at much greater length later in the book, but it is rather obvious that the ability to challenge media portrayals of people of color and of White people and to propose constructive alternatives, both depend on being able to analyze media texts effectively and convincingly. Neither a wooden use of statistics and contrived categories, nor claims based purely upon personal intuition, are likely to have any purchase on the policies of media executives and professionals.

Let us now turn to a critical evaluation of the principal concepts used in this arena.

Image

'Image' is a term with currency across art history and cultural history, media studies, and advertising.[5] It may be used with specific reference to the visual dimension of media, and thus especially in relation to photography, cinema, television or the internet. Or it may be used to indicate a basic difference between pictorial and verbal communication methods. Alternatively it may be accepted more generally to denote a condensed summary of perspectives held by particular groups of people about other groups.

At this latter point it easily becomes a term contrasted with reality, particularly in the sense of biased 'racial' imagery that bears no fair or factual relation to the people so imagined. 'Image' then becomes, rhetorically, a fabrication, implicitly malicious and certainly malign. In the influential book *The Image: or What Happened to the American Dream?*, Daniel J. Boorstin (1963) used the term thus to attack what he saw as US citizens' readiness for self-deception via comforting but artificial media images that sugared over much less pleasant realities.

The term has also sometimes been used with good intentions but in a severely reductionist manner, to focus on whether media images of people of color or White people could be said to be positive or negative. But this use has flawed policy implications. On a very elementary intertextual level, it is indeed unquestionable that if the only coverage of Latinos on US television is as criminals, or the only representation of Native Americans is as whooping warriors of a bygone age, or the only time we see Arab Muslims is when they are portrayed as terrorists, then there clearly exists a serious deficiency with the tight little boxes in which these groups are permitted to breathe. At the same time, a policy refusal to portray negative characters of a given ethnicity would fall into precisely the same trap, squashing the variety of an ethnic group into a tiny tub of virtue. There are examples of this. For some decades in Hindi cinema, for example, a Muslim character would almost inevitably be played as a 'good' person, which both defied reason and discouraged more imaginative portrayals. It is hard to imagine that this practice played any constructive role in communal relations in India.

Furthermore, that which is perceived as positive or negative in portrayal cannot be simplified to a thumbs-up or thumbs-down. First of all, who is to decide and on what basis the way to turn the thumb? A very striking example of this dilemma is the video image of African American Rodney King being systematically beaten by four Los Angeles policemen with clubs. Fifty-six violent blows, several stungun blasts and heavy kicks, a partially paralyzed face, nine skull fractures, a broken cheek bone, a shattered eye socket and a broken leg were the result (Baker, 1993: 42). For the police officers' attorneys, however, and for the virtually White Simi Valley community jury that exonerated them, the four men were faced with a dangerous unknown Black man who rushed at them, and were simply defending themselves and subduing him. Enough said, said the jury ... The attorneys took great care to concentrate on the first few seconds when, for whatever reason, King rushed in the direction of the police (perhaps to try to break through them and escape what he believed was coming), whereas many others focused on the relentless violence meted out to him as he lay upon the ground. The definition of 'negative' as regards image cannot be abstractly fixed.

Second, the components of what is positive or negative have to be separated out. If a minority-ethnic actor plays a criminal successfully, in other words acts well, makes a dent upon our consciousness, leads us to ponder the psychology and sociology of criminal behavior, does that mean that all s/he has communicated is the dangerous quality of all members of her/his ethnic group? If the same actor plays a milk-and-water positive role, making interminable politically correct remarks and smiling beatifically under attack, does that chalk up one for the angels? If a White character is shown to be a racist psychopath, is that a strike in favor of anti-racist honesty, or is a portrayal of banal everyday racist behavior and attitudes more of a challenge to the comfort-zone of White self-congratulation on not being racist?

In particular we need to face a central policy question: are we starting from media as a series of art-forms, or from an expectation of naturalistic realism in media, or from an expectation of correct propaganda in media? Without an answer to this question, image-analysis is liable to lose the plot.

Third, how do we evaluate a film or TV show in which the premise of the action is flawed, but the individual performers put in strong and varied performances? An example would be the US television police show, *NYPD Blue*, in which there were fairly varied Black and Latino characters, both continuing and occasional. Yet a fundamental premise of the show, repeated time and again, was the necessity for all police officers verbally to intimidate suspects into giving up their right to remain silent, an unlawful form of pressure which virtually always produced results with which a law-abiding audience would nonetheless feel at ease, namely confession followed by apprehension of the guilty. Arguably, the endemic denial of suspects' rights by US police officers to members of minority-ethnic groups and their consequent huge over-representation in the prison population were thereby excused, lending both space and legitimacy to this behavior.

In other words, a 100 per cent focus on positive and negative ethnic images risks very reductive assessments of key processes in the public's use of media texts.[6]

The term 'image', however, does not itself force us down that path. Given its more conventional dictionary sense of image as not a necessarily naturalistic or total reproduction of something – distinct from Boorstin's spirited attack on image-as-falsehood – it is hard to avoid the term as one conceptualization of media depiction. Beyond this again, 'imagery' conveys in media as in the arts the intentional aesthetic modeling of a human (or non-human) reality, yet one which the creators' intention *cannot* necessarily encapsulate or fix the public's interpretation of the modeling.[7]

In other words, if we disposed of the term 'image' we would immediately be compelled to invent a synonym. That does not excuse us, however, of the need to specify in what sense(s) we are deploying the concept. 'Image' is a term whose fuzziness is liable to breed fog.

A related term that has acquired some currency is 'the imaginary', used as a noun. This to some degree fuses the notion of image with that of ideology (see below).

Stereotype

At first glance representing virtually a synonym for 'image,'[8] this concept is derived metaphorically from rotary press technology for printing newspapers. Having set the raised print letters on flat metal plates, it was next necessary to curve the plates so they would fit around the rotary cylinder of the press. To do so, the flat plates were imprinted on thick soft cardboard at colossal pressure, four hundred tons to be precise. The cardboard could then be bent to form an arc and act as the mould for the curved metal plate. From this, a figurative stereotype becomes a social and psychological definition of an ethnic or other social group, as something produced as a result of enormous, irresistible pressure that in consequence is completely fixed, 'carved in stone' so to speak, totally resistant to change or adaptation. It may be hostile or it may be supportive – White people over the past half-millennium have often held supportive stereotypes of themselves and negative stereotypes of those they colonized – but it is rigid.

Implicitly, the notion of a stereotype draws attention to the psychological dimensions of ethnic (or gender or other) image-formation and retention, and particularly to the intransigence with which people will often cling to these images in the face of all kinds of reality-tests and reality-shocks. The 400 tons of pressure utilized by the rotary press rather powerfully evokes the tireless media reproduction in varying forms of racist stereotypes, day by day, year by year, decade by decade, ever since the centuries of colonialism and slavery began.

The discussion of stereotypes has often concentrated exclusively on White stereotypes of people of color, such as the 'Yellow Peril' definition of East Asians. On one level, this emphasis is appropriate, given the tremendous damage they cause. On another it is extremely limiting, for two reasons. Chief among these is the neglect of stereotypes of Whiteness, that White people are civilized and humane (as World Wars I and II, colonialism and slavery so amply demonstrated), natural rulers of the planet, intelligent, organized, energetic, visionary.

White stereotypes of Whiteness have included the 'civilizing mission' of the European colonialists, and the 'manifest destiny' of White settlers in North America to rule from the Atlantic to the Pacific, as well as the common Latin American enthronement of 'whitening' (*blanqueamiento* in Spanish-speaking nations, *branqueamento* in Brazil), that is, the supremely positive evaluation of European phenotypes. The neglect of Whiteness stereotypes also leads to the implicit restriction of the adjective 'ethnic' to people of color, and the implicit enthronement of Whiteness as normal, or at least planetarily central. A small flood of studies of Whiteness emerged during the 1990s, some of which tended toward narcissism, some of which cut new ground (see for example, Lipsitz, 1998; Hill, 1997).

The other limitation produced by exclusive emphasis on White racist stereotypes of people of color is the neglect of stereotypes produced by people of color, whether Japanese, Chinese, or South Asian stereotypes of each other, or of Africans, or within African nations by members of different tribal peoples. A colleague of our acquaintance once congratulated a Nigerian graduate student on his excellent class-paper on stereotyping, and asked him how the process operated in Nigeria. The student said that the concept did not apply there, and upon then being asked about relations between the Yoruba and Ibo peoples within Nigeria (numbering many millions respectively), answered that – he was himself Yoruba – Ibos really *were* grasping, greedy, money-grubbing, untrustworthy, unpatriotic ...

At the same time, in academic discussion definitions of the racial stereotyping process have also developed some less clearcut edges. First, stereotypes are generally reckoned to be particular aspects of a more general process by which humans categorize the world and thereby make sense of it for practical daily living (Abrams and Hogg, 1999). Social psychologist Henri Tajfel (1982) indeed argued that cognition typically operates by reducing the complex flux of social reality to bi-polar categories, suggesting therefore the psychological normalcy and ease with which racial stereotyping is accomplished. Turner (1987) and Capozza and Brown (2000) have further proposed that the ego-involved dynamic of judgement leads to value-based distortions in any inter-group comparison, so that stereotypes are by definition dynamic entities.

Second, stereotypes are argued to be capable of change over time, as in the story of how the Irish population of the USA gradually lost its earlier stereotype as more or less equivalent to African and gained White status (Ignatiev, 1995).[9] Historians have similarly traced the shift from religiously based negative stereotypes of Africans to those exploiting primitive physical anthropology and biology (Jordan, 1968; Haller, 1995; Fredrickson, 1971), and subsequently Barker (1981), Entman and Rojecki (2000), and other scholars cited in the previous chapter have analyzed the emergence of culturalist racial stereotyping since the latter part of the last century.

The most economical 'Ockham's Razor' explanation of these ideological switches would have to lie in the enduring persistence of racial oppression despite changes over time in hegemonic cultural frameworks and in the mechanisms of oppression (for example, the shift in the USA from slavery, then to share-cropping, and then to urban migrant labor).

Third, rather than being pure fictions, unresponsive to any counter-evidence, stereotypes are argued to have some connection with social reality, however partial and thereby distorted. As a result they gain in plausibility precisely because they appear to lock on to a kernel of self-evident truth. The stereotype of the Mexican man sitting asleep on the ground against a wall in daytime, a huge sombrero over his head, or of the Roma family traveling in a caravan that is also their home, or of the Arab woman with her head veiled, all scrape against a certain reality. Yet not only is the reality fragmented, but very often a negative interpretation of the fragment hangs in the background without needing to be explicitly stated. Thus Mexican men appear as torpid bums, Roma families as improvident, Arab women as powerless and repressed, and somewhere between contemptible and pitiable.

Fourth, an important aspect of racial and ethnic stereotyping is their overlapping, for example by gender and 'race', so that very often women of color have been defined as pliant and sexually available to White men, even aflame with desire for them, whereas men of color are depicted as troublesome and hostile. There is little doubt that stereotypes of social class overlap with those of 'race' and ethnicity as well, particularly in situations where a first generation of unskilled migrant workers from rural backgrounds is re-adjusting to industrial capitalism and urban existence. If those workers are also of a different ethnic group, national or international in origin, there is typically a fusion of both types of negative stereotype in their regard – they are *all* ignorant, noisy, dirty, disorganized, thieving, drunken, rambunctious. These are class stereotypes lent additional traction by racist ideology. This gender and/or class fusion process tends to lend extra vitality to racial stereotyping because it draws on more detail, or offers a variation in 'knowledge' about supposed differences in 'the others'.

Recent work on stereotyping in cinema (Ramírez-Berg, 2002) also examines the ways in which films and other media may present contradictory stereotypes, or how particular actors may use their performance skills to overflow the stereotypical roles they are allotted by Hollywood. (At this point we find ourselves drawing closer to literary discussions of text and textuality that we examine further below.)

So where does this panoply of meanings of the term 'stereotype' leave us? It seems on the face of it as though its uses render it contradictory in many ways. From the 400-tons-of-pressure analogy rigidly categorizing ethnic groups and implicitly overwhelming all resistance to its sway, to the historical switches in the specific content of racial stereotypes, from the presence of contradictory stereotypes to their derivation from the normal ways we make sense of the world, and from their emotive anchoring to their anchoring partially in fact, all in all the concept seems extraordinarily slippery. If stereotypes are so powerful and emotionally invested, how come they change? If so all-encompassing, how do mutually incompatible examples pop up in the same text? If so normal as a way of making sense of the world around us, and if at least partially grounded in reality, is it merely quixotic to try to challenge them?

Our response is that the very variety of these multiple dimensions of the term 'stereotype' acknowledges the complexity of cultural representation, for they are not mutually exclusive. For example, it is important not to fuse personal psychology with the sweep of history: a rigid racial stereotype someone holds to passionately for the duration of their lifetime does not have to stand the test of centuries. Bi-polar framing may be normal – dark-light, good-bad and the rest – but we are capable of thinking outside of binaries, and ever more so in the culturally hybrid planet that global migration patterns have influentially accented since the end of World War II. By and large, too, members of minority-ethnic groups have always been less likely to be prisoners of majority-group stereotypes and more able to differentiate between individuals than vice versa.

And because a stereotype is powerful, it does not mean it is sole king of the hill. Competing stereotypes can and do operate, as Watkins (1998) dissects so well in his discussion of the popularity of young Black hip-hop musicians and the success of Black cinema in the USA around the turn of the last century, contrasted with the simultaneously widespread stereotype of young Black men as criminogenic and unproductive. Indeed the very fact of conflict and change in stereotypes is a major reason why it is feasible to challenge them. Realistically acknowledging their dangerous power and reach is not the same as according them invincibility.

Perhaps the conceptual difference between 'stereotype' and 'image' is that the former suggests more by way of public and personal buy-in, while the latter focuses more upon the components of the content. The former tilts our attention toward media users, the latter toward media construction. Both, however, direct our attention to the constant interactive process between ethnic group roles – majority and minority – in the social structure and media texts. The urgent practical questions are, how might media break these racist moulds, where have media succeeded in breaking them, how can media which perpetuate them be brought effectively to account?

We now move from terms that identify one component or sub-component in the cultural and mediatic definition of ethnic communities, minority and majority, to a series of wider and more inclusive terms: framing, ideology, representation, discourse, text.

Framing

This is a concept used more so far in news analysis (Reese et al., 2001) than elsewhere in media research, though in no way exclusively with regard to 'race' or ethnicity. It is largely deployed in two senses, one to indicate that something of importance may be excluded from the media picture, the other to concentrate rather on what is actually in frame, in the photographic sense.

For example in the 1990s, in the realm of reporting ethnicity issues in the USA, a local TV news frame was typically (a) a crime story frame or (b) an ethnic cultural festival frame (Heider, 2000). In both cases the frame excluded pretty well everything else about the life of the communities of color in question, and zeroed in on a single 'negative' or a single 'positive' dimension instead. The term implicitly suggests that this framing is ongoing, an entrenched practice. Thus while the crime or the ethnic festival themselves may be reported in a 'racially' unprejudiced manner, the continual framing bestowed by the coverage over time is extremely restrictive and blocks out the potential in media for wide-ranging communication between various ethnic groupings.

The concept of 'framing' has definite value, in that it notes how something unsaid, out of frame, may be as (or more) important in representing ethnicity or 'race' as what is said.[10] It also encourages us to consider the motivations, conscious or habitual and in the latter case rarely reflected upon, of those media professionals who daily reproduce these frames – for frames may be habitual, but did not emerge either from a clear blue sky or fully armed like Athena from Zeus' forehead. 'Framing' also prompts us to explore the long-term impact on audiences' definitions of social reality, whether minority-ethnic audiences who find themselves systematically excluded except in repetitive and limiting news scenarios, or majority-ethnic audiences, with only superficial work-contacts at best with people of color, who draw their perspectives *on themselves* as well as on people of color largely from these frames. And lastly, the concept directs attention away from interpreting a single news story exclusively from its specifics, which in and of themselves may be unexceptionable, and towards the ongoing flow of coverage.

Examples are numerous. Coverage of the African continent virtually entirely in terms of wars, coups d'état, famines, AIDS and other diseases, corruption, all arguably has an immensely powerful framing role in defining people of African descent in White-majority nations, whatever the contents of an individual news story about them (Fair, 1993). The same could be said of framing Arabs as Muslim fanatics and terrorists bent on a second Jewish Holocaust (Shaheen, 1984; 2001). Covering people of color in Britain as immigrants ('even unto the third and fourth generation'), or

Mexican Americans, the largest Latino grouping in the USA, as immigrants, frames them as not belonging, as not being integral to the nation, as not being stakeholders in the common good (cf. Hartmann and Husband, 1974; Perea, 1997). Restricting African Americans in TV entertainment largely to sitcoms frames them in a buffoon role (Gray, 1995; Means Coleman, 1998).

These frames, such as the 'immigrant' frame, the 'African disaster' frame or the 'Black comedian' frame, are maintained even while telling with compassion the tragic story of undocumented Latin American workers dying of exposure in the Arizona desert, or of a truck in Britain crammed with undocumented Chinese workers dead from asphyxiation. Or in reproducing heart-rending news photos of emaciated African infants, or – at the other extreme – in a witty Black stand-up comedy act. If the media frame excludes depth and variety at the same time as it obsessively focuses on one trait or a mere handful of them, individually brilliant comedy acts, video games or news reports do not generally succeed in subverting the frame.

Lastly, framing is a useful concept for our focus in this study precisely because of the centrality of the visual in 'race' and ethnic relations, and in media. In cinema, television, video games, press photos and advertising, the simple presence/absence of people of color in frame is immediately an issue, even before we address the equally significant question of the roles they play. At the time of writing in the USA, for example, although African Americans were more visible in television and cinema than ever before, the same was in no way true of Native Americans, Latinos, Asian Americans or Arab Americans. If tens of millions of people are almost out of frame, literally, visually, they are scarcely even dignified with a media stereotype! There is not even an image to contest!

This is the principal reason why minority-ethnic media and progressive alternative media are so important, for in one way or another they at least put people back in frame. A commercial Spanish-language radio station in the USA that programs nothing but Latin hit numbers and only makes money for its White owners still serves that purpose. A Turkish corner-store in Germany and a South Asian corner-store in Britain or Canada that rent homeland films on video, also serve that purpose. The issue is not purely one of being in or out of frame though, as Naficy's (1993) study of Iranian television in Los Angeles showed, along with the Australian studies of Asian migrant media in Cunningham and Sinclair (2001) and Gillespie's (1995) study of Indian families' TV viewing in London. Within, and inevitably between, migrant generations there is a degree of cultural hybridization that defies binary exclusiveness. Zuberi (2001) has engagingly traced the diffusion of cultural hybridization in popular music through the British younger generation at large.

Ideology

This word has a considerable history (Larrain, 1979). Its most common contemporary sense is pejorative, defining ideologies as sets of false ideas that *other* people share, never oneself, such as Christian fundamentalism, Trotskyism or Mahayana Buddhism, belief-systems with an evolutionary lineage and dynamic of their own.

In more recent cultural theory, neo-Marxist uses (Williams, 1977: 55–82; Althusser, 1971; Gramsci, 1971) have been prominent, placing four facets of the term uppermost. First has been the notion that in capitalism's historical evolution its dominant economic classes have not only been active economically, but have also heavily influenced common understandings of the world and of the purposes of existence, (in essence, ideology). Second is the notion that these common understandings mostly operate to underpin, or at least rarely to subvert, the capitalist process. Third, that ideology is not made up of free-floating ideas, but ideas realized in institutions and codes of conduct that continuously enact them in all kinds of practical everyday ways.

Last is the notion that these understandings are not automatic, stable or permanent, but part of a continuous and emergent negotiation process, over decades and longer, between the centers of power and the masses. Ideological understandings may even disintegrate entirely in times of social pressure and crisis, such as the Russian belief, as World War I dragged on, in the divinely appointed Tsar and the Orthodox Church hierarchy. Or the American belief, as the decades lengthened after World War II, in the merits of women staying home to work unpaid as housewives and mothers. Or the Afro-Brazilian endorsement of their nation's racial hierarchy and its ideology of 'whitening',[11] both of which began to erode substantially during the 1990s.

A term given considerable play by Gramsci and Williams, and indeed by quite a number of researchers following in their footsteps, is the notion of hegemony.[12] The concept basically endeavors to focus our attention on the non-coercive dimension of political power, on the construction of a functioning if imperfect consensus in *national* self-understandings that enable over time within a given nation a certain level of political stability and a certain direction of capitalist development. The scenario is neither Aldous Huxley's *Brave New World* nor George Orwell's *1984*, that is, some form of total public subordination, but rather a scenario in which the capitalist order is acknowledged most of the time but far from always, in which that order is subject to intermittent challenges, large and small, and in which the recasting of common public understandings becomes a far from easy task if those challenges are to be surmounted ideologically and business is to be as usual. At the turn of the millennium the anti-corporate street battles in Seattle and from city to city across the planet represented one instance of such challenges to the capitalist order.

Thus racist ideology and its media expressions past and present are not a one-size-fits-all-forever phenomenon, but an evolving cluster of responses, sometimes internally contradictory one with another, to centuries of challenge by people of color to slavery, to colonial rule, and to the institutional racist practices of the post-slavery and post-colonial epoch. A case in point is the partial shift in emphasis since World War II which we have already referred to, from a biologically/genetically defined racism to a 'cultural' racism (Barker, 1981; Guillaumin, 1995), or 'modern' racism (Entman and Rojecki, 2000).

In this overall framework, the ongoing roles of media in articulating racist frameworks and stereotypes are of central significance, because it is precisely their overall role *daily* to define and massage the present and the past for us. But that vocation is not straightforward and is never 'done'. New challenges constantly present themselves. In this sense we could think of mainstream media as workshops of today's *and tomorrow's* racist ideology.

Thus the term ideology, in this definition, can offer a richly sociological and historical lens through which to address media framing of 'race' and ethnicity, in ways that framing itself and image and stereotype do not. It draws our attention to the specific societal sources of the understandings of 'race' and ethnicity commonly saturating media frames. Media may sustain and develop these understandings, but are only one vector in a whole cultural complex consisting of historical, economic, educational, political and religious forces and institutions.

We are not proposing the term as essential, any more than any other single term, only as useful. Indeed Roland Barthes, in his famous essay 'Myth today' in his *Mythologies* (1988), endeavored to substitute the term 'myth' for ideology. He did so in part to challenge the conviction of French Communist Party ideologues that they had a singular lock on exposing and dissecting capitalist ideology, and also to propose that not least they themselves were in the business of producing some pretty energetic if threadbare ideology, not simply the glorious truth.

Yet Barthes' attempt to capture ideological processes while cutting loose from the word itself needs to claim our attention a moment more. One of the most quoted examples he offers in the essay cited is a cover of the chic French weekly *Paris-Match* from the mid-1950s, showing an immaculately turned out African soldier in the French army saluting the *tricolor*. He argues that this entirely caption-less visual address was ideologically designed to 'prove' the loyalty of most of France's colonial empire to the Mother Country. In the context of the colossal French military defeat in its then-colony, Vietnam, at the 1954 battle of Dien Bien Phu, and the beginning of Algeria's liberation war against French colonial rule in the very same year, such reassurance may have come as some solace to the magazine's elite readers. Barthes suggests that the cover poses a 'natural' order of things, in which grateful Africans are only too ready to fight and if needs be to die for their colonial masters. Questions, mild and awkward alike, are effortlessly disposed of by the unadorned 'obviousness' of the photo.

The analysis is brilliant. Yet the tendency is still present to perceive the ideological 'naturalization' as seamless, overwhelming and almost invincible, rather than as often a holding operation in the face of repeated challenges, constantly in need of repair and remodeling, with competing and sometimes discordant institutions responsible for doing so. Barthes' implicit reduction of this untidiness is a wooden element derived, despite his own critique of it, from sloppy Marxist definitions of the public as simple dupes, and in addition from the symptomatic reading approach typical of literary studies that discards any uncertainty as to how users will actually appropriate a text. It is an interpretation that clashes with the much more change- and conflict-oriented uses of the term 'ideology' to be found in Gramsci and Williams. Those uses are pivotal for the disjunctions involved in analyzing 'racial' and ethnic dimensions of media.

Let us now take two instances to illustrate this. Hall and his associates (1978) analyzed a newly intensive British news media campaign in the mid–1970s highlighting street assaults – 'mugging' – by young Black males in Britain. They argued the trumpeting of the term, previously not even part of British everyday vocabulary, had to be understood in the context of a deep political crisis consisting of extensive labor unrest and social militancy since the 1960s, the ultimate roots being in the long-term decline of the British economy. Some circles of power with very good access to news media sought to deflect the challenge through the gradual ideological creation of a 'menacing Black American' stereotype for the Black younger generation. It effectively criminalized Black social resistance, reframing as a generally threatening and international public presence the bitter opposition by young Black people, not to White people as such, but to very extensive racial discrimination by employers, police and other authority figures.[13] Previously the dominant stereotype for people of color had been 'immigrants', but with the emergence of new generations of British-born people of color that term had lost some steam. Enter, instead, the pan-national Black figure of the young 'mugger', the nightmare of American streets, now homegrown. If the police repressed 'him', so much the better.

The second example comes from Australia in the mid–1990s, with the emergence of Australia's racist One Nation movement,[14] led by former Member of Parliament Pauline Hanson. This was also given very substantial and sometimes sympathetic play in Australian news media. It drew upon a still vigorous ideology of (supposedly dead) White Australian identity, saturated by the many historical decades of official 'White Australia' immigration policy, hostility to olive-skinned immigrant workers from southern and south-eastern Europe, and to new Asian immigrants, and centuries-long anti-Aboriginal sentiment. It too emerged during a period of sustained economic downturn,[15] which One Nation capitalized upon by claiming special privileges were being allocated to everyone except 'normal' White Australians.

Both of these are instances in which we may make the analysis of media and racism considerably more coherent by utilizing the term 'ideology' (in its neo-Marxist sense), with its inbuilt focus on conflicts and challenges to the status quo, together with the interconnections between media culture and the historical formation of a nation's majority self-understanding. It also points us to the multiply determined and mutually interacting processes, economic (the downturns), political (the racist backlashes) and international (migrant workers), included in both cases. The mediatic framing, stereotypes and images involved were all parts of what took place, but only made full sense in their intimate linkage with wider processes on which the term 'ideology' helps us focus as well.

The term has one final component that we feel is especially valuable and motivated us, indeed, to write this book. 'Ideology' in the neo-Marxist sense also pushes in the direction of doing media analysis to help bring about constructive change, rather than an ivory tower exercise. The latter may merely produce an entirely unjustified sense of moral superiority vis-á-vis media professionals, or consummate itself in pointless lamentation at how dreadful racism is in the media. After all, in perhaps his most famous aphorism of all Marx did remark that people had very frequently sought to understand the world, but that the key issue was to change it. Our consistent question is, how may this ideologically racist framing be combated, in and out of the media, in the interests of developing a more just and open society? The chapters that follow are designed to point precisely in that direction.

Representation

The most influential modern source of this term in the cultural context, rather than in the context of political representation, is Durkheim's *Elementary Forms of Religious Life* (1995), where he used the term 'collective representations' to denote the religious culture of Aboriginal Australians (or rather, what anthropologists of his day claimed those cultures to be). He proposed religious culture to have evolved over time in an emergent process in which it expressed the fundamental awe of earlier human beings at the enormous force of social/tribal bonds and the expectations they experienced constantly from birth. Hence 'God' and associated religious tenets were, Durkheim argued, a displaced expression of that very awe of society's overwhelming power over them.

The kernel of Durkheim's proposition was thus that fundamental conceptualizations of the world and the meaning of life were neither philosophically, nor theologically, but societally derived. The power over everyday understandings of the world that the Marxist tradition located in dominant social classes, Durkheim relocated in the tremendous force human society as a whole exerted over its members.

However, the term representation did not freeze at that point. At a later date it even became reclaimed within a Gramscian/Barthesian analytical tradition (see for example, Barthes, 1988; Hall, 1996b). Indeed the word at the time of writing has become a preferred expression for the process of imagery construction, including in the title of our book. A series of major analyses of 'race' and communication in the USA addressing the issues generally (Gandy, 1998: 155–92), in relation to African Americans (Hooks, 1992; Gray, 1995: 70–92; Guerrero, 1993: 113–55; Watkins, 1998), to Arabs and Muslims (Karim, 2000; Steet, 2000), to Native Americans (Kilpatrick, 1999), to Latinos (Noriega, 1992; Noriega and López, 1996; Valdivia, 2000; Ramírez-Berg, 2002) have taken the term as central to their arguments.

What does it signify in these later versions? Hall (1996a) proposes two levels of representation, the first linguistic, in which words denote particular things and processes. However, he quickly moves on to classic arguments by De Saussure concerning the arbitrary character of words/sounds as denoters. He sees De Saussure's work as able to be extrapolated from language alone to a 'constructionist' approach to all forms of representation such as narratives, imagery and discourses: 'If the relationship between a signifier and its signified is the result of a system of social conventions specific to each society and to specific historical moments – then all meanings are produced within history and culture' (Hall, 1996a: 32).

He then proceeds by way of this transition to a radically societal and relativist definition of representation, drawing heavily upon Foucault and denying that representation either simply mirrors reality or conveys without further ado the intentions of its makers. He concludes that much insight may be drawn from Foucault's notion of historically specific conceptual frameworks – 'discourses', in Foucault's terminology – that have come to define authoritatively, often with the back-up of laws, how we represent ourselves and others, indeed how we understand our existence and roles in various zones of life (psychiatric illness, sexual behavior and crime being some instances).

These frameworks allocate us roles, or 'subject-positions' in Foucault's terminology (and here once again we stray into a discussion of media users). For example, when a TV newscaster of color presents a story portraying a person of color being handcuffed by the police – the example is ours, not Hall's[16] – the combined discourses of criminality, 'race' and objective journalism might be said to place (a) us as viewers/law-abiding citizens, (b) the newscaster as channeling fact, (c) the police as defenders of public safety, and (d) the person being led away – guilty or not – as emblematic of the criminogenic character of 'minority subcultures'. From the rest of Foucault's work it is reasonably clear that he was not suggesting we were terminally trapped in those subject-positions, merely that they were the line of least resistance to our being discursively placed.

Thus media 'racial' and 'ethnic' representation, in this enlarged sense of the term, does more than present us with images or stereotypes for us to accept or reject, to learn or forget, or maintain at the back of our minds. It provides us with a well-worn script for a very familiar 'racial' play in which we are *all* performers in some regard or other, unless we consciously choose to walk off the stage. The handcuffed prisoner of color does not, of course, have that option, but since the rest of us don't have to leave our seats, our option to 'walk' may also be rather moot. After all, we have seen this show before many times. Why fuss?

Hall's discussion of representation is not one that figures in most of the other authors whose work was listed above, who quite often simply deploy the term without further conceptual clarification. This is not to say that there is not a great deal to learn from how they do deploy it. Gandy (1998) has a valuable chapter 'Reflection and representation' in which he summarizes a body of research critical of the shortcomings of mainstream media in this area. Gray (1995) helpfully traces the impact of a small number of Black TV professionals on developing some more nuanced representations of African American life.

But the actual term 'representation' is mostly used either to signal presence or absence of people of color from media, or constructive vs unconstructive portrayal. Gray uses it as a launching pad to analyze continuing US struggles over televisual representation of African Americans, Guerrero (1993: 113–55) to discuss the Reagan era 'racial' backlash in Hollywood movies, Steet (2000) to track the changing emphases of Arab world portrayals in *National Geographic*. But the term is used in a much more neutral, almost enumerative manner, rather than the layers of significance suggested for it by Hall and those he cites. There is no authoritative way to determine which type of use is more appropriate. The only issue here is to note the differences in its deployment as a concept – and, more to the point perhaps, the way in which Hall's more extensive version strives to reach beyond the text to audiences' and readers' responses, an issue we will revert to when we conclude our discussion of text and move on to reception.

Discourse

This term is another which relates the specifics of particular images or stereotypes to a larger context, in the first place within a larger *verbal* reasoning process – maybe just as emotive or more, than rational as a process – in which they flourish and to which they lend their sap. The term has effectively become almost commandeered by Foucault and his followers, and we summarized above the bare bones of that reading of the word. However, other more generic uses of the term have been applied to racism and media (van Dijk and Smitherman-Donaldson, 1988; van Dijk, 1988: 135–254; 1991; 1993), as well as Foucauldian treatments very close to our theme, such as Said's discussion of Orientalism (1978).

Van Dijk's approach has begun from a position very close to Bakhtin's (1986), namely the analysis of language communication in terms of a whole utterance (*vyskazyvanie*) rather than the sentence taken as the fundamental unit of analysis (the classical method of linguistic science). Thus an 'utterance' could be an editorial, a novel, a play, a *telenovela*, a documentary, a news bulletin, a computer game. The structure and logic of the communication would then be defined in terms of the whole, not chopped up into separate sentences or words as in some versions of content analysis. However, van Dijk has consistently taken this position a significant step further by urging the priority of 'critical discourse analysis', namely a rigorous questioning of discourses regarding their implications for or against social justice and, in his own work, particularly in relation to 'racial' justice.

Van Dijk has focused especially on the Dutch, British and American press and its typical inability in each nation to acknowledge the harsh realities of ongoing racist practices, while frequently contributing a great deal to racist paranoia in the White majority by use of xenophobic and overheated language when dealing with 'racial' issues. 'Uncontrolled immigration' panics and refusal to acknowledge systematic police violence and judicial injustice against people of color, are two of the topics he explores, while reserving a particular eye for the seemingly articulate and acceptable racist discourses of well-placed sectors of society, such as academics, educators, politicians and corporate leaders (see especially, van Dijk and Smitherman-Donaldson, 1993).

His approach is largely an empirical one, picking apart the assumptions, glossings and silences in 'racial' news discourses to expose their underlying drift. While utilizing certain basic concepts at certain points, such as schemata, stylistics, topic, rhetoric, his specific analyses have considerable resonance with standard literary-critical method. He does not, however, engage with the analysis of visual imagery.

Said's analysis of Orientalist discourse owes a great deal to Foucault, although he does not join the latter in his dismissal of the importance of particular writers in the promulgation of discourses. He restricts himself to British, French and US discourses concerning the so-called Near East, i.e., the Arab, Persian and Turkish world, while acknowledging Orientalism's discourse, historically, to have covered Central, South and East Asia. Unlike van Dijk's or Reeves' emphasis on discourse as contemporary public utterance, Said follows Foucault in tracking the genesis and development of certain still-influential literary, scientific and administrative tropes initially coined in the course of British, French, and later on, US struggles to dominate the region. These continued from Napoleon's 1798 invasion of Egypt and the 1869 creation of the Suez Canal to the past century's drive to control oil supplies and profits.

Said traces how frequently Western writers have insisted upon the ignorance, backwardness, emotionalism, Muslim fanaticism, of the 'Orient', the consequent irreconcilable gulf between 'East' and 'West', and upon the Olympian privilege of Western commentators in explaining to the world at large, including the so-called Orient, its true character. The continuity he points out between past and present in this regard is often very striking. Unlike Foucault, however, and more like van Dijk, Said's emphasis is consistently empirically tied to the continuing dynamic of 'racial' colonialism and neo-colonialism, as well as to a close reading of the terms of the discourse.[17]

The merit of discourse analysis in these forms is that it also invites us to perceive how 'racist' discourse interpenetrates other verbal discourses of gender, nation, class, youth, region, thus moving away from a sociologically unrealistic divorce between it and these other social sources of division. As we noted above in our discussion of stereotypes, the tenacity and vigor of racist sentiment and perception is much more easily grasped once this basic dimension is in focus, namely the typical over-determination of racist media discourses by their articulation and overlapping with others. In our discussion of 'ideology' likewise, we stressed the value of its enmeshment of racist thematics in wider historical and societal processes. On the other hand, given the tendency toward logo-centrism in discourse analysis we may gratefully refer back to discussions of imagery and the imaginary, in which the visual is accorded full significance.

The Text

As currently deployed, the term implies a specific formal entity – a popular song, a monument, a tattoo, a radio play, a feature article, an ad. Its overlap is evident, potentially or actually, with the concepts of discourse just discussed. There is no presumption that the text, however, has any necessary purchase on the stability or unity of its meaning as interpreted by viewers, readers, listeners, whereas in van Dijk's or Said's discussions of 'discourse' its hegemonic role tends to be assumed. To appreciate the difference one only need think of the ferocious struggles that have taken place over the interpretation of the Bible or the Qur'an, although the producers of symptomatic readings sometimes appear not to wish to acknowledge this problem.

However, there are still two major aspects to current concepts of the text that need noting. The first consists of the multiple voices (perspectives) often present within a single text. In a play or movie this is all too obvious, but normally this reality is equally significant, if not so immediately evident, in the novel, short story, stand-up comic act, documentary or computer game. This recognition trains us to look for the different strands in media texts, and not to assume they are unitary. For the analysis of 'racial' or 'ethnic' content, this is very important (see for example, Smith-Shomade, 2002). A film or a pulp novel may well contain, and not by the conscious intention of its creators, highly contradictory threads – indeed often does – so that it cannot be neatly written up as anti-racist or written off as racist.

The second aspect is the almost analogous notion of texts as 'spaces' within which different perspectives may clash, versus texts as homogeneous. Both exist. Gray's (1995) analysis of the construction of Blackness in US television is exemplary in this regard, stepping with consistently finely-tuned precision through the nuances of 'race', gender, class, genre, and declining to fuse the multiple with the unitary. For example his discussion of the Black-cast *The Cosby Show*, the tremendous US television success of the later 1980s, notes the way it moved beyond both assimilationist and pluralist perspectives while retaining significant elements of both. Yet he emphasizes by contrast how many of its look-alike shows projected

> a homogeneous, totalizing blackness, a blackness incapable of addressing the differences, tensions, and diversities among African Americans … Discursively, the problem of racial inequality is displaced by the incorporation of blacks into that great American stew where such cultural distinctions are minor issues that enrich the American cultural universe without noticeably disturbing the delicate balance of power. (Gray, 1985: 88–89)

Yet in assessing the text of US media handling of the upsurges that followed the 1992 not-guilty verdict on four policemen who had been charged with assaulting Rodney King, Gray establishes a striking internal contradiction:

> In the search for a hook or an angle from which to cover the crisis, the national press seemed at once *paralyzed* by an inability to speak coherently about 'race' and *spellbound* by the action, the drama, the spectacle. (1995: 170, his emphases)

Analysis of this contradiction almost inexorably draws us deeper into consideration of the public avoidance of honest discussion of 'race' endemic within US culture, the obsession with stunning visual images prized within US media culture, and how they combined to rob the

US public of understanding in the crisis. Gray's treatment is both fine-grained and, in Walter Benjamin's famous expression, brushes 'history' against the grain.

Yet, in conclusion on this point, the symptomatic readings frequent within cinema studies circles are normally content, unlike Gray who locates his study firmly within an analysis of the political economy of Reaganism in the 1980s and early 1990s, to analyze texts purely in terms of their own internal logics, narrative or semiotic.

This criticism must be balanced, however, by recognition of two invaluable emphases within the textual study approach, namely on genre and narrative and, within the theatrical and musical branch of textual study, a further emphasis on performance. While extensive discussion of these dimensions is beyond our scope here, we have already noted, in assessing empiricist content analysis, how that methodology usually irons them out of consideration altogether. Yet the role of genre in framing audience expectations is extremely powerful, and oftentimes the public deeply desires the repetition, with slight variations, of a given genre.

In relation to our study, the Hollywood Western, with its typically demeaning representation of Native Americans and Mexicans, and the virtual absence of African Americans as either cowboys, soldiers or farmers, is a classic example of a genre tremendously popular over two or three decades that succeeded thereby in hammering home these stereotypes and frames often in passing (Buscombe, 1988). In *Red River* (1948), for example, the action taking place within a mere ten minutes has a small boy orphaned, single survivor of an attack by bloodthirsty Indians; has John Wayne's character crossing Red River into Texas, looking out over the classic huge empty expanse beloved of so many settlers' historical portraits of America, and proclaiming 'That's all mine!'; and has Wayne's character shoot dead, with zero emotion, a Mexican who rides up to dispute his ownership and who with unthinkable *hubris* thinks he can beat the Duke's character to the draw.

Genre need not necessarily, we should emphasize, be a reactionary force. Genre-bending media texts, such as the multi-ethnic sci-fi *Star Trek* TV series and films, may push into new and constructive territory. But genre is a vital dimension of textual communication. What means one thing in a police drama may not mean the same on news, and what flies in a soap opera may not have the same drift in reality TV. At the same time, genres are not absolute or watertight, and mixed-genre media offerings are not uncommon. Nonetheless, neglecting genre considerations is distinctly inadvisable in the interpretation of texts, including media dealing with 'race' and ethnicity in one way or another.

A dual instance of middle – hybridized – ground in the news genre is to be found in Rodríguez's (2000) study of *Noticiero Univisión*, the US

Spanish-language news service. She found that its news values were virtually identical to US network news with the single exception that it paid much more attention to stories from Latin American nations. Simultaneously, to appeal to the widest audience, it cultivated a Spanish of which the vocabulary and pronunciation sought to find a median point among its various nationally specific versions.

Narrative and performance likewise, in their separate ways, are neglected to the detriment of understanding the dynamics of textual communication. (We have touched upon performance above, and will not pursue it further here.) Narrative is not only to be found in fiction. News coverage also organizes narratives, such as the US local TV news coverage of Black and Latino crime suspect stories that Entman and Rojecki (2000), Campbell (1995) and Heider (2000) found so prevalent.

Of course it is possible to produce media counter-narratives. The documentary *The Return Of Navajo Boy* (2000) traces moments in the life of a Navajo boy, actually named John Wayne after the actor, who had starred in a film set next to his home in Monument Valley, Utah. Soon afterwards, in a pattern grimly familiar from many Native American and Native Canadian children's experience since the mid-1800s of being forcibly relocated huge distances from their homes and culturally reprogrammed, the little boy was fostered out to a White family some four hours' drive away in New Mexico and was not permitted to retain contact with his own family. The actor John Wayne was contacted by the foster mother with a request for money for the boy, and sent a single check for $100, which the boy himself never saw. Meanwhile the original family found itself repeatedly used as a 'poster' Navajo family on picture postcards, in tourist snapshots, and in other movies as local color, largely because of its Monument Valley home. Due only to an extraordinary sequence of events, the family was reunited some forty years later, a moment the film very movingly records.

Nevertheless, the disparity in distribution just between *Red River* and *The Return Of Navajo Boy*,[18] let alone between such counter-narratives and the body of films in the Western genre, many still running on cable movie channels, needs no further comment from us. We will however return to the question of minority-ethnic media below.

We will summarize the observations on textual content at the close of the chapter. We turn now, at considerably less length, to three further dimensions of research on racism, ethnicity and media: the production of media, the uses of media, and the roles of minority-ethnic media. The brevity of the discussion that follows has everything to do with the relatively miniscule quantity of research that has been undertaken on all three in connection with the theme of this book.

Production and Media Political Economy

This dimension of the issue embraces everything from the macro-level of media corporations and their roles within global political economy, through the micro-level of routines, organizational dynamics and professionals' ideologies of media production. Both levels, very obviously, are intimately interrelated but do not automatically operate in functional harmony.

The two book-length studies of which we are aware on the organizational dimensions of media with specific reference to 'race,' were done some twenty-five years apart by the late Philip Elliott,[19] *The Framework of Television Production* (1972), and by Simon Cottle, *Television and Ethnic Minorities* (1997). Elliott's was a quasi-ethnographic study of a BBC TV production team as it put together a six-part magazine series on 'race' relations. The topic was fortuitous: Elliott simply wished to study the organizational process, and this happened to be the series theme. The series project was redolent of the high-minded, socially progressive and also elitist ethos to be found in a number of quarters in the BBC at that time.

Perhaps the most striking index of that ethos is the way the team began to assemble the outside people it proposed to involve in some fashion in the series, as information sources, interviewees, or as links to still further individuals with some special claim to knowledge. Out came the address books for friends and contacts, out came the off-the-cuff suggestions for individuals who had been in the news on the subject one way or another in recent months or years. Transparent in this process was the virtual lack of personal contact with the objects of racism, with such people as community organizers, schoolteachers, clergy, advocacy group leaders. It was a well-intentioned production about, but *not* with or from, South Asians, West Indians, Africans, Chinese.[20]

Cottle's study was based upon interviews with three sets of television producers, namely in-house multi-cultural specialists in the BBC, independent producers contracting at intervals with both the BBC and the commercial channels, and minority-ethnic cable company operators. He focused principally upon the constraints they reported on program themes, and found that each set of producers, notwithstanding internal distinctions, was forced to maneuver within an increasingly competitive business climate. Even for the BBC, these pressures were interpreted as favoring programs with wide appeal, while for the major commercial channels as for the start-up minority-ethnic cable channels, risk-taking was even more likely to be shunned. Equally, the inherited conservative cautiousness of the BBC as of the mid-1990s, and its internal structure of bureaucratic fiefdoms, were neither of them conducive to pushing the boat out and engaging imaginatively with communities of color.

Aside from a multi-national collection of essays, *A Richer Vision* (1994), edited by Husband, which focused on training and recruitment programs for people of color in the communication industries, but did not examine news or entertainment production in and of themselves, Elliott's and Cottle's studies to date remain the landmark organizational analyses. Amongst the limited research in this area Heider (2000) has studied some of the routine professional assumptions that dominate journalists' work when reporting on 'race' in the USA, and Zook (1999) has analyzed a period of some years over the 1990s in the Fox Television network in the USA when the corporation's attempt to break into the traditional network triumvirate of ABC, CBS and NBC led it to experiment with Black-cast shows.

Clearly this paucity of studies has a great deal to do with the reluctance of media professionals to have researchers hanging around them as they work, perhaps leaking their under-pressure behavior to other news outlets, and their creative ideas to competitors, or perhaps just getting in the way. A production or print media feature focused on 'race' and ethnicity is liable to have media executives especially nervous – not that this nervousness, sadly, usually translates itself into an active listening posture vis-á-vis people of color.

Yet understanding how 'race' and ethnicity are filtered through this very complex mesh would be tremendously valuable. We know from newsroom studies (see for example, Schlesinger, 1987; Gans, 1979; Tuchman, 1978; Berkowitz, 1997) and from a major study of the overall organization of commercial TV entertainment in the USA (Gitlin, 2000), that the media production process consists overall of a blend of professional routines, editorial controls, advertising constraints and pressures, personal career goals, legal frameworks, and owner/executive priorities. And some accidents. We also know that in White-majority nations, media organizations, with the advertising industry probably currently in the lead, are very White indeed at the top.

It would be possible to focus on top executives, though practically very difficult indeed to gain access, on the ground that media are hierarchical organizations like most others, and the top is where 'racial' priorities are set. Instances such as the deliberate squelching of a BBC survey report, which found viewers of a 1960s comedy show[21] to feel much freer to express racist views as a result of what they had witnessed on the show, seem to underscore that understanding of power in media. The BBC's refusal to share figures on minority-ethnic staff even with its Equal Opportunity Advisor (Cottle, 1997: 29) was a further signal of executive power and sensitivity. Sensitivity of a different kind was hardly evident however in the reported comments of Hollywood executives refusing to cast Halle Berry, daughter of a Black father and White mother: 'We love Halle, we just don't want to go black with this part'; '... milk is milk until you add a little Hershey[22] ... It doesn't matter if you add a little Hershey or a lot' (Lyman, 2002: 1).

Yet we know enough about the sociology of business organizations to know that priorities may be set at the top, but are operationalized by others, who in that process sometimes carry out the exact intentions of chief executives, but who also often reshape them, not always intentionally. We also know that there are powerful informal channels of communication that often out-maneuver the business's official flow-chart. Strictly focusing on the summit is liable to suggest that a change of attitudes at that level would solve the problems of racism in media. That presumes there is a complete vacuum of power at the middle levels, that entrenched routines and codes can dissolve overnight, and not least that racist attitudes are the peculiar preserve of those at the top (and that they are universal there). It further presumes that there are conveyor belts bringing fresh talent of color to the doors of media firms on a daily basis, an assumption about schools' and universities' institutional commitment to educating students of color for this industry that resembles nothing so much as cloud-cuckoo-land. Indeed the diagnosis presumes, as is so often the case, that racism is simply a matter of the wrong attitudes, an assumption we hope to have savaged successfully in the course of the previous chapter. It further presumes that there are no challenges and zero changes in the media industries (see Chapter 7).

In short, there is a huge amount of research to be done on the mesh between corporate cultures in the media industries and the production of 'racially'-inflected news, entertainment, ads, computer games, popular music and the rest. More particularly still, there is tremendous need for research that is ultimately designed to help bend corporate codes in constructive directions. In some circles within minority-ethnic groups in the USA, anti-Semitic 'explanation' takes the place of coherent analysis in evaluating why Hollywood fails to operate more constructively, pointing to the considerable number of Jewish executives in the industry, past and present.[23] That fetid cul-de-sac, representing 'the socialism of the idiot' as August Bebel once put it, not only needs denouncing for its racism, but illustrates how crucial it is to produce searching political economic analysis that can actually get us somewhere in the struggle against racism.

Media Users

Just as the different terms used in textual/content analysis position us differently in relation to the issues we study, so too inevitably in reception analysis do the terms employed influence our research focus. Quite often, to speak of 'audiences' suggests market research on consumers (of commodities, including media products); to speak of 'publics' implies an actively participating body of media users in a democratic culture; to speak of 'spectators' implies film and television viewers; to speak of 'fans' directly focuses on enthusiasts; to speak of 'readers' implies active individual users of print media and the Web. Academic research never quite gets to the point of dignifying 'couch potato' with category status, but the notion at times seems implicit in definitions of audiences as tendentially passive.

Broadly, there are two basic categories for research into users of both majority- and minority-ethnic media (we will address the latter in the next section). One is users' discursive and action responses to media racism, namely to extreme, and to less aggressive but still harmful, shortcomings in coverage. Examples of the extreme would be the identification of people of color as legitimate pogrom targets, but also, frankly, the blunt refusal to acknowledge the prevalent harm of racism or (except glancingly) the existence of communities of color. Examples of less aggressive but still damaging coverage would be the ghettoization of people of color into TV sports and sitcoms, their repetitive identification with criminality in news and drama, the absence of reference to their economic and cultural contributions.

The second is the identity-responses of media users to the lifeworld definitions rehearsed in media. In a satellite and VCR era, and in an era of affluent brain drain as well as impoverished migration, these media and the definitions they provide are far from univocal. Nor, to judge by the few user-research studies accomplished, do they have anything resembling general – or, in terms of individuals – unalloyed impact. On the other hand, the research literature on Whiteness (see for example, Dyer, 1997; Hill, 1997) powerfully suggests that over many decades the media perpetuation of the normalcy of White status, power and culture has, in a number of nations, solidified the majority-ethnic public's widespread acceptance of the incontrovertible normalcy and legitimacy of its own power. In other words, before even there is any question of hostile feelings or perceptions toward individuals or groups of color, there is already a presupposition that the 'racial' hierarchy is a given, that minority-ethnic groups are an anomaly. White status and power are taken as self-evidently the fabric of the real, and coterminous with the definition of fundamental national identity. The USA, Canada, Australia, Britain, Germany, France, 'are' White countries with some marginal variations, not multi-component nations (where in addition the components are set in a very definite and historically entrenched pecking order).

This does not mean that the 'Whitist' mindset excludes additional and logically contradictory perspectives. White wage-workers are generally very well aware of the pitiful poker hand they have been dealt, and how far down the pecking order their everyday lives are. Yet one response by disenfranchised White workers, especially in places where the industrial guts have been ripped out of their economies, but even where they have not, is to use people of color as the condensing rod of their discontent. The experience of being reduced to unwanted status after a history of already being used and abused in the hard grind of industrial labor is one very difficult to take out against a seemingly abstract persecutor (the global economy, competitiveness, even executives' fatal errors),[24] while communities of color, already resented, are an accessible, low-power target, typically suffering from police violence rather than protection. The Le Pen phenomenon in France, the 1990s attacks on migrant workers in eastern Germany and southern Spain, California's 1996 referendum denying basic rights to immigrant workers (Proposition 207), are only a few instances of seemingly common place occurences.

It is a contradictory response economically, because their targets hardly had the power, had they even wished it, to be the agents of White dispossession or labor exploitation. Yet framed consistently over many decades by media which represented ordinary White people as always on the winning side of the global and national 'racial' divide, if only by inches, White rage was extremely predictable when Whites found themselves cast unceremoniously in large clusters into the abyss, or even if threatened with being pitched over the line. On this plane, no contradiction at all. Only deep fear, outrage, and therefore in a number of instances, loathing.

The Whiteness vector also plays a major role in Latin American nations (Downing, 2003b), sometimes including communities of color. Afro-Brazilian documentarian Joel Zito Araújo readily admits[25] how as a boy he was entranced by Brazil's mass audience *telenovelas* and at that time never really thought about their overwhelmingly White casts (in a country where at least half the population enjoys some African ancestry). Yet later in life, he wrote a book and directed a documentary, both entitled *The Denial of Brazil* (2001), which searchingly critiqued the Brazilian media establishment's racism. Other Black commentators have acknowledged how as children watching Western movies they would cheer for Tarzan or the White cowboys, and never think of identifying with the Native Americans on screen. The 'racial' hegemonic process can be extremely powerful. But as is also clear from these examples, this acceptance need not be permanent (or unitary, for it may also coexist with jokes satirizing the pretensions of the majority-ethnic group). Moving beyond these more general insights, we find that as with organizational and political economy studies in this area, there is a remarkable dearth of research related either to majority-ethnic or minority-ethnic audiences and readers. Commercial user data in the USA and some other nations may include ethnic status among their categories, but do not pursue in further detail *how* people process media texts in relation to ethnic issues. The issue considerably complicates the already difficult business of audience-research, not only because it adds the multiple, often highly charged, and sometimes expressively dense dimension of 'race' and ethnicity, but because further dimensions such as class, gender, age, language, migration and refugee status are essential to make full sense of both 'race' and ethnicity.

An early academic media-user study in this area was the 1969–70 stratified sample which one of the present authors researched in collaboration with Paul Hartmann, consisting of six surveys, two each in low-immigration, high-immigration and average-immigration areas of Britain (Hartmann and Husband, 1974). The similar nature of 'racial' perspectives registered in all areas of Britain strongly suggested that media, rather than the opportunity for face-to-face interaction, were acting as major definers of immigrants of color. However, the methodology involved correlating users' views with available media content, not an examination of how they went about interpreting or applying media frames.

A limited number of academic focus-group studies has investigated the reception process. For example, Bobo (1995) reports on discussions among some Black women in the USA of the film *The Color Purple* (1985). Hunt (1997; 1999) reports, respectively, on Los Angeles focus group reactions to TV coverage of the tumults following the 1993 'not guilty' verdict in the Rodney King trial, and in his second study on focus group reactions to coverage of the O.J. Simpson murder trial. Gillespie (1995) reports on the uses of English, Indian and Australian television by some Punjabi families in London. Jhally and Lewis (1992) studied urban audience responses in Massachusetts to the TV sitcom *The Cosby Show*. Schlesinger et al. (1992) studied the responses from a multi-ethnic group of women to various kinds of violent media content. Ross and Playdon (2001) provide a number of short studies of users, both of domestic and satellite TV, in Europe, the USA, South Africa and Australia. Out of the studies cited above, some are of mono-ethnic media users, others of multi-ethnic users, some take dimensions such as gender into account, others do not.

These, and other, studies are therefore very hard to summarize in their entirety, but often reiterate certain common themes, such as the cumulative frustration of not seeing members of your ethnic group on the screen, or if present, only in demeaning and limited situations of one kind or another. As regards the negotiation of self-definition, some suggest (see for example, Gillespie, 1995) that older generations of immigrants and indigenous communities use satellite TV services for reinforcement of their original identity, while younger generations use domestic TV as a way of plotting out their own lifeworld trajectories. Bird's (2001) study in particular engages with both the frustration and the potential agency of Native Americans with regard to media representations. Younger minority-ethnic generations often find themselves having 'to navigate between more layers and worlds of meaning, producing many, not just one, senses of belonging.'

Visibly missing are in-depth studies of majority-ethnic audiences' and readers' appropriations of media texts. In our discussion above of Whiteness, much of our argument was exploratory, albeit based upon careful analysis of long-established media patterns. How in practice do different White audiences and readers handle these issues, and how do they relate them to other vectors in their lives? Which responses are likely to have social and political consequences, in which situations?

How too do media operate in pluri-'racial' situations, particularly where traditional binary definitions of 'race' have become vastly more complicated by the presence of additional ethnic Others – in New Zealand, for example, where the Maori/Pakeha divide has been joined by Pacific Islander and Asian migrant groups, or in the USA where numbers of Latinos, all told, now slightly outstrip the number of African Americans? As of the beginning of the 2000 decade African Americans were appearing in significantly more numbers on TV and in films, while Latinos, Native Americans and Asian Americans were generally conspicuous by their absence, even though kicking hard on the door to get in. Indeed, with a growing number of individuals born to parents who do not share the same ethnic background or nationality, how do such individuals relate to media on a banal daily basis in defining their own identity and citizenship?

Furthermore, we need not stop at individual, family or secondary group audience responses. What are the roles of media users' advocacy organizations in pressuring mainstream media for constructive change? How far are accurate minority-ethnic consumer statistics and information able to be used to galvanize better quantitative and qualitative representation, including behind the camera and off the page? How far may media monitoring research be deployed to challenge the pretensions of media corporations to ethnic inclusiveness and perceptive representation?

Minority-Ethnic Media

Minority-ethnic media are characterized by a dramatic variation in scale of operation, by the specificity of intended audience and by much else. Some such media are well-funded, the commercial dynamics of their operation are basically similar to mainstream media (albeit highly niche-oriented), and their contents are politically conservative. We might instance some of the Arabic language press in France and Britain, and in the USA the Russian newspaper *Novoe Russkoe Slovo* and sections of the East Asian press on the West Coast. The particular case of *Univisión*, the Spanish-language TV channel in the USA that historically has been dominated by Mexico's giant Televisa corporation, has been interestingly analyzed by Rodríguez (2000). Many Spanish-language radio stations are owned by

Anglos. At the other end of the spectrum are indigenous people's media (see Chapter 5), migrant workers' media, refugees' media. The study by Park (1970 [1922]) of the working class immigrant press in the USA was indeed one of the first occasions when media and ethnicity were systematically analyzed (primarily to check out loyalty to the US government in World War I), but his pioneering work was not followed up for quite a number of decades.

All these minority-ethnic media, however, are of interest inasmuch as every one in some degree contributes to a pluralizing dynamic. They may not do so on a permanent basis. The Yiddish press in the USA, for example, which was so strong a hundred years ago (along with many other examples of Yiddish culture) has virtually vanished. The Black press in the USA still has its exemplars – the *Amsterdam News*, the *Pittsburgh Courier*, the *Chicago Defender* – but they play much less of a role and are much fewer in number than was the case some fifty years previously. Nonetheless, in carving out communication spaces specifically targeted at minority-ethnic publics, even for example purely commercially-driven radio stations playing music popular with immigrant groups from their homelands, media with minority-ethnic content significantly complicate the national picture. VCR and satellite options have significantly expanded the menu for recent migrants.

There have been a few, yet notable contributions to analyzing such media. Over and above those mentioned, and beyond standard histories of one or other minority-ethnic press publications, the work of Appadurai (1996), Naficy (1993), Zuberi (2001) and of the authors in Cunningham and Sinclair (2000), merits particular attention. Appadurai principally focuses on two empirical global features of the contemporary era, namely media and migration, and argues that both separately and together they are serving to refashion the world in unprecedented ways. Media, especially electronic media, 'offer new resources for the construction of imagined values and imagined worlds ... they tend to interrogate, subvert, and transform other contextual literacies' (p. 3), '[their] consumption ... throughout the world often provokes resistance, irony, selectivity, and, in general, *agency*' (p. 7). Migration, now prominently including the brain-drain as well as the transfer of more traditional agrarian, industrial and service skills, has created vast numbers of people whose experiences have had to adjust to global as well as traditional realities. They have created numerous 'diasporic public spheres' (pp. 21–23), especially within the brain-drain sector of labor (pp. 195–97). 'Those who wish to move, those who have moved, those who wish to return, and those who choose to stay rarely formulate their plans outside the sphere of radio and television, cassettes and videos, newsprint and telephone' (p. 6). Appadurai stresses here the powerful fusion of media and interpersonal communication flows among migrants, and between them and their communities of origin. The contemporary expansion of air travel to enable intermittent visits to migrants' countries of origin further intensifies this meld of communicative and cultural flows.

Cunningham and Sinclair (2000) have re-worked the notion of 'diasporic public spheres.' They simultaneously take up an argument by Gitlin (1998) that there is no longer a unitary public sphere à la Habermas, but that fragmentation into 'sphericules' – a term of abuse for Gitlin – has become the order of the day, where groups only communicate internally. As distinct from these interpretations, they propose (along with a series of Australian examples detailed in the chapters of their book), that minority-ethnic media may often provide in the broadest sense the daily education in dual cultural citizenship that migrant populations need. This is clearly a much less alarming reading of the contemporary media conjuncture than Gitlin's. It confirms, rather, both Naficy's analysis of the functions of Iranian television in Los Angeles in the 1980s, and Zuberi's discussion of the hybridization of popular music in England by Caribbean and South Asian influences during the 1980s and 1990s. In both these instances, the cultural quasi-segregation that Gitlin fears is absent. Instead, cultural negotiation of dual nationality and dual citizenship, of past and present, is the order of the day.

The wide spectrum of minority-ethnic media, indeed, is part and parcel of the variety of minority-ethnic social locations. Questions of ethnic cultural identities, of migrants', refugees' and aboriginal peoples' rights, of the considerable range of diasporic situations, and not least of varying responses to White racism, all jockey for position in such media. We are remarkably under-informed, however, about how people use them, and how their uses interrelate with majority-ethnic media uses by people of color, immigrants, refugees and others. We are also remarkably under-informed about their political economy, which varies all the way from those very well-funded by affluent expatriate business, to those which are low-budget and local-circulation only.

Conclusions

We have focused here on the contemporary, or near-contemporary dimensions of these issues. We need equally to engage with the issue of accumulated cultural content. Studies of racism and the representation of ethnicity over the centuries in the visual arts, literature, theatre, popular music, popular science, educational textbooks, religion, all need to be integrated into the study of 'racial' visual representation in film, photography, television and the press. At times these representations show a remarkable thematic continuity, at other times they register significant shifts in perception and established definition, for example in the tendential move toward a culturally conceptualized racism from a purely genetically defined one. But is this only, as implied in the terms just used, a question of a succession of functional equivalents to legitimize continued White privilege, or do differences between these equivalences offer greater or lesser options for ideological resistance and/or greater flexibility and suppleness in justifying 'racial' subordination? And is there a way to assess the true social weight of the *accumulation* of multi-mediatic representations of 'racial' inequality over the centuries in the determination of its tenacity and pervasiveness in the present?

Notes

1 From its original unique location in literary studies the term 'text' has migrated to cover any form of communication, from bodily to architectural to musical to legal to computer code.

2 If this were the case, communication and media researchers would be out of work.

3 Like the term 'mass communication,' 'content analysis' has a restricted meaning in conventional US media research, denoting empiricist methodology as uniquely 'scientific.' There is no *a priori* reason why these terms' meaning should be constrained in this way.

4 Examples were legion, but the otherwise useful series of US media research conferences entitled 'Consol(e)ing Passions' will serve as just one instance.

5 In this zone, cf. David Dabydeen (1987), *Hogarth's Blacks: images of Blacks in 18th century English art*; George M. Fredrickson (1971), *The Black Image in the White Mind: the debate on Afro-American character and destiny, 1817–1914*; Raymond Bachollet et al. (1992), *Négripub: l'image des Noirs dans la publicité*.

6 For an excellent and detailed further discussion of this, see Gray (1995), especially pp. 3–7, and Ramírez-Berg (2002).

7 This sense is much looser than the original meaning of the term 'symbol,' which for the ancient Greeks signified an exact correspondence, namely a piece of ceramic broken in two, one piece being taken by a messenger and subsequently re-joined to the other to confirm the authenticity of a message. (The contemporary meaning of 'symbol' is much closer in its generality to that of image.)

8 Stereotypical media roles over the twentieth century have included the Black domestic servant, the Mexican field hand, the whooping Indian warrior, the inscrutable and dangerous East Asian, the mystical South Asian, the crafty and deceitful Arab, the Latin woman spitfire, the White executive.

9 Brodkin (1998) addresses similar issues regarding Jewish Americans, while David A.J. Richards (1999) discusses the historical racialization of Italian Americans.

10 In this sense, it is analogous to the term 'structuring absence', initially coined by French Marxist cultural and textual analyst Pierre Macherey.

11 In much of Latin America the notion has been prevalent that the closer people are to White, the more cultured, intelligent, beautiful, and worthy of respect they are. And vice versa. The strict binary racial divide of the USA – you're black or you're white and that's that – has not been in force, even though whiteness is clearly equally prized. As a person of color one could and should strive to be Whiter, through marrying someone with lighter skin, associating with light-skinned people, and in using skin-bleaching and hair-straightening agents (the 'whitening' ideology).

12 The discussion of the term has been considerable. See Gramsci (1971: passim), Williams (1977: 108–114 and passim), Femia (1981), Hall (1996), Lears (1985), Portelli (1984), Showstack Sassoon (1987); and for briefer discussions, Downing (1996: 199–204; 2001: 14–18).

13 As with every stereotype, this is not to say there were no Black muggers. The question is how far their numbers and activity were inflated.

14 For an understanding of the context of this development see Gray, G. and Winter, C. (1997) and Jayasuriya, L. et al. (2003)

15 We do not subscribe to the frequent commonsense view that racist upsurges nearly always emerge in conjunction with economic downturn. On the other hand, their conjunction may certainly be exploited to intensify racist sentiment.

16 Hall, in this essay, despite other contributions on the topic (Hall et al., 1978; Hall, 1990; 1996: 411–75), says relatively little about 'racial' representation.

17 For a sympathetic but critical analysis of Foucault's failure to address colonialism and racism systematically, see Stoler (1997).

18 For the sake of completeness, we should record that the documentary won a prize at the Sundance Festival and a Cine Golden Eagle Award, which meant it traveled worldwide in a package of US documentaries whose screenings were organized by local US embassies. Nonetheless …

19 Academic colleague of Charles Husband, and external PhD examiner of John Downing. His intellect and personality continue to be missed.

20 The BBC was exceptionally White at that time, to the point that Trinidadian Trevor MacDonald, long-time BBC radio journalist, was repeatedly passed over for television positions and was eventually hired as a reporter by the commercial news program ITN, for which he had never worked. As British readers will know, he went on over the next thirty years to become an iconic TV newscaster.

21 *Till Death Us Do Part*, screened in the latter 1960s, which featured an older White working class Londoner whose put-upon condition and raucously scripted racist persona became instantly popular among many White British viewers. The show spawned look-alikes in Germany and the Netherlands, though was taken off quickly there because broadcasters responded appropriately to their audience research. It was the template for the US show *All In The Family*, which ran for years as a comic soap opera rather than as a series, and initially stimulated the same responses, but in which over the life of the show the chief protagonist comes to change his opinions, slowly, but consistently in an encouraging direction.

22 Hershey has been the biggest chocolate manufacturer in the USA for a century. Ms Berry won an Oscar in 2002 for her role in *Monster's Ball*, though this had no bearing on the mind-set of the Hollywood executives quoted in Lyman's article.

23 For the history of anti-Semitic discourse concerning Hollywood in its earlier decades, see Carr (2001).

24 Readers of John Steinbeck's *The Grapes of Wrath* may recall how he portrays some wretchedly under-educated Oklahoma farmers dispossessed of their land during the 1930s, picking up their shotguns and announcing that once it had been explained that it wasn't the repossession agents' decision to foreclose, they were going to go 'kill the banks.'

25 Araújo (2001).

3 Racism and the Media of the Extremist Right[1]

We now focus on the first of the areas which we consider has received insufficient research attention, namely racist media produced by the extremist right.[2] Some commentators appear to think they can eliminate the threat posed by these media simply by voicing contempt for them ('a bunch of repulsive atavists'), while others trumpet a misdirected alarmism ('a Nazi revival is at the doors'). We will begin with a working definition of the ultra-right, trying to steer past these confused responses, and examine some US examples of how these political forces use media channels. We will then address three questions: (1) the ways in which ultra-rightist racist media call into question both some widely accepted theoretical approaches to media, including those current in broadly progressive circles, and the foolish dismissal of small-scale media as without significance; (2) the relation between ultra-rightist media and free-speech legislation; and (3) what we see as the actual and intensifying nexus between the following vectors: ultra-rightist media and movements, sometimes termed 'neo-populist'; mainstream conservative media and political parties; and the roles of law enforcement and immigration control apparatuses. We will propose that this emergent constellation of forces we see developing already for some decades in a number of OECD nations can be characterized soberly, and without spin, as an *ongoing low intensity pogrom*[3] – very different from a plain recrudescence of Nazism, but notwithstanding that, both serious and dangerous. This discussion will then lead into the succeeding chapter on media, ethnicity, civil war and genocide.

Defining the Extremist Right

Researchers define the extremist right differently. Caldiron (2001) offers a highly informative map of developments in Europe, Russia and the USA, and Melilli (2003) more briefly updates it, but their accounts suffer from their lack of categorization. On the other hand, they successfully avoid the dangerous analytical trap of segregating the extremist Right from the mainstream Right, a trap that we will analyze in more depth at the end of this chapter. Caldiron's title, *The Plural Right*, and Melilli's secondary title, *Old and New Fascisms*, serve to flag the multiple historical strands and current interconnections involved. Caldiron, for example, includes in his survey such examples as former New York mayor Giuliani's widely imitated 'zero tolerance' law enforcement policies (pp. 195–203), along with the Swiss ultra-rightist Democratic Union of the Center, at the time of writing in 2004 the leading party in the Swiss parliament, and with the vigorous Nazi skin movement among some young Swiss (pp. 237–44).

Let us try to move beyond Caldiron's and Melilli's rather grab-bag approach and offer a provisional typology of right-wing extremism. Berlet (1998, pp. 250–251), a leading US researcher of the ultra-right, categorizes the extremist Right – his typology is nationally specific – into the secular conservatives, the theocratic Right and the 'hard Right'. Effectively, the secular conservative Right covers groups with strongly reactionary views but normally working electorally and without recourse to terrorism (though some of their inner circles may operate clandestine violent campaigns). Within the US this would signify a spectrum from the Heritage Foundation to the John Birch Society. In France it would cover the *Front National*, in Belgium the *Vlaams Blok*, in Hungary *Fidesz*, in Italy the *Alleanza Nazionale* and the *Lega Nord*, in Germany the *Republikaner* and some other groups, in Russia Zhirinovsky's *Liberal'naia Democraticheskaia Partiia*, the Austrian Freedom Party (*Freiheitliche Partei Österreichs*), the British National Party, and *One Nation* in Australia. These are in no way marginal, but have received significant public backing at elections: the *Front National*, for example, along with another party which had split off from it, received 5½ million votes in 2002; *Fidesz* got 41 per cent of the Hungarian vote in 2002, just missing being elected; the *Alleanza Nazionale* and the *Lega Nord* have twice been members of a coalition government with Berlusconi's *Forza Italia* party; and the Austrian Freedom Party was admitted to a coalition government with a mainstream conservative party in Austria in 2000, and again in 2002, although it lost considerable support over 2002–2003.

The theocratic Christian Right – a particularly US phenomenon, though also to be found among US-backed fundamentalist sects in Latin America, and in the secretive lay order Opus Dei, much favored by Pope John Paul II[4] – also works within the system, and in the USA covers a spectrum from the Christian Coalition to Focus on the Family and National Empowerment Television (Kintz and Lesage, 1998).

The 'hard Right' covers white supremacists, anti-Semitic activists, the militias, and signifies their frequent readiness, even eagerness, to work outside the system, including the use of targeted violence. The nail-bomb attacks on Black people and gays in London, England, in April-May 1999, the murder of African American Joseph Byrd in Jasper, Texas, and of

Matthew Shepard, a gay man, in Laramie, Wyoming, shootings of Jewish schoolchildren and a Filipino American mailman in Los Angeles in 1999, of Asian students in Bloomington, Indiana in 1999, and the steady drumbeat of racist attacks in a number of European countries, are partly the direct work of these groups, partly the work of individuals who share their poisoned outlook.[5] The 1995 Oklahoma City bombing was an illustration of the lengths to which such groups will go. The KKK is the longest-running US group, but Christian Identity – which despite its name appears to have no Christian theology of any brand whatsoever – is perhaps the strongest of such groups in the US at the time of writing.

Berlet's focus on the USA is an important one given the unnerving number and luxuriant variety of extremist right-wing groups there[6] – although Russia offers some strong competition in this respect[7] – and the particularly strong international links of some US groups. However, in Canada, many European nations, Australia, or Japan, the spectrum would assuredly vary from the taxonomy he proposes. There are only rather minimal correspondences elsewhere with much of the US Christian Right's ideology, or with the patriot/militia movements' tactics in the USA. The fascist legacy, for example, is much stronger in Europe, although some commentators (see for example, Camus, 2002) argue that explicitly neo-fascist parties are very marginal in most European countries, and that the ultra-rightist parties which are doing well are those which have shed that rhetoric, and embraced the democratic 'game' along with very extreme free market, law-and-order and xenophobic policies. Others argue that for some young people Nazi symbols' shock value constitutes their key attraction.

Three crucial points need underscoring at once though. First, it is essential to recognize that activists in Berlet's three categories of the ultra-right typically *share* ideological positions on – especially – racism and anti-Semitism, but also abortion politics and gender issues, homophobia, and anti-labor and anti-welfare politics. Second, hard Right groups, despite their other ideological disputes, often have in common a commitment to racist violence. Lastly, as already emphasized, it is particularly important to acknowledge that there is no major firewall between the extremist Right and the mainstream Right, whether the American Republican Party, the British Conservative Party, the German Christian Democrats, the French RPR and UDF, the Italian *Alleanza Nazionale* and *Lega Nord*, and similar parties elsewhere.

In this third regard, many of the issues and themes dear to the mainstream Right zone are equally honored within the extremist Right, as per the ideological list just provided. Certain members of the US Congress and parliamentary deputies in other countries effectively act as legitimized spokespersons for a number of extremist Right positions. There is some circulation of personnel between these political zones as I have broadly defined them here, as well as the psychological lure of absolutist convictions for those frustrated by the compromises demanded within organizations which work within the electoral and legal system. Just as some dangerously misguided individuals in the Italian far Left back in the late 1970s and early 1980s defined the terrorist Red Brigades as 'erring comrades', so too an analogous mentality of ambiguous tolerance for the extremist Right most certainly exists within the more mainstream Right. (Sometimes this will break down for specific reasons, as for example in the case of Jewish rightists who predictably shun the anti-Semitic forces on the extremist Right, Catholic rightists in the case of anti-religious groups, or gay rightists vis-à-vis homophobic groups.) Toward the close of this chapter we will return to this pivotal issue of the relationship between the mainstream and the extremist right. Next, however, let us focus on some US illustrations of ultra-Right media activism.

Shortwave Radio and Internet Use by the Extremist Right

We will now illustrate this brand of media activism from current right-wing extremist uses of shortwave radio and the internet within the USA. We need to acknowledge that these two media technologies are only two amongst those used by such groups.[8] Print publishing,[9] television, video, rock music, are amongst the others and provide a depressingly varied symphony of hatred and rage.

Those who primarily use shortwave radio and the internet amongst these groups are within the hard Right, the reason being that within the USA both the secular and the theocratic Right have much readier access to radio, television and magazine channels. Legally speaking, shortwave users within the USA are required to broadcast only internationally, but in practice the medium has become popular among some of the most paranoid anti-governmental groups for domestic as well as international communication. This is because of the difficulty of being traced from shortwave broadcasts, as opposed to the internet, where only fairly advanced cryptographic methods offer serious protection against source identification. Much of the shortwave broadcasting from these groups is in English, which implies a US audience, although it also makes their messages accessible in much of Canada, in Britain, in Australia, in South Africa, and also in Germany and Austria where a considerable segment of the under-50 generation has enough English to listen in if they wish to do so (or, even more so, to access an English-language website).

The cost of producing programs on shortwave is considerably less than AM or FM. There are estimated to be 600 million shortwave receivers across the planet, and 17 million within the USA.[10] Shortwave radio use by these groups also includes toll-free call-in shows and toll-free order lines for selling 'books, subscriptions, newsletters, and memberships.'[11] Titles of some of the most active and widely listened-to programs include *American Dissident Voices*, produced by America's Promise Ministries, hosted by David Barley; *Scriptures For America Worldwide*, on Christian Identity, hosted by Pete Peters; and *Freedom Calls*, hosted by Bo Gritz on WWCR (World Wide Christian Radio), perhaps the leading extreme Right shortwave station at the time of writing. Other stations include WRNO (Worldwide Radio New Orleans), WHRI (World Harvest Radio in Indiana), WRMI Miami, WGTG in Georgia.[12]

Their themes, spread variously among them, include the following[13]: Freemasons are taking over; US sovereignty is threatened by allowing foreign troops on American territory; the Catholic Church is Satan's instrument; there is urgent need for politicians inspired by biblical teaching; income tax is illegal; children born today will be taxed to 85 per cent of their income by the time they are adults; the danger of the 'New World Order'; the Nazi Holocaust is a fiction; the 13th and 14th Amendments to the US Constitution, abolishing slavery, should not have been passed; militias need to be prepared for coming government crackdowns; buy gold to protect yourself from coming financial disaster; fight for the White 'race'; stopping abortion is the number one issue; the USA is administered by a Zionist Occupation Government; African Americans and Latinos are 'mud' people; and conspiracies are everywhere.

Seemingly paradoxically, there was a spurt in the growth of these short-wave stations after the Oklahoma City bombing. Many of the programs broadcast extremist Right groups' propaganda, arguing that the Federal Government itself bombed its own building in order to create public hostility to the militias. One might speculatively deduce that the growth spurt was testimony to the recognition, even within these wildly over-heated quarters, that the bombing was a monstrous act that indeed signified the very considerable public danger constituted by many of these groups, and that consequently they needed to distance themselves publicly. Enter the increase in shortwave extremist broadcasting, in order to offer an alternative explanation that might serve to exculpate the extremist Right.

Turning to extremist use of the internet, the Southern Poverty Law Center produced a list in Winter 1998[14] of 28 KKK websites, 38 neo-Nazi websites, 27 racist skinhead[15] websites, 25 Christian Identity websites, 9 of the National Association for the Advancement of White People, and 33 others from a smattering of organizations, all based within the USA. The Anti-Defamation League has identified more than 2000 such 'hate' websites,[16] and Hatewatch lists a number in a range of nations – Australia, Belgium, Brazil, Canada, Denmark, Finland, France, Germany, Italy, the Netherlands, New Zealand, Norway, Russia, South Africa, Sweden, and the UK – while noting that each list is certainly only a small sample from each country.[17]

Scanning these, as with listening to the extremist Right on shortwave radio, demands a fairly strong stomach. However, aside from visceral reactions, it is important to try to assess how effective these media are. In what follows, we will try to pose this question as carefully as we can, both conceptually and methodologically.

What may be the Impacts of such Media?

We will begin by commenting on the way consideration of this subject-matter may both significantly complicate major frameworks we custom-arily use to understand media and information (civil society, public sphere, cybercommunity, globalization), and call into serious question the commonly encountered dismissal of small-scale alternative media as insignificant. That is certainly one type of impact of these media, and although obviously far from the most lethal one, we need to take it into consideration first in order to clear the ground for our analysis. We will then turn to explore the relation between these media and their users.

One impact of these media, then, is on the taken-for-granted thinking of media and information researchers, most particularly as regards civil society and the other concepts listed above which we currently habitually deploy. Fundamentally, much of the scholarly discussion of these topics has had an optimistic and positive undertow, if not as a description of current realities, then at least as an account of what could be the case in imaginably different circumstances.

One of us well remembers, for instance, Russians and Poles talking to him with more than a little excitement in 1988–90 about the emergence and then quite rapid growth of what they termed 'civil society', that is media and other spaces in which they could more and more freely debate how to construct a new Russia and a new Poland without the shackles of the post-Stalinist state. A number of Latin American thinkers in nations which not long previously had emerged from under the shadow of US-backed military dictatorship, were using the same civil society terminology during the 1990s to apply to their urgent and hopeful attempts at democratic transition and consolidation, away from the US-backed military dictatorships that had plagued them. Civil society was indisputably defined in positive terms, and implied the imminence of a higher plane of human existence, an idealized Athenian agora. The internationally influential Zapatista move-ment in Mexico, ever since its public emergence in 1994, has underscored the positive effects of developing a 'global civil society.'[18]

Similarly, the current debate over the battle in a highly commercialized culture between the status of citizen and the status of consumer (cf. García

Canclini, 2001), rests upon the notion that citizens are struggling to function as such in the face of their redefinition as mere consumers. But the implication is, clearly, that their constructive citizen status is there if they will only insist upon it energetically enough. The possibility that citizen movement activism might take the form of banishing any other movement activism, or at least rendering it very risky, or unleashing a wave of racist attacks, is not immediately apparent from such debates. We forget all too readily that Italian Fascism and German Nazism were social movements before they succeeded in colonizing the state, and the examples analyzed in the next chapter from former Yugoslavia and Rwanda provide further evidence for this ugly dimension of social movements.

The notion of *Öffentlichkeit*, the public sphere, has become especially widespread in anglophone academic circles since the English translation of Jürgen Habermas' 1962 book in 1989.[19] Yet Habermas, in his original 1962 version, pursued a rather pessimistic argument, directly citing C. Wright Mills' withering critique[20] of McCarthyite America in support of his own contention that the sphere for informed public exchange was shrinking at high speed in liberal democracies, a notion he later reconceptualized as the colonization of our lifeworld. In contrast, quite a lot of those who have deployed the concept, including one of the present authors, have done so in a much more hopeful and varied direction than that, focusing on the facets of contemporary society in which some kind of free and constructive public debate is actually to be seen at work despite the obstacles in its path.[21]

Yet in view of the public realm created by extremist Right media, were we not being wilfully blind to the full range of possibilities in a public realm? What should we make, for instance, of the public sphere constructed in US gun shows, which are a prime location for extreme rightist booths, publications, and mutual confirmation by gun-obsessives (Pitcavage, 1996). Caldiron (2001: 140–51, 173–80) even speaks of a Gramscianism of the Right, signifying some European groups' long term strategy of diffusing and suffusing popular media with rightist content among the general public in order to create, gradually, a climate of opinion and a social base for their full-throttle operation. He cites the phrase 'the LePenization of minds' (p. 143) as a way of acknowledging the reach of *Front National* perspectives among the French public, well beyond that substantial number prepared to vote for it. There as well as earlier in his book, he traces the thoroughgoing efforts of the *Front National*, and of *Alleanza Nazionale* in Italy (pp. 48–58), to build a constituency among industrial workers and young people.

The widely circulating concepts of public sphere, civil society, and citizen are all thrown into some disarray once we begin to contemplate extremist right movements. Their presence and activity, even discounting circles such as those 'patriot' and 'militia' groups that shun public communication, in no way contribute to the processes of debate, discussion, review and, ultimately, public empowerment, that these concepts envisage. Anti-semitism, white supremacism, misogyny, homophobia, anti-labor activism, hostility to welfare claimants, visceral and paranoid anti-statism, religious fundamentalism and authoritarianism, are not positions about which extreme rightists think there is any negotiation. This is not to say that individual rightists cannot change their minds, just that open dialogue is institutionally defined within those circles as off the agenda (even though their public rhetoric often claims to speak for a 'racially' oppressed White public excluded by an arrogant elite from being heard): 'My way or no way.' In general, the term 'public sphere', as one of us has argued elsewhere (Downing, 1996: 24–6), suffers from an overly ratiocinative bent, and has little illumination to offer in the areas of the fierce political and cultural emotions capitalized upon and stirred up by the extremist Right.

Cybercommunity is another notion that a number of people have seized on with glad cries, seeing in the Internet an opportunity for new forms of warm and nuzzling communal nurturing just when the size, scale and speed of contemporary societies seemed set to iron out any such options. A classic exposition of such a view can be found in Howard Rheingold's *The Virtual Community*.[22] Elsewhere (Downing, 1999a) one of us has argued that the notion of 'community' underpinning arguments of this kind is typically loosely defined, but generally perceived as something positive and encouraging. What then of the communities constructed with the help of media and information technologies whose driving purpose is the extrusion, expulsion or even extermination of people of color? May not the 'community' of ultra-conservative interests, rage, self-righteousness and paranoia, enabled to feed its own growth through shortwave, the internet, rock music and the other media forms touched upon above, turn out to have far more impact than any conventional internet community, say for example Trekkies (Star Trek fans)? Maybe even more than human rights networks (though we surely hope not). We do not suggest that the extremist right is about to forge itself into a single strike force – its divisions based on mutual paranoia, contempt, and conviction of ideological rectitude are too powerful for that to happen – but for its various components to have a major impact, that implausible scenario is quite unnecessary.

'Globalization' is perhaps rather more ambiguous a term. Journalists and economists mostly use it to capture the very rapid expansion of worldwide economic links and processes. Labor unions in industrially advanced economies use it to decry the flight of jobs to nations with cheaper labor-costs. Media and information scholars use it to begin to talk about international cultural flows, the planetary cultural dominance of the USA, and issues of cultural hybridization. Nonetheless, it has the pulse of the future inscribed in it, and that seems to be exciting.

Or is it? As we survey these growing and increasingly straightforward and accessible international links between extremist rightists across the planet, does the future also portend one in which the re-establishment of the extremist right in larger numbers, and its links with the supposedly 'game-playing' right wing, will come to bear bitter fruit as it forms a kind of global community? There is the further irony that part of the appeal of a number of rightist extremist groups, such as the Austrian Freedom Party, the Italian *Lega Nord*, the French *Front National*, is their denunciation of globalization, the European Union, and what they define as Islamicization or, at other points (for example, the *Front National*), supposed anti-popular global conspiracies by Jews and Freemasons. The paranoid obsession of some US extreme rightists with the threat of a 'one-world government', of which the precariously tottering UN is supposed to be the harbinger, falls into the same category.

We are faced therefore with two separate paradoxes. One is that hostility to globalization is not a leftist preserve. (Indeed many leftists have come to prefer the term 'corporate globalization' in order not to sacrifice their own internationalism.) The other is that precisely those extreme rightists who decry it, just like the Taliban, are more than content to utilize all of its communication options to propagandize their chauvinist – or sometimes regionalist/separatist (the *Lega Nord*, Austria's *Kärnter Heimatdienst*[23]) – agendas.

There is even a third paradox here, in that in principle regional autonomy is a perfectly reasonable democratic aspiration, something very much in line with the socialist anarchist tradition, and reflected in the German Green Party's call over a decade or more for a 'Europe of the regions'. Yet like many generic principles, it contains almost diametrically opposed directions, the anarchist drive to domesticate the state, the petty regionalism and – historically at least – racism of the 'States' rights' movement in the USA, and the attractions of a de-centralized state for transnational corporations' negotiating purposes. There is much more here than can be ventilated properly within the confines of this chapter, but suffice it to say that consideration of the media of the extreme right presses us in a number of cases to consider very carefully indeed what we mean by globalization.

Alternative Media and Their Users

Such media may also lead us to reconsider standard research definitions within Communication and Media Studies of both alternative media and their audiences. The former have frequently been defined as petty flotsam and jetsam, romantic, irritating, ultimately marginal. Contrasted with News Corp, Sony and TimeWarner, why would anyone divert much research energy into them? Yet disregard for the alternative media of the extremist Right is arguably at least as wrong-headed as refusal to take seriously the alternative media of the far left (Downing, 2001). In particular, this is where the question of their audiences arises, very poorly researched (if at all) in the case of alternative media.[24]

For focusing specifically on extremist Right alternative media, one thing is or should be abundantly plain: their core audiences, though statistically a small minority, may be one of the strongest instances of the so-called 'active' audience, going far beyond simply an alert posture in regard to media content. These are political activists, including in a number of cases people fascinated by and committed to violent street activity. There is substantial, if totally misdirected, energy in these quarters, and some commentators have suggested that the conviction of being connected up with a national and international community through short-wave and the internet can provide a feeling of not being isolated,[25] of being part of a struggling, do-or-die global network of White supremacist warriors who will go down fighting if they have to.

Focusing on a different sector of the US extreme Right, both Lesage (1998) and Hardisty (1999: chapters 1 and 3) have also emphasized the vigor and importance of existing religious Right networks in diffusing extremist media content, including amongst women whose beliefs traditionally would have steered them away from political activism. This kind of audience networking was also, it is worth noting, a dimension of politico-religious organization that played a significant part in the overthrow of the reactionary but secular Shah of Iran and the return from exile and into supreme leadership of the religious reactionary Khomeini (Sreberny-Mohammadi and Mohammadi, 1994).[26]

We might further compare the comments of Mark Hunter (1998a), an American journalist who spent considerable time in and around Le Pen's *Front National* and whose findings resonated with the 'Gramscianism of the right' strategy mentioned already. He noted how extremist right-wing organizations in Europe were often now the only ones to maintain an active presence in depressed neighborhoods and people's everyday haunts, whether the Flemish *Vlaams Blok* in Antwerp's poorest quarter, or Italy's *Lega Nord* in bowling alleys, videogame arcades, sports stadiums. He further noted that France's *Front National* despite its size, has never depended on mainstream media coverage in the same way as other political parties, preferring to maintain direct organizational links with its support bases.

Thus these media may be embedded in existing religious and political networks, and may communicate national and global 'racial' community to isolated racist skinheads, and White supremacist activists of varying stripes. Moreover, beyond the 'umbra' of the dedicated core, there is also a larger penumbra of those sympathetic to their perspectives. On the other hand, we should not neglect the possibility that *some* of these websites and shortwave radio programs, as with some books and fliers, may have no particular impact at all. The fact that a website exists and is perceived by most as repugnant does not simultaneously and automatically lend it power.

We need also to integrate consideration of these hardcore ideological media with an understanding of how many right-wing extremist movements are able to capitalize upon *both* mainstream 'quality' media disdain for them *and* tabloid media hunger for the sensational. This has been evident with Australia's One Nation party (Horsfield and Stewart, 2003), with the *Lega Nord* (Biorcio, 2003), with the *Front National* (Birenbaum and Villa, 2003), and with the Austrian Freedom Party (Plasser and Ulram, 2003). From within this perspective the elite media become icons of the jaded, possibly corrupt, place-seekers who dominate the political system. The tabloids, by contrast, make their money from a good fight, including scrappy rightist political figures who elect to pursue a populist strategy of publicly denouncing the elite on behalf of the 'little' (White) people oppressed by 'racially' alien immigrants and neighbors. The net result of these combined processes is that there may be three distinct categories of media, yet effectively working in the same direction in their particular ways.

Racist Media and Free Speech Rights

The question of racist websites, in particular, leads Canadians and Americans straight into a discussion of their respective freedom of speech legislation and philosophy, but not only them. Because of the communication liberties enabled by that legislation, especially in the USA, some European nations such as Germany, with explicit laws banning Holocaust denial, the formation of explicitly Nazi parties and other extremist Right activities, find these laws flouted with impunity in consequence of US extremist Right websites.

This raises not one, but three questions: do such nations have the right to see laws enforced for which they have voted? And, whatever the answer, is there currently even more danger of an extremist Right resurgence in some European nations, for example the Czech Republic and Slovakia, with their tolerance of anti-Roma violence and humiliation, than there is in North America? How far are the ongoing waves of violent racist attacks, especially in former East Germany, but also in many other European nations large and small, likely to gather momentum, despite the very creditable attempts of many Germans, Spaniards and other European citizens to stand up against them and be counted?

For Canadians and Americans, though, the free speech provisions of Section 2 of the Charter of Rights and Freedoms and of the First

Amendment are of pressing importance.[27] Often it is the Left that pursues these principles, given its historical experience of being denied free speech rights. Better, in this view, to plug for the rights of fascists to speak than to give up those rights for the Left.

Much too often in the USA, however, the First Amendment is regarded as a kind of magic talisman, a piece of historical constitutional wizardry that effectively preserves the USA from extremist right-wing groups achieving power. The more such groups talk, the more people will be outraged and disgusted, runs the argument, almost in a Durkheimian mode that argues crime to be good for social solidarity and cohesion (see Downing, 1999b). But this is by way of a hopeful prediction or hypothesis, not an established fact. The presumption that there will indeed be a shocked and militant reaction should not be a foregone conclusion: all too often, North Americans (that is, Canadians and Americans) will simply shrug their shoulders and say, 'Well, they have the right to say these things, don't they, even if they are repellent.' Sooner or later someone will speak with great seriousness about dying if necessary for the right of someone to express an opinion contrary to their own – for the time being a rather cozy assertion in either Canada or the USA.

There is little attention to the close practical links *between* speech and action among rightist extremists, and yet it is these links which are at the heart of the problem. Europeans, with the experience of fascism and sovietism behind them in the past seventy years, tend to be much more intuitively attuned to this question than North Americans, with the exception, to some degree, of African Americans, for reasons that must be rather obvious.

The US shibboleth that 'bad speech requires better speech' is normally just that, a shibboleth: neither speech nor action are forthcoming, let alone any sustained organization of oppositional activism. This degree of political sluggishness will not be galvanized into a combative mode by the mere existence of First Amendment (or analogous) legislation. And so people mostly hope the problem will simply go away of its own accord, and half-shut their eyes to some real outcomes: assassination of abortion clinic staff and of low-level law enforcement personnel, attempted or actual bombings of targeted public figures and/or their institutions, physical attacks on immigrants and people of color, especially Black people and Roma, and on gay men. It needs recognizing, moreover, that hate crimes are often perpetrated with a particular degree of sadistic viciousness, way beyond the average robbery with assault.[28]

All the same, are we not making a mountain out of a molehill? Admittedly these groups are unpleasant and potentially lethal, but does their danger compare significantly with, for instance, either general street crime or traffic fatalities and injuries, in almost any industrially advanced country we might mention?

The Nexus between the Extreme Right
and the Mainstream Right

The answer depends in significant part on our evaluation of two linked issues (1) how we see these groups interacting with more established conservative forces, and (2) the increasingly powerful presence of those forces internationally since 1979–80, the years in which first Thatcher became British premier, and Reagan then became US president. Now there are, clearly, both policy and sectarian differences amongst extremist Right groups, and between them and the established Right, as witnessed by the withering invective directed by some extremist Right groups against the harshly rightist US radio commentator and talk-show host Rush Limbaugh (Hilliard and Keith, 1999: 6, 131–36; cf. Danky and Cherney, 1996). The assassinated gay Dutch far rightist Pim Fortuyn, the petty regionalist Umberto Bossi (of the *Lega Nord*), the US religious fundamentalist Pat Robertson, the neo-liberal 'post-fascist' Joerg Haider, are further examples of diversity within the political right.

But that does not create a firewall between these groups, encouraging as these divisions might appear at first glance. To some extent, rhetoric is rhetoric. There is in practice a constant circulation and permeation of both tactics and individuals among the proliferating rightist organizations and movements, one that needs mapping much more carefully than has been done to date.

Examples are many. We might instance the decline of the National Front in Britain during the 1980s following the election of the harshly conservative Thatcher government in 1979, which simply meant that National Front activists switched to or re-joined the Conservative Party. Party allegiance may change without it signifying a change of mind.

We might also note the frequent presence within mainstream conservative parties of individuals whose views in many respects belong to the extremist Right, of whom perhaps some of the best known are the late unlamented Enoch Powell, MP, in Britain, former Senator Jesse Helms in the US Senate, Oliver North and Patrick Buchanan in the Reagan Administration, Trent Lott, Senate Republican Majority leader at the close of the 1990s, Edmund Stoiber, Bavaria's Christian Social Union leader from the 1990s through to the time of writing. These names are of an older generation, admittedly, but were not a passing phase. They helped to build the present 'racial' conjuncture.

We need, also, to note the well-established competitive dynamic of political parties of the right and the left which, when faced with uncertain electoral outcomes, have repeatedly tried to garner some extra voting strength by trying to steal the clothes of the extreme Right – and have helped push the political spectrum toward the extreme right in consequence. Examples include the Labour and Conservative Parties in Britain, and the competition between them since the 1960s (Dummett, 2001:

89–153) to show how strict they can be in reducing immigration (that is, the immigration of people of color). They also include the RPR and the UDF conservative parliamentary parties of France, which have frequently pitched themselves as anti-immigrant, even to the point in some areas of working with the *Front National* to vote to exclude candidates of the left (Orfali, 1990: 41–42; Tévanian, 2001: 114–15; Caldiron, 2001: 151–54). In Germany, although ultra-rightist parties have had only fairly fleeting electoral successes to date, their influence on the agenda of the major parties regarding issues of 'race' and German nationality laws has been considerable (Casasus, 2003; Decker, 2003).

Furthermore, as noted above, industrial worker communities hit by recession and corporate globalization, young people of the popular classes, women, all have been systematically wooed by Italy's *Alleanza Nazionale*, Belgium's *Vlaams Blok*, the French *Front National*. Many such groups and parties have worked very hard to move out of the political mini- ghettoes often inhabited by rightist extremists in the past. Some have managed to push the whole political spectrum to the right. The role of segregationist US presidential candidate George Wallace in 1968 and 1972 was a major instance of this shift-phenomenon, effectively developing a social base among Northern as well as Southern White working class voters who would later support not only Reaganism[29] but also the rightward retreat of the Democratic party to the political agenda of the Clinton administration – and that rightward shift moved even faster with the brazenly extremist agenda of the second Bush administration.

Within the USA and Canada, we need equally to note the pumping of very substantial money over the past twenty years into new rightist think-tank organizations such as the Heritage Foundation and Cato Foundation in the USA, or in Canada the Fraser Institute and the Northern Foundation (Himmelstein, 1990: 145ff.; Covington, 1997; Jeffrey, 1999: 420–31). Six major foundations of this kind (Bradley, Olin, Scaife, Smith Richardson, the Koch Family, and Castle Rock) are listed as the 8th, 11th or 12th richest – depending on the researcher (Hardisty, 1999: 61) – in the USA. One of their favorite causes is the funding of militantly rightist campus organizations, in the hope, and currently with the effect, of developing a corps of dedicated activists among students.

Lastly, we need to take serious account, at least within the USA, of the feverish rhetorical pitch of conspiracy paranoia, religious extremism, and White supremacism that came to characterize both much of AM talk radio (Land, 1998), as well as the forces even further to its right, from the earliest months of the Clinton administration in 1992 onwards (Alterman, 2003). Above we noted the way ultra-rightist alternative media meshed in certain ways in certain countries with tabloid and elite media, and rightist talk-radio provides yet another instance of this mesh in action (mesh, that is, not unison).

The attacks of 11 September 2001 subsequently gave tremendous leeway to US Attorney General Ashcroft and the Bush administration to target and profile Arab Americans and individuals with Muslim names, locking up a large number and incarcerating them for very many months without trial, whilst placing mosques and other bodies under continuous surveillance. Of the 762 incarcerated after the attacks, many for already three years at the time of writing, a handful was found to have any links with terrorism, yet Ashcroft continued to press for even more repressive measures.[30] Nor is it only in the USA since then that terrorism has legitimated racist actions against immigrant workers, as Negrouche (2001) makes clear in his analysis of France.

Thus neither historically nor currently are extremist Right organizations and voices detached from a wider political influence. We see today the growth to prominence and increased respectability in the USA, Canada, Europe and elsewhere, including India, of ever more reactionary and dangerous political forces (Betz and Immerfall, 1998; Hunter, 1998b; Camus, 2002; Mazzoleni et al., 2003; Caldiron, 2001; Melilli, 2003). That being the case, even if we are prepared to play statistical games with the numbers of those injured and killed on the roads versus those brutalized and killed by hate groups, it is most unwise to segregate out these smaller groups from the whole picture. Politics today is in constant flux, not fixed by the boundaries of what was considered reasonable or imaginable at any given moment in the past. Brooke Jeffrey, in his account of the growth of neo-conservatism in Canada, puts it well:

> ... the fact is that the ignorant gladiators are no longer on the outside looking in. Instead, through a combination of good timing and deliberate manipulation by others, they have been surprisingly successful in moving to the centre ring, if not the centre of the political spectrum. They have achieved a degree of legitimacy and, in some cases, political power, unimaginable even a decade ago ... Their surprising rise from humble beginnings to their current status in such a relatively short period of time is understandable only if it is put in the context of the very substantial assistance they have received from the corporate elites and single-issue interest groups whose causes they promote. (Jeffrey, 1999: 403)

Neo-Populism and Racist Media

Closely related to our case above for seeing ultra-rightist racist media and movements as much more than marginal or powerless, is an argument with considerable recent currency that in Europe and elsewhere there has emerged over the past decade or more a multi-nation right-wing neo-populist wave (Betz, 1994; Betz and Immerfall, 1998; Jeffrey, 1999;

Ihl et al., 2003; Mazzoleni et al., 2003). The importance of this debate for the understanding of ultra-rightist media is not only directly connected to the needed re-evaluation of the marginal standing of ultra-rightist groups, but also to a necessary acknowledgement of the point made above that ultra-rightist media audiences and readers are not just conventional media users, but are people actively mobilized in, or somewhere within the penumbra of, political movements (Downing, 2003a). In the US context, this phenomenon has been a strongly mediatized one, centered as noted above on talk radio.

Despite the notorious vagueness of the terms populism and neo-populism, the former potentially covering everything from the groups we focus on here to Portugal's anti-fascist movement of 1974–76 or the Russian and American agrarian radicals of the 19th century, we still think the terms serve to underscore something useful, namely that in seeking to assess as accurately as possible the contemporary impact of the ultra-Right we must come to grips with rightist social *movements*, not just with elitist military coups and authoritarian regimes. These movements, as Betz (1994) and others argue, are often in response to widespread feelings of political betrayal (in 'rustbelt' zones, for example), or fears of not having a viable function in the economy of the future, or of the imminent erosion of national cultural homogeneity, or of a dangerous decline in public and private ethical standards. Corporate globalization may spur radically rightist reactions, especially if these are fostered by activist ultra-rightist groups, not just the 'Another world is possible' responses of the 1999 anti-WTO Seattle protests and their ongoing manifestations around the world.

An inaccuracy in the term 'neo-populist', however, as Himmelstein (1990) argues in relation to the USA, is that the intellectual and financial sources of these movements and shifts to the right are very often to be found in long-established conservative and extreme conservative circles. For example, the linkages were tight during the 1990s and beyond between the far rightist AM talk radio programs already mentioned, and the right wing of the Republican party. As we argue in this chapter, there are various symbiotic (though certainly not seamless) relationships between these movements and established political parties; and, importantly, between them and police, court officials and prison officers; and, not least, between all of these and government policies and bureaucratic practices regarding immigration. We are usually *not* just faced with a sudden and spontaneous street upsurge, whatever the usual slew of minimally informed pack-journalists or overly specialized sociologists may propose to the contrary. Yet neither are we faced with a singly orchestrated or smoothly lubricated political phenomenon, notwithstanding the gravity of post-9/11 state repression initiatives.

Fundamental to our argument in this chapter, however, is how often the connective tissue that binds together differing extreme rightist groups, that binds all of them together with more mainstream conservative groups, which in turn gives both sets of political actors a common cultural discourse with the more general public, is precisely White racism, often mixed in with anti-Semitism and Islamophobia. The five hundred years of Western colonialism, neo-colonialism and slavery have left in their wake not only facts and structures, but also vibrant ideological discourses, capable of discursive reformulation, and seemingly always available to the Right and the extremist Right. And these forces' use of media technologies old and new is helping to nourish and activate that ideology and practice above all. Little else appears to explain the extraordinary speed with which racist populist movements and groups have grown in so many European nations – not just movements denouncing jaded and corrupt elites, or harsh economic policies, either of which would be entirely understandable, but movements whose energy and cohesion are derived in significant measure from the specific appeal of racist emotions and perspectives. Indeed Bouillaud (2003) urges that the terms 'populist' and 'neo-populist' be dropped in favor of 'overtly anti-immigrant parties'. Especially in certain eastern European countries, 'anti-Roma' needs adding to his list.

As we noted in chapter 1, the long-standing discourse of racism has often been reformulated in recent years in culturalist terms, ostensibly distinct from the genetic and biological tropes of 19th and earlier 20th century pseudo-science. The French *Front National* proclaims the right to cultural difference as one of the two justifications for its fiercely anti-immigrant propaganda (along with its clearly untrue equation of unemployment figures with immigrant worker numbers). The Danish Peoples Party, Belgium's *Vlaams Blok*, the Austrian People's Party, Italy's *Lega Nord*, are only some of the extreme rightist European parties which have revamped their racist policies in this 'culturalist' rhetoric. Sometimes anti-Semitism has been discarded, at least on the surface, in the growing movement among US Christian fundamentalist extremists and some others – for example, Italy's 'post-fascist' *Alleanza Nazionale* – to identify explicitly with the Israeli Right and extreme Right, mostly in power since the *Likud* party's first electoral victory in 1977. Sometimes legislation prohibiting certain forms of racist expression has generated public relations claims by extreme rightist political leaders not to be racist, typically evidenced by conceding – as a fleeting aside – that not *all* immigrants are criminals or living on welfare, an example of the 'discursive de-racialization' analyzed by Reeves (1983).

Some detailed studies of the language[31] used in *Front National* documents and in speeches by its leader, Le Pen, give a remarkable insight into the issues on which the party has sought to capitalize, and the modalities by which it has gone about this task, including what Pedon and Walter (1999) term 'photopopulism' (the use of simplified single-issue still images). Terms such as 'mental AIDS' for 'elites cut off from the people', 'cosmopolitan lobbies', and 'planetary immigration invasion' are blunt and brutal (cited in Taguieff, 2002: 139).

But there are also more subtle, but equally significant examples. Krieg (1999), for instance, disentangles the superficially trivial use in parentheses of the Latin word (sic)[32] in *Front National* publications (exceptionally frequently as compared to the mainstream or leftist press). She found it was almost ritually used to cap quotations from political figures whom the *Front National* loathed. She proposes that its insistent rhetorical deployment rather efficiently served three *FN* goals. It avoided engaging in reasoning with its opponents' positions, simply jeering at them instead (she draws a parallel with Nazi propaganda's similar approach), whereas leftist publications mostly specified the grounds of their disagreement. It encouraged a sense of superior community within its rightist readership circles, who could pride themselves on knowing how to interpret their opponents' statements in line with *Front National* dogmas. And by this coded sneer, it could also steer clear of making directly racist statements which, given French laws on racist expression, its opponents might use against it in the courts. We might add a fourth goal to Krieg's list, namely that the frequent use of a Latin word was an implicit counter-attack against the accusation of crass stupidity and lack of education regularly leveled at *Front National* supporters by a section of the French intellectual elite.[33]

Taguieff (2002: 117–21), along with other researchers whom he cites, has taken the populism argument further still, suggesting that a feature of contemporary political culture in a number of countries is the bypassing, through the immediacy of television, of traditional political party communication, organization and affiliation. He instances two-time Italian prime minister Berlusconi, owner of the major private TV channels as well as ultimate authority over the three state channels, as the emblematic figure of this shift, but also references the American Ross Perot, the Swiss leader of the Democratic Union of the Center, Christoph Blocher, and Brazilian President Fernando Collor de Mello (1990–92), amongst a group of politicians who have come from nowhere and soared to prominence, if not always high office, through the instantaneity and lack of time for deliberation enabled by current media technologies. He refers to the roles of television and the internet in this regard as 'telepopulism', in which such media, or some instances of them, effectively become harnessed to rightist political movements, in a form of temporary colonization.

Stimulating as it is, Taguieff's analysis appears a little superficial and rushed. Perot and Collor, for example, are dimly remembered if at all by now, the former removed from the public sphere because of his small-town solutions and style, the latter chased prematurely out of office because of his arrant corruption. Both outcomes rather strongly suggest that 'telepopulism' is not as embracingly determinative as suggested. Berlusconi himself only managed to come to power through a coalition with the *Alleanza Nazionale* and the *Lega Nord*. And as the studies in Mazzoleni et al. (2003) show, different sections of the mainstream media may respond differently, attacking rather than facilitating rightist movements (and as noted, some of these have successfully utilized the attacks, in populist vein, as evidence of the elite's conspiracy against them).

Most particularly, Taguieff's 'telepopulism' notion seems to downplay one of the two typically fundamental factors (the other being racism), in the appeal of these so-called 'neither left nor right' third ways: an accumulated deep disillusionment with traditional political configurations that we have noted in the Netherlands, Belgium, France, Austria and Italy, and also manifest in both India, with the decline of the long-dominant Congress Party and the rise of the extreme rightist BJP (Rajagopal, 2001; McGuire and Reeves, 2003), and Australia, with the prominence for a while of One Nation (Horsfield and Stewart, 2003). The use of television to bypass conventional political procedures and parties was a way of discrediting them as out of touch and unresponsive, not merely for convenience and speed.

On the other hand, Taguieff has a productive thematic analysis of ultra-right ideologies in the contemporary conjuncture, with direct implications for the continuing virulence of racism in Europe and probably beyond. He suggests (*op.cit.*, 125–35) that two dimensions of this right-wing populism, distinct but not necessarily mutually exclusive, are 'protest' populism and 'identity' populism. The former focuses on an attack on traditional elites, the latter on the assertion of particular national, 'racial' or analogous identities. The *Front National* combines both, as do the *Vlaams Blok*, the Austrian Freedom Party, the Danish People's Party, the late Pim Fortuyn's *Lijst Fortuyn* in the Netherlands, and the *Lega Nord*. The late Enoch Powell was in some ways a precursor of many of these trends, in his unashamed and aggressive racist nationalism, in his self-positioning as a champion of ordinary British people against the elite and in his melding of ultra-Right and mainstream Right roles.[34] In this political scenario, it is typically claimed that the elite are heedlessly importing undesired and undesirable foreigners – immigrants and/or refugees and/or Muslims – in great numbers, in total disregard of the everyday public's cultural identity, economic plight, and safety from crime.

The attention we have given Taguieff's analyses here should not be taken to imply endorsement of his practical stands on anti-racist policy in France. Tévanian (2001: 66–73) offers a trenchant analysis of Taguieff's status as the 'racism guru' of French news media, noting not only his public endorsement of former government minister Chevènement's 1998 law enacting even more exclusionary immigration controls, but also Taguieff's moral equation of anti-racist activists ('extremism', 'totalitarian spirit', 'taste for civil war', 'media lynchers') with Le Pen supporters. There is no room here to pursue this issue further, but it is important to be aware of the extent to which, as we already mentioned in Chapter 1, the French official doctrine of republican *laïcité* – the rejection of State affiliation to any religion – may easily lead to a refusal to engage adequately with issues of difference. This was very evident in battles during the 1990s until today over the right of Muslim girls to wear a headscarf (the *foulard*) in French state schools (Battegay and Boubeker, 1993: 148–50; Rabbah, 1998: 173–209; 273–300).

Law Enforcement, Immigration Control, and the Ultra-Right

The other element in what we have suggested is a nexus between the ultra-Right, its media, and wider social forces, is the contemporary development and administration of law enforcement and immigration control policies. The United States is in the lead, with its police force and court officialdom only too ready to shunt dismaying percentages of Black and Latino men, in particular, into its jails, and with its militarization of the Mexican border (Davis, 1998; Gilmore, 1998; Parenti, 1999; Pintado-Vertner and Chang, 1999–2000; Gilmore, 1999–2000; Wacquant, 2000; Dunn, 1996; Bauman, 1998: 103–27). We are nonetheless compelled to recognize that the same basic law enforcement and immigration control processes are in operation in the practices and doctrines of Fortress Europe (cf. Maschino, 2003), in the Schengen Agreement, and in Australia's successive Howard administrations' policy on immigration, refugees and Aboriginal Australians. The jails in these nations, from Canada to the Netherlands, are disproportionately filled with people of color, who are correspondingly likely to have some kind of police record, and who also figure quite disproportionately on probation lists (thus often making it much harder to be employed). In a number of American states, as the 2000 presidential contest showed in Florida, they may be permanently disbarred from voting.

The racist behavior of German, Swiss, French, Italian, Spanish, British and other police forces toward people of color is often excerpted from this larger picture and defined purely in terms of poor training, attitudes and motivation amongst people who take up police or prison work as a career. Yet since quite often law enforcement agents' behavior in this regard is contrary to professional codes, official regulations, and even the law, and since by and large it is also rare for the offending officers to be sanctioned in any serious manner, it is no less than sensible to consider these patterns as emergent *de facto* policy, not as training failures or negative psychological syndromes. The racist practices of British immigration officials were typically codified over time by the Home Office (equivalent to the US Justice Department), and then enshrined in the annexes of constantly updated immigration laws.

We wish to suggest therefore that what people of color are currently collectively subjected to in country after country, even if it does not directly impact each and every individual, is a kind of *ongoing low-intensity pogrom*. This emergent phenomenon is the overall result of *intertwined* mediatic, political and law enforcement agencies, each one working according to its own dynamics and routines, and none of them going entirely unchallenged on this front, including within the ranks of the professional agents of these social institutions. Post-9/11, of course, these intertwined processes have considerably intensified.

Traditionally, pogroms – anti-Semitic onslaughts in Tsarist Russia, the attacks on Armenians in Turkey leading up to the 1915 genocide, episodes such as the attacks on California's Chinese settlements in the 1870s and 1880s, the so-called 'race riots' in East St Louis in 1918, Chicago in 1919, in Tulsa, Oklahoma in 1921, in Rosewood, Florida, in 1923, in Los Angeles (the 'zoot suit riots') and in Detroit in 1943, in Watts, Los Angeles, in 1965 – were initiated at high government levels, national or local as the case might be. The last Tsar, Nicholas II, regularly set anti-Semitic pogroms in motion in order to disperse and divide political opposition (Klier and Lambroza, 1992), and anti-Armenian pogroms were also green-lighted by Turkey's national government (Reid, 1992). A standard feature of these episodes was that the police stood by, refusing to prevent the murder, rape and mayhem, sometimes actually joining in. Very often the press and media inflamed public opinion long beforehand, and subsequently justified what happened as very unfortunate but predictable. Not that such events could not recur, and not that they have not already done so: the January 2002 slaughter in Ahmedabad, India, of over two thousand Muslim men, women and children in 'reprisal' for the wanton killing of some 60 Hindu pilgrims in the state a few days earlier, displayed exactly this pattern.

Our suggestion is that while far less dramatic and concentrated than pogroms of the traditional kind, and while not tracing their origins to anything as simple and unidirectional as an absolute emperor such as the Tsar, the cumulative patterns of racist prisonization and police repression visible across the affluent nations ultimately represent a technology of control with some distinct analogies to conventional pogroms of the past. They too have a lethal chemistry of repression, racism, media, politics and economic turbulence.

In media terms, the continuous diet in US local and national news, and in TV police 'reality' shows, of coverage of crimes being committed by people of color (Campbell, 1995: 69–82; Entman and Rojecki, 2000; Heider, 2000: 39–44; Fox and Van Sickel, 2001: 151–82), has built up over at least two decades to tendentially criminalize entire populations.[35] Back in the 1970s in Britain Stuart Hall and his colleagues (1978) similarly noted how the media figure of the 'mugger' was being deployed to criminalize young people of color in the public mind. Reeves and Campbell (1994) have documented the racist impact of the Reagan administration's 'War on Drugs' of the 1980s in terms of both its media coverage and state repression of people of color.[36] Mexican and Latin American immigration has been systematically represented in *The Los Angeles Times* and other Californian media by verbal metaphors of dangerous waters, disease and animality (Santa Ana, 2002: 65–103). Gerbner and his research teams over the years found a large proportion of US citizens, especially those who watched TV a great deal, exceptionally prone to believe they lived in a scary world: the media history of this process is a long one (Gerbner et al., 1999).

Consequently, it has become no surprise to media users to be told the perpetrator of a crime was a person of color or 'immigrant' or 'refugee' (whatever the actual truth of the matter); no serious concern to the public to think such large numbers of people of color are in jail, often with sentences many times longer than White inmates' for the same offenses; and even a relief to citizens outside the jails to think that the level of threat to one's daily safety has receded because most of the dangerous people have been locked up (though 'of course unfortunate mistakes are sometimes made'). Certainly Le Pen and the *Front National* have had a field day with inflating and inflaming people's fears in France concerning immigrants of color and White people's street safety (Souchard et al., 1997: 47–82; Bizeul, 2003: 99–116), and this kind of political message from the mainstream Right and the ultra-Right about criminality and skin-color is very common across Europe and beyond.

Thus we see an emergent trend toward operative collaboration between the ultra-Right (inside and outside extremist groups as such), general law enforcement policies and procedures, and common, though not universal, media representations of people of color. These representations are all the more effective for not having been planned from a central source. Mainstream media, unlike many ultra-rightist media, do not incite to individual violence, but they generate a defining framework within which it is easier for ultra-rightist media to operate, a kind of common ground of negative, fearful and hostile perceptual schemata and radically inadequate and distorted information about communities of color, from which the ultra-Right can advance its 'policy solutions' to 'the problem'.

We view this as certainly short of a pogrom in the strict and traditional sense, but in light of its common appearance across nations, its duration over the past quarter-century or more, and its degree of impact, the term *ongoing low-intensity pogrom* seems appropriate. It involves rather few actual killings as compared to the scores, hundreds, or even more who die in 'conventional' pogroms – and even those horrors are intermittent, not ongoing events. Nonetheless, across the majority of OECD countries the overall pattern of racist repression and violence from state law enforcement agencies and ultra-rightist movements, either tolerated or simply marginalized by many mainstream media, is severe, has been cumulative, and shows no sign of slackening, indeed the reverse. The conceptualization of the prison-industrial complex as 'social death', of which the mainstream media silence on prison realities is a key component, is an important part of coming to terms with the linkages between all these agencies of power. Again, there are different opinions and even collective initiatives from inside the prison-industrial complex, which is not a monochrome entity, although HoSang (1999–2000) argues that the various police reform initiatives over the past decade and longer represent an attempt to fine-tune the system rather than substantively change it.

The situation and our proposition need more detailed research, and it is certainly possible that the crisis is more accentuated currently in the USA than elsewhere. Nonetheless, it is a very dangerous and chilling trend, one which saps the foundations of opportunity, freedom and social justice, in the process eviscerating citizenship and democracy. If there is a more adequate term to denote this syndrome than 'ongoing low-intensity pogrom', we have not found it. In the next chapter we will explore this notion further in relation to still more violent and dangerous processes of dealing with difference and the Others.

Conclusions

Here, as in later chapters, we have been more concerned to summarize the directions in which we judge it important to pursue further research than to offer perfectly safe and thoroughly footnoted findings. Thus the principal task this chapter has set out is the detailed mapping of interconnections in the perpetuation of racist structures and processes among (1) extreme rightist groups, right-wing neo-populist movements, and their media; (2) established media, including local media and especially tabloid-style print, radio, TV and internet publications; (3) mainstream rightist parties and organizations; and (4) national and local government agencies in charge of law enforcement, immigration control, anti-terrorism and related spheres.

Critical discourse analyses of the extreme Right's media language and racist rhetoric are part and parcel of the research task we have posed. Equally central, and preferably closely linked, will be studies of audience uses of ultra-Right media, and their political economy. Having said this, however, we also conclude that research would be valuable on anti-racist media activism within religious, labor, and center to center-Left political parties, as well as within mainstream conservative parties (which should not be demonized, but analyzed). On the principle that all that is necessary for evil to happen is for decent people to stand by and do nothing, tracking the *absences*, failures and successes of such media activism among union activists, progressive community groups, feminist groups, lesbian and gay rights groups, human rights activists, environmentalists, would also be a productive exercise.

Notes

1 An earlier version of this chapter was published as 'International communication and the extremist right,' in Manjunath Pendakur and Roma Harris, eds., *Citizenship and Participation in the Information Age*. Aurora, Ontario: Garamond Press (2002), pp.137–46.

2 Not every rightist or extremist group is racist: the Unification Church of the Reverend Moon, the Branch Davidians of Waco, Texas, some of the militias, did not and do not have racism as part of their ideology. Racism is not necessarily foregrounded within the contemporary Christian Right, though it is very rarely targeted there as a *structural* reality to oppose, only – at best – as an intra-group issue among the sect's devotees.

3 The phrase is adapted from the military strategy term 'low-intensity warfare'. Cf. Klare and Kornbluh (1987).

4 The highly secretive Opus Dei, with toward 80,000 members in 80 countries, is at the other end of the spectrum from a populist movement. Its origins were in Franco's Spain, and its founder was spiritual advisor to the Generalísimo. He was super-fast-track canonized by John Paul II in 2002. It seeks influence by methods which in Europe of the 17th and 18th centuries were typically characterized as 'Jesuitical,' namely having members in very high places. Examples include General Pinochet, the butcher of Chile, for whose release from house arrest in Britain the Vatican militated very actively; and in earlier decades after World War II, a whole nest of Croatian Ustaše (see the next chapter). Highly placed members were involved at that juncture in the secret exfiltration program of Nazi officials to Latin American countries, especially to Argentina, Brazil and Bolivia, and in the process of 'cleansing' former Nazis and collaborators in European countries so they could reassume their influential positions. In 2000, others were pivotally influential in the process of defining Austria as readmissible to functioning membership of the European Union following its expulsion on account of the victory of Joerg Haider's Austrian Freedom Party (see below). A current passion is the 'civilizational war' against Islam. For more detail see the French website Réseau Voltaire: http://www.reseauvoltaire.net/opue-dei.html, and Walsh (1992).

5 In the USA, such crimes are seriously undercounted: 'Discounting Hate,' *Intelligence Report* 2003 http://www.splcenter.org/intel/intelreport/article/jsp?aid=157. In European nations, different categorization and enumeration procedures can produce quite loopy contrasts, clearly with no basis in reality, for instance nearly 50,000 racial violence incidents in Britain in the same year that France recorded a mere 30! For a European survey, see the British magazine *Searchlight* 1997 [www.s-light.demon.co.uk/stories/fascism.htm#GE]; Hunter (1998b); Pfefferkorn (1997); 'Keine Entwarnung vor rechten Skins,' *Die Tageszeitung*, Berlin (2/19/99) [www.taz.de/tpl/1999/02/19/a0203. nf/stext? Name=ask10578aaa&idx=1]; Govaert (1998).

6 Over 700 such groups as of 2002, a high proportion operating websites, according to the Southern Poverty Law Center's Intelligence Project: http://www.splcenter.org/intel/map/hate.jsp

7 Laqueur (1993).

8 Parry (1995).

9 For print media, see Danky and Cherney (1996); for television, see Frankl (1998) and Williams (1998); for video see Johnson (1998) and Kintz and Lesage (1998); for rock music see Hilliard and Keith (1999, pp. 220–21), and 'Profiteering From Hate: the lucrative world of the nazi music industry uncovered,' in the long-running British anti-fascist magazine *Searchlight* (February 1997), research conducted jointly with the Swedish anti-fascist magazine *Expo*: www.s-light.demen.co.uk/stories/musicfeb97.htm

10 *Minneapolis Star Tribune*, 6/21/95, 11A, cited in Hilliard and Keith (1999, p. 96).

11 James Latham, 'The rise of far Right hate programming on the short-wave bands,' *Vista* (April 1994), cited in Hilliard and Keith (1999, p. 95).

12 These radio stations are surveyed and monitored by Global Community Forum at Radio For Peace International in Costa Rica: sufpicr@sol.racsa.co.cr

13 Listed from *Vista* (Radio for Peace International) website in Hilliard and Keith (1999, pp. 127–28).

14 Southern Poverty Law Center, *Intelligence Report*, Winter 1998; reproduced in Hilliard and Keith (1999, pp. 118–23).

15 There are also anti-racist skinhead groups, whose work is to be respected.

16 Cited in Political Research Associates homepage (publiceye.org) under American Sociological Association press conference report, 1999.

17 Hatewatch.org See also Whine (1997); Zickmund (1997).

18 See Kaldor (2003), 50–77, for a more detailed treatment.

19 *Strukturwandel der Öffentlichkeit* (1962), Neuwied/Berlin, Luchterhand; English language edition *The Transformation of the Public Sphere*, Cambridge, Massachusetts, MIT Press, 1989.

20 C. Wright Mills, *The Power Elite*. New York, Oxford University Press, 1956, ch. 13.

21 Cf. Downing (1988); Calhoun, ed. (1993), especially the essay by Fraser; François and Neveu (1999).

22 Howard Rheingold, *The Virtual Community: Homesteading on the Electronic Frontier*. Reading, Massachusetts, Addison-Wesley Publishing Co. (1993).

23 The Carinthian Homeland Service, a provincial political organization in the Austrian province of Carinthia (its' leader Joerg Haider's geographical base), which lent crucial support to the formation of the Austrian Freedom Party. The Kärnter Heimatdienst had been founded in 1920, had enthusiastically endorsed the Nazis' annexation of Austria, and had been banned for a dozen years after World War II, but was re-established in 1957. ('Service' in German (*Dienst*) regularly though not necessarily carries a military connotation.)

24 See Downing (2003).

25 Some studies suggest that rightist extremists are often socially isolated individuals. Mark Potok, editor of the Southern Poverty Law Center's quarterly *Intelligence Report*, has argued that 'These people who felt like outcasts ... are getting in cars and driving to rallies and meeting soul mates from the Internet'. Cited in Michel Marriott, 'Rising tide: sites born of hate', *The New York Times* Circuits section (3/18/99). Cp. Zickmund (1997, pp. 199–204), who argues precisely the opposite, namely that the activism, within some Internet hate group discussions, of vocal challengers who dispute racist statements 'is a step towards forcing subversives into open interaction with society' (p. 204). While this may happen here and there, Zickmund arguably underestimates the widespread commonalities of racist sentiment and ideology. In these times 'society' at large is very doubtfully *anti*-racist.

26 It has to be said that the roles of the religious ultra-Right in perpetuating racism are yet to be carefully analyzed. As we note below, some ultra-Right religious groups explicitly eschew racism amongst their own devotees, although this intra-communitarian commitment has no implications of any significance for an attack on institutionalized racism in the structures of society at large.

27 For a helpful summary of the Canadian legal position on freedom of 'expression' (broader than speech), and its relation to hate speech, see Hogg (1992: Chapter 40), especially p. 22 of that chapter. I am very grateful to Mathew Englander and Gary Yabsley of Ratcliff and Company, Vancouver, for making this reference available to me.

28 See 'What are the aggregate patterns of hate crime in the US?' at www.publiceye.org/pra/hate/hate99ASA-03.htm#P129_8730

29 See the extensive documentary *George Wallace: Settin' the woods on fire* (dir. Paul Stekler, 2001, U.S. Public Broadcasting System).

30 Eric Lichtblau, 'Ashcroft seeks more power to pursue terror suspects,' *The New York Times*, June 6, 2003, A1, A14 and the outstanding survey of the Guantánamo saga by Isabel Hilton, 'Held in contempt', *Financial Times FT Weekend*, 28–9 August, 2004, W1–2.

31 See the articles in *Mots/Les langages du politique* 58 (March, 1999) on extreme rightist discourse in France; and also Souchard et al. (1998).

32 Literally signifying 'thus,' but also used in academic writing to signal a misprint or grammatical error in a cited passage.

33 The French elite, like elites elsewhere (Van Dijk, 1993), seemingly could only attack racism in subordinate classes by manifesting elitist contempt for their crude racism, apparently assuming it would immediately shrivel and vanish as a consequence. And that they, in their glory, did not – more covertly and delicately – ascribe to the same root ideology.

34 When he was dropped from the Conservative Party's Shadow Cabinet in April, 1968 for the first of his notoriously inflammatory speeches, timed and released with great care to capture maximum news attention, his removal meant no loss of salary whatsoever, let alone loss of his job. Yet what intensified the energy of a number of those who marched in his support was the perception that the elite had ganged up on him and fired him for speaking his mind. He did zero, of course, to disabuse his supporters of their sense of righteous indignation and solidarity.

35 We need to keep in mind in this context the normal, ongoing relationship of law enforcement agencies nationally and locally with their media counterparts at both levels. Studies by in Britain and Canada by Chibnall (1977), Ericson, Baranek and Chan (1991), and Schlesinger and Tumber (1994), have demonstrated both the key role of the police as a continuous news source for the crime stories that local news media lap up, and also the very careful courting of journalists by law enforcement officials at the highest levels.

36 '... we also can state that coverage on all of the networks, including CBS, periodically [encouraged] such strong identification with police action that it [became] little more than propaganda for the expansion of state power in the surveillance and repression of visible and vulnerable populations in America's inner cities ... From its sanctification of Middle America as a place of endangered purity, to its dehumanization of urban drug transgressors, to its approval of the reactionary privatized community, to its indictment of educational permissiveness, to its unfavorable portrayal of the 1960s, the routine news coverage of the crack crisis, in many instances, represented mainstream journalism's ideological convergence on – and moral conversion to – the once-extremist views of the New Right and Religious Right ... Ultimately, such cracked coverage made it easier to dismiss the disadvantages experienced by the black and brown urban poor as self-inflicted – matters of individual choice and self-indulgence, not matters of economic history, social structure, and racial inequality (op.cit., pp. 32, 161)'.

4 Violence, 'Race' and Media: Comparative Perspectives

It is relatively commonplace to contrast contemporary patterns of 'racial' and 'ethnic' subordination with other social divisions, notably 'religious', 'national' and 'tribal', and thereby downplay the significance of 'race', on the ground that whatever problems exist, they do not operate on the same scale as, for instance, the low-intensity civil war in Northern Ireland since 1969, the high-intensity civil wars in ex-Yugoslavia in the 1990s, or the Rwandan genocide of 1994. Hanging in the air is the unvoiced but pregnant implication that while White people may have something to answer for in their past, in the present era serious mayhem cannot be laid at their door, and consequently that people of color should get their own house in order and look at how ugly life can *really* be in some other places, before crying 'racism!'

The planetary homogenization of all people of color in this discourse betrays its opportunistic intent (and no doubt its lack of sincere interest in the Irish, Balkan and Rwandan tragedies), but at the same time it will serve as a useful point of departure for a comparative analysis of how media operate in 'ethnic' and 'racial' scenarios, and in scenarios where the 'cultural markers' (over-determined and essentialized signifiers), and therefore their mediatic processing, are different. Language-conflicts (for example, Belgium, Sri Lanka) and caste would constitute further examples, though we shall not explore them here. The 'cultural marker' comparison, therefore, is one question to address, and in the discussion of Northern Ireland we will begin to do so.

The other is the roles of media in situations of extreme collective violence. The specific illustrations we have chosen are all from dismayingly to terrifyingly intense confrontations and repression, taken from 'civilized Europe' and from the so-called 'Third World'. The focus on conflict and violence represents a certain distortion, since in practice, both historically and currently, most members of different ethnic and other socially categorized groups rub along most of the time without evident friction.[1] While the absence of overt conflict during any one period may not betoken the absence of deep conflicts of interest, it is also the case that many groups have no particular conflict of interest, certainly not an endemic one. In the

21st century, for example, it is frequently taken as axiomatic that Jews and Muslims are inexorably at loggerheads, but historically they have enjoyed long periods of peaceful co-existence and co-operation, as have Hindus and Muslims. Racism may also entail a distorted form of admiration, such as obsession with the supposedly exotic qualities of the Other(s).

That said, our focus here is different. While it is important to avoid assuming ethnicity is somehow inherently explosive, and to search out systematically what may be favorable media scenarios for constructive interrelation, it is also the case that we need to think very hard indeed about the roles of media in relation to the worst explosions of 'racial' hatred, just as we need to understand them in partly analogous explosions of 'religious', 'national' and 'tribal' hatred. Our priority must be to try to fathom their roles (1) in helping generate these huge traumas, (2) in sustaining them in motion and in memory (or forgetting), as well as (3) in resisting them and in helping to draw lessons from them for establishing a grounded and enduring peace. Their ongoing roles over decades, as regards (1) and (2) will particularly absorb our attention in this chapter.

These traumas vary from the ongoing low-intensity pogroms we argued are characteristic of 'racial' scenarios in many of the OECD nations, to severe pogroms, to civil wars and violent expulsions,[2] to actual genocide. What any and all of these entail is far removed from the standard international media stereotype typically trotted out to explain their viciousness, of spontaneous atavistic violence. The situations we shall examine belong firmly to the modern world, not to the weird survival of a blood-soaked barbaric past (although the horrific bombs falling on Afghanistan and Iraq as we were preparing this book render minimal the violence of club and spear). The Nazis, too, notwithstanding their Nordic god-craziness, were outstandingly modern. Indeed, the *local* uses of mass media technologies, and of state law enforcement agencies and other bureaucracies in these conflicts, demonstrate rather precisely how embedded they are in modernity, as – not least – do the interventions of *international* media in depicting them.

Indeed, in riposte to the apostles of not taking racism seriously, there is no magic (White) wall that blocks off the escalation of contemporary low-intensity 'racial' pogroms into full-scale pogroms, or further still. The Rwandan genocide had as its precursor a 3–4 year civil war, and behind that an intermittent series of blood-drenched confrontations stretching back at least thirty-five years. The civil wars in ex-Yugoslavia and Northern Ireland did not explode out of a clear blue sky. And the Nazi genocide itself had very deep roots. Paul Massing's classic study *Rehearsal for Destruction* (1949) demonstrates the variety of versions of anti-Semitism in Germany from the 1880s through to the close of World War I: the absolutist-biological, the antecedent of Hitlerism; the religious-traditional, defining Jews as Christ-killers; and the large farmer class's resentment of petty economic middlemen, quite often of Jewish background. To these was added a sizable semi-educated segment of the intelligentsia, often devoid of religious belief, but pouring into German nationalism and imperialism the energies of religion. After Germany was blocked from acquiring more colonies by the longer-established imperial powers and 'the march towards a place in the sun was stopped, anti-Semitism, the 'twin-brother of extreme German nationalism' made the defeated nation itself the new battleground and redefined the enemy' as the Jews (*op.cit.*, 148). Massing also notes how most of the organized Left failed to register the tenacious virulence of anti-Semitism with sufficient seriousness, casually dismissing it as passing political backwardness or simply a distorted version of class resentment, both of them due to melt away with the victory of socialism. Not least his account documents how political leaders repeatedly played the Jewish card or connived with anti-Semites for temporary political gain, thus continually extending the legitimacy of anti-Semitism. This experience connects intimately with our discussion in the previous chapter of how vitally important the linkages may be between the ultra-Right and the mainstream Right.

We will begin our media analysis in each case with a very brief introduction to the conflicts in Northern Ireland, former Yugoslavia and Rwanda, and then proceed to examine the roles media played in each situation. Distinct from our focus in the previous chapter, we shall consistently find ourselves in this one engaging with the roles of international as well as local media. This has a lot to do with the fact that although Northern Ireland and the Balkans are in Europe, they have traditionally been regarded as peripheral zones, colonized, Slav-ized and/or Islamized, and therefore more akin to the 'Third World' or Russia than 'Europe proper'. For sure, European media comment regularly on the 'racial' scenario in the USA, and vice-versa, but their authority to frame those scenarios is not matched by their capacity to lubricate foreign policy and to affect the global play of forces governing their outcome, as has been the case in the three situations under consideration here. By foreign policy we mean both actions and the refusal of action, the contrast between foreign intervention in ex-Yugoslavia and its absence in Rwanda being a perfect illustration of how both matter. (Readers should realize, however, that unless already familiar with the three complex situations presented in this chapter, it will likely be unproductive to try to master its detail and argument at a single gulp.)

Low-intensity Civil War, 'Religion' and Media: Northern Ireland

A very common approach to defining religion's role as a vector in social conflicts, especially by secular researchers, is to perceive it as (a) atavistic, or at least a medieval survival, and (b) supremely hypocritical, given the major world religions' self-professed goals of peace and order. Such a perspective posits the altogether rosy scenario that it is possible to exorcise these conflicts through shaming the participants into confessing their lack of modernity and/or spiritual consistency. In reality, religiously-defined conflicts have rarely been centrally driven by purely theological issues, even though religious differences have certainly been part of the story, serving as a combined everyday cultural marker[3] and condensed symbolic shorthand. The same is true of 'nationality' and 'tribal' conflicts, as indeed it is of 'racial' ones.

Indeed the only productive way to address the 'cultural marker' comparison, in our view, is to begin by recognizing its primary fallacy, namely the assumption that an everyday shorthand – skin-color, tribe, nationality, religious sect – conveys a sufficient explanation of the scenario under consideration. Rather, it is the *over-determined and essentialized* character of these shorthand cultural markers to which we must direct our attention. In almost all of these conflictual scenarios, the dynamics of social class, gender, age, and not least of state law enforcement agencies, also spin into and only very occasionally out of the saga. Young angry males, sexually voracious younger women, submissive women employees, permanently unemployed neighborhoods, well-to-do urban professionals, uncouth migrant workers, sets of people with privileged access to state resources, other sets of people targeted by law enforcement agencies: all these socially constructed categorizations and the realities behind them can be found at work in the examples of 'race', 'religion', 'tribe' and 'nationality' we examine here, never mind many other situations beyond the compass of this book.

This is not to *reduce* the specificity of religious sect and the rest to 'objective class forces', patriarchy, generational clashes or any other single, simple category. It is not to say that 'racial' strife is *really* all about social class. It is to say that these trees have multiple roots, and while their leaves – nationality, tribe and so on – are how we typically identify them in everyday interactions, and are indeed vital components of the trees, we can no more stop at the leaves than we can forget them, if we wish to grasp the issues at stake in their entirety. Equally, the argument popular among US neo-conservatives (Thomas Sowell, Dinesh D'Souza and others) and Marxists alike, that 'race' has passed away or never really existed, is a wretched simplification.

Introduction to Contemporary Northern Ireland

As with the next two case-studies, it is hard, if not on the edge of absurd or cheap, to write a postage-stamp-sized summary of the issues in order to review their media dimension. But it has to be done, so we hope that for those for whom it is the first time of venturing into this terrain, they will follow up some of our cited references, and that others familiar with it will not grind their teeth to powder.

Overt conflict emerged in 1968 and by the time of writing had taken well over three thousand lives, not to mention those physically maimed and psychologically traumatized. The terms used locally to denote the contending groups were quite often not Protestant and Catholic, but loyalist (that is, to the British state, the predominant position among Protestants), and nationalist (that is, in favor of reuniting Ireland as a single nation, with Dublin as its capital, a quite common preference among Catholics). These terms much more accurately defined the core of the conflict than the religious ones. It was a conflict substantially linked to eight centuries of British colonialism, which from the late 1500s also meant repression by an officially Protestant state. In the 1600s this state extensively allocated tracts of north-eastern Irish farmland to poor Protestant settlers from Scotland. Hence the demographics of the North-East, inaccurately termed 'the North' (County Donegal is also on Ireland's northern coast).

For nationalists Northern Ireland was, understandably, a political fiction, 'the Six Counties' ripped out of Ireland's 32 counties in 1920 and re-named Ulster, instead of the nine constituting the original northern province of Ulster. When the British government ceded independence to the other 26 counties, was also the moment at which those six north-eastern counties combined a localized majority of loyalists with a minority Catholic labor force concentrated in two of them. This constituted an economically viable micro-state, with a Catholic reserve army of labor, but securely in loyalist hands. For loyalists, it was the 'Province' (of Britain), proud possessor of the heavy industrial port city of Belfast, which was then unmatched in economic terms by Dublin or any other Irish city. Not only were Belfast's shipyards and textile industry then important to the British economy, but part of the British elite maintained an ideological attachment to the loyalist elite in Ireland's North-East. Thus throughout the 20th century, to be marked 'Catholic' by the loyalist majority in the micro-state stereotypically meant not only a political charge (disloyalty to the British state), but also an economic one (unskilled laborer, field hand, hard-scrabble farmer, or unemployed). In turn, a quite frequent ideology among Protestants was that this economic status betokened Catholics' poor work ethic, meager talents and subordination to popery and priest-craft (not the result of past colonial policies, cemented by entrenched discrimination from government and private institutions alike).

Similarly, on an everyday level, Catholics' stereotypes of Protestants – with, as usual, a partial hold on actuality – defined their lifestyle as emphasizing taut austereness, primness and discipline, contrasted to a Catholic lifestyle which was more likely to value warmth, liveliness, wit and knowing how to have some fun. Certain features of each sect's religious practice were typically scorned by adherents of the other. Protestants despised the Catholic confessional and the prohibition on birth control, saw devotion to the Virgin Mary as sacrilegious, and Catholicism as generally retrograde and pre-modern, while Catholics found Protestant services singularly aseptic, and as hypocritical the systematic discrimination and contempt Protestants handed out to them in the name of a superior brand of Christianity. Deference to the Pope and loyalty to the British Crown thus fused rather tightly with both religious and political commitments and antagonisms, and with quotidian experiences.

What was *not* available was any instant identity-marker by skin color or language. Certain last and first names, though, could serve as instant clues. Segregated neighborhoods, especially those well known for militant loyalism or nationalism, likewise. Because education was religiously segregated, knowledge of which school a person had attended would also nearly always immediately identify someone's sect, so that especially from the 1970s onwards, questioning a stranger 'Which school did you go to?' or 'Where do you live?' would be read as dangerously provocative.

The question of religion was therefore *neither* the core of the Northern Irish conflict, *nor* purely epiphenomenal. It served as a hugely condensed symbol of a great deal else, both historically and in people's current everyday lives. And as the Troubles lengthened their sway and their pain over the years, so in distrust and for security's sake many people shrank back into their sectarian grooves, whether or not religious beliefs themselves played any significant role in their lives. The British military intervention, ostensibly 'to keep the two sides apart' and to 'maintain law and order', was in reality an exemplary case of low-intensity warfare strategy,[4] including both extensive media management and targeted assassinations. The elitist militarism of the Provisional IRA (Irish Republican Army) was for many purposes, though far less resourced, the British army's mirror-image, and was equally bankrupt of ideas for constructive resolution of the conflict.

The Roles of Media

As with former Yugoslavia and Rwanda, issues in media representation were both local and international. What roles did local, British, southern Irish and global media play in the Northern Ireland conflict of the last third of the 20th century? We have relied upon a series of different studies for the following analysis,[5] but one of the difficulties we faced in writing it was the lack of systematic interrelation of the varied media in play during the civil war. The nearest to a connected account over the first three decades of the civil war is Parkinson's (1998) study of British media representation of Ulster loyalism, but which is concerned with the likely impact of coverage in Britain rather than on the Irish public, North and South.[6]

What follows is consequently sketchy at intervals, but one point is crucial to establish from the outset, namely the *longevity* of media which had reflected and reinforced the sectarian segregated educational system and political structure of the territory. The *Belfast Newsletter*, reflecting the aggressive determination of Protestant Loyalists never to be swallowed up by the South, had been founded in 1737; the *Belfast Telegraph*, founded in 1870, represented the wealthier, publicly less strident segment of the Loyalist community; and the *Irish News*, founded in 1891, voiced the desire for reunification common among Catholics, not least because it would free them of the systemic discrimination they lived under. Evaluating the roles of media in the conflict is not therefore something that can usefully be done simply by a content analysis from 1968 or during some period of aggravated crisis. It is their cumulative impact over generations that needs to be the primary focus. In this regard, media in Northern Ireland, like media in former Yugoslavia and Rwanda, raise significant research questions which typical approaches to media research often skate over because of their obsession with the contemporary.

Traditionally, broadcast media inside Northern Ireland had routinely avoided reference to the Catholic third of the population or to the Irish Republic's affairs, and thus by systematic silence had communicated the normalcy of Loyalist domination (Butler, 1991). Furthermore, the BBC's pan-national broadcasting policy had meant that programs rejected by its Belfast outpost would not be broadcast anywhere else in the UK either. This effectively led to a virtual media silence throughout the UK on anything controversial regarding Northern Ireland, not least including the structural subordination of the large Catholic minority. This held until the mid-1960s introduction of a commercial TV channel which, in search of an audience, ran material that while not politically controversial, at least engaged with the one-third or more of the public who did not identify with Protestant loyalism.

Mentioning English media, however, compels recognition that, like the Irish Republic's media, they were *both* a foreign *and* a domestic presence simultaneously in Northern Ireland, depending on whether you were loyalist or nationalist.[7] Attitudes to British or Irish media in the two communities, especially to the press, could and did move into routine distrust and contempt. Curtis (1984) presents a series of case-studies accounting convincingly for nationalist resentment of British news media. This combination of local (but variously conflicting) British and Irish media representations made for a particularly complex mediascape.

Irish media in the Republic, after an intense initial identification with northern Catholics' plight in 1968–72, paid less and less attention to ongoing stories from the North as though weary of and even embarrassed by them, but inflated any signal that peace was on the horizon (Trench, 1991). As regards Irish media inside the North, Rolston (1991b), analyzing the two Belfast loyalist newspapers and its one nationalist daily some twenty years into the Troubles, characterized two as having moved toward representing a new 'post-sectarian' professional elite from each community, whereas one of the loyalist dailies had shifted to an ever shriller assertion of its traditional fundamentals. Curtis' (1984: 262–74) brief account of the newspaper *Republican News/An Phoblacht* and the Provisional Irish Republican Army's media policies, focuses almost entirely on war reporting issues, and does not explore wider representational matters in nationalist media. After her study was published, and with the rise of a legal political party linked to the IRA (Sinn Féin The Workers Party) which engaged with social policies as well as the war, the newspaper's contents became much wider in scope. Its distribution, however, never remotely matched the diffusion of mainstream media.

In 1967–68, as noted, English media representation briefly shifted from virtual disinterest over decades in Northern Irish affairs to sympathetic coverage of the student-based civil rights movement of the mid-60s. This mirrored coverage of the US civil rights movement. But this did not take long to change into a framework redolent of traditional colonialist optics: as Butler (*op.cit.*, 110) puts it, 'prior to April 1969 "reasonable" Catholic grievances versus "unreasonable" Protestant wrongdoing were the major concerns; now the conflict was represented as a dispute between equivalent warring tribes'. Former *New York Times* correspondent Jo Thomas (1991: 125) similarly characterized the terms in which the conflict was officially discussed in British media as 'law and order, terrorism and counterterrorism, or religious sectarian battles in which both sides are portrayed as equally bigoted, equally powerful, and equally unreasonable.'

This binarist framework, in Butler's analysis, generated (a) an obsessive focus on IRA terrorism[8] to the exclusion of all other dimensions of the nationalist community, along with (b) a virtual symbolic annihilation of the loyalist community, the 'Bad' and the 'Ugly' as he puts it (*op.cit.*, 115). The 'Good'[9] were the British, trying to hold the ring and return British peace and reasonableness to these unregenerate contenders. Sometimes the issue was reframed as one in which extremists on both sides were holding a reasonable majority hostage, but this framing also drastically reduced the complex issues in the conflict to moral virtue stifled by terror.

Not long after this change a 'reference upwards' system was instituted in 1971 for UK broadcast journalists. This had a strongly chilling effect on reporting the conflict, because it meant that news professionals had to get a green light from top management before they could even begin a Northern Ireland story or seek interviews (Curtis, 1984: 173–89). Journalists with a good career in mind were consequently likely simply to avoid the topic, thus reducing its coverage. Repeated British government attacks over a 20-year period on any coverage dissonant with its orthodoxy culminated in a 1988–94 ban on even permitting IRA members to speak in broadcasts (their words had to be spoken by an actor's voiceover).

Digging deeper was no more on the international than on the British news media agenda, or if it was for some genuinely professional journalists, editorial controls over which stories could be pursued frequently dissuaded them too from further investigation. *New York Times* correspondent Jo Thomas was initially discouraged by British government officials from pursuing her stories, and then ordered back home by her newspaper. Some US media though, particularly in handling a 1988 outrage involving the street assassination of three unarmed IRA members by British commandos (Miller, 1994: 160–201), did provide a picture that included the violence of the British state as a vector in the situation. Soviet media, through 1991, covered the continuing British military repression, but more, as Soviet leader Nikita Khrushchev once put it, by way of continuing the game of West and East 'throwing dead cats at each other' than out of any more principled involvement.

The point here, in terms of this book's focus, is not to move into a generic discussion of censorship and self-censorship, but to underscore the extent to which the international media representation of conflictual relations – in this case with a connection to religious adherences – may very well have contributed to a dangerous lack of understanding and sympathy within global publics for the people involved. Holland (1996: 399) notes the frequent expression of boredom among US journalists reporting on Northern Ireland with the supposedly insoluble conflict, a vision of the situation which left a great deal of space to a fatalistic acceptance of the British government's line on how to deal with the conflict. We already noted the similar disinterest among media in the Irish Republic. Thus the constant admixture of stereotypes and silences among media based outside Northern Ireland arguably had serious practical and long-lasting consequences for the prolongation of the conflict inside, freeing up the British state to pursue its handling of the conflict as the only permissible or imaginable one. As elements of global civil society have begun to crystallize with the increasing advent of global media, the possibilities for global social movements to exert effective international pressure have grown. Yet in this instance, global news publics were not fed from sources that might have seeded alternative strategies and asked inadmissible questions.

This is a very different approach to the role of media in the Northern Irish situation from one which focuses solely on negative mutual stereotypes and their media endorsement or challenge. We have emphasized the crucial historical role of partisan media in Northern Ireland, but by itself that tends to simplify the issues greatly by relying on an implicit notion that a newly responsible and imaginative media coverage would over time soften people's fears and hostilities. But the actors involved in Northern Ireland were not just 'the two communities' and 'the media'. The British state, in particular, was a hugely significant actor, as to a lesser degree were the US and Irish governments. Thus including both states' power and international media roles in the analysis of the media is essential. The British state's interest in the territory was rather consistently read in mainstream English and international media as that of keeping the peace and maintaining law and order, notwithstanding intermittent 'errors', 'overreactions' and 'tragic consequences'. The core *raison d'état*, that it refused to lose face by allowing itself to be perceived internationally as having been gunned out of its legally defined territory, was rarely if ever on the media agenda. Furthermore, especially in England itself, which clearly had a huge influence one way or another over the situation, attempts by television and other journalists to open up the situation for public debate were consistently met, as we saw in the case of the 'reference upwards' system, with blockages at the highest levels (Schlesinger, 1987: xxiii–xxvii, 205–243).

High-intensity Civil War, 'Nationality' and Media: Former Yugoslavia

As noted below[10] the terms 'tribe' and 'nationality' are often used to denote rather similar realities, the distinction being in significant measure ideological rather than sociological (tribe = atavism, nationality = modernity). At the same time, 'nationality' has several senses: it may indicate people's citizenship in and cultural membership of an internationally recognized nation state; the same, for people's connection to a nation contained within a larger multi-national state (for example, Québec inside Canada); and the same too for people's adhesion to one of the separate peoples, previously constitutionally defined as nationalities and/or federated republics, emerging from the collapse of the Soviet bloc and Yugoslavia 1989–91.

There is a huge literature on nations, the nation state and nationalism (see for example, Gossiaux, 2002: 5–66; MacDonald, 2003: 15–38). Anderson's endlessly cited study (1983) pivots the issue on what brought about mass public adhesion to nations globally over the past three centuries, as opposed to more limited and localized community identifications. For him, the way national loyalties seem to have come to supersede all others, whether in the First World War (class loyalties) or the 1979 war between Communist Vietnam and Communist China (Marxist-Leninist loyalties), are proof positive of the ascendancy of the nation as a form of social cohesion in the modern era.

Whether, however, that apparently fundamental simplicity either explains those wars or sheds light on the nation-form, needs a closer look. The need in wars for incessant internal propaganda, the penalties for desertion, the bellicosity of some regimes and leaders, the rising determination as war continues to avenge fallen comrades or family victims, and to defend one's fighting unit, all considerably complicate the notion that people readily leap into combat based on national identifications. Anderson is certainly far from the only writer to lean on such visions of nationhood's visceral power, but given his prominence it is worth stepping back from his starting point as a way of disputing 'from the top' the visceral passions so often taken as endemic in this arena. Nation state, nation and nationality are very doubtfull watertight categories reducible to a single global theory, as a comparison of the 19th century unification of Germany or Italy with the disintegration of Federal Yugoslavia should make clear.

Introduction to Former Yugoslavia

Along with the Russian-Chechen wars, the Yugoslavia nightmare of the 1990s[11] was widely interpreted as a universal explosion of nationality hatreds, once the Communist regimes' lid had been taken off. However, this was a wild exaggeration. Though we shall concentrate on the Yugoslav case, in actuality the vast majority of these transitions were entirely peaceful (Kahn, 2000). This is an important observation, one which mirrors our observation that historically most tribes, Jews, Muslims, Hindus have rubbed along just fine much of the time. Our analyses, while focused here on overt conflict, must also engage with that contrasting reality. And with the further reality that in some situations signs of peace and harmony may be deceptive, especially to the outside observer, but also even to insiders: many Yugoslav citizens had difficulty believing the descent into hell was actually happening.[12]

At the same time, as we shall see, while there was clearly a vicious civil war between Serbs, Croats and Bosnian Muslims, and later some violent strife between (ethnic) Albanians, Macedonian Slavs, and Serbs, there is considerable reason to dispute that the Serb forces were attempting genocide against Bosnian Muslims, and also whether US, French and British media reports of the *scale* of killings, rapes and tortures were based on evidence or cumulative hearsay (Hammond and Herman, 2000; Johnstone, 2002). The charge of 'genocide' was thrown about very freely, both by Serb and Croat propagandists at each other, and by international commentators surveying the situation of Bosnian Muslims and Albanians. This use of the term, which confused savage dispossessions, bombings, murders and rapes designed to create Serb-free, Croat-free and Muslim-free zones, with the intention systematically to liquidate entire peoples, was grossly and dangerously ill-judged. It both blotted out the actual dynamics of the civil war and almost criminally banalized the actual Nazi Holocaust (Pergnier, 2002: 135–140).[13] Furthermore, the contrast with the more or less contemporary refusal by Western authorities and media to acknowledge the *real* genocide in Rwanda, is striking. The consequences of that refusal, as we shall see later on this chapter, were terrifying.

Confusing the issue in the former Soviet Union and Yugoslavia was their previous nationalities and 'autonomous republics' policy, which defined as nationalities and/or as distinct mini-republics not only groups with a prior existence as such (Estonia, Georgia, Slovenia), but also groups which elsewhere might typically be referred to as ethnic and/or regionally-located minorities. For example Soviet Jews were a nationality (a hangover in this instance from Czarist practice), Chechnya was an autonomous republic, Bosnia's Muslims were declared a nationality in 1968, and Kosovo an autonomous republic in 1974. Yet all these designations had rather limited real entitlements within the framework of a highly centralized power structure in Moscow and Belgrade. And just as some Russians insisted the Soviet system made them second class citizens in their own land, so too did some members of the largest single Yugoslav group, the Serbs, see the Federal state as depriving them of their rightful place. (Perhaps needless to say, other nationalities were prone to see matters quite differently.)

Slammed together as a nation in 1918, and first named 'Yugoslavia' (South Slavia) by its then Serb monarchy in 1929, the component parts of the country were produced, like so many African and 'Middle Eastern' countries, by drawing artificial lines on a map. These lines chopped Albanian territory roughly in half in order that the mythic Serb homeland of Kosovo to the south would stay with the Serbs, and included both ethnically homogeneous Slovenia in the far north, which historically looked to Austria to *its* north, and Croatia, to Slovenia's south, which had strong ties to Germany and Italy. The borders as drawn also generated significant groups of Croats and Serbs living outside their republics' territory in Federal Yugoslavia, which from the perspective of multi-national citizenship mattered not at all. In the climate of the 1980s when citizenship and nationality came increasingly to be defined in mono-ethnic mutually mistrustful terms, it produced a lethal situation, one readily exploited and intensified by the reactionary Croatian, Serb, Bosnian and Kosovar Albanian (the KLA/UCK guerrilla) leaderships.

There were many turning points in this grim narrative, but certainly a constitutive one was Germany's and the Vatican's almost instantaneous endorsement of Slovenia's[14] and Croatia's secessionist declarations of national independence. The Serb-dominated Yugoslav Federal state defined the secessions as military rebellions against internationally recognized government authority, which simultaneously threatened to leave the Serbs in Serbia as a truncated entity, with their co-nationals in Croatia, Bosnia and Kosovo subjected to severe discrimination and loss of rights. Slovene, Croat and Bosnian Muslim leaders counter-defined the Federal army's actions as the Serbs' military hammer, bludgeoning the other nationalities into fealty to a Greater Serbia. Almost inevitably, the experience of the ensuing wars cemented the distrust, and in the widespread cases of forced removal and the attendant violence, often fomented fierce mutual hatred.

There were two principal phases of the conflict, namely from Milošević's accession to power in 1987 through the 1995 Dayton Accords, and subsequently the mounting tension between ethnic Albanians and Slavs in Kosovo and Macedonia, marked by NATO's bombing campaign in 1999. The focus here will be principally upon the Bosnian-Croatian-Serbian triangle, which achieved an unstable peace in the mid–1990s, but whose typical coverage by international media generated a definitional framework that later permitted, even encouraged, Western public acceptance of the 'humanitarian' NATO bombings of Serbian targets in 1999 to resolve conflicts in Kosovo (Hammond and Herman, 2000). We will dwell on this latter turn of events briefly at the close of this section on ex-Yugoslavia.

There are some longer historical features of this violent saga which need to be taken into account, partly to acknowledge their significance, but more particularly to register their intensive mythicization, especially from the mid–1980s onwards, by Serb and Croat propaganda machines. 1989 marked the sixth centenary of the Serbs' defeat by Ottoman colonialism at the battle of Kosovo, an anniversary that Premier Milošević exploited intensively in his late 1980s bid either to run Yugoslavia via Serb dominance, or to create a new Greater Serbia. 1940s Serb-Croat history was even more easily mined. During the Nazi-backed Croatian state of 1941–45, members of the Ustaše (the Croat fascist militia) had executed hundreds of thousands of Serbs, along with Jews, Roma and others. Surviving grandparents were still there to tell the story. Furthermore, some Bosnian Muslim units had been recruited as auxiliaries in the same attacks. Thus by linking the Kosovo anniversary with other bitter Serb defeats that had taken place within living memory, he lacerated the Serbian public with a chain of past tragedies, provoking amongst some a savage determination to right them immediately and for good. More generally, the role Bosnian Muslims had played well into the twentieth century, namely as landlords to Serb sharecroppers, and as the elite in Sarajevo and other cities, injected a powerful class dynamic into the mix of factors.

The Yugoslav nationality divisions were also to some extent religious (Perica, 2002). Serbs' religious tradition was Eastern Orthodox Christianity, and they had had an independent national church for centuries. Many

Serb clergy were among the most impassioned proponents of a Greater Serbia. Croats were overwhelmingly Catholics, to the point that the 1990s regime elevated Alojzije Stepinac, Croatia's World War II Nazi-sympathizer cardinal, into the father of modern Croatia and set up statues to him in every town. The remainder of Bosnians were Muslim by tradition, although typically referred to by hostile Croats and Serbs as 'Turks,' signaling their forebears' historical conversion to Islam under the centuries of Ottoman rule. A further twist on the religious front came about during Bosnia's civil war, when the rightist Muslim leadership brought in some thousands of hardline Islamist fighters, which tilted the scales away from the more secular and pluralistic Muslim culture of Bosnia, especially of Sarajevo. Religious differences were, however, wildly inflated during the 1990s. Croat propagandists, for example, claimed to be the West's bulwark against both Islamic fundamentalism and the backward eastern variant of Christianity practiced by Slavs, and they eagerly latched on to the half-baked stereotypes perpetrated by Harvard political scientist Samuel Huntington in his much-bruited (1993) *Foreign Affairs* article 'The Clash of Civilizations'.

The nationality divisions were to a degree linguistic as well (Gossiaux, 2002: 71–73). Serbs, Montenegrins, Croats and Bosnians spoke Serbo-Croatian, with dialectal variations that often did not overlap with ethnicity or religion, the Slovenes and Slavic Macedonians different Slavic languages, and the Kosovar and Macedonian Albanians, Albanian. Croatian and Serbian ultra-nationalists in the late 1980s promptly elevated the Serbo-Croatian dialects into separate national languages (with, naturally, a glorious history). Thus the 'cultural markers' became increasingly essentialized and over-determined.

This republic/nationality structure was inherently likely to increase appetites to expand the limited entitlements the centralized federal state offered (culminating in autonomy demands), appetites that were thus virtually bound to issue in a series of zero-sum stand-offs between different groups. As Gossiaux (2002: 98–103) confirms, the fusion of democratic demands for majority rule with a discourse of mono-ethnic nationality easily oiled the wheels for the attempted creation through force of state territories in which, respectively, neither Croats, Serbs nor Bosnian Muslims lived (other groups were permissible as ethnic minorities). Furthermore, the history of a single Communist Party lent itself to being morphed into a series of mono-ethnic national government parties with a bear-hug over media output. Referring to Slovenia, but with implications beyond it, Johnstone rather sourly notes a third factor, namely how

remarkably little attention has been paid to one of the most compelling motives for the leaders of a small community of under two million to create their own independent state: the huge increase of prestige, power, and income it affords to those who occupy the top positions in the new government. Editors of small journals may suddenly become cabinet ministers and ambassadors, not to mention arms dealers and import/ export tycoons. (2002: 139)

The Roles of Media

There have been a number of studies of the domestic and international roles of news media in Bosnia, Croatia, Serbia and Kosovo during the civil wars.[15] Iordanova (2001) also offers a fascinating review of how Balkan film-makers constructed their own discourses about the region through to the end of the 1990s, although regrettably the distribution of many of these films has been very thin, not least in sub-titled versions. Here, however, we will focus rather on broadcast and print media, television being the most important, and divide the topic up by 'nationality'.

(1) It could be said that the very first chapter in the immediate genesis of the conflict was a highly controversial media news story in 1987. This was at a point when Serbian television news was for the first time reporting separately from the Federal service. Premier Milošević visited Kosovo, the poorest of the Yugoslav territories, in which the majority ethnic-Albanian population had long chafed against economic neglect and a semi-apartheid political system (precious as Kosovo was in the ultra-nationalist Serb imaginary, Serbs had been deserting the area for decades, but still retained a rather privileged local status). At a Serb demonstration in which the demonstrators threw stones at the police, and the police responded with baton charges, Serb TV *only* showed the police beatings, followed by Milošević's pugnacious and demagogic proclamation afterwards to the demonstrators that 'no one shall beat you again!' In the other Yugoslav territories the entire episode was shown. The result was both a surge of pro-Milošević feeling in Serbia, where the truncated version was shown over and over again, and very considerable alarm in the other Yugoslav republics at Milošević's evident readiness to engage in the crudest media manipulation and the explosive implications of his chosen road to power.

Indeed in Serbia, Milošević's control over major and most[16] minor media in the Serb republic during the latter 1980s was essential in inflating Serb nationalism and in denying a voice to anti-chauvinist currents among Serbs:

The national consensus, however, was not easily achieved. It was the fruit of several years' labour by the government, which used its power to marshal media workers who either volunteered for nationalist service (through conviction) or were press-ganged (by economic pressure, fear of professional isolation, reprisals, or ingrained habits of obedience).

Journalists who opposed the government faced marginalization or, in government-controlled media, demotion and sacking, while others departed in the face of government pressure. (Thompson, 1999: 52)

These controls became more intensive than ever during the 1990s, the January 1993 mass firings in broadcast news being a watershed (Thompson, *op.cit.*: 81–82). Thompson also notes (*ibid.*: 106) how in the early 1990s a variety of independent media voices were available in Belgrade, but characterizes the situation as a 'safari park', namely a situation that held nowhere in Serbia outside the capital, but could be used by the regime to protest to the outside world that it had a free media system. Nonetheless, by 1996, even the 'safari park' had vanished. The same media monopoly was asserted in northern and eastern Bosnia in the six months building up to the 1992 outbreak of armed conflict. This was done by seizing Bosnian TV transmitters covering half of Bosnian territory, and thenceforth broadcasting non-stop Serb propaganda (*ibid.*: 214). Thus military and media strategies for the colonization of Bosnia were two sides of the same coin.

During the war years, TV and press silence concerning Serb-organized mass expulsions and bombardments reigned virtually complete in Serbia, and the parts of Bosnia controlled by the Bosnian Serb army. Serb media addressing Serb audiences insinuated that Muslims and Croats were equally oppressed by fascists and fundamentalists and glad to see them chased out by brave Serb fighters. Bosnian Serb media lumped Bosnian Muslims together as fundamentalists, *mujahedin, jihad* warriors. Often all Croats were stereotyped as *Ustaše*. Allegations of genocidal intent and practice were thrown at the Croats, just as the reverse was the case, partly for domestic and partly for foreign consumption. MacDonald (2003) analyzes in considerable detail the tremendous power of allusion to the Shoah, the Nazi Holocaust, by both Serb and Croat media, and how the fears they evoked of a repetition of wartime and postwar atrocities played into the new civil war between the two peoples. The role of Serbs as victims, acting out of desperate necessity in their own defense and against virtually global odds (Russians alone seemed to be morally on their side, but no tangible support was feasible following the Soviet empire's collapse), was thus underwritten by the propaganda hijacking of the Shoah.

There were numerous Serb protests that took place, many with large numbers, against controls over their media, but in the near-absence of other fairly independent domestic information sources such as the TV station Studio B, and later Radio B92 (Collin, 2001), and especially after the 1999 NATO bombings, fear, isolation and defensiveness reigned (Thompson, 1999: 114). Yet even though surveys indicated deep distrust of the major broadcast channels, people still watched RTS, the main TV news. Thompson surmised that the reason may be precisely that RTS is the voice of political power. In a society unaccustomed to any independence in the media, many people may not want independent information (especially given that independence in this context is associated so strongly with [*national*] 'treachery')... The rivals ... offer conjectural weather reports about the storm of Serbian politics; RTS sits in the citadel beside the divinities who shape the weather. The point is that RTS reflects the reality of power. (*op.cit.*: 109)

Serb (and Croat) propaganda to Muslims, by contrast, came via actions. Executions of women, children, the elderly, the destruction of mosques and homes, were intended to send a message that return was out of the question, and simple survival the most that could be hoped. The actual physical repression was often undertaken in the name of national self-defense by local and regional gangsters and thugs (not too far removed in their social characteristics from the Interahamwe activists in Rwanda whom we discuss below). These groups operated in general with the knowledge and consent of the Serbs' leadership, even if they undertook specific actions on their own initiative.

(2) The new Croat state's media structure and propaganda drive were mirror opposites to the Serbs'. Strict central control was maintained over all major and most minor media, despite the governing party's pre-election guarantee of media freedom, and notwithstanding the outstanding performance of Croatian media in the months leading up to the first post-Communist election (Thompson, 1999: 137–47). Journalists with any sense of ethics or responsibility were fired *en masse* after the election, especially if they were of Serbian origin, and often replaced with the crudest of hacks. So just as a Serb media presentation of an event would depict Serb aggression as motivated by defensive considerations, so too would Croat media coverage, simply switching the embattled heroes' national identity. Where a Serb account would omit all mention of atrocities committed by Serbs, including foreign media versions, so equally would Croat accounts in the case of Croat atrocities. Serbs were presumed to be wholly united in trying to crush Croatia. Journalists were required to refer to Croats who fell in military engagements as having 'fallen for Croatia's freedom' or as 'heroes in defense of the homeland.'

Laws banning defamation of public figures were used to intimidate journalists who sought to convey the truth. Such individuals were also systematically sidelined and fired in considerable numbers, and sometimes physically attacked. They were regularly defined as traitors, as agents of either the Serbs, or the Bosnian Muslims, or both, or of a criminal nostalgia for the old Yugoslavia whose perpetuation would have denied Croats their mythic thousand-year dream of an independent state. Dissident media, such as the regional *Slobodna Dalmacija* or the alternative paper *Feral Tribune*, were starved of newsprint, or in the case of would-be radio stations, denied broadcast frequencies. New private media waited endlessly for legislation to permit their existence.

Like Serb media, Croat media defined the Bosnian Muslims as the lowest of the low. Hatred for Serbs was normal, but total contempt was reserved for the Bosnian Muslims: aggressors, criminals, hordes, extremists, *mujahedin*, Islamic fanatics (even Ottomans!). This reflected a common conversational culture of Serbs and Croats before the eruption of war, who would unite in telling jokes that ridiculed the supposed stupidity and sometimes the treachery and lack of principle of Bosnians (read Muslims). Such was the seemingly harmless preparatory role of ethnic humor for eventual violence. At a later date, when the diplomatic links between the USA and the Croatian regime became stronger and the regime became the unofficial channel for weapons shipments to the Bosnian Muslim army, there was an officially dictated easing of this barrage of media hostility.

A particular Croatian theme, however, directed externally as well as internally, was that a Muslim Bosnia would constitute an Islamic thrust into Europe, with only the Catholic Croats standing in its path. The Bosnian Croats' destruction of the exquisite bridge at Mostar, built by order of Ottoman emperor Suleiman the Magnificent, was propaganda by vandalism in service of this claim. The bridge had no strategic value.

In general, to cite Thompson's study once more, the logic of war functioned as a vortex:

> War enabled the [Croatian] government to tighten its grip on news and media. It produced emotionally heightened situations in which it was easier to advance propaganda, disinformation and lies, and more difficult for its audience to distinguish lies from truth, commentary from fact. It gave a pretext for the enactment of Presidential decrees ... in the name of national security ... The war added to the insidious pressure on journalists to censor themselves 'for the sake of the people', although the beneficiary was the government, not the people. (1999: 187–88)

Certainly there was virtually no attention given by Croat media, any more than by Serb media, to a major humanitarian crisis in 1995, when the Croatian military uprooted southwards over a third of a million Serbs from eastern Croatia (and slaughtered many hundreds of elderly Serbs who failed to escape from their homes). For Croatian media, this was merely a repossession whose huge refugee consequences were of no consequence, while for Serbian media it was a signal, dismal failure of the Milošević regime, one which needed to be muted at all costs.

(3) Like the government and territory of Bosnia-Hercegovina, so too its broadcasters soon effectively came to fall into three camps, which in many regions meant a 100 per cent Serb, Croat or Muslim coverage, but in the

capital Sarajevo meant a three-way coverage on the same channel. Thompson cites an American observer thus:

> Many of those grey Communist journalists had colourized into Serb, Croat and Muslim journalists … none could be disciplined by the studio bosses without provoking the wrath of their co-religionists in the government or in the streets. You could usually predict the slant of a piece by the name of the reporter … This had the interesting effect of making Sarajevo TV coverage simultaneously narrow-minded and broad-based. (1999: 227)

From 1993 onwards, admittedly with the departure of a substantial number of Serb and Croat TV journalists and with a precipitous decline in staff overall, the channel's identity and the circles of influence within it became both more and more confessional (Muslim), and also more and more tightly tied into the ruling Muslim party's strategy, which was to try to defend itself by negotiation and by trying to avoid provocation. There was also a deep reluctance among many elite Bosnians to admit that the Serb army was ready and willing to invade and seize territory regardless of human rights or suffering. The result was that reverses quite often went unpublicized in the earlier phases of the conflict, and that the channel became more of a soap-box about sovereignty and national unity than a news service. However, the Sarajevo newspaper *Oslobodenje* (Kurspahić, 2003; Thompson, 1999: 241–44) struggled against endless odds, including not only shelling by Serb forces but also quite often the enmity of the Bosnian Muslim leadership, to produce a news service untainted by the ultra-chauvinism dripping from so many media sources in ex-Yugoslavia at that point.

We will move in a moment to review international media coverage of the conflicts, but before doing so, one general observation is in order. Notwithstanding the high-pressure funneling of nationalist loyalties by these extremely authoritarian states, which had no qualms about their bear-hug of the news media, in all three instances we have had occasion to note both the struggles of a number of media professionals and the resistance of many members of the public against these bear-hugs. A splendid example is from 1996 when 40,000 protestors marched in freezing rain past the Serbian state TV and the government newspaper *Politika*, hurling abuse and eggs at the buildings, and when at the main evening TV news hour, thousands of Belgrade inhabitants would bang pots and pans, blow whistles and ring bells (Thompson, 1999: 114). This consideration suggests both some hope and some disquiet. Hope, because the public and media professionals were not successfully welded into a single piece of inert metal. Disquiet, because despite this, the Serbian and Croatian power elites, in particular, were still successful in activating their lethal nightmares for years on end.

Internationally speaking, many media commentators resorted to atavism as their explanation of choice in describing the war, the pogroms and the so-called 'ethnic cleansing' that took place over the 1990s. The French TV channel Antenne 2 repeatedly attributed the conflict to 'ancestral hatreds' and the Balkan 'cauldron' (Charaudeau et al., 2001: 134). Iordanova (2001: 29–86) provides a stellar survey of how the Balkans, economically the least privileged part of Europe, have been portrayed by both scholars and media pundits as the historic homeland of barbarism, blood-feuds, religious wars, in terms not so distinct from the 'tribalist' discourse we examine below (indeed the term 'tribal' was sometimes deployed). They were the 'Third World' zone of Europe, the only location of centuries-old Muslim communities.[17] They had even, on one loopily ahistorical account, collectively 'caused' the First World War through the assassination of the Austrian Grand Duke in Sarajevo.

As in Rwanda and Northern Ireland, so too in the Yugoslav conflicts that exploded during the 1990s the varying interventions by outside powers were made all the more possible by international media portrayals of the region as beyond regulation or salvation, as sunk in irretrievable blood-feuds. Paralleling the Serbs with Nazi war criminals organizing concentration camps and 'genocidal' attacks against Muslims, identifying all Serbs with Milošević, and keeping near-silence concerning Croat atrocities, not least the expulsion of 350,000 Serbs from eastern Croatia, all contributed to a dangerous reduction of vision.

Wall (1997b) argues that in contrast to Western media accounts of the Rwandan genocide, global coverage of Bosnia at least noted the twentieth century historical dimension of the conflict and thus made it comprehensible on some basic level, unlike the supposed inexplicability of the Rwanda conflict. Presumably, therefore, however much the Balkans were Europe's 'Third World', the frame for understanding them was implicitly a rationalistic one, unlike the historically loaded racist definitions of 'tribal Africa'. Yet in part she fails to acknowledge the way in which, as MacDonald (2002) stresses, that history itself became mythologized by Serb and Croat propagandists, inflating past atrocities committed by the other side and muting those of their own, with the result that the highly *contemporary* sources of the slaughter were befogged and thus minimized in the accounts of many international commentators. Not only was this a consequence, but the way also needs to be recognized in which the Bosnian Muslims were defined by international media sources within the framework of the Shoah.

Johnstone (2002: 68–77) notes how this theme played internationally, with the Serbs identified as Nazis, not the Croatian regime, despite its evidence of enthusiastic Nazi collaborators in the World War II era and the new regime's trumpeting of that period. She particularly stresses the role played in this global media process by the American political public relations firm Ruder Finn. For the first two years of the war, the Bosnian Muslim leadership relied on the indisputable evidence of Serb and Croat aggression as its basic propaganda material to try to draw effective international support. In the siege of Sarajevo, mortar bomb and sniper attacks against women and children were all easy for journalists to cover. Being barred from Croat and Muslim concentration camps meant that stories from the rest of Bosnia were harder to follow up, but nonetheless the evidence for sustained atrocities by the Serbs was overwhelming.

At the same time, there is evidence that the particularly widely distributed news photograph of a gaunt young Muslim man naked to the waist, standing behind barbed wire with other men of various ages, was seriously misleading in that there was no barbed wire around the site as a whole and those present had no physical barrier to stop them leaving. The photographers themselves stood behind a short length of barbed wire fencing to take the shot. The Auschwitz echo, however, was deafening, especially when underscored in countless news reports (Johnstone, 2002: 72–5; Pergnier, 2002: 32–4; Krieg-Planque, 2003: 32–66).

Very little else was available to the Bosnian Muslim leadership, since the international arms embargo left them militarily very weak against the already heavily armed Serbs. The world powers were notably unresponsive to their pleas for help, beyond slow-acting sanctions against Serbia. Only when the US-sponsored Croat-Muslim alliance took shape in 1994, and some weapons began secretly to be shipped to Bosnia via Croatia, did the Muslims have a military potential. (For Croatian leader Tudjman, this meant the Serbs would be tied down elsewhere, so that Croatia could extend its territory, violently driving out hundreds of thousands of Serbs.)

The Bosnian Muslim leadership also tried to convey to the world that it was in favor of a multi-ethnic country, and not planning a fundamentalist regime. Partly this was to counter Croat and Serb propaganda to the contrary, partly it was true of many members of the general public; but it was not true of the leadership. The Bosnian Muslim president, Izetbegović, was well known for his view – as were some influential figures around him – that Islam could only be practiced properly in an Islamic state. The leadership, as already noted, appears to have had a strong sense that world perception of Bosnians as victims was the best way to attract major-nation backing against the Serb and Croat armies, and thus utilized atrocities suffered by Bosnian Muslims as a form of victim-propaganda directed to garnering that support.[18] A study of the three French TV news channels found the strategy had some degree of success, in that Serb soldiers were termed as 'Serb irregulars', 'Serb militias', 'Serb paramilitaries', while Bosnian soldiers were normally not so identified, or if given a noun, were 'Bosnian combatants', which fits the binary 'aggressor/victim' rather closely (Charaudeau et al., 2001: 71–72, 75–77). Indeed international officials circulated rumors to journalists that the Bosnian

Muslims were not only exaggerating the destruction, but that some units were even creating incidents in order to suck the Western powers and the UN into the vortex.[19] Similar allegations were raised concerning the months-long Serb siege of the charming Croatian town of Vukovar, namely that the Croatian leaders allowed it to continue much longer than militarily speaking they had to, in order to generate world sympathy. They had already manufactured an apparent Serb shelling of historic Dubrovnik for the consumption of foreign journalists located offshore, who could not gain direct access to the site, but heard guns firing and saw plumes of black smoke rising from inside the city – and duly filed their reports about Serb barbarism.

The public in NATO countries was therefore mostly offered a simple choice between longing for the 'ethnic' carnage to cease and being forced to hope that their governments' and NATO's pronouncements and actions (though actions were noticeable by their absence), would some-how lead to that goal. Yet in actuality the interventions that did take place skewed those conflicts still more grotesquely. Examples include the pre-tense of protecting Bosnian Muslims and Croatian Serbs, the NATO bombing of Serb civilians in the Kosovo crisis, and the idiotic blueprints for resolving the Bosnian crisis promulgated by a series of Western offi-cials (Britain's Owen, Norway's Stoltenberg, America's Vance and Holbrooke). The scenario was one of blind *Realpolitik* (UN, NATO and major-nation officials) leading the blind (the general run of big power news media professionals), and in turn blinding the shocked, misin-formed, confused and impotent general public in those nations.[20] The problem appeared to be one in which western governments, used to justi-fying military spending and preening themselves on their military capa-bility, found themselves having to explain why that military capacity should not or could not be used in a policeman role to put a halt to the daily mayhem on their publics' TV screens. Eventually, having failed to do so in Bosnia, Serb *civilian* targets were bombed as proof positive of NATO's moral virtue (Hammond and Herman, 2000) and its govern-ments' determination to protect the rights of Muslim Kosovar Albanians (always with an eye to Turkish public opinion and the 'Middle East').

Essentially, once television images of the war's horrors became preva-lent it was important for the international players to convince the rest of the world and their own publics that they were using their power to end the slaughter. At the same time, the US, French and British governments greatly feared electoral unpopularity through actually sacrificing their own troops to do so. Death-free military engagement, especially bombing, was thus the order of the day. Thus it was for the UN and its agencies also, although in all cases, however half-hearted the investment in addressing the slaughter, it was much more active in Bosnia than in Rwanda. One way of handling this conundrum of constructing a death-free armed intervention was to avoid it, by defining Bosnia as an individual human rights and entrenched 'ethnic' issue, rather than as violent dispossession in the interests of creating for the future the largest possible Croat and Serb state territories. Once defined in the two former ways, the demonic Balkan stew could then be isolated as the uncontrollable culprit. The other approach, adopted by those who wanted some kind of intervention to halt the slaughter – often in the name of an explicitly racist humanitarianism, – '*this* should not be happening in *Europe*' (as though two world wars had not) – was to allege as we have seen, that a new Shoah was in process. This absurdly over-defined the dimensions of the issue, almost parallel to its under-definition as 'just the Balkans again'.

While therefore there is some consensus on the roles of Croat and Serb media, there is none in the interpretation of global media roles in the nationality conflicts in Bosnia and Yugoslavia. Many in the 'West' would note how energetically news media reported on and warned against the horrors committed and impending, and might just take the story as a sad object-lesson showing how impotent media are to change behavior, or at least governments' behavior. Kolar-Panov (1997) studied how expatriate Croatian and Macedonian groups in Perth, Australia, became fixated on watching videos of the war and its atrocities, and how Perth's former Yugoslav community disintegrated as a consequence. Johnstone's intention, by contrast, is not to paint the Serbs as somehow the victims after all, but to analyze the conflict that wrecked the lives of so many people as an *interaction* between (a) three new mini-states, each with its reactionary leadership, and (b) between them and certain leading world powers, each of which had its own agendas as well.

Her ultimate purpose is to warn against the recent ascendancy of the human rights rationale for using military force against other nations, with a particular eye on the 1999 NATO bombings of Serbian targets in the name of preventing 'another' genocide in Kosovo. For her, this is the latest in a series of noble doctrines justifying self-interested imperial intervention, such as The Civilizing Mission (British Empire), Manifest Destiny (decimation of Native Americans and seizure of their lands), Protection of Minorities (Britain's refusal to decolonize Cyprus), Restoration of Democracy (Iraq, 2003), Defense of Free Trade (the Opium Wars), Prohibition of Slavery (seizing Lagos to unseat its slave traders, then proceeding to colonize Nigeria), or Containment of Communism (support for a whole shipload of dictators). As such, the human rights rationale's media reproduction is likely to enshrine in international public opinion the centrality of 'ethnicity' and 'nationality' (or in some cases 'religion' or 'tribe') as the wellspring of what is happening, rather than a sober analysis of the entire field of forces (for example, French-American rivalry with regard to Congolese mineral resources, and its role in the Rwandan genocide next door). In turn, insofar as such definitions become hegemonic, they are liable to bring with them internationally as well as locally untold negative consequences.

Genocide, 'Tribe' and Media: Rwanda

The terms 'tribe/tribal' and 'tribalism/tribalistic' in everyday use are almost synonyms for primitive, atavistic, bestial, Thomas Hobbes' 'war of all against all'. In White discourse they connote the entire African continent, but also jungle-dwelling Amazonian Indians, desert-dwelling Aboriginal Australians, Arctic-dwelling Inuit and remote mountain-dwelling Papuans: in other words, the other pole away from Us, the modern and civilized. In recent times, no case appeared to sum up the witheringly poisonous charge of these terms so decisively and incontrovertibly as the Rwanda genocide of April-July 1994, in which some 800 thousand people, or 75 per cent of the Tutsi population of Rwanda, along with Hutu accused of supporting them, were exterminated in the space of one hundred days.[21] A quarter century before, the Nigerian Civil War, pitting mostly the Yoruba and Hausa 'tribes' against the Ibo 'tribe', resulted in at least a million fatalities.[22] Thus when people learn that in the single nation of Cameroun there are 200 'tribes', their instinctive vision of the country – about which they know nothing at all – is quite likely to be a Hobbesian one (cf. Downing, 1990; Fair, 1993). We need, however, for the sake of clarity of understanding of both tribes and White people, to step back from these pregnant simplicities and take a longer look.

Introduction to Rwanda

Inasmuch as this horrific episode involved substantial numbers of the Hutu majority killing men, women, children, the aged, with machetes, spears and clubs,[23] and in many cases celebrating and laughing at their victims' torments or in recounting their exploits to each other afterwards, it exactly fits the image of 'Nature red in tooth and claw' or, if we prefer, Freud's violence instinct (the 'death drive'), victorious in its insurgency against civilized life. When we learn that Tutsi and Hutu all spoke the same Kinyarwanda language and were overwhelmingly Christianized, 80 per cent Catholic, and that even some Hutu clergy of various denominations, and some Hutu nuns, took active part in or condoned the massacres – though a number sought to protect the victims, and often paid the ultimate price – the force of a seemingly innate 'tribal' savagery may seem to be demonstrated beyond the possibility of further dispute.

Yet whereas we would characterize the Nazis' extermination policies as evil, and the slaughter of some two million English, French, Germans and others in the 1916 battles of Verdun and the Somme River as a monumental tragedy of war,[24] we would take neither case as demonstrating the British, French and Germans, let alone all White people, to be universally 'tribal,' atavistic, prey to violent compulsions beyond their control, feasting upon slaughter.

If we react to the Rwanda genocide in the same analytical manner[25] as we would to these other hideous events, we find some multiply disturbing complexities to the story. Some reach right back into the chancelleries and offices of the USA, France, Britain, Belgium, and the United Nations (Melvern, 2004; Barnett, 2003; Gouteux, 2002), and others were linked to the vast mineral wealth of neighboring Congo, then Zaire (Braeckman, 2003). Rivalry between the US and French elites for access to that wealth, especially coltan, diamonds and copper and more generally for hegemony in Africa, also played its part, though rarely in plain view. We also find that, internally, the basic organizational impetus for the Tutsi genocide lay in the fierce determination of the long-running Rwandan regime, corrupt and despotic, to preserve its power in the face of two threats that had sought to undermine it from 1990 onwards. One was a mounting challenge from inside the country to the ruling elite's sway (by 1994, even with a recent switch to a multi-party system, the president and his coterie had been in power 21 years). The regime's principals mostly hailed from and had their base in the northern part of the country (Pottier, 2002: 35–7), also the zone most directly affected by the civil war that began in 1990, yet their Hutu 'tribal' identity did not easily persuade southern Hutu to link up with the northern elite: so the southerners' allegiance had to be won. The second threat was an armed incursion in the northern part of the country, fighting for the right to return to Rwanda some 600,000 Tutsi refugees in Uganda, whose older generations had been forced to flee the country in 1959–60 and 1963–64 as a result of lesser but still terrifying bloodbaths.

Then two events in particular gave the planners of genocide golden opportunities to foment anti-Tutsi sentiment. Firstly, in October 1993, the Hutu president of the neighboring nation of Burundi (Rwanda's equally small southern neighbor), who had been a voice for reconciliation and peace, was assassinated by some Tutsi army officers. Then in April 1994, descending to land from peace talks in Tanzania, the Rwandan Hutu president's plane was shot out of the sky, with all aboard killed, including the new Burundian president (also Hutu). For a corrupt Hutu elite struggling to retain power and for its murderously anti-Tutsi ideologues, these attacks were propaganda gifts which it exploited relentlessly.[26] Its intentions had been made fully clear a year earlier, at the outset of 1993, when the northern elite cut off peace talks with the Tutsi invasion leadership, and Colonel Théoneste Bagosora, the genocide's prime organizer, told the Tutsi leaders 'I am going to prepare the apocalypse for you' (Chrétien et al., *op.cit.*, 155). Melvern (2004: 19–47) details the meticulous accumulation of planning for genocide over the four years before it began.

For example we find that between January 1993 and April 1994 the machetes that played such a dominant role in the genocide had been imported at double the normal rate (nearly 600,000, or one for every third adult Hutu male) by a Rwandan businessman very close to the regime. We find that the local district mayors (the *bourgmestres*), all Hutu, were a network carefully organized and directed from on high to oversee and complete the exterminations within their jurisdictions, and that they continually submitted detailed written reports, albeit usually in veiled language ('the work', 'pacification'), of their extermination activities. We find that the identity cards specifying tribal membership, a system in place from Belgian colonial days, provided a modern and perfectly bureaucratic method of identifying who were Tutsi in every location. We find that the shock troops of the genocide, the Interahamwe, were formed in 1991, and the Zero Network, a death squad, was founded in 1992. We find that *daily* two radio stations mobilized for genocidal attacks in specific locations. And far from least, we find that Western governments, especially France, but together with the UN, long delayed specifying the slaughters as a planned genocide, thereby avoiding any compelling reason to send an intervention force to help halt them.

This disaster therefore bore no marks of a spontaneous outburst of 'tribalism', tragic and gruesome, but 'typical of the African continent'… This was a struggle for political and economic resources in the most heavily populated (but tiny) country on the continent, where by the early 1990s through deforestation, soil erosion, and the multiplication of micro-farms, two-thirds of Rwandans had access to 200 less calories per day than the basic health minimum, where unemployment was 30 per cent in rural areas, and where at least half a million people had been turned into refugees because of the returnees' armed incursions (Gasana, 2002). Permanently unemployed young village men were, in significant numbers, easily recruited to the Interahamwe genocide squads. Meanwhile the regime's Hutu elite had consolidated its land holdings, its stranglehold over large-scale commerce, and its positions in the state. It chose to try to defend its acquisitions by mobilizing all Hutu against all Tutsi, and equally against any and all Hutu who sought to protect them.

As General Roméo Dallaire, the UN force commander in Rwanda who was persistently denied sufficient troops of quality to protect Rwandans, wrote in his account of the genocide

> The massacre was not a spontaneous act. It was a well-executed operation involving the army, Gendarmerie, Interahamwe and civil service. The identity card system, introduced during the Belgian colonial period, was an anachronism that would result in the deaths of many innocent

people. By the destruction of their cards, and of their records at the local
commune office, these human beings were erased from humanity ... The
men who organized and perpetrated these crimes knew they were crimes
and not acts justified by war, and that they could be held accountable for
them. The Interahamwe returned to destroy the evidence. The faceless
bureaucrats who fed the names to the militias and destroyed the records
also played a part. (2003: 281)

The Roles of Media

The study of the role of media inside Rwanda by Chrétien, Duparquier,
Kabanda and Ngarambe (2002) focuses mostly upon a fortnightly newspaper (*Kangura*, Wake Him Up) and two radio stations. Symptomatic of the
elite's political strategy of channeling popular discontent into anti-Tutsi
hatred, the newspaper was started as a seeming continuation and look-
alike of a combative underground monthly called *Kanguka* (Wake Yourself
Up), which in 1987 was one of the first to challenge the regime, and had
become quickly popular, but was fairly soon shut down. While the focus of
Chrétien et al. is on hate media, they also note (*op.cit.*, 47–8) how progressive alternative media were very much part of the scene initially, vigorously
denouncing the elite's bloodthirsty threats and racist lies.[27]

Kangura, however, was from its first issue in 1990 proposing genocidal
solutions to both general discontent and to the specific traumas induced
by the armed incursions in the north. Its language was unremittingly
violent, as were its cartoons (Chrétien et al., *op.cit.*, 24–42, 180, 189, 236,
254, 256, 271, 274, 295, 361–79), dwelling endlessly on bloodshed and
announcing the imminence of a war to the death for Hutu survival.
Copies were read at public meetings and at Interahamwe rallies. Its early
editions were produced by a government printing press. It repeatedly
diffused fake documents, such as one describing a purported Congo
colonization and domination plan by the exiled Tutsis dating back to 1962,
and the notorious 'Ten Hutu Commandments' which echoed the Protocols
of the Elders of Zion in their allegation of a Tutsi conspiracy to enslave.
The vicious propaganda of this publication, echoed by another dozen
such, then began to be amplified in August 1993 in a major way by the
launching, once again by members of the northern elite, of Radio Mille
Collines (Thousand Hills Radio) (Kellow and Steeves, 1998).

This station and (once the genocide began) the government station
Radio Rwanda, were the most dangerous of all the attack-media, though
not the only ones. They were the most effective because no literacy was
needed to receive their messages,[28] no payment was needed to hear them,
and 'during the genocide, when communications and travel became difficult, the radio became for most people the sole source of news as well as
the sole authority for interpreting its meaning ... Those who had no

radios visited neighbors who had them so they could know what might be coming next' (Des Forges, 1999: 71, 316). Both stations, on a daily basis, identified specific places where genocidal actions should be perpetrated, and individuals who should be hunted down.

In the case of Mille Collines (Thousand Hills), a number of further factors played a very significant role. It was founded in August 1993 in significant measure to combat the growing reach and appeal of Radio Muhabura, the returnees' station, which could not be heard in all parts of the country, but which consistently de-emphasized divisions between Hutus and Tutsis, and focused on the machinations of the regime's northern elite. Mille Collines' founders and key staff were overwhelmingly members of that elite. It broadcast on the same frequency as Radio Rwanda between 8am–11am, lending some of the official authority of the government station to its broadcasts. In January 1994 it increased its range with an additional transmission tower. In its first months, establishing itself, it mostly broadcast popular music and live chat, presenting a much more animated diet, in everyday language, than Radio Rwanda. Two of its most popular personalities were singer Simon Bikindi, whose lyrics were fiercely hostile to Tutsi (Chrétien et al., *op.cit.*, 341–60), and announcer Kantano Habimana, possessed of a highly effective radio voice and a witty and barbed tongue.

After its first few months, Mille Collines' tone became ever more violent, constantly reporting rumors and inventing scare stories designed to make Hutu feel in danger, and encouraging bloody retribution against Tutsis. For example, in November 1993, following the rape-murder of six children and the adult with them, a crime hard to pin realistically on the invading army because it was 100 kilometres away the other side of mountains and dense forest, but quite plausibly an atrocity perpetrated to smear the invaders, Mille Collines proceeded to recall the crime every single day in its broadcasts and to denounce the UN contingent for not having located the guilty parties (Melvern, 2004: 75–8). As soon as the full-fledged massacres began in April 1994, the director of Radio Rwanda was forced to flee for his life, and the government station became the country's second radio voice mobilizing for genocide.

The term most used for Tutsis was the *inyenzi* (cockroaches), but other terms such as 'insects', 'snakes' and 'rats' were also frequent (Des Forges, 1999: 75, 162, 401, 419; Chrétien et al., 2002: 162). This paralleled the mutual dehumanization common in both US and Japanese World War II propaganda against the other nation (Dower, 1986: 81–94, 242–59), a dehumanization that opened the door in the Japanese case to Hiroshima and Nagasaki, and in the Rwandan case to extermination.

The Tutsi were also framed as descendants of invading Ethiopian conquerors who had historically enslaved the Hutu. This semi-accurate ethno-history[29] was well entrenched in Rwandan educational and official culture.

The Catholic White Fathers order and the Belgian colonial administration had for generations institutionalized a school curriculum that defined the two groups as radically distinct.[30] Rwandans' identity cards had carried their ascribed tribal membership ever since the 1930s.[31]

Chrétien et al. (2002), Kellow and Steeves (1998) and the Human Rights Watch account (Des Forges, 1999: 74–83, 255, 296–7) summarize other propaganda themes as follows: (1) All Tutsi are infiltrators, including dominating the economy and higher education, forging their identity cards to pretend to be Hutus, acting as a fifth column for the returnees' armed incursions, and even using their women to seduce well-placed Hutus and foreigners working for powerful international agencies, so as to poison any concern for Hutu rights; (2) Tutsi are plotting to restore their former domination, from the time before the massacres of 1959 which had driven such large numbers of them to flee the country, and this would mean they would reclaim their land-holdings. Weapons and incriminating fifth column documents were frequently summoned up to prove the imminence of an anti-Hutu pincer onslaught between the returnees' army and local sympathizers; (3) Hutus' only chance of survival is therefore to fight back with as much or more ferocity than the Tutsi, who were vociferously accused of engaging in massacres of up to 20,000 at a time,[32] and even of cutting out the hearts, livers and stomachs of their victims. As the genocide proceeded, women, children and the elderly were also caught up in the bloodbath, for the regime and its media even began to assert that Tutsi women could only produce Tutsi babies (completely recasting the traditional male line of descent), and thus that Tutsi babies, if not killed now, would grow up to be the same threat to all Hutus as their parents and ancestors.

The logic of racialization was complete. The uses of media to propagate it were extremely intensive, a poisonous crescendo of fear-mongering, gross lies, incitement to genocide, and specific mobilization, day by day, to exterminate. Songs stirred murderous hatreds, cartoons dwelt on (mostly invented) atrocities that cried out for vengeance, and the choices were made stark: slaughter or be slaughtered, annihilate or be enslaved. Particularly for groups of young, angry, permanently unemployed Hutu, the Interahamwe provided a mobilizing mission which racist media fed moment to moment.

As regards international media representations, it was a struggle in which, as the Human Rights Watch/Fédération Internationale des Ligues des Droits de l'Homme book puts it:

> Well aware of how easily foreigners accepted explanations of 'ancient, tribal hatreds', the [Rwandan regime] repeatedly underlined the 'tribal' nature of the killings when called to account by the international community. They insisted that they had been simply unable to control the

outburst of spontaneous, popular rage. Then, turning the explanation into a plea for additional foreign support, they would express regrets that the government was so poor that it could not supply its officials with the resources to keep order. (Des Forges, 1999: 91)

Dallaire similarly characterizes the genocide perpetrators' politically attuned and astute deductions:

> ... the hard-liners I had met on my reconnaissance of Rwanda had attended the same schools that we do in the West; they read the same books; they watched the same news; and they had already concluded that the developing world, as represented by the Organization of African Unity, would not have the resources or the means to deploy in force to Rwanda. They had judged the West far too obsessed with the former Yugoslavia and with its peace-dividend reductions of its military forces to get overly involved in central Africa ... I believe they had already concluded that the West did not have the will, as it had already demonstrated in Bosnia, Croatia and Somalia, to police the world, to expend the resources or to take the necessary casualties. They had calculated that the West would deploy a token force and when threatened would duck or run. They knew us better than we knew ourselves. (2003: 79)

Perfectly reflecting this ideologically collusive framework, a major UN Security Council statement on Rwanda spoke of 'mindless violence' and UN Secretary General Boutros Ghali of 'deep-rooted ethnic hatreds' and of a military out of control (*ibid.*, 631, 637; cf. Barnett, 2002: 120). France's President Mitterrand was cited as saying 'In those countries, a genocide doesn't really signify anything', and one of his advisors, Bruno Delaye, that 'among Africans, massacres are a common practice that is hard to eradicate'.[33] Meanwhile the French government was both denying the seriousness of the situation, and would assist many of the leading perpetrators of the genocide to escape. The US government, fresh from its 1993 panic-stricken retreat from Somalia, was heavily invested in avoiding a further entanglement. Perhaps, needless to say, mainstream global news media did little or nothing to pinpoint or challenge these miserable realities.

Rather, as Wall's study of the general Western press coverage of Rwanda (1997a and b) shows, five predominant themes surfaced: tribalism, barbarism, the conflict's inexplicability, the incapacity of neighboring African nations to surmount their own barbarism to help, and the West as the sole remaining policeman. The racist obfuscations of the term 'tribal' in the Western news media have rarely been more blatant, or more destructive of the lives of the innocent. In analyzing the roles of Rwandan media in this horror, we need constantly to bear in mind the complementary roles of Western media, for in the global North they both echoed and formed the passive and complicit elite and public reactions to the genocide.[34]

Pottier (2002) adds some important further reflections on the roles of international media and NGOs in the aftermath of the genocide, although his media analysis focuses entirely on reports by certain journalists in elite American, Belgian, British, French and Dutch newspapers.[35] He proposes that, almost in parallel with the genocide planners' utilization of the racist meaning of 'tribe' to deflect international intervention, so the victorious Tutsi army leaders utilized the West's shame over its failure to intervene in order to generate a very successful 'hands-off' policy regarding the leadership's invasion of eastern Zaire/Congo and liquidation of unknown numbers of refugees. The 'screen' which blocked the West's vision in this subsequent round of slaughter was basically that these many hundreds of thousands of refugees were probably all perpetrators of genocide, because predominantly Hutu. And no Western power was sufficiently committed to justice to engage its wealth in the process of weeding out the killers and enabling the refugees to go home safely (many NGOs were constantly badgering them to return, with no notion of how, for instance, their homecoming would be handled in terms of disputed land rights in a land-scarce country). Pottier does indicate that the Belgian and Dutch press sources he examined covered these realities quite well, certainly much better than the American, British or French press. But neither the Netherlands nor Belgium wield major influence on the world stage.

Conclusions

The comparison of religion, tribe and nationality with 'race' and ethnicity and their media renditions is only at the beginning.

We have already seen how it is vital to include the roles of international media along with those of local and regional media, and how it is possible for local forces to manipulate the standard assumptions of 'Western' news professionals and aid agencies about such matters as tribalism, the Shoah, or 'the ethnic factor'. We have seen how these conflicts are perfectly compatible with at least formally democratic institutions[36] and modernity, while their intensification is also fully feasible through overwhelming, if never total, media control by the given regime in conjunction with organized action by its control agents (for example, the *bourgmestres* and the Interahamwe, or the paramilitaries and gangsters in the post-Yugoslav republics, or – less drastically – the Orange Lodges and the B-Special police officers in pre–1968 Northern Ireland).

We have seen how local media can cumulatively ratchet up existing fears and help create a binary crisis, in the sense that the choice of action is made to seem stark and inevitable: be a victim no longer, survive by attacking or disappear. We have seen how 'history' can be summoned up in purely invented and/or mythicized form to present this choice as urgent, the final chance to right historic wrongs, to be at last the great people long denied its greatness. This is a story which has been replayed many times, by Afrikaners and Japanese, by Russians and Israelis, by Serbs and Croats, by Hutus and Tutsi, by Irish nationalists and Protestant loyalists, by rightist Hindu and Han nationalists. Far from every member of these peoples loves to get drunk on this stuff, but in the midst of war it can be defined as pudding-headed and even dangerous, not to do so.

What is missing from analysis and urgently needed, is scrutiny of the emotive power of these identifications and markers for the committed, and the roles of media in generating and sustaining that process. For the hundreds of thousands of 'Yugoslavs' who migrated around the world to escape the situation, for the Hutu who strove to protect Tutsi, for the Protestants who did the same for Catholics and vice-versa, this question is of little or no importance. But a purely rational analysis of the 'field of forces,' as we put it above, or even an analysis of what was systematically excluded from media coverage, always falls short of explaining the degree of passion needed among the activists and *particularly* their penumbra. Is fear the only dimension, or does it combine with the joy of channeling aggression? What else is in the mix, and how do media feed – or starve – the cathectic process?

Second, what is also missing is analysis of the roles of internet use, something rather minimal in the early 1990s while many of the conflicts discussed above were being enacted, but by the time of writing an every-day component of mediated communication on such issues as these. The methodology of assessing internet uses is still rudimentary, so the question is not easy to handle, but it demands to be addressed.

Third, we need more precise consideration of how media representations of 'race', 'tribe', 'religion' and 'nationality' parallel each other, and what are their distinctive differences. We also need to be able to describe much more precisely than we currently are able to do, how social class, gender, age and language interact with these factors, and by which mechanisms they may be collectively overdetermined, in significant part by media. What is distinctive about the definition of someone's ethnic status as contrasted with the definition of their religious adhesion? How far is the latter in fact religious, in any committed sense, at all ('nationalist' vs 'Catholic' in Northern Ireland, 'Turk' vs 'Muslim' in Bosnia, 'Muslim' vs 'Pakistani' in India)? Is nationality taken to surpass ethnicity, in the sense that it summons up an historical player on the global or regional stage, as contrasted with the role of a sector within such a global player? Is it important that nationality may register choice, whereas ethnicity, as we argued in Chapter 1, is capable of being fluid, especially over time, but is often taken to be purely a given, particularly in highly conflictual situations?

Fourth, we have noted the great role played by *the accumulation of media framing over time*, over years and decades, in generating extremely explosive and dangerous situations. Whether the standard silences of Northern Irish and English media for decades on the second-tier status of Catholics in the Six Counties, or the quickening intensity of genocidal media content from 1990 onwards in Rwanda, or the mutual demonization via media in the Croat, Serb and Bosnian Muslim conflicts, or the decades-long multi-dimensional build-up to genocide in German culture, this gradual but unceasing process is one that media researchers, often accustomed to snap-shot studies of contemporary media, are liable to be blind to, not by will so much as habit. It is a process which, looking back to our discussion of ongoing low-intensity pogroms in the previous chapter, we disregard at our peril. It may come over time to have the hardness and sharpness of a coral reef, not something which can be simply wished away or preached out of existence.

And finally, whether looking at the media dimension of Serb irredentist military strategies or the relation of Radio Mille Collines to Rwandan *bourgmestres'* citizens' lists, much of the foregoing has eschewed media-centric analysis of media. It is the synergy of media with other social forces which gives both their influence. In line with this, we need to conclude with the acknowledgment that mediatic definitional frames of 'race', 'religion', 'nation' and 'tribe' are not only sustained, or challenged, by media. As Thompson observes in connection with ex-Yugoslavia;

> ... people's bedrock attitudes toward the wars in Croatia and Bosnia are not created by the state media; rather, the media play variations upon those attitudes, which derive from other sources (national history, family background, education, oral culture). Media did not inject their audiences with anti-Muslim prejudice or exploitable fear of Croatian nationalism. The prejudice and fear were widespread, latently at least; there was a predisposition to believe 'news' which elicited and exploited the prejudice. Media could not produce a nationalist society; without the media, however, Serbia's leaders could not have obtained public consent and approval of its extreme nationalist politics. (1999: 108–09)

At the same time, the issue Thompson raises of 'latent predispositions' does pull our attention back to the issue raised in the previous paragraph, namely the long-term *cumulative* impact of media frames in harsh conflict-situations of the kind analyzed here and in the previous chapter.

Notes

1 Guillaumin (1995: 30–31) has rightly warned against reducing 'race' to 'aggressivity,' i.e. conflict-proneness.

2 Expulsions rather than 'ethnic cleansing', an unacceptable term because it euphemizes the process, implies there is indeed something undesirable in those expelled and does not properly convey the Slavic words used in the nations of former Yugoslavia and elsewhere, which all incorporate the notion of 'purging' (Naimark 2001: 4–5). By pogrom, we mean

violent attacks on neighbors or neighborhoods calculated to induce terror and timidity but not removal or extinction. By genocide we mean the plan or the effect of physically exterminating an entire people or a major section of that people. Planned exterminations have included Armenians in Turkey, Jews in Nazi-occupied Europe and Russia, Tutsi in Rwanda. The extermination of countless millions of indigenous Americans by European diseases constituted unplanned genocide, on top of the many individual barbarous onslaughts on the colonizers' part.

3 Cf. Guillaumin (1995: 138–144).

4 See Schlesinger, 1991.

5 For accounts that address a number of these dimensions, see Elliott (1977); Curtis (1984); Schlesinger (1988); Rolston (1991a and b); Miller (1994); Rolston and Miller (1996); Horgan (2001); Parkinson (1998).

6 Parkinson's account is simultaneously useful but rather dazing because of its very extensive detail. His effort to be scrupulously fair is commendable, but in the end his argument more or less boils down to (1) the news media failure to understand the devastating impact of ongoing terrorism on the Loyalist community, or to give it the same level of news attention as mainland terrorist attacks; (2) the obsessive media focus on the most recalcitrant and sectarian members of the Loyalist community, rather than the spectrum of opinion actually existing within it; and (3) the effect of fear of being jettisoned into reunification with the Republic by a British public and parliament uninterested in the Protestant community's loyalty to the British monarchy.

7 Though the study by Parkinson suggests that severe anxieties among Loyalists concerning the potential for betrayal by the English authorities may also have put English media on the edge of being 'foreign' too, for that community.

8 For an excellent discussion of both fictional and news TV representation of terrorism in the Northern Ireland saga, see P. Schlesinger, G. Murdock and P. Elliott (1983).

9 Alluding to the Clint Eastwood classic *The Good, The Bad and the Ugly* (dir. Sergio Leone, 1967).

10 See n. 22.

11 First Slovenia seceded, then Croatia, and then the rest of the Federal republic disintegrated. See Donia and Fine (1994), Silber and Little (1996), Vulliamy (1994), Glenny (1999) and Johnstone (2002), for varying accounts of the strife. Different accounts of the conflict and its media coverage (see n. 12) strike different basic poses, some strongly pro-Bosnian Muslim, some pro-Serb, others more detached. I have done my best to evaluate the accounts independently in order to steer my own course through the thicket of interpretations.

12 Witness the outstanding documentary *Comrades* (2000) by Mitko Panov, professor of film at the University of Texas, depicting the entirely friendly relations in the early 1980s among young multi-national military service draftees (he was one) into the Yugoslav Army. Later, some were compelled to end up fighting for opposing sides. Others emigrated.

13 The tendency is widespread and needs resisting. For example Parkinson (1998) scatters through his book allusions to 'border genocide' waged by Provisional IRA groups against Protestants with homes near the frontier with the Irish Republic. That violent attempts were made to clear the border zone of its Loyalist inhabitants is not in dispute, any more than the burning out of whole streets of Catholics' homes in Belfast in 1969. But genocide it never remotely resembled, and the casual use of the term disgraces its users.

14 It goes beyond our scope here, but Gow and Tilsley (1996) mount a very interesting argument that the Slovenian international media strategy was the most successful of all the new successor republics.

15 Gow et al., 1996: 63–100; Thompson, 1999; Kurspahic, 2003; MacDonald, 2002; Collin, 2001. For analyses of international media coverage, see Gow et al., 11–59, 103–178; Hammond and Herman (2000); Krieg-Planque, 2003; Charaudeau et al., 2001.

16 For a lively account of the story of Radio B92, see Collin (2001). For further accounts of the Bosnian newspaper *Oslobodjenje*, of Croatia's *Feral Tribune* and its *Danas*, subsequently *Novi Danas*, and other minority voices against the various new regimes, see Kurspahić (2003).

17 Iordanova (op.cit., 55–70) explores as well in her rich and nuanced work what she terms the 'consensual self-exoticization' that filmmakers and other intellectuals from the Balkans have produced, feeding into these stereotypes. (She further notes how far a cry was this collaboration in myth-making from the militant challenges to European racial stereotypes by a number of post-colonial filmmakers and novelists from the global South.)

18 Johnstone (2002: 109–118) questions whether the notorious 1995 onslaught on Bosnian Muslims in Srebrenica, which came to stand as the archetypal icon of Serb exterminism, may have been cynically forecast and permitted by the Bosnian Muslim leadership precisely in order to garner global public support. The November 1999 UN Report on the Srebrenica massacre cites some surviving members of the Srebrenica delegation as claiming that Izetbegović had told them he had learned a NATO intervention was possible to defend Bosnia 'but could occur only if the Serbs were to break into Srebrenica, killing at least 5,000 of its people (Johnstone op.cit.: 112)'. She also queries the refusal of then US Secretary of State Albright on security grounds to make satellite images of the alleged burial field publicly available, and notes a series of reports that some thousands of Muslims vanished and turned up later because they had managed to escape through the heavily forested region. Johnstone's purpose is not to deny a terrible massacre took place, but to query the quality of evidence for its having been even half of the 7000 people conventionally claimed, let alone the 12,000 initially claimed. The debate will no doubt rage for a long time, but in determining the roles of media in exacerbating or reducing ethnic conflicts, the question of collusion between under-informed journalists and unscrupulous elites is unavoidable. See also Pergnier, 2002: 35–36, 55–56, 113–23.

19 Johnstone (2002: 65–68) argues that this allegation might not have been fantasy, in that all three bomb massacres given prime publicity in international news media took place shortly before major UN and NATO decisions were due, and were not rationally speaking in Serbian interests (they made the Serbian side look particularly loathsome). She also notes the presence of several thousand extremist foreign Muslim fighters of the Al-Qaeda type who could have been responsible, for whom the lives of secular Bosnian Muslims were not necessarily of much account, any more than the lives of the hundreds of innocent Kenyans and Tanzanians blown to bits in the 1998 US embassy bombings in Nairobi and Dar Es Salaam.

20 At the risk of oversimplifying, however, it might be said that if journalists writing for the everyday global public had originally begun by identifying the basic character of the three *leadership* groups in the Bosnian conflict – gangster (Serb), fascistoid (Croat), religious reactionary (Bosnian Muslim) – and subsequently introduced them to some of the specifics and complexities, the scenario might have begun to jell in people's minds in a way that made adequate sense, as opposed to the 'ancient ethnic hatreds' scenario that was in fact deployed.

21 See the discussion of different estimates in Melvern, 2004, 150–151.

22 While there is no space here to explore it as we have done in the case of Rwanda, the Nigerian Civil War was similarly defined in Western media as an orgy of tribal hatred, though the three major 'tribes' in question numbered each one dozens of millions of people and thus were at least akin to a nationality or a nation (are the Swedes or the Slovenes a tribe?). These three groups, with many other smaller ones, had been jammed together in one nation by the British just three generations previously, and in ways that had consistently empowered extremely conservative northern Hausa elites at the expense of the two major southern peoples. It was a little like – a century ago – forcing England, France and Germany to be a single nation. After northern anti-Ibo pogroms in 1966 following two military coups just months apart, a section of the Ibo leadership sought secession and to form the new nation of Biafra – but one which would enjoy unique access to Nigeria's oil-producing zone. The harshness of the civil war that ensued for three years was greatly amplified by the weapons supplied Biafra by the French, and to the other side by the British, Americans and Soviets. But how could a civil war between regions over access to oil, abetted by foreign governments, sensibly be reduced to atavistic tribalism?

23 I have argued elsewhere (Downing 1988) that international reaction to the fascistic violence of the Salvadoran elite was at its height when killings, maimings and torture were

by hand, but following the industrial high-tech phase of the war permitted by US military aid, the personal horror level became muted through the apparent abstractness – the wartime inevitability – of the violence.

24 Freud's development of the notion of the death/violence instinct as a parallel human drive to the sexual instinct owed much to his horrified reactions to World War I's indescribable slaughter.

25 My analysis here is based upon Chrétien et al. (2002); Des Forges (1999); Gouteux (2002); Kayimahe (2002); Braeckman (1996; 2003); Gasana (2002); Guichaoua (1995); Pottier (2002); Melvern (2004).

26 The perpetrators of the plane to attack have, predictably, been presumed to be either Hutu extremists convinced the president was selling them out, or Tutsi military. No final determination has been reached at the time of writing.

27 This may be the place to attack the endless use of 'moderate Hutu,' which continues to serve as the term of choice to denote those Hutu who did not participate willingly in the genocide. It implies that the normal way of being Hutu is to be extremist and genocidal, and effectively reinscribes a tribalist definition of the Hutu people and of the crisis itself. As Pottier (2002) argues, this framework in turn permitted the slaughter of hundreds of thousands of Hutu refugees in Zaire/Congo during the years following the genocide.

28 One-third of Rwandans were illiterate.

29 By the time of the genocide, intermarriage between the groups was not uncommon, and political alignments did not tidily mirror ethnic identities. Those Hutu who protected Tutsi friends and neighbors, at great risk to and often at the cost of their own lives, should be remembered with honor. For a careful account of the history of Tutsi and Hutu, including in Zaire/Congo, see Pottier (2002: 9–52).

30 See Braeckman (1996: 58–100) for a comprehensive overview of the Church's role in Rwanda.

31 The invading Tutsi forces' political platform called for the elimination of these identity cards, a proposal which was violently assailed by extremist Hutus who argued that their cancellation would lead to Tutsis being able to take over all positions of power, because power-sharing could no longer be monitored. New identity cards, with no ethnic identifiers, were supposed to be printed in France and shipped to Rwanda, but their delivery kept being mysteriously delayed, and the genocide took place before they ever arrived.

32 The returnees' army, the Rwandan Patriotic Front, did commit certain atrocities over and above the destruction typical of battle, but the elite's propaganda machine freely multiplied them.

33 Cited in Gouteux 2002: 110, 113.

34 For a critique of French news coverage, see Gouteux, op.cit., 179–230. Barnett (2003), in his account of the UN's roles in the genocide, explicitly focuses on the question of ethical responsibility in an international bureaucracy. While his emphasis is perfectly appropriate, omitting the roles of media and public culture in the equation leaves a serious lacuna in an otherwise very interesting analysis.

35 It also suffers a little from overly simple correlations of NGO officials' statements with journalists' judgements.

36 It was in the move away from one-party rule in Rwanda that both progressive and newly regressive media began to be noticeable, just as it was in the *glasnost* era in the former USSR that Russian anti-Semitism revoiced itself in the public arena.

5 The Distinctive Challenge of Indigeneity[1]

Molnar and Meadows (2001) drawing upon their extensive work on indigenous media introduce their analysis of indigenous communication in Australia, the South Pacific and Canada with a statement that can usefully inform all analyses of indigenous media. They argue that:

> Through the title *Songlines to Satellites* we [also] suggest that the use of information technologies by Indigenous people remains linked to traditional forms of communication. If this link is broken, the nature of the communication changes. Technology does not replace traditional communication forms; rather it offers Indigenous communities another tool for communication. In this way, Indigenous media producers appropriate technology for their own ends. At the same time, there can be a constant tension between traditional processes of discussion and decision-making and the 'modernising' constraints of time and technology in program production (Barclay, 1990, p. 9). This is because the link between traditional communication forms and communications technologies is not seamless; rather it involves a process of negotiation, because what is being created is a new cultural product that grows out of the traditional form. (2001: p. xii)

At the heart of this statement there is a necessary challenge to understand the nature of the indigenous peoples' experience. It requires a recognition of the historical relations between indigenous peoples and those who usurped their rights, physically displaced them and imposed alien definitions of identity upon them. History is always relevant to contemporary understandings of the location of indigenous communities within modern nation states. Their exclusion from the official history of the 'nation' always creates fissures in the current labored discourse of national identity. Historical practices of the physical exclusion of indigenous peoples to the territorial peripheries and genocidal ambitions of obliteration have failed to eradicate indigenous peoples. Consequently, in many instances their continuing survival and presence is a perpetual repository of guilt for the dominant communities.

Indigenous peoples are never merely a distinctive demographic entity. They cannot be an unproblematic unit of ethnicity, treated as variants of ethnic diversity within the discourses of contemporary multiculturalism. Their historical relation to contemporary nation states gives them a distinctive foundational basis for particular legal and moral claims on the state, which we will explore in more detail below.

Just as Cunningham and Sinclair (2000) insist upon the necessarily unique historicity which has shaped any diasporic experience, so too indigenous peoples' experiences and transformations should not lightly be reduced to any assumed homogeneous category. The time frames that define the processes of dispossession and exclusion may differ markedly: for example, if the assault upon the indigenous communities in Australia may be loosely dated to the 1788 colonization (Hughes, 1987), then the dispossession of the Sami may be understood as an ongoing process from the middle ages onwards, related to the interests of the emerging states in Fennoscandia (Niemi, 1997). And, whilst the Eurocentrism eloquently articulated by Shohat and Stam (1994) may have informed and legitimated the seizure of indigenous peoples' lands and the usurpation of their rights in very many instances, it should not be thought that such actions were, or are, in some way uniquely European. The experience of the indigenous people of Taiwan is but one relevant example (Kung, 1997); and the history of Berber peoples since the seventh century Arab invasion of North Africa is yet another. The unique temporal framing of the processes of exclusion, and the distinctive ideological justifications for such actions at the time, and currently, cannot be subsumed in some universal morally righteous opposition to the current oppression of indigenous peoples. The specificity of these historical variables have continuing and critical relevance to an understanding of current circumstances.[2]

Only through a concrete grasp of this distinctive historicity can the *current* political struggle over the situation of specific indigenous communities be understood. The vigor of indigenous peoples' demands in contemporary 'Latin' America, especially in Mexico, Guatemala, Ecuador, Peru and Bolivia, but also in Argentina, Brazil and Chile, provides ample evidence of this reality. The capacities for political mobilization and creative identity politics of indigenous communities themselves can only be adequately understood through such a perspective. And in this chapter we will, whilst referring to other instances, quite deliberately develop our argument in relation to the specific cases of the Aboriginal Peoples of Australia and the Sami of the Nordic states.

Indigenous Peoples and the State

If ethnic diversity has constituted a challenge to the modern nation state then the identity and status of indigenous peoples has proved particularly troublesome. Their resilience and continued coherence as distinct communities stand as unlooked for markers of the processes of genocide and exclusion that have typically been central to their contact with dominant usurpers. The very notion of indigeneity has within it a necessary claim to precedence and territorial primacy that sits uncomfortably with the chronic marginalization within the nation state that is their typical current condition. Consequently, where the state, and the dominant ethnic populations within that state, are confronted by the challenges of indigenous peoples that they have special rights, behind any such legal claims there lurks a moral demand for reparation and remedial action for past offences. Having historically constructed the indigenous peoples as 'Others', the guardians of national identity are now faced with the consequences of this 'othering' in the vehemence of indigenous identity politics. The contemporary political agitation of indigenous movements typically holds up a mirror that reflects the historical brutalities of the 'othering' process: as both material usurpation and cultural deracination.

Faced with this challenge the state and the dominant socio-political system has a number of uncomfortable questions to address. Amongst these, two are likely to be highly visible in the political negotiation of the demands of indigenous peoples. One is the potential economic and territorial costs that may follow from taking seriously the demands of indigenous peoples over land rights. As the Australian case has illustrated, moves toward addressing indigenous land right claims immediately attract the resistance of powerful vested interests, such as mining corporations. But second, the rise of indigenous political assertiveness necessarily opens an uncomfortable Pandora's Box of questions about the self-image and moral certitude of the dominant ethnic communities. If, as we shall briefly see below, the stereotyping of indigenous peoples has been central to the construction of the legitimating ideology for their oppression, then their claims to equity require a necessary complementary deconstruction of the supporting stereotypes. Claims for reparation are supported by detailed accounts of past, and recent, atrocities visited upon them by the dominant community.

In the last two decades there has been a significant movement in the development of international law relating to indigenous peoples, (see Anaya, 1996, for a valuable overview, and also Aikio and Scheinin, 2000) and a strong international mobilization around indigenous peoples' rights. Consequently, in the context of this book it is both appropriate and necessary that this issue should be addressed. But, at the outset it is important to recognize that it is not easy to 'ring fence' the domain of indigenous politics and identities. As we shall see the *internal* heterogeneity of Indigenous populations is a recurrently complicating factor. And, the legal and political inter-face between indigenous peoples and other minority populations is not as easily established as some might want. As Kymlicka (2001) has noted, the emergence of new international norms relating to indigenous peoples has been linked to a broader shift regarding the rights of 'national' minorities. He states:

> By national minorities, I mean groups which have been settled for centuries on a territory which they view as their homeland: groups which typically see themselves as distinct 'nations' or 'peoples', but which have been incorporated often voluntarily into a larger state. The category of national minorities (or what others call 'homeland minorities') includes indigenous peoples, like the Inuit in Canada or Sami in Scandinavia, but also includes other incorporated national groups, like the Catalans in Spain, Scots in Britain, or Quebecois in Canada. These latter groups are sometimes called 'stateless nations' or 'ethnonational groups' to distinguish them from indigenous peoples.
>
> There is no universally agreed criteria for distinguishing indigenous peoples from stateless nations. (2001: 122)[3]

This problematic overlap of indigenous peoples and national minorities raises a number of issues. At one level, the recent success of 'stateless nations', like the Catalans or Basques in Spain, and Scotland within the United Kingdom, in achieving degrees of autonomy within the state, demonstrate, by implication, the viability of indigenous peoples' aspirations. And, of course, reciprocally the potential comparability of the two cases may serve to reinforce resistance to meeting the claims of either category. As Kymlicka (*ibid*: 127) notes that there are many instances where countries have systematically denied the claims to language, self-government and control over land and resources of both kinds of groups.

But indigenous peoples know who they are and there is a growing legal framework which aims to address their claims. At the first major UN inquiry into the situation of indigenous peoples, in 1986, Special-Rapporteur Jose R. Martinez Cobo provided the following definition:

> Indigenous communities, peoples and nations are those which, having a historical continuity with pre-invasion and pre-colonial societies that developed on their territories, consider themselves distinct from other sectors of the societies now prevailing in those territories, or parts of them. They form at present non-dominant sectors of society and are determined to preserve, develop and transmit to future generations their ancestral territories, and their ethnic identity, as the basis of their continued existence as peoples, in accordance with their own cultural patterns, social institutions and legal systems. (Martinez Cobo: para. 379)

The existing ILO Convention 169 on the *Rights of Indigenous and Tribal Peoples in Independent Countries* and the *UN Convention on the Rights of the Child* explicitly recognize the distinctive identity and claims of indigenous peoples. And there has been a developing view that the needs and rights of indigenous peoples differ from, and may be expanded beyond, the rights of minorities (see Alfredsson, 1998; Daes, 2000). Equally, it has become increasingly recognized that some form of autonomy or self-government may be necessary for realizing the rights of indigenous peoples (Hannum, 1996; Heintze, 1998). Article 31 of the draft UN *Declaration on the Rights of Indigenous Peoples* (1993) states that:

> Indigenous peoples, as a specific form of exercising their rights to self-determination, have the right to autonomy or self-government in matters relating to their internal and local affairs, including culture, religion, education, information, media, health, housing, employment, social welfare, economic activities, land and resource management, environment and entry by non-members, as well as ways and means for financing these autonomous functions.

It is clear from this that indigenous peoples would not have the right to independent statehood, nor indeed would this be what all indigenous peoples would seek. The designation of indigenous populations as 'peoples' has in some quarters provided a basis for anxiety about the nature of the political claims of indigenous peoples. For Article 1 of the United Nations Charter states that all 'peoples' have a right to 'self-determination'. As Kymlicka (2001: 123) has argued, this may be regarded as being 'too strong' as the basis for the determination of indigenous peoples' rights since it has been interpreted, following the re-mapping of Europe after World War I, to include the right to form one's own state and has consequently been significantly limited in its interpretation in international law. Clearly, the resistance of contemporary states to the claims of indigenous peoples would be likely to be routinely robust if they felt that in every instance the bottom line was an aspiration to break away and form an autonomous state. Kymlicka (2001: 125) in responding to Anaya's (1996) argument, provides a useful phrasing for the nature of self-determination demands that fall short of creating an independent state. He suggests that if instead of seeking full independence 'the aim was instead to "rearrange the terms of integration" within existing states', then what is needed is 'a conception of self-determination which sets limits on state sovereignty, rather than a conception of self-determination which simply relocates state sovereignty'. That would sit comfortably with the expectations of Article 31 of the Draft Declaration, and be supported by current arguments. (Anaya, 2000; Myntti, 2000)

One potential basis for the difference between the reasonable expectations of indigenous peoples and the territorial anxieties of the dominant communities regarding the territorial sovereignty of the state lies in the latter's failure to comprehend the different spiritual and philosophic relationship between indigenous peoples and their land. As Professor Daes, Special-Rappoteur on indigenous peoples noted, there is a need for non-indigenous peoples to comprehend the interrelation of spiritual, social, economic and cultural values in indigenous peoples' relation to their land and resources. In her United Nations report she stated that: '... indigenous peoples have illustrated the need for a different conceptual framework and the need for recognition of the cultural differences that exist because of the profound relationship that indigenous peoples have to their lands; territories and resources' (Daes, 1997: 17). Self-determination for indigenous peoples involves a recovery of their relationship with their land, rather than just a simple legal claim to territory. As Henricksen (2001) has noted in a valuable review of self-determination and indigenous peoples:

> A major reason for the impasse on the question of the right of self-determination for indigenous peoples appears to be that many governments view the issue within the traditional de-colonization context, while most indigenous peoples approach this question from an angle that does not correspond to this traditional approach. Indigenous peoples view this matter from a political and philosophical angle founded on the principle of equality and non-discrimination: calling for equality with regard to the right of self-determination – without necessarily wishing to establish their own state. One should bear in mind that the western nation state concept is not the most natural way of implementing or exercising the right of self-determination for the vast majority of indigenous peoples. (2001: 14)

From this perspective the challenge presented to the extant nation state by the claims of self-determination by indigenous peoples is not a simple threat of fragmenting the state in order to create an independent state founded on historical territorial claims. The challenge, in fact, is typically more complex; but potentially just as threatening. It requires a reflexive deconstruction of the dominant communities' understanding of *their* relationship to the state, territory and 'nation'. It requires a willingness and capacity, to engage with an indigenous peoples' world view. And, it requires a willingness to negotiate a meaningful self-determination for indigenous peoples within the state: possibly through an exploration of differentiated citizenship within a multi-ethnic society.

The contemporary circumstances of indigenous peoples most powerfully demonstrate the critical relevance of the legal and political status of minority communities in determining their media environment. In their introduction to *Songlines to Satellites*, Molnar and Meadows note the key role of the media in empowering indigenous communities, and they state that: 'Central to this empowerment is the ability of Indigenous communities to control the means of production of culturally specific media products' (2001: xii). As we shall see below, such control is significantly dependent upon the legal and political leverage available to specific indigenous peoples. And, whilst the centrality of the media recognition of minority or indigenous rights has been recognized in international legal instruments such as Article 9 of the *European Framework Convention for the Protection of National Minorities*; Article 11 of the *European Charter for Regional and Minority Languages*; Article 17 of the *UN Convention on the Rights of the Child*, and Article 17 of the draft *UN Declaration on the Rights of Indigenous Peoples*; only the draft *UN Declaration on the Rights of Indigenous Peoples* refers to the media as part of indigenous self-determination.

The current demography of indigenous communities, whilst historically determined, has powerful implications for both their political mobilization, and the political economy of their media environment. For example, the territorial dispersal and internal linguistic variation of both Australian Aborigines and the Nordic Sami, where both are numerically small minorities within the relevant states, sets them in a very different context to some of the Pacific Island communities who, whilst sharing extensive linguistic diversity, are a demographic majority within their state.

Reciprocally, the history and current formation of the nation state within which indigenous peoples are located provides a further unique feature of their current struggle. For example, 'mature' liberal democracies such as the United States of America, New Zealand and the Nordic states find themselves vulnerable to the legal claims of their indigenous populations because of the logics of their own political settlement and their legitimating political philosophies. The historical oppression and current exclusion of their indigenous populations sit uncomfortably with their de facto citizenship status. Such political ambiguities were not readily apparent in a Soviet Union informed by Stalinist policies of 'ethnic' management, nor in contemporary China. And in the on-going nation building of the contemporary Pacific islands the absence of an institutional infrastructure and political stability that would be a forum for indigenous political struggle provides yet another distinctive context for indigenous mobilization. As we shall explore more fully below, the political structures of the state currently regulating the historical territory of indigenous peoples critically shapes the formation of the indigenous media environment. By determining the legal status of their resident indigenous population, by developing mechanisms for recognizing their distinctive cultural and political demands, and not least by its shaping of the national and local media environment, the state apparatus defines the field of struggle, and of opportunity, for indigenous communities.

Negotiating the Past in Contemporary Politics: The Case of Australia

Something of the specificity of the historical, territorial and cultural dislocation of indigenous peoples can be illustrated in relation to the case of Australia. Here the dissonance between the genocidal history of white settlement sits uncomfortably with the contemporary self-image of a progressive liberal modern multi-ethnic state. And, echoing the emphasis of the early part of this chapter, the legal and political processes have been central to the struggles of the Aborigines for recognition, reparation and self-determination. As Hartley and McKee have asserted: 'Indigeneity is a "semiotic hot spot" of contemporary Australian political and cultural life' (2000: 6).

In Australia near genocide against the indigenous peoples has been recognized in many historical analyses (Hughes, 1987; Reynolds, 1999). However, the history of this historical account of Australia's indigenous peoples and the construction of 'Aborigines' is itself a powerful illustration of the hegemonic manufacture of history by the dominant players in a country's social relations (Hemming, 1992; Attwood and Arnold, 1992). In 1968, the anthropologist W.E.H. Stanner in a seminal contribution to the ABC Boyer Lecture Series entitled 'The Great Australian Silence' identified Australia's established capacity for forgetting Aboriginal people and their views in what he described as a 'cult of forgetfulness on a national scale' (Stanner, 1968: 25). The decades since have seen a contested struggle to confront this forgetfulness with the realities of the past. The fundamental problem has rested with the issue of whose voice shall be heard in the telling of these realities, and what lexicon of moral and political discourse shall inform the understanding of them; for the critical appraisal of national identity does not take place in a vacuum. For the relatively young nation of Australia the three decades since Stanner's painful accusation have seen a rapid transformation of Australian life. The racist White Australia policy has given way to a de facto active multi-ethnic society in which state multi-culturalism has been concretely expressed in federal and state institutions, and in social policy. This remarkable transition has seen the emergence of a viable multi-cultural socio-political environment; yet one within which the Australian indigenous communities still remain anomalous and essentially excluded. The new Australian populace, until recently predominantly of European origin, found a perverse bonding with their new homeland in their spontaneous capacity to integrate into an historical marginalization of Aborigines (not unlike the anti-Black racism which European, Asian and Latin American immigrants alike evinced as they settled themselves into United States social life).

The bitter irony of this process lay in its being concurrent with a painful, fractured, but nonetheless significant emergence of the

Aboriginal voice within Australian life. Aboriginal resistance to their oppression most certainly did not only begin in the 1960s (Miller, 1985; Lippman, 1981). But the Deaths in Custody inquiry and the struggle over land rights provided very specific foci for the articulation of indigenous peoples' rights and the public exposure of their experience.[4] (Just as the Alta River Dam Project which flooded traditional Sami territory catalyzed Sami politics in the Arctic.) The issue of Aboriginal deaths in custody provided a challenge to the complacent belief of the equitable rule of law in 'the lucky country'. And the issue of native title and land usage challenged the foundational belief of the Australian nation in their acceptance of *terra nullius*. The 1992 Mabo case, which decided that British colonization in Australia did not *ipso facto* erase Aborigines' rights relating to land, raised a wide range of moral, legal and political questions for all Australians (Stephenson and Ratnapala, 1993; Rowse, 1993).

For the majority, 'White', Australians it caused a fundamental rupture with the founding assumptions of Australia's mythic origin in the earlier convict settlements so vividly described in Robert Hughes' (1987) historical account *The Fatal Shore*. It recognized the prior occupation of the continent by indigenous peoples, *and* the continuity of their presence in it. For the vast economic interests of mining companies and the extensive territorial claims of pastoralists it was a veritable nightmare of possible dispossession and exclusion from 'their' land. For the Aboriginal communities it represented a famous victory and a new measure of the Australian state's capacity to deal equitably and honestly with them. In essence the question was, and is, how will the process of law and politics operate in the interpretation and implementation of this ruling? To say that the jury is still out would be both naïve and optimistic. Mabo provided a new focus for a political struggle that remains massively unequal between Aboriginal and other interests.

And, important as these judicial/legal events were in shaping the developing understanding of Aborigine majority relations in contemporary Australia, again they were but one significant element in the complex interplay of forces over the last three decades. For simultaneously over this period there has been a growing visibility and range of activity in the Aborigine creative and expressive world of arts and letters. Certainly in the world of literature the Aboriginal experience has found both a voice, and a commercial possibility, in the expansion of Aboriginal literature. The biographic stories of Sally Morgan, the plays and poetry of Jack Davis and the 'retrieved' oral history of Kangkushot (Read and Coppin, 1999) are merely illustrative of this process. In film too the Aboriginal experience has penetrated into the world of cinema (Langton, 1993; Molner and Meadows, 2001).

Throughout the last three or four decades in Australia the majority non-Aboriginal population has changed dramatically in its ethnic demography, with initial extensive European migration being supplemented by more recent flows of labor power from Vietnam, Cambodia, Japan and China. And the demographic transition has been complemented by a complex reflexive process of awkward reappraisal. The quiet certainties of mateship and identity that underpinned the idea of 'the lucky country' have metamorphozed into a less homogeneous, and less myopic, self-understanding within Australia. After the UK's economic and commercial shift toward the European Union exposed the trading relations of Australia and moved it to closer economic ties with its near neighbors in the ASEAN states, so too the demise of 'Mother England' and the Commonwealth as political and cultural referents opened up a space for the re-examination of Australian identity in the light of its new demography and its emerging socio-political translation into a Pacific-rim nation. The 'cultural cringe' in relation to the European past was being challenged by an assertive celebration of Australia's home grown popular culture in books such as Fiske et al.'s (1987) *Myths of Oz*, whilst at the same time a strong republican movement sought to sever Australia's political ties to the British monarchy (Winterton, 1986).

This opening up of the cultural space of Australia in the 1980s and 1990s created an expansive canvas on which all Australians could challenge their well-rehearsed collective forgetfulness. At one level this provided the context for a cumulatively self-critical exhumation of White Australia's history of racism and exploitation. From the earlier work of Bottomley and de Lepervanche's (1984) *Ethnicity, Class and Gender in Australia*, through analyses such as Pettman's (1992) *Living in the Margins: Racism, Sexism and Feminism in Australia*, critical scrutiny of Australia's past, and present, discriminatory practices and exclusionary ideologies has become a powerful analytic genre. The late 1990s saw a series of highly critical, and visible, books which extended this analysis, including Stratton's (1998) *Race Daze: Australia in identity crisis*; Webb and Enstice's (1998) *Aliens and Savages: Fiction, Politics and Prejudice in Australia*; Hage's (1998) *White Nation* and Mickler's (1998) *The Myth of Privilege: Aboriginal Status, Media Visions, Public Ideas*.

In the light of this particular trajectory within the majority Australian public sphere it is perhaps not surprising that Dixson in her (1999) conservative analysis *The Imaginary Australian* claims to have identified the presence of a 'subliminal self-dislike currently running through Anglo-Celtic Australia'. She notes:

I am not alone in sensing it. In his 1992 Boyer Lectures, the historian Geoffrey Bolton refers to 'self-hatred', 'the besetting sin, the corrupting and crippling thing on the Australian scene'. Cultural analyst Meaghan Morris notes 'a tendency for critics to run polemics suggesting that ... Anglo-Celtic is bad and Australia is the most vicious country in the world'. The playwright David Williamson urges us to 'stop feeling ashamed of ourselves'. (*ibid*, p. 2)

Dixson's argument is not that such self-doubt does not exist, but that as an inchoate self-doubt it is not healthy to the continuing political role of non-Aboriginal Australians. In essence her argument is that:

> Since the Anglo-Celtic core culture plays a key cohesive role, during a period of consolidation it must develop a less negative, more realistic and more assured sense of itself. That more assured sense, vital to living over the long term with the richness and challenge of difference, demands public debate about identity, and especially the kind of debate which probes its imaginary dimensions. (*ibid*, p. 3)

Certainly, the reactive xenophobia and racisms of Pauline Hanson's One Nation Party demonstrated how assaults on the 'forgetfulness' of White Australians do not necessarily invite a rational and open-minded moral enquiry on the part of those collectively implicated in the critique. Nor should the populist chauvinism of Hanson's supporters be any comfort to the educated and politically sophisticated. The calculated exclusionary nationalism of Prime Minister John Howard's government's response to asylum seekers and his stolid refusal to utter the 'S' word ('sorry') in relation to Aboriginal oppression was a proven successful political strat-egy at the last Federal elections.[5]

The Australian case aptly illustrates the important distinction between the exposure of racism and exclusion and a political, and emotional, capacity to successfully negotiate its implications. The Australian Bicentenary in 1988 brutally revealed the on-going divisions within Australian self-identity (Bennett et al., 1992). The attempt to formally and extensively celebrate the Australian nation exposed the continuing power of hegemonic ideologies to inhibit attempts to translate reflexive critiques of past, and current, oppression into realistic appreciations of their politi-cal implications. Like the Mabo decision, a fracturing of the legitimacy of the status quo does not easily translate in policies and practices that equi-tably address the new recognition and new rights of those previously excluded.

However, if cultural shifts do not readily translate into political changes this should not result in a dismissal of the change in consciousness. The anxious self-assurance of 'White' Australia policy is now long gone. And, if majority 'White' Australia has undergone a painful deconstruction of its origin myths, neither has it entirely given up on its recognition of its virtues. The Australian Human Rights and Equal Opportunity Commission's 1997 report, *Bringing Them Home*, provided detailed and heart-breaking analysis of Australia's treatment of young Aboriginal children. It was a further exposure of the failed humanity of majority Australia in its relations with the Aboriginal communities. And yet the popular success of the 2002 film *Rabbit-Proof Fence*, which addresses this relatively recent period of history, suggests that some part of contemporary Australia can own the truth of its past and seek to negotiate an on-going wish for positive change. The director of the film, Philip Noyce, is quoted as saying: 'The popularity of the film shows that most people … want to come to terms with the issue. It says that white Australians needed a vehicle to express this huge shift that everyone has made' (Abley, 2003: 6). This is perhaps somewhat Pollyannaish; but the recognition of contemporary progress is as vital to understanding contemporary Aboriginal-majority relations, as is the revelation of past and current excesses.

A detailed critical history of past relations between indigenous people's and dominant settler populations may provide a stick with which to beat those responsible. But, it may simultaneously provide a baseline against which continuing progress may be measured. The brief synopsis of the Australia experience sketched above presses home the specific dynamics of historical nation building and contemporary political infrastructures in shaping the state's response to the demands, and rights, of their indigenous populations. These same forces can be seen to be in play, but with different substance and weightings, in the Canadian response to the Inuit where very real self-government rights have been extended to them in the creation of Nunavut within the Canadian federal system. Or again, in the recent, and varied, response of the Nordic states to the claims of the Sami.

To sum up, in every instance the current role of the media, and their potential role in the future, can only be adequately understood by a prior grasp of the historical relations between the dominant ethnic communities and the indigenous peoples and the manner in which these are incorporated into the contemporary politics of the state.

Media Representation and Indigenous Identities

Just as other chapters in this book have dealt with the issue of the representation of minority ethnic identities, so too that is a critical issue in relation to indigenous peoples. It is critical in that a core element of self-determination is a capacity to construct and report your own reality. And, it is also critical in that the power of non-indigenous media in determining the majorities' perceptions of indigenous peoples has been, and is, a central plank of the hegemonic determination of indigenous peoples' worlds. If we recall Hartley and McKee's (2000) location of indigeneity as a semiotic hot spot in contemporary Australia, then the very specificity of the history and current circumstances of the Australian Aboriginal communities should act as a powerful reminder that the polysemic possibilities of indigenous identities must always be approached in relation to their unique history.

We have already noted the long potency of Eurocentric thought in its construction of its understanding of the known world in terms that juxtaposed civilization and primitivism. The 'strangeness' of the indigenous peoples and their world was routinely reported in ways that flattered the self-image of the author and the assumed reader. However, it should not be assumed that the depiction of indigenous people was inevitably and uniformly negative. Cannadine (2001) has provided a persuasive account of 'how the British saw their Empire'; and a key thesis throughout this analysis is his insistence upon the translation to accounts of new worlds and new peoples of the very systems of accounting for social relations that were operative in the metropolis of the time. Thus, he argues that:

> ... when the English first encountered the native peoples of North America, they did not see them collectively as a 'race' of inferior savages; on the contrary, they viewed them individually as fellow human beings. It was from this pre-Enlightenment perspective that the English concluded that North American society closely resembled their own; a carefully graded hierarchy of status, extending in a seamless web from chiefs and princes at the top to less worthy figures at the bottom ... In short, when the English initially contemplated native Americans, they saw them as social equals rather than as social inferiors, and when they came to apply their conventionally hierarchical tools of observation, their prime grid of analysis was individual status rather than collective 'race'. (2001: 7, 8)

Thus, from Cannadine's perspective across the historical and geographical range of the British empire there can be traced the ebb and flow of a process of seeking to replicate in the Empire, a hierarchical social structure modelled on that which was thought to be operative at home. This necessarily requires an awareness of the complexity of the grid of analysis that any usurping power may bring to their understanding of indigenous peoples. There are many parallel, and possibly contradictory, threads that form the discourse of self-regard of dominant oppressors. If you are exterminating Tasmanian or North American Native Peoples you cannot sustain a pre-Enlightenment view of their equivalent status systems. Rather the harsh politics of social Darwinism and 'race' theory will serve you well (Kiernan, 1969). The nature of the material relations between groups powerfully shapes the ideological construction of 'explanations' of the legitimacy of the pattern of relations between peoples, as Jordan (1969) meticulously demonstrated in his account of British relations with 'Black' populations in America and the Caribbean.

Consequently, among other issues, there needs to be a degree of caution about 'what conventionally hierarchical tools of observation' may be employed by non-indigenous actors when engaging with indigenous peoples and issues. The trans-global emergence of indigeneity as an increasingly salient political issue should not obscure the very different stereotypical images imposed upon indigenous peoples, and the quite different ideological frameworks (Eurocentric; Japanese; Indonesian) that have spawned them.

Even in the case of 'progressive' actors seeking to argue for the recognition of the distinctive rights of self-determination of indigenous people, it cannot be assumed it is not possible that their virtue may be undermined by accompanying ideological frameworks. Kymlicka (2001), for example, warns that one reason for the international communities' emerging new norms in relation to indigenous peoples may be more than a sincerely held wish to remedy past wrongs. He suggests that another Promethean current often fuels this desire: namely, a belief that the cultural differences between majorities and indigenous peoples are much greater than with stateless nations. This is a liberal-progressive variant of the civilized-primitive trope in which:

Indigenous peoples do not just constitute distinct cultures, but they also form entirely distinct forms of cultures, distinct 'civilizations', rooted in a premodern way of life that needs protecting from the forces of modernization, secularization, urbanization, 'westernisation' etc.

He concludes:

I suspect that, for many people, the basis for singling out indigenous peoples is not their history or mistreatment, but their cultural 'otherness' – in particular, their isolation from, and repudiation of, modern ways of life. (2001: 128, 129)

The situation of indigenous peoples in their representation within and through the media has much in common with the partial and stereotypical portrayal of other minority populations; and has similar routes. The historical exclusion of indigenous peoples from 'mainstream' media has left the task of recording and explaining their experience, aspirations and cultures in the hands of majority professionals, with virtually inevitable consequences.

Historically, detailed descriptions of indigenous groups by colonial explorers, settlers and scientists provided accounts of indigenous peoples in which an emphasis was often placed on the differences between the 'civilized' and the 'primitive' in ways which emphasized the primitiveness and strangeness of the indigenous peoples. From travelogues and journals such (mis)representations moved on to 'scholarly' literature, literary fiction and newspapers, and from there to radio, film and television. (See, for example, Fairchild, 1928; Berkhofer, 1988; and Weston, 1996, for examples of the historical continuity, and internal contradictions, of media images of indigenous peoples.)

This trajectory can also be traced in the Sami/non-Sami relations in the Nordic countries. Lehtola (1995, 1997, 1999) has demonstrated how travel writers, historians and novelists, as well as physical anthropologists, have been active in recording their perceptions of the Sami over the centuries. Cumulatively, elements in these accounts have tended to represent the Sami as an uncivilized, under-developed, and even untrustworthy people. Lehtola points to the relevance of such imagery in serving as a justification for humiliating and offensive treatment of the Sami (Lehtola, 1995; Isaksson, 1996; Wilmer, 1993: 10–11).

In summarizing the research on the contemporary media representation of the Sami, Markelin (2003b) identifies a number of recurring tendencies in the relationship of the Nordic majority media towards the Sami population. The first is a marginalization of the Sami and Sami affairs. For most national and regional news media outside of the main Sami areas, including areas with a large Sami population, the Sami seem to be significantly under-represented (Berg, 2001; Furuly, 1994; Idivuoma, 1999; Lehtola, 2000; Pietikäinen, 2000; Skorgerb, 2000b). Effectively, the Sami appear to be absent in the national media, and in the regional press. Sami issues appear to be included mainly in relation to conflict, or when something conventionally interpretable as 'newsworthy' takes place. Thus, in this respect the Sami *per se*, and indigeneity and Sami rights, are not in themselves routinely newsworthy. (Compare the strikingly different current situation in Australia discussed below.) Consequently, the manner of their representation in the Nordic news media is comparable to that of minority ethnic communities elsewhere: they are vulnerable to the logics of *news values* as intuitively and conventionally interpreted by majority ethnic media professionals within their epistemic community.

And, in a phenomenon that is comparable to the Australian context, Markelin also notes the related stereotypical representation of the Sami as inexorably 'traditional'. Rather than the old perceptions of the Sami having been allowed to fade, it seems the Sami and Sami culture can still be linked to a specific 'otherness' and a romanticized traditional past. (See for example, J. Lehtola, 2000; Pedersen, 1997 and Skogerbø, 2000.) As Markelin observes: 'Indeed, in some instances, it seems it is precisely as a mythical element of national history that the Sami are today included onto the 'national narrative of the state' (2003b: 7). This selective investment in indigenous peoples as esoteric relics of a past 'traditional' facet of early state formation by majority ethnic communities is echoed in the schizoid image of Native Americans held by successive generations of 'White' Americans. As Weston reported:

> Basically, images of the Indian have embraced two contradictory concep-
> tions: the good Indian (or noble savage) and the bad Indian. The two
> images – the noble red-man and the bloodthirsty devil – have persisted in
> literature and popular culture from captivity narratives of the seventeenth
> century to made-for-television movies in the late twentieth century.
> (1996: 11)

Whilst 'bad Indians' may be useful ingredients for 'good' movies, 'good
Indians' provide ecological nostalgia for distressed urban North Americans.

Even in the formulation of their historical status as indigenous peoples
it is the majority media professionals who have the power to interpret the
contemporary relevance of indigenous communities to national agendas,
not the indigenous communities themselves.

The situation of the Sami in the Nordic media has strong similarities,
and some distinctive differences, from the situation of the Aborigines in
Australian media. Writing in 1993, Langton reported of the Australian situation that: 'Aboriginal and Islander people were still virtually invisible
on three commercial television networks' (p. 21).

This was a situation that was confirmed by a further contemporary
study (Bell, 1992). More recently, however, Hartley and McKee have provided a more complex and nuanced insight into the representation of
Aborigines in the Australian media in the mid–1990s. They report that:

> The most compelling result of our survey in numerical terms is a simple
> discovery: Aboriginality is over-represented in the Australian news
> media in *factual* stories. While Indigenous *fictional* characters portrayed
> in popular culture are quite rare, Aboriginality turns out to be a massive
> *presence* in Australian journalism. Aboriginality and 'Aboriginal issues',
> continue to draw headlines, comment columns and editorial opinion
> with a frequency unjustified statistically by the population of Indigenous
> people. Indigeneity has become central for Australia's status as a nation.
> It remains as Australia's 'running story', a story that just keeps on going.
> It is the point around which political debates – debates about social
> justice, fairness and the adequacy of social structures – take place in
> Australia. (2000: 209)

This statement is consistent with the argument above about the increasing
significance of indigenous rights and reconciliation as a *political* issue in
Australian life throughout the 1990s. As such, it can usefully be compared
with the much quieter, and emotionally and morally cooler, emergence of
Sami rights within Nordic political life over the 1980s and 1990s. It also
indicates that the extent of visibility, and the nature of the representation
of indigenous peoples, may simultaneously differ markedly depending
upon the medium and genre which is being monitored.

The salience of indigeneity as an issue not surprisingly impacts upon the apparent relevance of indigenous peoples to journalistic news values, and potential soft news and entertainment audiences. Thus, Hartley and McKee note how coverage of Aboriginal issues in 'hard news' varies across the continent through the ways in which dominant *state* news media respond to specific issues such as land right claims. However, where Aboriginality becomes salient to media professionals there remains the question of who will speak, of how Aboriginal peoples will be represented. And, here too Hartley and McKee provide a range of insights, amongst which are:

> It seems that while the Aboriginal public sphere was well developed in terms of culture, arts and sports, it had no public infrastructure in party political or financial terms. The basic construction of Indigeneity in the Australian public sphere is as what Marshall Sahlins once called the 'original affluent society' – people who were culturally rich but politically and economically poor. (*ibid*: 228)

and:

> Who actually appears to comment on and represent Indigenous issues and questions? As can be seen from Figure 11 ... the most visible Indigenous public figures were mostly drawn from the world of sport and entertainment. (*ibid*: 228)

and:

> By contrast, the non-Indigenous people who are involved in the Indigenous media sphere can be characterized much more easily: they were party-political politicians (see Figure 12). Since speaking on this subject was their job, it is no surprise to find that prime ministers, state premiers, Aboriginal Affairs ministers and other MPs represented almost the entire profile of this sample. (*ibid*: 228)

This again is consistent with the demographic location of Aboriginal peoples within the Australian public sphere. With few exceptions they are absent from the dominant economic and political sphere; and like minority persons in other countries are positively celebrated only in their exceptionality as sportsmen and women and as entertainers. The nature and significance of Aboriginal political structures and systems of accountability are not recognized as authentically 'political' by the majority society.

Significantly, the 'authenticity' of Aboriginal life and culture was defined in the media in a way that powerfully echoed Kymlicka's warning, noted above, that indigenous peoples may be fleetingly and perversely 'celebrated' for their perceived 'isolation from, and repudiation of, modern ways of life'. Thus, Hartley and McKee report that their analysis revealed that:

> The culture of Aboriginal Australia was presumed to be part of nature: from a non-Indigenous perspective, the two collapsed together.
>
> Nature magazines and their advertisements constructed a public, addressed as explicitly white, who wanted to discover Australia, who desired meaning, and who could find it 'ecotouring with the elders'. Aboriginality was an essentially Australian object, a place that could be visited by white Australians by means of travelling, moving through space and, it was implied, through time. 'Experience what life was like in Australia 60,000 years ago' … It was the language of tourism that one of the few appeals to 'authentic' Aboriginal culture was carried out in the mediasphere; and here, that appeal was relentless. (2000: 245)

This particular construction of the authentic otherness of indigenous peoples is, ironically, rooted in a determined *insistence upon* their historical indigeneity. For the Australian Aborigines, as for 'Eskimos', this formulation purposefully claims the excluded indigenous communities as national treasures, as 'ours': whilst simultaneously executing a convenient historical vault over the indecencies and brutalities of their historical dispossession and exclusion. Rooted in a deep national history they, the indigenous peoples, are reclaimed in their 'pure' state, and by inference their relation with the majority populations remains unsullied by intervening realities.

The media representation of indigenous peoples shows clear similarities to the portrayal of other minority ethnic populations in majority media. The basis for the similarities can be found in the comparable processes of exclusion, and the problematic political economy of access to the processes of media ownership and production. And, as has been emphasized throughout this chapter, some of the distinct differences have their roots in the specific historical relation of indigenous peoples to their contemporary nation and state; and to the contemporary location of indigeneity as an issue in national politics

The Political Economy of Indigenous Media

Just as with other minority media systems, the development of indigenous media cannot be determined solely by the virtue of the indigenous peoples' claims and the commitment of their activists. The brutal realities of the political economy of the media impact powerfully on the viability of indigenous media (Browne, 1966; Molnar and Meadows, 2001). The emphasis within this chapter on recognizing the particularity of the historical and current location of indigenous peoples in relation to the surrounding apparatus of economic and political power takes on real urgency through this perspective. As Molnar and Meadows have argued in relation to the role of the media in empowering indigenous peoples, a central issue '… is the ability of Indigenous communities to control the means of production of culturally specific media products' (2001: p. xii).

A critical feature of guaranteeing such control is the ability to generate an adequate revenue stream. However, as we have already noted the spatial dispersal of indigenous peoples, the degree of linguistic diversity and their absolute numbers may render them highly problematic as commercially viable audiences. The case of Imparja Television in rural Australia is a telling exemplar of this dilemma (Batty, 1993; Molnar and Meadows, 2001). Having won the licence to operate the central zone footprint of the Remote Commercial Television Services network in 1988, against an alternative publicly funded community bid, Imparja has found the financial imperatives of its operation has dramatically undermined its capacity to act as a platform for an Aboriginal voice. As Molnar and Meadows report: 'Largely because of commercial constraints, Imparja Television is committed to broadcasting selected programmes from Australia's three commercial networks with well over 90 per cent of its output being standard commercial fare' (2001: 57). There is nothing inherent in commercial media that render them anathema to indigenous media, but the economic logics of production and dissemination do make servicing small and/or dispersed audiences potentially fraught.

However, it is not only the brute realities of profitability that determine the viability of indigenous media for in the political-economy of the media the domain of the political is equally relevant. States in their regulation of the media environment may bend the arm of commercial interests and enable the viability of non-commercial enterprises. One of the major factors in shaping this reality is the legal status of indigenous peoples within their state, and its consequent expression in state policies. As the multi-national studies of Morris and Waisbord (2001) have effectively demonstrated, even in an epoch of economic liberalization and globalization the state continues to have a central role in shaping media environments. As the case of Maori in Aotearoa (New Zealand) has powerfully illustrated, the legal confirmation of the status of indigenous peoples has a significant impact in providing a platform of legitimacy from which they may struggle for their media rights (Fox, 1993). In the case of the Sami, Markelin (2003a, 2003b) has also shown how the different legal recognition of the Sami, as indigenous peoples within the states of Norway, Sweden and Finland, contributes to the dynamics of the policy from within which they must contest their rights. Furthermore, her carefully nuanced analysis shows how legal recognition is but one factor in shaping the development of indigenous media policy in these states. As we have already seen above, the salience of indigeneity as an issue *per se* within the political structures of each of these Nordic states may be seen as a further critical variable.

The role of formal state policy on indigenous media is a far from simple issue. Molnar and Meadows in their review of the Australian situation state that: 'The Indigenous broadcasting sector in Australia has developed in spite of an almost complete lack of policy on Indigenous media and varying levels of support from the relevant Australian government departments' (2001: 5). And yet this requires careful reading for whilst their analysis does reveal the absence of a coherent government *policy* on indigenous media, this is not synonymous with the absence of a policy *debate* about this issue. Indeed, the remainder of their chapter details a sequence of inquiries and formal reports by various government agencies from the early 1980s through to 2000. Over the last two decades, there has been a series of significant, and expensive, government funded initiatives in indigenous broadcasting in the absence of a coherent policy. Appropriately, these authors recognize this in quoting (*ibid*: 5) the former manager of the Central Australian Aboriginal Media Association (CAAMA) as saying 'Policy is something that happens behind us'. As this quote indicates, formal policy may follow upon actual practical innovation. The space of the possible made available by the absence of state negative constraint, may, in some circumstances, be as important as the potential for development made available by active, and positive, state intervention.[6]

Clearly, in any national context a formal policy guaranteeing recognition of indigenous peoples' cultural and linguistic rights, and a media policy linked to this, gives indigenous people a legal and political resource to seek to develop their own media environment. But, just as such a policy does not guarantee the *de facto* realization of these rights, so too the formal absence of a policy is not of itself a sufficient deterrent to their development.

And, if the role of government policy is important but not unilinear in its impact, then the nature of the governmental institutions through which policy is formulated and implemented is central to this complexity. Since 'generically' media policy is a product of multiple and contested interests then it cannot be expected that indigenous media policy, embedded as it is in the national context, can be an exception to the rule, even though it will, of course, have its unique constituent elements. Just as the Sami case study has indicated the range of organizations, agencies and governmental bodies that are engaged as players in shaping policy and practice, so too the Australian situation confirms the general rule of complexity whilst simultaneously underlining the distinctive nature of each national case.

The ability of indigenous peoples to pursue their own interests within such a context is itself partially a function of their structure and the coherence of their own power base within the state political apparatus. As Molnar and Meadows illustrate, the Australian expression of self-government rights for Aboriginal peoples may also generate fragmentation of purpose and priorities at community level, and heavily compromised representation through ATSIC (The Australian and Torre Straits Islanders Commission). And, in the case of the Sami, Markelin has shown how the quite different vigor and role of the Sami Parliaments as representative organizations of Sami interests in Norway, Sweden and Finland, have been a further significant element in shaping the Sami media environment. Thus, the ways in which states formally recognize the status of indigenous peoples, and the institutional means whereby they claim to facilitate degrees of self-government for them, are key variables in determining the political environment in which indigenous media policies and structures can be developed.

An inevitable correlate of this is the economic resource base available for the development of indigenous media. In every instance this is critical for the development and sustainability of indigenous media. A heavy dependence on the state through direct funding brings with it inevitable constraints, as for example, in the case of Australia (Molnar and Meadows, 2001). Or, where state funding is mediated through the national public service broadcaster, as in Finland, Norway and Sweden, (Markelin, 2003a and b), then the internal priorities and dynamics of those organizations have a major impact in shaping the consequent indigenous media organizational structure. And finally, where commercial enterprises carry the responsibility for facilitating indigenous media, there are predictably depressing instances of profit, not formal policy, shaping programming policy.

Conclusions

The relationship of indigenous peoples to the mass media demonstrates many of the characteristics that are found in the review of minority ethnic communities' relation with the media; they suffer from extensive misrepresentation in the majority media. However, whilst their frequent relative invisibility from particular media genres is typical of minority representation in general, there are also distinctive echoes of the Rousseauesque 'Noble Savage' to be found as the historical continuity of indigenous peoples' relation to their territory is given a partisan gloss by the majority media. And the claims of indigenous peoples for self-government rights over their traditional territories also provide quite specific foci for competition and conflict with majority ethnic interests, which then in turn become dominant issues in news media coverage.

As with other minority ethnic populations the unique demography and location of indigenous peoples within the political fabric of their society has powerful implications for the economic viability of their media. However, the unique status of indigenous peoples in international legal instruments provides a distinctive feature of their relation to the state. As we will explore more fully in Chapter 9, the status of indigenous peoples in relation to *differentiated citizenship rights* provides them with a legal basis for making specific claims upon the state. As the examples of the Sami and the Australian Aboriginal Peoples have indicated, the state can be a critical player in facilitating a minimal media environment for indigenous peoples. In an era where much media research literature has become fascinated with the processes of economic liberalization and globalized media systems, the state remains a demonstrably relevant, and potentially potent, player in shaping national media environments. Through both media regulation, and direct subsidy, the state can significantly contribute to the profile of the indigenous peoples' media environment.

The viability of indigenous peoples' media is not only of central importance in allowing indigenous peoples to sustain a media environment which can reflect their experiences and sustain their values and cultures. In multi-ethnic societies indigenous media are critical components of a public sphere in which diversity is sustained as a feature of the media environment of all. Indigenous media institutions not only generate media content which in various ways penetrate the majority media environment, they also develop and train media professionals who, when recruited into the 'mainstream' media industries, take with them a distinctive sensibility which may enrich the professional repertoire of those media. Indigenous peoples have a specific history and distinct legal status in contemporary society; the quality of their media environment is an unobtrusive measure of a state's commitment to participative democracy and the availability of communication rights.

Notes

1 This chapter has benefited extensively from the four year research project into Sami Media in the Nordic States, funded by the Ethnicity and Social Policy Research Unit (ESPR), at the University of Bradford. We are indebted for the advice of Dr Lia Markelin, whose Ph.D *Media, Ethnicity and Power* provides a magisterial review of the contemporary dynamics of Sami media. We would also like to acknowledge our indebtedness to the many colleagues in the Sami media, and beyond, for their kindness, openness and generosity, without whom the Sami analysis would have been impossible.

2 Not least in terms of their current significance for Indigenous politics and identities are the ways in which the historical experiences of exclusion, and dispersal, have impacted upon the current internal diversity *within* indigenous communities. The relative viability of languages within indigenous peoples may well have been differentially effected by varying patterns of dispersal and migration over time. Equally, the movement of indigenous persons from traditional homelands into current urban conglomerates can generate a fragmentation of existential connection to traditional mores between those communities continuing to reside in traditional homelands and those now located in urban environments outside their traditional lands. (See, for example, Langton, 1993)

3 As the international political struggle to establish a coherent policy on the guaranteeing of the rights of indigenous peoples to self-determination continues, (see, for example, Aigio and Scheinin, 2000) so too the distinctive capacity of *national* initiatives in advancing this program has been recognized. As Henricksen observes in a valuable brief overview *'the international process is influenced by national political processes, which often tend to be more pragmatic and flexible than the international process. National experiences of indigenous self-determination, or self-government as some would call it, directly influence the international debate and thereby move the discourse forward'*. (Henricksen, 2001: 7)

4 The relation between indigenous peoples and majority communities and the state typically become focused around specific *cause celebres*. In the case of Australia an inquiry into the disproportionate numbers of Aboriginal people dying whilst in custody initiated in 1987 and reporting in 1991, provided just such a catalyst. (Bourke et al., 1998)

5 Pauline Hanson's unsophisticated cant provided a clear focus for a widely shared sentiment, called by Mickler (1998) *The Myth of Privilege*, which perceived Aboriginal People to be singled out for unjustifiable special treatment. This specific targeting of Aboriginal Peoples was, moreover, entirely consistent with her broader view that Anglo-Australians were losing out to the special interests of minorities. Her own political moment may have collapsed from, amongst other things, internal discord in her party, but the rhetoric of Anglo-Celtic Australian ascendancy continued to flourish in the 'one nation' rhetoric she shared with John Howard (see Stratton, 1998).

6 See the discussion of the role of 'first generation' human rights principles in shaping the multi-ethnic public sphere in Chapter 9.

6 Media Monitoring and Codes of Practice[1]

As this book has proceeded there has been a cumulative critical account of the roles played by the media in shaping attitudes and framing understandings of difference in the multi-ethnic world. In pursuing this agenda there has been a wealth of relevant data to be drawn upon. The activities of the media are subject to extensive monitoring and critique. The amount of individual and organizational effort that goes into this process is unmeasured, but must be truly enormous. From the individual concerns of committed young scholars pursuing their own agendas in masters and doctoral research, through to the funded activities of organizations such as Fairness and Accuracy in Reporting or Accuracy in the Media, the media are subject to continued scrutiny. 'Media performance' has become an established concern of academics, media professionals and the public. This effort is, of course, not co-ordinated, not always methodologically sound, and frequently propelled by foregone conclusions in pursuit of supportive data.

Doubtless the first attempts at stone age graffiti received a critical response, and for centuries religious authorities and the state have frequently shown themselves to be eager to monitor and control the presence of the media in public life. Alternatively, in the modern world, the media are widely seen as the necessary handmaidens of democracy (Dahlgren and Sparks, 1991; Keane, 1991; Garnham, 2000.) It is the perceived power of the media which feeds both an anxious concern for their free availability and a deep distrust of their immediate and subterranean effects.

In a recent account, Nordenstreng (2003) seeks to trace the roots of contemporary initiatives to promote coherent and systematic media monitoring and finds a number of trajectories. From Walter Lippmann's (1922) concern about the 'pseudo-environment' created between the audience and the world by the mass media, through to MacBride's (1980: ii) suggestion that 'it would be very useful to devise some system for monitoring the extent to which certain newspapers and chains of newspapers distort news concerning disarmament in the world', and the subsequent MacBride Round Table (see Vincent, Nordenstreng and Traber, 1999); and via, *inter alia*, the more recent Cultural Environment Movement initiated by George Gerbner and the Third World Network in Malaysia, Nordenstreng perceives a momentum building around the issue of media monitoring. Indeed, his own corpus of work constitutes a personal academic and political pursuit of establishing an integrated trans-national media monitoring organization (Nordenstreng and Griffin, 1999). Such instances as have occurred of international comparative media monitoring around specific issues have proved to be illuminating, if not exactly potent, in their impact upon media performance. As we shall see in the later discussion at the close of this chapter, the methods of media monitoring are multiple and the relation between their methodological rigor, expense and practical impact far from linear.

However, before returning to media monitoring it is both necessary and appropriate to look at its awkward policy cousin, media industry codes of practice. For if the media have suffered a long history of critical scrutiny, they have learnt to develop defensive strategies. Principal among these has been the development of professional ethics, and their practical adjuncts, codes of practice. In the contemporary world, codes of practice are ubiquitously present in media industries across the world (see Husband and Alam, 2001). They are a practical and explicit statement of the professional ethics of specific media. And, as such; they declare the espoused values and professional competencies expected of individuals working within a specific media profession. They are the platform upon which claims for self-regulation are built (Nordenstreng, 1999, 2000). They are both a declaration of integrity *and* a benchmark for monitoring media performance along lines established by the media themselves. As such it is appropriate to scrutinize their nature and function before returning to the question of media monitoring.

Codes of Practice

These codes have not of course emerged in a professional vacuum. Indeed, news and broadcast media have an established tradition of constructing an ethical framework within which professional practice routinely operates (Belsey and Chadwick, 1992; Kiernan, 1998; Nordenstreng, 2000; Christiens et al., 2001). As we shall see shortly below, this 'in-house' engagement in formulating an ethical agenda for media performance is not necessarily an entirely disinterested and selfless act. However, in developing a discourse and practice around media ethics media professionals have not lacked in external advice and guidance. From the contentious MacBride Report of 1980, through to the Council of Europe's 1993 resolution and recommendation on the ethics of journalism, to Article 13 of the Treaty of Amsterdam, there has been a plethora of recommendations and requirements provided by extra-media bodies which would aim to guide their operation. And more specifically in relation to the issue of ethnic diversity, the Vienna Monitoring Center on Racism and Xenophobia published a report of its European Media Conference entitled *Racism and Cultural Diversity in the Mass Media* (ter Wal, 2002), which provided direct recommendations for the functioning of the media in multi-ethnic Europe. Again, within the Tuning in to Diversity Project, colleagues at Online/More Colour in the Media (in Utrecht) are generating a review of the very many recommendations relating to the responsibilities of the media in operating in a multi-ethnic context that has been produced by governmental, NGOs and professional bodies. Thus, codes of practice relating to the role and responsibilities of the media in representing ethnic identities and constructing agendas around inter-ethnic relations exist within a context which strongly supports their legitimacy. The existence of such codes also makes reasonable the general public's expectation that they should be seen to have an effect on media performance.

However, the reality is somewhat different. Not all codes of practice contain explicit statements relating to ethnicity or racism. Neither are all professional bodies committed to engaging with their responsibilities in regard to the representation of ethnic relations. Whilst the International Federation of Journalists (IFJ) has, through its International Media Working Group on Racism and Xenophobia (IMRAX), pursued an active program of sensitizing the world of journalism in regard to the reporting of ethnic relations and racist organizations, it could not be said that their initiative has met with universal enthusiasm. The British National Union of Journalists, as well as the Netherlands and Finnish unions have, for example, produced specific guidelines pertaining to ethnicity, representation and diversity for their members. And, currently, in 2004, there is a major initiative to promote a 'European Manifesto for Minority Community Media' (www.multicultural.net). But this concern with an ethical professional sensitivity to reporting ethnic diversity and racism is far from a universal practice.

In fact we may usefully reflect upon the manifest and latent functions of professional bodies and media organizations producing codes of practice and guidelines for their performance in relation to ethnic diversity. In examining the wide range of codes and guidelines that are available, it is noticeable that the content typically has a variety of *types of statements*. Many documents contain *value statements* which indicate the moral and ethical bases for the proposed actions. These statements position the proposals within the document in relation to external framing discourses, *inter alia* of professional responsibility, human rights philosophy and theological belief. They provide a legitimacy for invoking specific values and behaviors. Such value statements are routinely complemented by *persuasive statements* that in general terms outline a range of behaviors and practices that are desirable. These statements provide the professional codex of the 'oughts' of everyday practice. Going beyond the general discourse of values, they provide a behavioral repertoire of good practice. However, much more rarely present are *prescriptive statements* that explicitly specify behaviors and practices that 'must' be implemented if the practitioner is to avoid charges of incompetence and bringing the profession into disrepute. Such statements do not invite the conformity of conscientious professionals to operate within a virtuous voluntary system of autonomous action; rather they require all members of the profession, on pain of sanctions, to comply with an explicit code of practice. Compliance by its nature does not necessarily attract individual commitment, but it does exact behavioral orthodoxy.[2]

A not too cynical interpretation of very many of these codes and guidelines is that they constitute a gestural rhetoric of 'professional standards' that represent sincere aspirations for the *collectively imaginable*, rather than an executive order for the regulation of the *collectively attainable*. As such, they are of course entirely consistent with the logics of professional bodies and the ideology of professionalism itself. A core function of all professional bodies is to define the terrain of their activity, to provide a self-evident legitimacy for their members' exclusive occupation of this terrain and to seek to guarantee *self-regulation* of their performance within it. In this respect, journalistic and media codes of practice express a generic 'professional' rationale. Their content provides an exposition of professional *values* that gives the practitioners their distinctive collective identity and legitimacy. The specification of professional behaviors, both persuasive and, where present, prescriptive, demonstrates their serious-minded commitment to self-regulation. The potential absence of any meaningful sanctions for failure to adhere to the code is of course not made explicit as a serious qualification to the credibility of these implicit claims. The ideology of professionalism provides a binding coherence to the relevance and meaning of such codes. However, we need only to look at the law, medicine, the church or academia, to sustain a justifiable scepticism about the adequacy of self-regulation of the professions.

Additionally, and importantly, it is necessary to remember that 'being professional' is not the same as being moral. Professional ethics and the normative routines of professional workplace cultures function to define individual's *limits of responsibility,* as much as to identify their means of meeting their responsibilities (Husband, 1995). Being professionally competent may not be at all the same as being morally responsible. Bauman (1990) provided a valuable perspective from which to view this dilemma. For Bauman, morality is found within the individual. It is driven by a *wish to be for* the Other. It is a proactive act of imagination and generosity which is not based upon some rational choice principle of exchange. From this perspective, ethics necessarily become heterogeneous external law-like systems of rules collectively generated. Bauman suggests an essential basis for this in modernity's pessimism regarding human goodness. He argues that:

> Throughout the modern era, echoing the concerns of the order-builders, philosophers deeply distrusted the moral self. That selves cannot be left to their own resources, that they have no adequate resources to which they can be, conceivably, left – was an assertion which did not depend for its truth on empirical findings; it did not generalise from reality; but defined the way in which (in the case of guardians of order) reality was to be shaped and (in the case of the philosophers) was to be thought about and interpreted. (1990: 63)

Thus this denial of the possibility, and reliability, of a human moral impulse provided the context for the apparently necessary *external* imposition of ethical guidelines, and their *coercive collective* regulation. And, as we have seen, ethics cannot stand as a self-evident code of conduct, but must themselves be legitimized through the invocation of foundational principles which allow for the recognition of right and wrong in human conduct. Such ethical packages are themselves normalized via the institutions which promulgate their existence and symbiotically regulate their enforcement. Ethics then are always subject to normative pressures.

For the operation of codes of practice and guidelines for the media professionals operating in an ethnically diverse world, it is possible to tease out some awkward implications arising from this reality. First, as we have seen above in the discourses around ethnic diversity and multi-cultural responsibilities, there is a noticeable lack of value consensus. The values invoked by media codes are quite capable of becoming ambiguous, open to contradictory interpretation, or to be simply contested when applied to ethnicity and racial ideologies in the contemporary world.[3] Thus it is conceivable that we may attain compliance within the behavioral requirements of codes in the absence of commitment to the framing values. As such, professionalism here becomes a superficial technical accomplishment. But everything that is known about ethnocentrism in everyday racism (Essed, 1991) suggests that the contrary values would leak into the professional performance, through acts of omission as much as commission.

Additionally the external collective carapace of professional ethics, and their attendant codes, are always open to alienating individual professionals from their unique moral agency. As already argued above codes not only specify expected behaviors, they also establish a normative limit to the 'reasonable demands' that may be made upon a professional. Thus the workplace culture of a media professional, through confirming the adequacy of an individual's 'professional' competence, may help to suppress their personal moral discomfort about their disengagement with moral responsibility which 'professionalism' all too frequently permits.

Setting limits of responsibility is particularly relevant since media professionals routinely operate in institutional structures that are hierarchical and firmly shaped by strong workplace cultures. Individuals may work *for* large corporations, but they work *with* a finite and relatively stable cohort of colleagues. These *communities of practice* (Lesser et al., 2000) provide social, interpersonal terrains of professional practice. Such is the nature of these communities that they provide the locus and means of socialization into the profession and the continuing collective discipline which regulates normative compliance. It is here where codes of practice are resisted or embraced, where requirements for sensitivity to ethnic diversity are given tokenistic existence in a shared glib discourse, or where through awkward persistence they are developed as a challenge to established routines. (The nature and power of communities of practice will be developed more extensively in Chapter 8.)

To extend the analysis from Chapter 1, it is exactly in such communities of practice that within the British context observers would expect to locate *institutional racism* (Parekh, 2000). Institutional racism exists where the unthinking routines of a work place, *in their effects*, are racially discriminatory. It does not require explicit intent but merely the absence of the imaginative morality of *being for the other*. Whilst not without its critics (Miles, 1989), the concept of institutional racism was central to the philosophy of the British 1976 Race Relations Act and is fundamental to much equal opportunities policy in Britain, including the Race Relations (Amendment) Act, 2000. As noted in Chapter 1, in recent years institutional racism was at the heart of a major inquiry into the death of a young man called Stephen Lawrence and the subsequent investigation provided an extensive review of the operation of institutional racism within the Metropolitan Police Service in London. The inquiry defined institutional racism as:

> The collective failure of an organisation to provide an appropriate and professional service to people because of their colour, culture or ethnic origin. It can be seen or detected in processes, attitudes and behaviour which amount to dissemination through unwitting prejudice, ignorance, thoughtlessness and racist stereotyping, which disadvantage minority ethnic people. (Stephen Lawrence Report, 1999)

To emphasize the relevance of this concept to the argument being developed here, its key insight is in recognizing that ethnic discrimination may be reproduced within an organization without the wilful intent of the individuals involved. In the context of national discourses on ethnic discrimination and exclusion, where it is quite usual to reduce racism to extremist (proto-fascist) politics, the essence of this concept is to assert that 'nice people' can discriminate. Organizationally, the concept of institutional racism moves the focus of attention away from an exclusive focus upon the malign behavior of 'prejudiced' individuals to a scrutiny of the effects of the routine practices of the institution.

Institutional racism in contexts such as this should not be seen as some unique syndrome that is cognitively and culturally sealed from other value systems and beliefs. In Chapter 1, reference was made to symbolic racism and enlightened racism. These concepts explicitly indicated how core racial beliefs are normalized by being intricately interwoven into other powerful belief systems in American life. Equally, we are familiar with the potent synergy between ideologies of the nation and distinctive forms of race theory (Weimer, 1996; Hage, 1998). In the current era we are still subject to imagery and polysemic representations that layer together race and gender in ways that are rooted in the histories of racism and the histories of imperialism (hooks, 1991; Kabbani, 1994; Grewal, 1996; Stoler, 1997). Even the healthy pursuit of sports may be not quite innocent vehicles of racial ideology (James, 1984). Thus, in considering the nature and powers of institutional racism it would be a mistake to only track enthusiastically the 'racial' content of workplace cultures. In an important early contribution, Williams (1985) stressed the importance of recognizing that racial practices may be sustained by non-racial ideologies. Thus, the normalized existence of hierarchies of professional status within the newsroom, or on the film set, ease the ready yielding of personal responsibility to the authority of a senior. Professional pride in the acquired skills of producing copy that is able to survive the critical intervention of the editor, or sub-editors, lubricates a socialization into the house style of a particular newsroom. Through such processes do liberal individuals generate right-wing, racially aggressive or dismissive copy. And, of course, in all of these circumstances a need to succeed, to climb the professional ladder of status and income, provides a quietly persistent urging in most professional careers. The many interacting values and belief systems that co-exist in the workplace have to be isolated and understood as the emergent building blocks of institutional racism.

Consequently, the purpose of introducing the concept of institutional racism here is precisely because it explicitly locates the individual within the normative context of their workplace. It requires codes of practice to have relevance to the organization and operation of media production as much as to the behavior of individual practitioners. Hence, it follows that media organizations that exploit codes of practice in order to uniquely locate responsibility for media performance with individual employees are exercising a deft, and indefensible, sleight of hand.[4]

It is precisely because media professionals operate within specific communities of practice that the pragmatic fragmentation of media monitoring into distinct domains of content (performance), production (ownership, human relations practices, economics) or consumption (audience size and audience appreciation) cannot be analytically sustained, or politically endorsed. Of course, within the logistical constraints of carrying out media monitoring, data can be collected from within these discrete domains. But any meaningful analysis of this data *must* frame it within a perspective that is alert to the dynamic interaction *between* these domains. And certainly a failure to sustain such an integrated understanding of the nature and operation of the media industries would be likely to generate analyses that are politically naïve.[5]

We need only to think of the institutional process of news production, including 'alternative' news, to have an immediate sense of the necessary interaction of these processes (Franklin and Murphy, 1998; Downing, 2001). Concerns about the impact of the ownership and control of news industries at a global and organizational level are well known (Herman and Chomsky, 1988; Herman and McChesney, 1997). The dynamics of interpersonal relations within the hierarchical routines of the newsroom, within the routine community of practice of news production, provide the social psychological crucible in which these dynamics are given effect (Heider, 2000). The ethnic demography of the newsroom cannot be divorced from the ethnic balance of media content, a consensus about the target audience, and related assumptions about news values requires a coherent workplace culture. Issues of media performance cannot be separated from the issues of recruitment and retention of staff. Obstacles to the entry of minority ethnic staff into media industries, and discriminatory constraints placed upon their utilization, and personal-professional development within the workplace, are recurrent features of mass media practice (see Husband, 1994).

The shared values, behavioral norms and taken-for-granted-knowledge of media professionals' community of practice can serve to isolate them from accountability to non-professional persons, communities and institutions. In this respect, professional identities demonstrate all the in-group/out-group dynamics that can be found in any process of collective identity formation (Capozza and Brown, 2000). Out-group critiques can strengthen in-group identities and additionally narrow the permissible diversity of values within the in-group. On these terms alone ethnically homogeneous work groups are hardly conducive to sustaining workplace cultures appropriate to representing a multi-ethnic reality. Although codes of practice are rational arguments for regulating behavior, it would be foolhardy to believe that they are implemented and negotiated in working environments entirely defined by rationality. Journalists, film makers and other media professionals, have a strong in-group identity and are highly resistant to external scrutiny and regulation. Thus, in essence, whilst it is quite reasonable to accept that many journalists are quite sincere in their endorsement of codes of practice, it is naïve to assume that they are institutionally well suited to implementing them.

Notions of autonomy, objectivity and professionalism all too easily smother critical reflections on routine practices. In order to become credible instruments of change, codes of practice endorsed by media professionals need to be implementable, monitorable and indeed must contain in-built mechanisms which allow adequate review and evaluation, including the possibility of professional sanctioning. At present, codes of practice are lacking in several aspects, illustrated through the process of news-making which is powerfully structured and subject to continuous internal monitoring and regulation but which, even so, leaves journalism regrettably weak in controlling racist and xenophobic content (van Dijk, 1991, 1993; ter Wal, 2002). It is evident that it does not require the presence of active intentional racists within the newsroom, or elsewhere within the media, in order to explain the lamentable record of the media in representing ethnic diversity, or in guaranteeing equity and access of minority persons to the media.

Consequently, in appraising codes of practice we must be realistic about the institutional context within which they exist and are required to operate. We must be equally realistic about the essential formal structures that must be in place in order for them to operate with any prospect of success. Codes of practice must not become instruments for launching ad hoc assaults upon individual media professionals who in many instances are institutionally blocked in their attempts to fulsomely implement them. For example, there has been an instance where a union of journalists wished to formally sanction a colleague for grossly inadequate reporting, only for the editor to refuse to implement it.

It is necessary to see codes of practice as *vehicles for change* and to understand that this process of change is only realistically facilitated when both individual commitment, and systemic organizational policy are appropriately linked in a co-ordinated program of action. Individuals alone cannot be reasonably expected to change a workplace culture if the discretionary powers operating at every level of the organization signal that the institutional stance on equal opportunities and responsible production values is purely tokenistic rhetoric. And equally, the world of equal opportunities and anti-racist initiatives has many examples of where heavy handed top-down managerial initiatives have generated powerful resistance and a negative backlash. When seen as necessarily collaborative, codes of practice become vehicles for change which must be given the sensitive backing of an executive power that is expressed *throughout* the organizational structure of the media industries.

Media Monitoring: A Routinized Research Practice or a Political Intervention?

In examining the nature and functions of media monitoring it is perhaps necessary to initially at least sketch the range of activities that might be included in this concept. At its simplest and not entirely banal level we may see the daily opinionated dialogue between friends and colleagues as they rehearse their response to the previous night's television or a current film as media monitoring. Here judgements are made, amongst other things, about production standards, framing of issues, adequacy of representation and enjoyability. And these judgements are typically partisan and highly ego-involved. All the participants are likely to claim a legitimacy for their argument, whilst simultaneously feeling no need to wrap themselves in the mantel of objectivity. Objectivity in discussions such as these is perceived as the arid discourse employed by academic pedants and alien 'experts'.

Nor are these discussions structured in such a way as to provide a systematic and coherent analysis of an issue. They are typically freewheeling, idiosyncratic and focused in the interaction itself. The dialogue, its vivacity, wit and familiarity, is itself a goal of the interaction. Its future impact on media practices and collective action has little salience. This *is* media monitoring but it is not credibly included in the practice envisaged by those who routinely use the term. For media monitoring is assumed to be serious in its intent, systematic in its execution and to be capable of claiming a legitimacy based upon some attempted invocation of objectivity. Thus, media monitoring starts from an anticipated impact; namely that it will change media practice. It starts from an assumption of privileged awareness and insight amongst those who would carry it out. And, explicitly or implicitly it lays claim to an appropriate methodology that is able to reveal the obscured or contested *truth*. Media monitoring is always a form of political intervention.

If this is so, we may reasonably ask who has the temerity to carry out media monitoring on behalf of whom? Starting from concrete instances reveals a great deal about this activity. In the UK, political parties recurrently carry out monitoring of the coverage of the BBC, accusing it of being politically partisan in its news reporting. Norman Tebbit in the Conservative Thatcher era was famously exercised by this issue and in 2002 the anti-European faction of MPs in the British parliament commissioned research on the BBC's coverage of the launch of the euro currency. In the US Accuracy in Media (AIM) is funded and supported by fundamentalist Christian groups whilst Fairness and Accuracy in Reporting has radically different politics and a different support base. The World Association of Christian Communication in 2000 monitored the gender patterns in news media in seventy countries on 1 February, 2000 (see Who Makes the News www.wacc.org.uk/index1.htm). In Denmark a small but vociferous minority ethnic organization Media Watch routinely critiques specific news stories. And, of course, academics worldwide pursue small and large projects of media monitoring on a wide range of topics.

One reasonable conclusion which may be drawn from such an ad hoc review is that very frequently a few people claim to act in the interests of whole categories of people (women, political interests, minority ethnic communities, the disabled and so on) in initiating, funding or executing specific monitoring exercises. This raises the question of the mechanisms for, and degree of, accountability such actors have to those they claim to represent. Additionally, it invites a complementary analysis of the means of communication between these actors and those in whose interest they claim to act. And finally, it raises important questions about the adequacy of the mode of dissemination put in place to optimize the impact of the monitoring undertaken.

Evaluating the adequacy and impact of media monitoring is an underdeveloped art, but we may start by locating the whole process of media monitoring within the general framework of the assumptions of deliberative democracy. The role of information, of publicity, in fuelling the dynamic operation of the public sphere is widely regarded as both fundamental and self-evident (Dahlgren and Sparks, 1991). However, the nature of the democratic participation of citizens themselves remains highly problematic, and the subject of much contemporary speculation (Kymlicka and Norman, 2000). Equally, the 'proper' organization of democracy in order to guarantee descriptive representation in shaping public discourse is far from consensually agreed (Mansbridge, 2000). And, assumptions about the 'standards of reasonableness' which should guide the subsequent dialogues remain elusively multiple in theory and barely identifiable in practice (Williams, 2000). Consequently, we should at least not assume an extant normative framework in coming to judge the adequacy of media monitoring. There is, in fact, a necessary prior research task which is to reveal the salient assumptions of the role of information and the nature of the public sphere employed by those engaged in media monitoring (see the discussion of the public sphere in Chapter 9).

This would almost certainly reveal an interesting array of elitist assumptions as proponents of specific monitoring initiatives *de facto* claim the authority and status of 'organic intellectuals' (Showstack Sassoon, 2000). More simply, they see themselves as practically advancing the interests of particular groups in contesting their disadvantaged location in a specific political context. For academics this comes relatively easily as an extension of their class and cultural location in society. They are the guardians of arcane knowledge, specialist techniques and have a privileged relationship to revealing truth (Bourdieu, 1988). For politicians and those who are self-declared as politically active, participation in media monitoring has a double-edged virtue. It enables them to declare *a priori* conclusions blessed with their tactical affiliation to a species of scientific method. Additionally, it is an activity that is likely, however temporarily, to sustain them in the public eye. Minority ethnic activists may logically be located within either of those categories, or may be instances of a distinctive fusion of the two.

Identifying the elitist credentials of a great deal of media monitoring is not the basis for an inevitable dismissal of this activity as flatulent self-indulgence. It is, however, a reminder of how any instance of media monitoring should be carefully examined in the context of its national political and cultural locale. It is also one variable which points to the difficulty of effectively carrying out meaningful international comparative studies. If, in the context of the concerns of this text, one function of media monitoring is to contribute to the eradication of racism and xenophobia then it must be rooted in concrete realities. It is consequently always appropriate to ask 'who is pursuing monitoring on behalf of whom; what does the monitoring aim to reveal; who are the intended audiences; is the methodology appropriate to these tasks and is a viable dissemination strategy in place?'[6]

Fundamental to addressing the above questions is the nature of the accountability of the media monitoring personnel to those whose interests they claim to represent. Demonstrating accountability is far removed in many instances from claiming authority. Nor is an absence of expressed disquiet from the claimed constituency a demonstration of adequate support. Self-governing and self-directed exercises in small scale media monitoring by poorly funded minority ethnic organizations are one strategic response to the frequently loose link between the media monitoring project and the marginalized minority population. Very often the money for large-scale media monitoring of ethnic representation is available from majority ethnic funders and is disproportionately accessed by majority ethnic researchers. This is not of itself a sufficient basis for rejecting outright the works of such majority ethnic researchers. (In those terms these two authors would be damned.) But the political economy of media monitoring is as important a topic for research as is the political economy of the media themselves. Many current initiatives examining ethnic representation in the media have, as an element in their *raison d'être,* an explicit attempt to close the gap between the research collectivity and the beneficiary ethnic community. By forging links between appropriate NGOs, research groups and media professionals, such initiatives aspire to build up lines of communication between key players in developing media monitoring as a legitimate instrument for changing practice.

The networks and alliances appropriate to any particular project will have a specific character. Depending upon the aims of the project, key players will be required who can facilitate access, provide contextual insight, aid analysis, facilitate dissemination or fight for implementation in practice. This will differ from project to project and in an international comparative project may differ from country to country. This reality underlines the necessity of the researcher recognizing that the exploitation and efficacy of the research is not solely in their hands.

Such alliances also address a further critical aspect of media monitoring; namely, the adequacy of the mechanisms for disseminating findings. Given the policy ambitions of media monitoring, an ability to convert data, and its analysis, into persuasive texts for specifically identified target audiences is a logically necessary component of the process. In all too many instances it is possible to argue that this element of media monitoring has received less detailed consideration in the planning phase and emerges as an ad hoc scramble by a monitoring group depleted of energy, and now devoid of funds. It is arguable that media monitoring must at a very early stage of its planning explicitly map the intended final dissemination phase; for both the sampling frame, the methodology and the mode of write up should be appropriate to the persuasive engagement with the intended audiences. As activists know, a single example, forthrightly exploited and vigorously defended, may have a greater impact than an extensive body of data subject to sophisticated factor analysis and theorized with elegant erudition. A great deal of media monitoring is avidly consumed by those who need no persuasion on the politics of the issue at hand, and the resistant target audiences are seldom consulted about their response to the uncongenial analyses. Media monitoring is in quite considerable need of systematic study as opposed to partisan advocacy.

In considering such a research agenda it is tempting to speculate that the political and policy impact of media monitoring is frequently inversely proportional to the cost and sophistication of the research. Certainly, cost and the time expended on a project are two of its most defining features. Figure 1 below suggests how a range of media monitoring initiatives may be mapped into the world defined by these two variables.

Through locating media monitoring strategies in a framework defined by time and cost, it is possible to begin to sketch a logistical structure in which resources may be related to research options. The options open to potential interested parties then become more apparent. It provides an initial step towards a modelling of media monitoring wherein the pragmatic alliances that are likely to be required for particular monitoring options become more readily apparent. If this is then related to the media to be reviewed and the demography of both the intended beneficiary

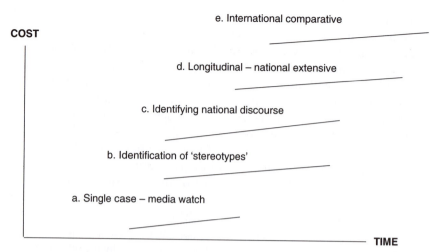

Figure 7.1 *Media Monitoring Taxonomy*

group and the intended target audience then further logistical realities will be exposed. A diverse target audience may require a range of research tools and a multi-faceted dissemination strategy. Media monitoring initiated from within a politicized marginal minority ethnic group may have highly developed internal channels of communication, access to free or non-market cost research staff, established links to media and key political players; and consequently their ambition may reasonably exceed their apparent resources. Certainly, at present, there is no reason to believe that there is a linear relationship between the resources committed to an exercise in media monitoring and its subsequent impact upon media performance.

Conclusion

In this chapter we have examined the role of codes of practice in shaping the media industry's performance in responsibly representing ethnic diversity. Such codes are in themselves expressions of particular value systems and are reflective of the culture and interests that generated them. We have found ample reason for being cautious about their potential effectiveness whilst recognizing that they do provide a benchmark for a monitoring of media performance. Media monitoring has itself been observed to be extensively practised, highly diverse, and often driven by conviction. Media monitoring has not itself been subject to adequate critical scrutiny, so that its relation to defining and policing media ethics and practices remains ambivalent and open to disputation.

Notes

1 This chapter draws on the work of Charles Husband and Yunis Alam carried out within the European Commission funded project – *Tuning in to Diversity*.

2 Whilst these grammatical distinctions within Codes of Practice are clearly discernible and may have relevance for their application we would wish to register a note of caution. To demonstrate the *fixed* meaning of such statements is almost impossible. The different values brought to the interpretation of the *denotative* meaning of codes, the very different national contexts and the pragmatics of language use in different professional communities of practice all work against a rigid interpretation of the significance of such statements.

3 Two points can be made here. One has to do with the media professional's perception of the limits that may reasonably be expected to govern the expression of the values in a code. Many journalists, for example, would seem to have a visceral fear of censorship which predisposes them to prefer codes expressed as broad statements of good practice; and to be reciprocally deeply resistant to proscriptive guidelines. Whilst affirming values of responsibility, decency and honesty they are unwilling to have non-professionals tell them how to do their job. Of course, given the many instances of state intervention in the operation of the media such resistances have their own historical basis. Secondly, given the analysis of the pervasive capacity of racist ideology to feed into everyday consciousness it is evidently the case that the values framing media codes may themselves be vulnerable to partisan interpretation when the subjects in a particular story are from a different ethnic community to the media professional. Journalists are not inoculated against the foibles of 'the limits of tolerance'; nor against the rewards of refusing to be 'politically correct'. (See Chapter 1)

4 The more extensive discussion of communities of practice in Chapter 9 makes clearer the interface between organizational features of media production (including institutional structures and managerial ideologies), and the attempt of media workers to construct and defend their professional identities. It is the dynamic interplay of this range of variables within a specific location that institutional racism emerges with the normative reasonableness that renders it invisible.

5 The desirability of nuanced multi-level programs of media monitoring sits in stark contrast to the typically *ad hoc* manner in which particular media monitoring initiatives emerge. There is a real scope for coherent analyses of the political economy of media monitoring.

6 It is a nice irony that one of the principal vehicles for the dissemination of the outcome of media monitoring are the media themselves. All the familiar issues regarding the ownership and control of the media; and of access to the media, thus become peculiarly relevant when optimizing the practical impact of media monitoring is at issue.

7 Pressurizing the Media Industry: Achievements and Limitations*

This chapter[1] focuses on a major series of attempts made over the period 1992–2002 to pressure the US television entertainment industry into more varied and richer representations of people of color. As well as the work of minority-ethnic advocacy groups, it addresses attempts by members of the professional guilds in Hollywood to create initiatives framed with the same goals in view.[2]

The focus on entertainment, rather than news, is not to downplay the importance of the latter for a democracy, especially a functioning multi-racial democracy. However, democracy belongs to the imagination and emotions as much as it does equally to reason and logical debate. If we cannot *feel* a multi-racial democracy we are very unlikely to plan it or even care much about it except in a purely defensive mode. Furthermore, at least within the USA, the appalling decline in the quality of television news – the public's primary information source – means that for some time now the real, as opposed to the hypothetical or vaunted, contribution of the news media to democracy has turned nearly to water. Therefore efforts to address entertainment, while only part of the necessary movement of public opinion to develop more democracy-friendly media, were and are more urgent than ever.

These efforts were not unprecedented. The NAACP (the National Association for the Advancement of Colored People) in its first decade protested *Birth of a Nation*, the 1915 feature film demeaning African Americans and glorifying the Ku Klux Klan, and the televised version of *Amos 'n' Andy* in the early 1950s. Noriega (2001) has provided a detailed account of how Latino activists protested the TV advertising campaign for the *Frito Bandido* in the 1960s, out of which emerged an independent Latino cinema movement. The 1981 New York City campaign against the shooting of the feature film *Fort Apache, the Bronx*, which framed Latino and Black residents of the Bronx as modern-day Apaches (thus succeeding in producing three different lampoons at once), was another significant moment in the generation of a media policy on 'race' by the public (Pérez, 1985). But during and after the last decade of the 20th century, the

---

*Mary Beltrán, Jane Chi-Hyun Park, Henry Puente, Sharon Ross and John Downing

sustained level of protest and generation of specific *practical* proposals for effective change, was something new.

In our view, this experience (continuing to the time of writing) is a very important one to assess – although, naturally, various individuals and groups will evaluate it in different ways – because of the global as well as national influence of US television, and because of its intimate interface with Hollywood's equally influential film industry. The assessment needs to be critical, not in order to whip ourselves into an orgy of fatalism, but in order to hone the most intelligently devised approaches we can muster to reorient media industries in constructive and stimulating directions. So while we shall not be able to answer all of the questions we pose in the next paragraph, each one is important.

The specificity of the USA needs acknowledging from the start. Many nations have culture ministries which frame cultural development policies, while in the USA, cultural policy on a mass level is developed by media corporations, and public support for the arts is frequently a football in a political contest between the puritanical conservative right on the one hand, and a whole spectrum of dissimilar but somewhat dissident positions on the other. How far does or even can the US experience of contesting industry practices represent a model for such goals elsewhere? Was the movement to challenge industry practices faced with inevitable structural limitations *however* successful it might prove in some directions? What would constitute necessary additional initiatives in complementary spheres of activity, such as education? Is the growth of national and international media oligopoly an institutionalized barrier to constructive change (McChesney, 1997), or do contemporary niche marketing and advertising strategies herald a diversification of media representation, at least for minority-ethnic groups with moderately affluent sectors (Tharp, 2001)? Are public service media more likely to be amenable to these shifts in direction?

Media monitoring, discussed in the previous chapter, is one attempt at public influence over major media institutions, which can be used to address 'racial' and ethnic content, and beyond content, professional practices and procedures. We shall see that monitoring was also a significant element in the overall strategy minority-ethnic advocacy groups and some of the guilds adopted in Hollywood, but only in conjunction with other methods too.

From 1992 through 2002, relations between minority-ethnic advocacy groups and the commercial television industry were mostly conflictual. We should state at the outset our view that while this strife was not unproductive, neither did it come close to improving the level or quality of screen representations, or of behind-the-screen employment, of people of color, such that US citizens, the TV industry, or the advocacy groups could or should feel remotely satisfied. Nonetheless, however we may evaluate them, these fairly sustained protests have in our view been far preferable to the previous decades of only intermittent public critique. For the first time the issue has been *continually* on the table through the advocacy groups' assaults on the Hollywood citadel. They have begun to frame a media policy for the public in this arena.

Yet to speak in terms of the industry as a citadel, accurately as it may convey the feelings of alienated citizen-viewers longing for diverse and exploratory programming, also fails to capture the intricate complexity and potential porousness of its decision-making processes. This second observation is not out of kilter with the first, that eleven years of strife from 1992–2002 were insufficient to steer the Hollywood liner on a different course. To understand why this apparent paradox is not one, namely the interactions between corporate cultural policy made from the top and the plethora of microscopic processes which enact media policy, we need first to take into account some basic features of the US commercial television industry, which also distinguish it in some ways from analogous industries in other countries.

Major Overall Features of the US Television Industry

There has been an increasingly competitive industrial situation ever since the advent of the Fox Channel in 1985, challenging the previous ABC, CBS and NBC oligopoly. As of the time of writing, this development has gone much further. Some cable channels have become established and quite prolific program producers, and there are two new mini-networks (WB and UPN). All this is combined with ongoing national and international mergers and acquisitions in the television and media industries.

To actually produce shows, there is an amoeba-like process of program production parceled out over time to thousands of different production units, with the result that a vast volume of lower-level hiring and script decisions quite often do not depend on the same people two seasons running of the same show (over and above the normal occupational mobility of Hollywood creative professionals between network, cable and movie companies). Naturally, there is strong overall financial control from on high, and some top executives have a reputation for minutely viewing the product and micro-managing it, but continuous detailed intervention from the very top is virtually impossible.

Control from the top is also exercised in general through the multiple filters through which any program must pass – talent agencies, focus groups, executive scrutiny from marketing, legal, and standards and practices departments, script meetings – before it sees the light of day (Gitlin, 1994). Corporate executives frequently make very rapid decisions on killing shows, even after they have been broadcast, on the basis of their interpretation of the initial ratings' promise. The division between the administrative and the creative wings of entertainment media, as of advertising, is a key one.

Just in case any readers should be in doubt, there is a normal dominance of business criteria over creative criteria in instances where they clash. It has been mooted in jest that Hollywood would film Marx and Engels' *The Communist Manifesto* if convinced that money could be made from it (though no doubt with some luscious starlets as Engels' live-in partners, and another as Marx's maid with whom he had a child out of wedlock). Technically speaking, if some top Hollywood executives judged that well-scripted and richly portrayed films concerning minority-ethnic group stories would be lucrative, their policies and procedures would quickly adapt. Some long-term industry insiders indeed argue that savvier marketing diagnoses are almost all that is needed to reposition industry priorities.

The very high stakes involved lead in very many ways to caution and the repetition of tried formulas. On the other hand, stale programming at some hard-to-forecast tipping point equals financial death. There are therefore simultaneous contrary pressures toward conservatism and toward finding a *successful* new formula. Given these parameters of intense uncertainty, informal networks of creative professionals are the stuff of daily life in Hollywood. They supply each other with leads and information for employment, or are able – like the 'show-runners', for example, who manage a given project's creative facets – from time to time to hire people with whom they have a prior history of working well. These individuals in turn may be able to bring in 'their' people to work in their unit, if they are not contracted at the time. This both cements relationships and offers a level of confidence to such professionals in what is in reality a high-risk gamble, that the project will work and so justify future contracts (rather than be the topic of negative gossip on the circuit and a dreaded albatross when looking for the next contract). The consequence of all these vectors for those people outside such informal networks – historically and currently typically including people of color and all women – is that access to jobs and the establishment of a career is a *great* deal more arduous still than for the average White male professional. For whom it is already often remarkably hard.

More tenacious even than specific acts of discrimination, of which there are plenty, are the professional and organizational routines that constitute the daily world of commercial television entertainment production and sales. Given the fierce competitiveness of the industry, there is a great deal of resistance to any sort of 'leg-up' in employment that is perceived not to be based on merit, indeed to anything that could be dismissed as 'affirmative action'.

Cronyism, however, hiring people you are familiar with and trust, is not perceived by most members of the Anglo majority as affirmative action, despite its significant role in perpetuating 'racial' inequalities in the industry. It is an insurance in favor of the individual who is making the hires (1) for the future when return favors will likely be needed, and (2) gives confidence that the already known individual's contribution will be well performed – which will mean the reputation of both hirer and hiree will not be a hindrance to getting the next contract. In other words, it is a combination often of a personal comfort zone with someone of the same ethnic group, and reassurance from prior experience that that individual has the professional talent and/or personal style to function effectively, and to not act as a drag on the entire production unit's performance. Mentoring practices and cronyism overlap in significant ways, in that mentors also tend to choose people of the same ethnic group to help. The contribution of those who do not mentor on this basis is critically important for the diversity of the industry.

Thus to sum up so far, and taking this whole array of forces into account, it should be clear already that advocacy group pressure is not and never will be *sufficient* to the task of effecting comprehensive change, precisely because of the industry's structural characteristics. The advocacy groups cannot be part of the daily decision-making and organizational process. There is no way they will be allowed that type of involvement in managerial prerogatives. Therefore they are compelled to be reactive. At the same time, this does not mean they have no clout at all, as we shall see. They are a necessary and in principle very praiseworthy part of the picture.

We will next focus in on some specific current dimensions of the industry which affect the quantitative and qualitative representation of people of color on the screen, as opposed to these overall structural dynamics.

Industry Patterns and Trends Impacting on People of Color

There is a huge lack of ethnic and racial diversity among network executives, particularly with respect to Latino and Native American Indian executives. There is also a lack of 'cultural competence' among many network executives to address issues of 'race' and ethnicity – many of them, on a daily basis, only have and only ever have had contact with Latino domestics and gardeners, or lower level secretarial and janitorial staff of color. There is also sometimes anxiety over in-depth discussion of these issues, with people actually out of their depth and refusing to admit it in case they have to confess ignorance.

There is a singular lack of accurate information about marketing issues and viewing patterns of particular ethnic groups. Latino audiences have for long been significantly under-counted by the Nielsen TV ratings system. Equally, there is a stereotype problem in part fostered by the Spanish-language networks, who like to claim all Latinos as their viewers, and in part coming from network executives who assume this is the case, thereby letting the executives off the hook of taking Latino audiences seriously.

In 2002, quantitatively speaking,[3] African Americans for the very first time in history appeared on the screen in approximate ratio to their percentage of the population. However, though welcome, this had no necessary bearing on the significance of their roles within the show or to the quality of the script. These might be walk-on and ensemble parts, not continuing characters, and in no case guaranteed the portrayals were credible or interesting. There is also a very strong tendency, one with deep historical roots, to bunch African Americans into sitcoms, comic roles, and stand-up comedy shows (Gray, 1995).

Quantitatively, the other minority-ethnic groups were not even within hailing distance of African American televisual representation, the situation being numerically most objectionable of all for Latinos, given they constituted 13 per cent of the US population. If included at all, Latino, Asian American and Native American actors were typically hired as ensemble or guest actors.

This had definite implications for the work of the various advocacy groups, whose constituencies' immediate needs were clearly at different levels: from basic inclusion (Native Americans, Latinos, Asian Americans, Arab Americans) to the quality of representation (African Americans).

These figures inevitably also raise questions about initial pipelines into the industry. While there is no doubt that the industry needs a major overhaul in this regard, it does not bear unique responsibility. The educational system, both in general and in terms of programs of study which could feed into jobs in the industry (everything from video and audio production on the creative side to management and marketing on the administrative side), has a huge responsibility which by and large it is not fulfilling. This does not only apply to junior colleges and universities, but also, on appropriate levels, to high schools and even earlier. Only some universities, community colleges and schools with media arts programs also offer the needed practical information about the entertainment business, industry internships, scholarships or other options. Nor do they often promote visits by industry professionals, especially by those with a commitment to a diverse industry labor force. The assumption that Hollywood is indeed a White citadel is common, and talented students of color do pre-censor themselves from getting involved. A visit from a professional reaffirming that however difficult the path, it can be taken, can have a dramatic impact on willingness to face up to the risks and motivation to push ahead.

Sometimes, particularly on the administrative side of the industry, law schools, business schools and advertising programs will provide a generic foundation on which industry entrants will base their specific expertise acquired on the job. This is not just relevant to a general abstract goal of seeing different faces in all departments of the media industries: so many creative decisions are effectively taken on the business side of the industries, that representation of people of color in discussions and planning on that side are particularly important.

All indications are that the various branches of the academy could and should outperform their overall current level of achievement in preparing minority-ethnic students for television and film industry careers, as well as for preparing all students to work effectively within an increasingly diverse workforce and marketplace. A critical national evaluation of all these gaps in educational provision has yet to be undertaken.

There is overall a dearth of discussion and/or collaboration between academics and TV industry professionals, as well as between academia and advocacy groups, despite goals held apparently in common. Misperceptions, mistrust and a certain mutual scornfulness are rife. Structured opportunities for mutual debate and education would be of great advantage.

The education system too, however, does not bear unique responsibility for the pipeline. High school drop-out figures among young Latinos and Native Americans cannot only be laid at educators' doors, but they obviously have a seriously negative impact on access to jobs of many kinds.

At the same time, the roles of the industry's own internal pipelines, its training programs, its provision of networking opportunities, its encouragement of mentorship beyond the ethnic frontier, are all vital beyond the initial entry point. Industry programs are highly vulnerable to cost-cutting and to changes in personnel at the very top, and require energetic outreach to minority-ethnic publics to ensure equal access for all in practice. Some, like Disney/ABC's year-long Writers Program, which began by being targeted to people of color, no longer are, and now depend very much on successful outreach for their utility to screenwriters of color. Outreach visits and programs in a country the size of the USA, however, are time-consuming and cost some money – not much by the standards of Hollywood expenditures, but a tasty morsel for the bean-counters.

The other influence on the internal pipeline has been the industry Guilds (the Directors Guild of America, the Screen Actors Guild, the Writers Guild of America), which have expended a variety of efforts with respect to diversity issues. Institutionally, their concerns are related to jobs rather than quality of representation. However, they have in recent years offered valuable programs, such as networking and the publication of minority-ethnic employment figures (the DGA), training workshops (the WGA), and – more intermittently – sponsored content research (SAG).

However, the Guilds have limited powers to affect change outside this realm, as the DGA found out when the courts bluntly refused it permission to lead a class action suit on ethnic diversity employment issues in the industry. (The decision was of a piece with the visceral anti-labor unionism which has characterized the US state for almost all of its history, and no doubt the minority-ethnic component of the DGA's attempt was hardly an advantage.)

This has been an exceptionally rapid overview of the US industry and of the roles and absences of people of color within it, and will likely leave insiders somewhat frustrated, but was necessary in order to set the scene for our primary topic, an account[4] of the tussles over ethnicity and 'race' that took place from 1992 through 2002. We will begin by a short overview of the minority-ethnic advocacy groups.

'Vinegar' or 'Honey'?

There are two fundamentally different, often opposed, strategies, summarized by this epigram which is sometimes used in conversation on the topic among activists. There are of course variants of both. The 'vinegar' approach – and it should be said that this is an epigram favored by its opponents – consists of being publicly strident, through press conferences, the issuance of denunciatory monitoring reports, demonstrations and the like. The 'honey' approach sees the industry's executives as having numerous priorities, and as most likely being simply alienated by threats and accusations, not least from groups which do not really have the resources to back them up with any action. Thus the appropriate strategy in this view is not to lambast the industry, but to praise it publicly for the times it does perform creditably, and meanwhile try to develop positive working relations with the more open-minded and thereby to massage the decision-making process in a positive direction, but off-camera.

It would take more research than has been done to date to prove it, but it is at least plausible that the stridency of the 'vinegar' groups makes the approaches of the 'honey' groups more attractive than they would otherwise be. They may not ultimately be antithetical, irritating as this thought might be to some of the more insistent advocates of either position.

The head offices of some groups (the National Association for the Advancement of Colored People (NAACP), the NCLR, the Arab-American Anti-Discrimination Committee, the Hispanic Arts Foundation) are in the Washington DC region, whereas some of the other advocacy groups, particularly those which focus exclusively on media, are located in Los Angeles. Obviously, three thousand miles apart, the potential was there for differences in focus and emphasis, with East Coast groups normally being oriented toward Capitol Hill and a variety of issues, not only media, and Angelenos focused on the immediacies of their city's industry.[5]

Advocacy groups are typically under-funded, especially regarding the resources needed to conduct effective public relations and advertising. Some, for example the Media Action Network for Asian Americans, receive zero funding. It is easy to critique their weak impact if this factor is not taken into account. In part also precisely because of lack of funding, as well as their absence from the industry's daily internal decision-making processes, advocacy groups focus for the most part on reactive strategies.

Within the spectrum of minority-ethnic advocacy groups, the NAACP has held a dominant role, both as the oldest such group, the largest, and as the single African American advocacy group. By contrast, there are multiple and sometimes mutually conflicting Latino media advocacy groups (NCLR, the National Hispanic Foundation for the Arts, the Imagen Foundation, Nosotros, the Latino Entertainment Media Institute, the National Hispanic Media Coalition). As one result, network executives have been able to choose which group with whom to work. It is not immediately evident that the National Latino Media Council, which was formed to try to bridge these divisions (and has an even larger set of Latino organizations as members), has managed so far to create a single effective voice.

Native American, Asian American and Arab American advocacy groups have a relatively weak voice. Pacific Asian Americans dominated Asian American advocacy activity until the beginning of the 2000s, but there are signs as the decade continues that South Asian Americans are beginning to make their presence felt.[6]

A major weapon deployed by some advocacy groups was the threat of channel boycotts, with some Latinos using the term 'brown-outs'. The ostensible objective was to signal to the advertisers that a particular channel was losing viewers because of its unresponsiveness to their concerns, in the hope that the channel executives in question would seek to act to reassure their advertisers that they would make significant moves to reassure their minority-ethnic viewers.

In reality, everyone knew that the advocacy organizations were not really generals of huge and disciplined armies of television viewers who could actually deliver on their threat. The underlying strategy was different: to make a statement which would receive publicity, and would likely have two outcomes. One, rather specific, was to get the protest amplified through one or more members of the Black and Hispanic Congressional Caucus in Washington DC, in the knowledge that the industry was always looking to Congress to help it in one way or another in the fast-changing global media environment. At the committee stage of a Bill, the position of just one legislator on a key House committee could make a great deal of difference to the framing of legal changes. The other, more diffuse but still with some traction attached to it, was that TV organizations usually had a smaller or larger raft of problems of various kinds to deal with, and often did not relish having them increased by public accusations of ethnic favoritism.

Research was also a tool utilized, with intermittent publication of in-house or commissioned reports documenting the quantitative under-representation, and sometimes the qualitative misrepresentation, of people of color in entertainment television. Some of these reports are referenced below. On one level it might be argued that reports of this kind simply gather dust like other sociological studies, and have a very short (if any) impact in an industry focused on today and tomorrow. At the same time, they represent systematically gathered data, not simply individual complaints and impressions, and their cumulative growth over time can provide ever more weighty arguments by using comparisons, for example that the industry has not progressed any further over the past X number of years, or has retreated to its dismal performance of X years back. (This recapitulates some of the discussion in our chapter on media monitoring.)

In 2000 a major new step was undertaken in bringing together the concerns of all minority-ethnic groups under one umbrella, namely the establishment of the Multi-Ethnic Coalition. This consisted of advocacy groups representing African Americans, Latinos, Asian Americans and Native Americans, with the Coalition's chair rotating every six months between these groups.

The MEC proceeded to start releasing quarterly public monitoring 'report cards' on industry performance, comparing companies' content output over the previous quarter. It is safe to say that most industry executives were less than fully appreciative of this ongoing contribution to debate. In news terms, they gave reporters a predictably recurring story to use at intervals, a boon to those who have to feed the Moloch of daily or weekly news, especially in *The Los Angeles Times* and the weekly and daily versions of the *Hollywood Reporter* and *Variety*.

However, in 2002 the NAACP withdrew from endorsing these report cards, thereby reducing their significance in some industry executives' eyes. The NAACP's reason was, plausibly, that simple inclusion statistics no longer served its constituency's purpose. Given what we have noted already, namely that quantitatively African Americans had reached for the time being a presence in approximate proportion to their numbers in the US population, a simple quantitative statement – for that is what the 'report cards' offered – did not address the continuing and even more complex problem of the *quality* of representation. Thus a purely quantitative measure could reduce pressure for further and much-needed change. Whereas for the other minority-ethnic groups, the 'first base' of being visible *at all* was still an urgent goal. In news media and industry perception the Multi-Ethnic Coalition tended to be dominated by the NAACP, and episodes such as this, virtually inevitable in the complex negotiations of coalition politics, tended to signal the accuracy of that perception.

Let us now summarize the main industry responses to these challenges.

Television Industry Responses

Industry executive responses ranged over a considerable spectrum, including dismissing or simply ignoring specific advocacy group claims, and promising to run a minority-ethnic themed show and not doing so. The networks have struck countless development deals with actors and producers of color in the last decade, which have never made it out of the development stage. They have also occasionally funded a minority-ethnic themed show and programmed it in order to reduce advocacy group pressure, but then taken the show off after a few weeks. They have sponsored or taken part in special one-off highly publicized seminars on minority-ethnic issues. In 2000 there was a sudden rash of appointments of Diversity Vice-Presidents, almost all of them African Americans (prompting speculation that the NAACP was a primary target of this move even though it initially appeared to be a response to the formation of the Multi-Ethnic Coalition). Estimation of their institutional efficacy is the matter of continuing debate among advocates of change, and this difference in evaluation may correlate with activists' overall adhesion to 'vinegar' or to 'honey' tactics. Consistently, however, corporate spokespeople have announced or repeated their firm's *unwavering* commitment to the fair employment and proper representation of people of color.

In some cases, this was followed up by actions, such as setting up training and recruitment programs for minority-ethnic writers and directors. A particular example is the energetic outreach activity to high schools and communities nationally organized within Disney/ABC, whose top executives, as of 2001–2, had gained a reputation as being committed to this goal. ABC has also established a program to foster minority-ethnic business executives. Over 2002, the networks established talent searches and showcases through which to promote the hiring of Latino, Asian American and Native American actors.

ABC/Disney and Fox were the most advanced of the Big Four networks in the early 2000s with respect to long-range diversity plans and a variety of initiatives to this end. Cable channels such as Showtime, HBO and Nickelodeon had also made some very serious commitments in this direction (it was rumored that HBO's initiatives had come about through quiet but insistent internal pressure from its employees of color). CBS was at that time widely regarded by advocates as least concerned to promote constructive change.

We will turn now to a blow-by-blow account of indicative challenges and industry responses developed over this decade of stepped-up public activity.

Key Moments in Advocacy Group Activity, 1992–2002

1992 The tendentially maverick Hollywood NAACP chapter issued a public 16-point proposal for improving minority-ethnic employment and on-screen image, the first in what would be a continuing series of reports of this kind by various groups. The National Hispanic Media Coalition tried to block the sale of Spanish language TV channel Univisión to a consortium representing Mexican TV interests. That attempt, although it failed, pinpointed the failure of *all* television channels to represent US Latinos, since Univisión was – and largely still is – using the USA as an after-market for Mexican programs.

1993 The NAACP publicly protested media coverage of Michael Jackson and other Black celebrities and announced it would conduct a study of media representations of African Americans. The Arab-American Anti-Discrimination Committee publicly protested a CBS show lampooning a wealthy Gulf Arab.

1994 The NAACP attacked News Corp owner Rupert Murdoch's right to a US broadcast license. The Reverend Jesse Jackson founded the Rainbow Coalition Commission on Fairness in the Media, and called for boycotting networks with bad minority-ethnic representations. The National Council of La Raza issued a report tracking Latino under-representation in TV since the 1950s. The Directors Guild of America founded its African American Advisory Steering Committee.

1995 Forty-five Latino organizations announced a boycott of ABC for its failure to include Latinos in its programs, focusing on its president's fail-ure to deliver on his promise 19 months previously to include a Latino-themed show the previous fall season. Criticism of the Rainbow Coalition Commission's inadequate efforts surfaced among other advocacy groups.

1996 The National Council of La Raza publicized a report it had commis-sioned showing a fractional if stereotyped improvement in Latino repre-sentation, but an ongoing drastic under-representation. Alex Nogales, director of the National Hispanic Media Coalition, publicly demanded a high-placed Latino executive in ABC/Disney reporting directly to its President on diversity issues, before the NHMC would reduce its public critiques.

1997 The Hollywood NAACP chapter protested the representation of African Americans on the Fox, WB and UPN channels, but without clearing its protest with the rest of the NAACP, and was forced to retract some of its initial positions. The National Hispanic Media Coalition announced a boycott of ABC/Disney, but was only joined by some other Latino advocacy groups and conflict surfaced between different Latino advocacy groups over the right stance toward ABC/Disney. The National Hispanic Foundation for the Arts was founded in Washington DC by members of the Congressional Hispanic Caucus and some prominent Latino actors, with a mission defined differently from the other advocacy groups, namely one of working within the industry rather than attacking it from the outside. This was the strategy equally pursued by the Imagen Awards Foundation, started in 1985 by the National Council of Christians and Jews. The NAACP formed a Los Angeles branch to offset its Hollywood chapter.

1998 A Federal Appeals court threw out FCC rules encouraging industry hiring of women and people of color, dating back to 1968. Despite FCC Chairman Kennard's efforts to repair the damage, neither the courts nor the National Association of Broadcasters showed interest in supporting him. Reports were issued both by Emeritus Annenberg School for Communication Dean George Gerbner, and by the new organization Children Now, documenting serious failures in the quantity and quality of minority-ethnic representation on television.

1999 The NAACP publicly attacked the industry for the absence of minority-ethnic actors. With the NAACP in the lead, the Multi-Ethnic Coalition began to be formed. The NAACP threatened a boycott of a network channel, which it later withdrew, and Latino organizations called for a one-week 'brown-out' of the networks. Two further studies were published, one by TN Media showing a numerical over-representation of Black characters on TV in ratio to their proportion of the public, and a huge under-representation of Latino characters; and the other by the Directors Guild, indicating a fall in the number of minority-ethnic directors. A major *Los Angeles Times* article (9 November 1999) by Greg Braxton on the industry's shortcomings in this arena drew considerable attention.

2000 ABC, CBS, Fox and NBC announced agreements with the Multi-Ethnic Coalition that they would hire more minority-ethnic individuals, ratifying these in separate memoranda of understanding. Diversity Vice-Presidents and similar roles began to be established at the networks. Nearly all the individuals appointed were African American women. US Labor Secretary Alexis Herman met with studio heads to discuss improving 'racial' diversity in entertainment. Children Now issued its second report, indicating that African Americans were most likely to feature in sitcoms, Asian Americans in drama, and Latinos in secondary roles (when individuals belonging to either of the two latter groups appeared at all). The report also noted that minority-ethnic characters were not so well developed as majority-ethnic ones. TN Media published a further study indicating sharp differences between Black and White television viewing patterns. The Screen Actors Guild released 1999 data indicating that while generally jobs were fewer, the proportion of minority-ethnic actors hired rose that year. The Directors Guild of America published statistics indicating a drop in the number of minority-ethnic directors the previous year.

2001 The NAACP and the NCLR presidents publicly criticized the networks' continued failures to improve 'racial' representation on television. The

Multi-Ethnic Coalition expressed its dissatisfaction with the Fall 2001 programming. Twenty-four network executives met with MEC leaders. SAG and ABC instituted the first showcase for minority-ethnic actors. Former SAG affirmative action official Peter Nguyen filed suit against the Guild alleging racial discrimination, and former affirmative action director Patricia Heisser Metoyer also filed suit alleging she had been placed on leave when she complained the Guild's statistics of its own 'racial' demographics were being falsified. Later in the year the SAG human resources director, targeted in these suits, was fired. Reports during the year in *Variety,* the *Los Angeles Times* and from Children Now concurred on the networks' continuing failures to improve their diversity.

2002 (through the end of August): ABC, Fox and NBC instituted new minority-ethnic talent programs. ABC greenlighted a $30 million mini-series on American Indian myths and legends, though contemporary portrayals of Native American life were still wanting. The Multi-Ethnic Coalition issued its report cards, but without the NAACP's participation. Some executives interpreted this rupture in the ranks as downgrading the attention they needed to pay to the MEC report cards.

Conclusions

The multi-faceted and conflictual character of these challenges to US entertainment television industry traditions indicates the range of voices and efforts going into them, and the responses indicate that the industry is not entirely deaf. Both findings signify progress. Indeed, we would argue that there is a substantial constituency within the industry, both on the creative and the business sides, which would like to see constructive change, and that this constituency needs nurturing and empowerment, composed as it is of individuals who often have insufficient mutual knowledge or support – and are also often working very intensive hours. Such a constituency, working in loose alliance with advocacy groups, with the Guilds' programs in this arena, with educators at all levels, and with academic researchers, could provide the detailed sense for the realistic options available even within the commercial TV entertainment industry for constructive and stimulating programming. Too often the fatalistic determinism of the cash nexus blinds even the willing to the existence of realistic options.

How to stimulate and develop this extensive alliance and networking would represent a major media policy undertaking on the public's part, one certainly in synch with a democratic culture if not the structures of democracy as they currently operate. It would represent a preferential tilt toward the public and away from untrammeled corporate decision-making. Although the discussion of this move would require much more space than we have here, and considerable fresh action-research, one extra reality must be noted. The roles of the advertising industry – either by silence or intervention, a huge potential influence – must be included in any assessment of the prospects for constructive change. Historically, that industry has been one of the very Whitest of bastions within the culture industries of the USA. There are signs that some forces within it are reconsidering the realities they have long taken for granted, and that change may slowly be emerging there too. But without some elements of the advertising industry also involved in some ways, the initiative we have sketched would be seriously weakened.

Notes

1 The research on which this chapter is based was carried out with a grant from the Education, Media, Arts and Culture Division of the Ford Foundation (now the Knowledge, Creativity and Freedom Division). Gratitude is due the Foundation for its support, but the views and findings here do not necessarily represent those of the Foundation or its officers.

2 The major minority-ethnic advocacy groups are listed further down in the chapter, but two of the largest and longest established are the National Association for the Advancement of Colored People (NAACP), principally representing African Americans, and the National Council of La Raza (NCLR), representing Latinos. Their remit is across the board, not just in relation to media. The professional guilds are long-established in Hollywood: the Writers Guild of America, the Directors Guild, and the Screen Actors Guild. They perform a number of the functions of a labor union, but also of a professional association.

3 For annual surveys of the representation of people of color on US television, beginning in 1999, see the Fall Colors reports on the website of the organization Children Now: www.childrennow.org. The research reports from this organization, based in Oakland, California, have contributed greatly to public discussion of these issues within the industry and on its penumbra, as well as in classrooms: a model of research contribution to the goals under discussion.

4 This account is based upon the study of *The Los Angeles Times*, *Hollywood Reporter* and *Variety* for the period in question, supplemented with interviews with advocacy group activists.

5 An example of the dislocation that may emerge between the two sites is the role of the Hollywood chapter of the NAACP, which issued one of the first of such reports in 1992 denouncing the industry for its failures in relation to people of color. As the decade moved on, members of the Hollywood chapter from time to time would make public statements seemingly on behalf of the parent organization, but without apparently getting them approved in advance at NAACP headquarters in Baltimore.

6 By contrast with these groups, Jewish Americans have sometimes been ascribed quite extraordinary influence over Hollywood, in part because of their historically strong presence within the entertainment industry, in part by anti-Zionist groups, on the ground that Jews in the industry have been accused of using their positions to bolster support for Israel. They have never, to our knowledge, been accused in recent decades of promoting Jewish-themed shows or characters, only on occasion of not having troubled to ensure that other minority-ethnic groups got a reasonable entry to the industry, or that demeaning ethnic stereotypes of other groups were avoided.

8 Communities of Practice and the Cultures of Media Production

Communities of Practice as Sites of Production

In the previous chapter we have examined attempts to pressurize the US television entertainment industry into more varied and richer representations of people of color. In this chapter we explore a more generic understanding of the institutional and professional context within which media content is generated. From this basis we then sketch a systems approach to countering racism in the media, and promotion of responsible media practice.

In the discussion of codes of practice the concept of 'communities of practice' was used in passing, but was not developed. Here we will briefly sketch a model of this concept and then employ it to explore some of the practical implications of our previous analyses. It is a concept that has recently been developed in relation to a detailed study of nurse socialization and practice, and which proved to be valuable in revealing the dynamics of identity and practice in that profession (Burkitt et al., 2001).

Lave and Wenger's (1991) account of communities of practice defines it as being comprised of any group involved in joint activities, who also reproduce the community over time by the gradual induction of new participants or learners. Thus, a community of practice is both an enduring organizational activity in which individuals work together through shared routines and interlinked skills, and it is the location where new participants in this process are socialized; where becoming a member involves learning the skills, knowledge and the values of the community. Consequently, practice and learning are inter-meshing processes in a community of practice, where both are specifically situated within the organizational and physical characteristics of the workplace. Learning in such a context is not merely a process of mastery of new knowledge, it is also learning through embodied performance that involves interaction with co-participants in joint practices. There is, in other words, an engagement with both 'discursive consciousness' and 'practical consciousness' (Giddens, 1979, 1984).

Discursive consciousness is the domain of our knowledge where cognitively available information enables us to engage in a professional practice in a manner we can describe to others: not only in terms of what we know, but also in terms of how and why we know it. It is a competence that is available to reflexive scrutiny. Knowledge of journalistic law, of the 'facts' of a story, of how to light a stage, or how to handle an editing desk might be examples of such knowledge.

Practical consciousness, on the other hand, is knowledge we cannot explain to ourselves or others. It is often based upon 'embodied' learning (Burkitt, 1999) where we have routinized professional skills as embodied performances. Thus, historically, journalists have spoken of journalists having a 'feel' for a good story. Equally, the aesthetics of lighting a set cannot be adequately reduced to technical knowledge of the profession; and a skill at manipulating the technology of an editorial process is not adequate to explain the practice that shaped the outcome. Professional competencies are very much a fusion of processes of discursive consciousness and practical consciousness that have been learned 'on the job'.

However, the development of professional competence within a community of practice is not confined to the acquisition of a specific skills base; it also involves the construction of an identity through participation in the community. Thus, professional skills are not developed in a disembodied and detached cognitive tuning. On the contrary, they are acquired in active co-participation with others, whilst being simultaneously linked with a reformulation of personal identity, within a particular community of practice.

Each community of practice has its own distinct characteristics. Each has its own organizational structure, with particular resources and staffing levels. Each has its own constraints of time, production processes and anti-cipated productivity that generate their own demands and pressures. And, each community of practice operates within the constraints of its own managerial style. Organizational factors such as these form the *institutional dimension* of communities of practice. However, as we have already noted, each community of practice is also a crucible within which individual, and shared, identities and values are negotiated. These constitute a *subjective dimension* of a community of practice.

Following the model developed by Burkitt et al. (2001) we can usefully represent these two dimensions as orthogonal axes defining a community of practice, within which any individual professional must negotiate their identity and practice.

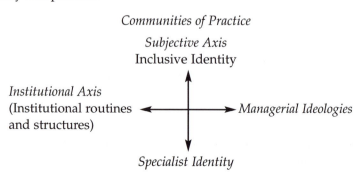

Communities of Practice

Subjective Axis
Inclusive Identity

Institutional Axis
(Institutional routines ←——————→ *Managerial Ideologies*
and structures)

Specialist Identity

In the context of nursing, the 'inclusive identity' was that of nurse. It was a generic identification with the profession and their shared commitment to 'delivering individualized holistic care'. And the 'specialist identity' was a subset of this, such as burns nurse, palliative care nurse, or accident and emergency nurse. Importantly, these specialist identities defined each other through comparison with others, and also through a common interpretation of their specialism in relation to the shared dominant values of the inclusive identity. It is possible to transpose this process to media industries where we may find inclusive identities such as journalist or film maker complemented by such specialist identities as foreign affairs correspondent, sports editor, crime reporter or financial journalist, and documentary maker, cameraman or Bollywood director. The literature on media careers and identities very fulsomely reveals just how strong such professional-personal identities can be. Importantly, they are not merely individually important as components of personal identity, they are also significantly the product of collective interaction and are sustained by peer pressure in the community of practice.

Again, in the context of nursing the institutional axis was readily identifiable in relation to the organization of health care delivery within specific specialisms, formally and informally structured in a hierarchy of power and status. Within any community of practice the specific dynamics of time, power and resources were easily revealed. The difference between the staffing ratios and the rate of patient turnover between, for example, an inner-city accident and emergency unit and a suburban hospice offered quite extreme comparisons. The managerial ideologies of the British National Health Service were readily identifiable and their impact could be traced through a very wide range of communities of practices (Traynor, 1999). The different organizational structures represented within the world of journalism offer similar substantive differences in the defining logics of news production. From the limited resources and personal management style of a small town weekly, to the extensive resources and complex management systems of global enterprises, journalists sustain their trade in very different environments.

Perhaps the key insight to be offered by this model of communities of practice lies in its capacity to reveal how individuals negotiate their professional identities within the unique pressures and constraints of a specific community of practice. Just as nurses develop specific collective workplace solutions to the *emotional labor* (Benner, 1984) of delivering care whilst handling pain, loss and disability, so too journalists develop collective strategies for handling the mismatch between their professional self-image and values and the pragmatics of meeting deadlines. We have talked above about the necessity of recognizing the specific history and dynamics of a particular diasporic community. So too, media professionals do not exist in reality as a generic category. Their current practice, and their capacity for change, are fundamentally determined by the characteristics of their unique community of practice.

Much of the literature reviewed in the chapters above has provided insight into the failings of the mass media in their engagement with ethnic diversity and with racism. A considerable part of this literature has focused specifically upon media content. Monitoring media content for its representation of ethnic diversity is a useful practical and political tool in providing a descriptive account of the status quo. And, over a period of time, repeat monitoring can reveal the nature and degree of change that may have occurred. Such data, however, of itself does not reveal the production processes, the managerial decisions or the professional ideologies that generated this data.

In order to intervene in media systems to improve the adequacy of representation of differences and the opening up of access to a rich range of media there must be a detailed understanding of the processes of media production. The virtue of this model of communities of practice is that it does not allow the production process to be reduced to the disembodied organizational structures of particular industries. Nor does it allow the evident failings of media industries to be explained away in terms of the personal pre-dispositions of individual professionals. It demands the necessary articulation of both the subjective and the institutional axes of communities of practice. It is a model that is entirely consistent with an attempt to reveal the dynamics of institutional racism in shaping media content. In principle, by approaching the challenge of improving the performance of mass media in representing diversity through the prism of communities of practice, a number of truths become apparent. Among these are:

- that individuals alone cannot be held responsible for the adequacy of media performance.
- that the actions of well-intentioned individuals can be subverted and negated by the force of institutional routines.
- that workplace cultures in the community of practice are the necessary unit of change.
- that organizational 'diversity policies', 'equal opportunities mission statements' and other such gestural expressions of benign ideological commitment must be judged by the resources committed to them – over the long term.
- that the commitment of resources in the absence of sustained managerial commitment is likely to be futile.
- that the 'professionalism' of the media worker may be both part of the problem and a potential leverage point for pursuing change.
- that strategies for change should be planned as strategies – with long-term sequencing of targeted benchmarks for change pursued through tactically sensitive interventions.

- that the interactivity of all the elements in a community of practice requires a framework of systems-thinking even when planning specific interventions.
  and most certainly of all:
- that real progress must be measured over years, not months.

Pursuing Change

There is a wide range of initiatives currently being developed and in operation that seek to actively promote responsible media practice in relation to the representation of ethnic diversity. Some are clearly addressing relevant elements of the institutional axis, employing a managerial systems approach to effecting change. Some, often promoted by professional bodies themselves, seek to work through the subjective 'professional' axis of personal ethical responsibility, and some employ variations on an integration of both (see Husband and Alam, 2002, and ter Wal, 2002). In the sections below the insights provided by examining media production through the prism of the concept of communities of practice are exploited in looking at two complementary approaches to promoting responsible media practice in representing diversity. Initially, organizational initiatives that address the institutional axis of media production will be discussed. This will be followed by a complementary analysis of media professionals' initiatives to counter racism in the media: an approach that typically explicitly invokes the individual's subjective identity as a media 'professional'.

Organizational Initiatives

Research approaches employing an organizational systems approach can draw upon literature on organizational change and upon the wide range of past experience in pursuing equal opportunities initiatives in relation to gender and 'race relations' (Collinson et al., 1990; Shaw et al., 1987). In fact, there are often extant guidelines that have been generated from relevant national government bodies such as the Commission for Racial Equality in the UK or the Office of Multicultural Affairs in Australia. Such governmental documentation typically grounds specific recommendations for 'good practice' in relation to relevant national and international legislation.

A Systems Approach to Countering Racism in the Media

A systems approach to implementing change within a media organization would typically include a planning phase, an implementation phase and a review phase.[1]

In the planning phase it is reasonable to be concerned whether those driving the process have an adequate sensitivity and experience in order to appropriately prioritize the program for change. Senior management, and departmental specialists from majority-ethnic communities or privileged class positions within minority-ethnic communities, may not necessarily possess the relevant knowledge. Consequently, we may reasonably ask who participated in the development of the initiative? And are the values that underpin it widely shared? In the planning phase:

> A wide process of consultation should be in place. Ethnic diversity should be built into the planning phase.

There is a necessary and intimate link between the planning and implementation phase since the planning process must allow for continuous review and development of the initiative as it proceeds. We have seen how discretionary power is located, and legitimated, at different locations within a workforce structure. Consequently, a critical element in the planning phase must be:

> The identification of likely points of resistance and the identification of allies for change who should be explicitly engaged in the planning of the implementation phase.

The interaction between the institutional and subjective axes in a community of practice makes it appropriate that dominant relevant values in the professional identity should be strategically invoked in planning the rationale for change. However, a rehearsal of collective ethical virtue of itself may generate a dangerous illusion of substantive change. 'Race awareness training', extensively pursued in Britain in the 1970s and 1980s, was substantially irrelevant to changing corporate equal opportunities practices (Gurnah, 1989; Sivanandan, 1981). Consequently, within the planning phase:

> Explicit, unambiguous and measurable – Targets for professional practice – must be set.

Within any context of media production there are almost certainly different professional identities in play and in any particular media organization there is almost certainly a number of relatively autonomous communities of practice. Consequently, one task of the planning phase must be to explicitly remain sensitive to the differing subjective identities in play and their own priorities and perspectives. It is not helpful if a cadre of journalists operating in news production actively support a strategy for change if, at the same time, the human resources department of the wider organization regard affirmative action as a 'politically correct' violation of their routine practice. Consequently, within the planning phase:

> The processes of change must be made organizationally relevant to all personnel, with the perspective of employees at different locations in the organization being identified, recognized and engaged with.

In the implementation phase all the concerns about the internal fragmentation of media production and the necessity of sustaining ownership of the program of change remain relevant. There must be clarity about ownership of responsibility for implementing change. There must equally be effective channels of communication which help to sustain the process of change as part of routine professional practice and managerial expectation. Initiatives can be easily stifled by collective resistance or complacency, particularly where it is perceived as having no managerial momentum.

> Individuals at each level in the organisation must be aware of their responsibilities for facilitating change.

Central to the implementation phase of an attempt at systemic change must be an iterative process of monitoring and adjustment. The purpose of setting clear benchmark measures for change in the planning phase is that progress may be monitored over time. Monitoring of routine performance can be anathema to any professional, and media professionals are no exception. But, in the organizational environment of late capitalism, routine monitoring of performance has become ubiquitous, and indeed some talk of living in an 'audit culture'. Where there has been a competent planning phase the rationale for monitoring should at least be understood, if not welcomed. And the pay-off for participation in monitoring is that it provides the evidential basis for a continued commitment of resources to the program of change. The managerial quid pro quo for professionals' commitment to initiatives for change must be a realistic planned commitment of resources to ensure the continuing viability of the project. If the resources are known to be limited the ambition of the project should be equally modest. Managerial statements about pursuing 'equal opportunity' or 'diversity' strategies without a realistic planning commitment of resources has all the sincerity of children making promises with their fingers crossed. Majority-ethnic management and minority-ethnic professionals, amongst other committed players, are likely to have widely differing views about what constitutes adequate resourcing of an initiative.

> The systems for monitoring and feedback must be explicitly agreed and resources committed in order to ensure that the process of change can be sustained over time.

It is the purpose of *the review phase* to convert the insight and data on current practice generated by the prior two phases into coherent information that can fuel the cycle of change. However, given the very many different perspectives of media professionals, and their audiences, the interpretation of the data generated raises all the issues about the ownership of the process that were aired in the planning phase. Professional self-interest and institutional myopia can easily combine to form an alliance of containment that would seek to manage the emergent implications of data arising from the earlier phases. Consequently, the more extensive the commitment to a shared and open evaluation of data, the greater will be the relevance and credibility of the analysis. Evaluation of media performance in terms of personnel, production and content requires a broad range of interests to be represented in the process. There is no single formulaic way of getting this right, but there are very many easily available ways of getting it wrong.

The review phase has the purpose of closing the circle of media performance management. It requires a sensitive and multi-layered strategy in which feedback from the processes of monitoring and evaluation is directed to different audiences and interests appropriately. Feedback must be purposive and directed toward sustaining change, rather than expressive and calculated to demonstrate good intentions. Consequently:

> There must be appropriate mechanisms for the sanctioning of the performance of individuals and the regulation of communities of practice.

And specifically:

> There must be institutionally supported positive rewards for relevant improvement, and negative sanctions for failure.

Organizational initiatives into monitoring recruitment and retention of minority-ethnic staff and the adequacy of the representation of diversity in content have been developed by a number of Public Service Broadcasters, including the BBC in the UK, NOS in the Netherlands and Sveriges Television in Sweden. These public service broadcasters have developed their own explicit 'diversity' policies and have generated a range of initiatives which cover recruitment and retention of minority-ethnic staff, monitoring of aspects of production and training in ethnically sensitive production techniques. Interestingly, whilst the BBC is allowed to formally monitor the ethnic profile of its staff, the Swedish Broadcasting Corporation is not allowed to do so under Swedish law. This serves to illustrate how initiatives within media organizations may be constrained, or facilitated, by the broader multicultural policies and legal frameworks operating within the country.

Ironically, the explicit policy commitment given by the management of such public service broadcasters to promoting equity and diversity within their organization can, in fact, serve to reveal the extensive nature of the challenge. Despite years of pro-active initiatives to widen the ethnic profile of their staff, the Director-General of the BBC Greg Dyke in January 2001 denounced the corporation as 'hideously white'. In his words:

> I think the BBC is hideously white ... I think the BBC is a predominantly white organization. The figures we have at the moment suggest that quite a lot of people from different ethnic backgrounds that we do attract to the BBC, leave. Maybe they don't feel at home, maybe they don't feel welcome. (*Observer*, 7 January 2001)

Dyke's forthright statement reveals something of the power of entrenched interests and routine practices to reproduce ethnic privilege in employment, even in an institution with a serious managerial commitment to ethnic diversity. The processes of institutional racism discussed previously, are permeated through many communities of practice and require a sustained commitment to be eradicated. One potential advantage of a systemic approach to institutional change is that it does reveal the gross limitation of 'quick fix' gestural initiatives.

Media Professionals' Initiatives to Counter Racism in the Media

Critiques of media performance in relation to the representation of ethnic diversity and the reporting of racism are known to virtually all media professionals. For many it is perceived as a persistent 'white' noise, that if you focus upon it becomes an irritant, but which equally can be easily ignored. It is a low-level professional tinnitus generated by outsiders who can be discounted. However, for others this same information is a source of deep professional disquiet and is a running sore undermining their personal job satisfaction and professional pride. For such persons these failings in their profession are something that can and must be addressed. There are indeed instances of sustained commitment by journalists, for example, to develop guidelines and recommendations for improving practice in this area. For example, the British National Union of Journalists has actively worked to promote improved professional practice, and was probably the first to ratify a statement of guidelines on reporting 'race'. Subsequently, the Working Group Migration and Media with the Netherlands Association of Journalists generated general recommendations for journalists entitled, in English, *Balance or Blunder* (Top and Doppert, 1993). Comparable publications have been produced by The Belgian Working Group 'Media en Migranten' of The General Association of Professional Journalists of Belgium (AVBB/AGJPB), and by the Finnish Union of Journalists. Indeed, the parent body, the International Federation of Journalists (IFJ) has for many years had an International Media Working Group Against Racism and Xenophobia (IMRAX) which acted as a 'think tank' and promoted initiatives for combating racism within the media. The professional challenge of responsibly reporting ethnic diversity and racisms in the contemporary world has increasingly attracted the considered attention of media professionals. (see for example Hafez, 2003; Nordenstreng, 1995; Nord-Süd Aktuell, 2001).

These instances of initiatives from within the world of journalism illustrate how professionals are able to find through *the language and values of their profession*, a means to address biased and racist practice. Interestingly, in looking at these publications and in talking to the committed journalists who are driving these initiatives, it is noticeable how other aspects of their professional identities impinge upon the policies they develop. For example, anything that smacks of censorship is robustly resisted, and it may be that one person's 'monitoring' is someone else's 'censorship'. And, for example, in the case of the Dutch initiative their publication speaks of 'recommendations' rather than 'guidelines' or 'codes of conduct'. In the Dutch context the latter terms are maybe seen as too prescriptive and likely to generate a backlash.

Such 'self-evident' considerations of the permissible limits of intervention are likely to exist within any community of practice. For this reason it is important that there are collaborative programs for promoting responsible media practice that draw together partners with different vested interests: professional bodies, ethnic community organizations, policy NGOs and training organizations. The mix of skills and perspectives available in such collaborative ventures are likely to be particularly effective in promoting relevant professional development. And certainly such initiatives do exist. For example, the work of On Line/More Colour in the Media and Mira Media based in Utrecht has provided a diverse range of training initiatives across Europe (see http://www.multicultural.net). However, before drawing this chapter to a close it may be appropriate to reflect upon what range of competencies should be addressed in promoting personal-professional responsible media practice.

An Agenda for Responsible Media Practice

An induction into competence in the technical accomplishments of producing media content, whether journalism, drama or film, is in the contemporary world only a necessary, but not a sufficient, basis for professional practice. The plethora of formal requirements, and persuasive injunctions about the responsibilities of the media in the contemporary multi-ethnic world ensure technical competence, but must be complemented by a carefully honed sensitivity to the dangers of unthinking professional practice. Unintentional as much as malicious acts of misrepresentation are the legitimate concerns of critiques of media performance. Responsible media practice, requires both specific knowledge and technical competence but also a very particular mind-set. Thus, in opening up the educational agenda for preparing media professionals for responsible media practice we may usefully look to the considerable literature on intercultural competence. There is an enormous body of literature, and university and commercially based training provision, in this area. However, for our purposes it is useful to pragmatically start by clarifying the conceptual language that will assist in helping to define the educational task and to provide a framework for operationalizing the content of relevant training. Kim (1992) provides a useful 'systems-theoretic' model which distinguishes between two complementary competencies: specifically she distinguishes between *intercultural communicative competence* on the one hand and *cultural communicative competence* on the other.

Intercultural Communicative Competence

Intercultural communicative competence Kim sees as a generic communicative skill that enables us all to be flexible and open in adapting to the challenge of intercultural interactions regardless of the specific cultures involved in the exchange. In arguing for the possibility, and necessity, of this competence she refers back to the stress that is inherent in all cross-cultural interaction. Unfamiliarity with the culture and behavior of other people, a concern at getting things 'wrong', an ambiguity about the real content and meaning of the information flow and a wish to control the interaction, all transpire to generate anxiety. Additionally, this anxiety is likely to interact with existing inter-group stereotypes and sentiments and feed a specific 'inter-group posture'. Namely, a perception of people of different ethnic identities through an 'us versus them' perceptual filter. As we have seen, stereotyping not only radically reduces ambiguity about what may be expected of other people, it also reciprocally makes relevant the individual's own identity and offers a spurious certainty about their own values and beliefs. This inter-group posture is, of course, itself made reasonable and non-problematic by the taken-for-granted world view that a person brings to any inter-ethnic situation. Thus, at the heart of inter-cultural communicative competence is a reflexive critical self-awareness of our own cultural baggage and agendas. In Kim's words:

> In other words, individuals who hope to carry out effective intercultural interactions must be equipped with a set of abilities to be able to understand and deal with the dynamics of cultural difference, intergroup posture and the inevitable stress experience. (1992: 376)

Whilst Kim's model is essentially intended to be applied to *in vivo* inter-cultural encounters, it clearly can be seen to have relevance for the range of activities encapsulated in the processes of media production. This is particularly so when her opening up of intercultural competence into three related dimensions is taken into consideration. She suggests that the adaptability at the core of this competence should be expressed in relation to three related dimensions of human behavior: the cognitive, the affective and the behavioral dimension.

In relation to cognition Kim draws upon the literature on cognitive styles in which cognitive simplicity, having a limited range of concepts, is compared with cognitive complexity, and cognitive rigidity is juxtaposed to cognitive flexibility. In relation to inter-ethnic relations the classic model of cognitive defensiveness and rigidity is, of course, expressed in the syndrome of the 'Authoritarian Personality' (Adorno et al., 1950). But social psychology has continued to provide rich insights into the cultural and psychological dynamics that interact in producing selective perception. And, in relation to the media, van Dijk (1991) has elegantly revealed the limited mental schemata that may be found in the shaping of news stories. Thus, the cognitive dimension of intercultural competence would aspire to sustaining a flexible openness in engaging with the world. It is a refusal to be dogmatic, and it is a practiced willingness to refuse to reduce new experiences to comfortable clichéd categories. In this respect it is entirely consistent with the emphasis on truth and objectivity in journalism and to the creative impulse of the entertainment media and the arts.

Kim's affective dimension is characterized by an emotional and aesthetic openness. It is defined by a rejection of ethnocentrism and prejudice. It requires a rejection of the emotional laziness of scapegoating where rigid stereotypes feed the expression of hostility and misplaced claims to superiority. On the positive side, the affective dimension of inter-cultural competence is characterized by empathy with others: not just knowledge of others but an emotional engagement with their lives and experience. Whether in news media, literature or film, there is a distressing body of literature revealing the negative emotional agendas expressed in, and evoked by, the contemporary media in multi-ethnic societies. Thus, this effective dimension invites a deliberate inculcation of a positive and other-directed emotional openness in our encounters with others, rather than an unthinking but active rehearsal of emotional closure and defensiveness. Exactly this fusion of cognitive and emotional openness is advocated in Stockwell and Scott's *All-Media Guide to Fair and Cross-cultural Reporting* (2000). This Australian handbook asserts that cross-cultural competence requires that:

> The media worker who aspires to tell the full story has to leave behind the familiar and approach the unfamiliar with curiosity, sensitivity, respect and the moral imagination to understand the world from a cultural perspective that may differ from their own … . Media workers should always be aware that their own values, beliefs and practices are influenced by their own experience of culture and are not the only 'right' view of the world. (2000: Section 5, page 10)

Additionally, the behavioral dimension of intercultural competence highlights our capacity to be adaptive and flexible in our behavior. In ethology, the study of animal behavior, the concept of 'behavioral repertoire' refers to the full range of potential behaviors an animal has available to it. Thus, in relation to intercultural competence the aspiration is to be comfortable with a wide range of behaviors, only some of which may be part of the daily routine. Again, the aspiration is toward optimal flexibility. The behavioral dimension, contrary to first impressions, does not relate only to face-to-face encounters; for example, whether a journalist would be comfortable with the different inter-personal social distance that is the norm in another culture. For behavior is also part of ideology; the embodied self has a 'practical consciousness' that regulates our actions just as much as the schemata of our 'discursive consciousness'. Consequently, the issue of openness, flexibility, and adaptability that was critical in relation to cognition and affect is equally central to our understanding of the generic relevance of the behavioral dimension of intercultural competence.

These three dimensions in dynamic interaction in the lived practice of any media professional define their readiness to be able to enter into an engagement with difference. It is a skills based disposition to remain reflexively self-critical and open to the difference of others, without prejudging that difference negatively and behaving accordingly. As such, it could be readily integrated into the curricula of courses of professional training, and most certainly into journalism training. It is the dispositional basis for engaging with the requirement to treat others equally by being prepared to treat them differently.

There is a great diversity between nation states in terms of their understanding and management of ethnic diversity. Additionally, as we have seen, the issues of pluralism and multiculturalism have become heavily contested political agendas. Consequently, in order to prepare journalists and other media professionals to work in this environment of highly politicized practices and debates around ethnicity and citizenship, they must be introduced to this debate in a considered and structured manner. They must be enabled to explore their own location in this debate, and to locate the dominant discourses in their country of origin, and of practice, into this context. Developing intercultural competence must always involve the individual in a process of revealing their own taken-for-granted worlds of ideas and values. Consequently, this in every instance involves exploring the interface of personal biography and the specific context of the individual's socialization. This can in itself be taxing and uncomfortable. However, when the conceptual language that might help in revealing an individual's own sense of national and ethnic identity is itself unstable and contested, this task becomes doubly difficult. It is for this reason that current academic and political debates about the nature of identity, citizenship, difference and multiculturalism, discussed above, should be examined as part of a generic process of preparing media personnel for practice in the contemporary multi-ethnic world. Developing a generic intercultural competence ironically requires the individual to interrogate the specificity of their own identity and culture.

In essence, the acquisition of intercultural competence requires that all media workers should be facilitated in acquiring a critically reflexive understanding of the belief structures and feelings they bring into their relationship with ethnic diversity. Equally, they should have the opportunity to reflect upon the adequacy of their own behavioral repertoire for efficiently interacting across a range of cultural settings. These issues can be raised in a specific short course, and then can be consolidated by tracing the implications of this learning into specific concrete agendas layered thematically throughout the curriculum and probationary practice. Since intercultural competence is defined as a generic skill it can reasonably be assumed to be of relevance over a very wide range of media practice.

Cultural Communicative Competence

However, whilst intercultural competence properly developed and applied, may empower a media professional in relation to any intercultural agenda, it will also leave them seriously exposed and ignorant in relation to any specific cultural context. Being in a general sense disposed toward openness and a non-pre-judgemental attitude toward difference facilitates the media professional's ability to seek information and to handle that information equitably. It does not of itself provide knowledge of other cultures and people. Consequently, Kim specifies the necessity of a complementary *cultural communicative competence*. Not surprisingly, this refers to the necessity when dealing with another culture or person of a different ethnic background, of acquiring specific relevant information about the history, cultural values, institutional systems and behavior of that society.

The essence of ethnocentrism lies in assuming that the behavior and values of one's own culture are a historical universal norm that may be applied in all other cultures, or that may be employed to judge them. Thus, the acquisition of culturally specific knowledge has two benefits. It provides for the accurate representation of that culture and its people and it supplies concrete experience of difference that feeds the practice of intercultural competence. Of course, the open disposition that is characteristic of intercultural competence is also a necessary prerequisite to the appropriate interpretation and employment of such culturally specific knowledge. The outsider's understanding of another culture is a fraught activity even for anthropologists with a supposed disciplinary expertise in the matter (James et al., 1997). For journalists seeking to report on another community, and for other media professionals whose work creates a representation of communities other than their own, responsible media practice requires that they equip themselves for the task through acquiring the appropriate cultural competence. It is reasonable to assume that schools of journalism operating in specific countries would provide within the curriculum an introduction to cultural competence in relation to at least the larger and/or most salient minority-ethnic communities in that country. This can be facilitated through self-directed learning modules and guidance to appropriate web sites, as well as placements with minority-ethnic media and community organizations.

Here again Stockwell and Scott provide a very useful illustration of the need to provide media workers with specific cultural knowledge when working with people of particular ethnic communities: in this case Aboriginal and Torres Strait Islander people. Amongst the specific cultural norms which they introduce are sensitivities around eye contact, modes of greeting, time, the significance of kinship, naming deceased persons and access to indigenous land. The information they offer illustrates eloquently the ease with which misunderstandings and resentments may be created in the absence of the appropriate use of culturally specific knowledge. Importantly, they also carefully and explicitly warn against the casual application of such cultural knowledge to all and any member of the Aboriginal and Torres Strait Islander communities. Such 'informed' stereotyping is as dangerous as ignorance. They, amongst other things, note that:

Indigenous communities throughout Australia have their own distinct history, politics, culture and linguistic experience. Although indigenous people may share many experiences and similar circumstances, they are not a homogenous group and no single person can speak for all indigenous people. (2000: 30)

It cannot be over-emphasised that Aboriginal and Torres Strait Islander communities are diverse, and, therefore, no tips on procedural matters, or definitive list of 'right' or 'wrong' approaches will be relevant to all situations. (2000: Section 12/13, pp. 30, 31)

This caution underlines the complex challenge of integrating intercultural competence with cultural competence in order to promote responsible media practice. The flexibility and learned ability to creatively tolerate ambiguity in a situation that is at the heart of intercultural competence, provides the appropriate relation to information collection and processing. It creates the space within which the relevance of culturally specific knowledge, in any particular instance, may be evaluated. It nurtures the 'moral imagination' to remain open to difference.

Intercultural Media Competence

Clearly, intercultural communicative competence and cultural communicative competence are highly interactive skills that are essential to the media professional operating in the contemporary multi-ethnic world. But, they are also equally relevant to the transcultural nurse and to the international business executive. However, for media professionals there are quite distinctive skills, embedded in their routine professional practice, which themselves demand a specific *intercultural media competence*.

Like the previous competencies much of the insight into their necessity and nature has been derived from critical reviews of past practice. As we have already seen above, there is a quite remarkable body of literature which has graphically revealed the nature and causes of media failure in the representation of ethnic diversity. Probably the major source of such failures is to be found in the unthinking and routine practice of professional skills. This is important for it points precisely to the fact that 'good professionals' are adept at bad representation of minority-ethnic persons and cultures. Thus, a core element of training in intercultural media competence lies in developing a critical reflexivity toward the dangers of the routine exercise of acquired professional skills. Once again there is no shortage of insightful and critical literature that can underpin the development of a critical intercultural media competence. This literature is actively embraced in the extensive range of university- and school-based courses in media education, where course curricula and texts provide a sensitization to the power of narrative and visual representation in normalizing extant power relations in society.

In any act of representation there is a necessary interpretative link between the represented and the represented to – between the subject and the audience. Typically, those represented by the process of media production have little or no input into the process of representation. And, typically, the process of production is permeated by an implicit understanding of who is the intended audience. Thus the audience, in coming to consume and interpret the news story, novel or film, routinely experiences no bewildering chasm of incomprehension when faced with the professionally generated product. The shared world view of dominant ethnic media professionals and dominant ethnic media audiences provides a hermeneutic symmetry that allows the transmission of meaning to be efficient, and multi-layered. The notion of the passive audience helplessly bombarded by media messages is long gone. The audience brings to media content an interpretative repertoire that is deeply rooted in their socialization, identity and current circumstances.

Thus, in encoding or decoding the narrative structure of a news story or a film plot, a powerful complex of cultural and political assumptions are brought into play. Consequently, the narrative structure of mainstream film has, for example, been extensively deconstructed to reveal the dominant ideologies of 'race' and difference embedded in them (Bernstein and Studlar, 1997; Davies and Smith, 1997; Young, 1996). Equally, as has been noted above, journalism's capacity to create highly partisan representations of reality is continuously exposed and critiqued. Indeed, it is the power of 'news values' that have been internalized as the core of a good journalist's practice, that have over a very long period of time been frequently identified as providing the impetus toward partiality and myopia in routine press and television reporting. It follows from this that one element of intercultural media competence must be a critical reflexive awareness of how these outcomes may be unthinkingly reproduced in routine professional practice. Appropriate instruction in avoiding such outcomes must be part of all professional training. Clearly, the transmission of facts and insight through such training would be a necessary, but not sufficient, part of professional education. For, in the absence of an appropriate disposition toward learning and practice, this information may be easily discounted. A complementary intercultural communicative competence is a necessary catalyst to the process of acquiring sensitivity to the dangers of narrative construction. And, again, reflexive insight into the dangers of ethnocentric dominant ideologies provides a basis for avoiding a variety of forms of negative misrepresentation; but it does not provide the substantive knowledge that must underpin accurate and appropriate representations of other cultures and people. A willingness to invest in the necessary labor of acquiring specific cultural competencies is also a necessary positive complement to the self-discipline of avoiding misrepresentation.

However, in relation to the visual media, the narrative is not independent of the visual construction of reality. In relation to photography and film the audience's capacity to read the conventions of visual representation has been opened up to scrutiny. It is again an acquired skill deeply embedded in unspoken cultural assumptions. Professional skills of visual production have been translated into an audience's normative competence in reading the visual. Reading the visual is a collusive partnership of the media and the audience in exercising complementary learned techniques of visual representation.

The visual framing of majority and minority ethnic interaction through the technical construction of a specific scene employs a range of professional judgements, including camera angle, lighting and location of persons in the frame, which paradoxically are routinely invisible but powerful. Responsible media practice consequently requires that an additional element of inter-cultural media competence must involve a self-conscious sensitivity regarding the potency of professionally routinized techniques. The subtlety and power of these visual codes makes them particularly dangerous tools of racist and ethnocentric media practice. Many, but certainly not all, racist elements of a verbal discourse are readily vulnerable to detection and critique, (certainly in particular European newspapers for example), but the very nature of the codes of visual representation frequently render them unobtrusive and routinely non-problematic.

Training for intercultural media competence requires a sensitivity to, and respect for, the expertise of the media worker, and appropriate media credentials in those who would offer the training. Mira Media and On Line/More Colour in the Media have provided just such courses and training in promoting responsible media practice in the European context.

Such training will regrettably often be seen as peripheral to the core purpose of professional socialization; namely, an acquisition of the skills of the trade that guarantee acceptance as a member of the profession. However, it has cumulatively become apparent in the review above that it is exactly these routinized skills which form the basis for the reproduction of dominant ideologies and racist imagery. Responsible media practice requires that as young people are inducted into all the media professions they are facilitated in acquiring a generic *intercultural competence* which will inform all their practice. Equally, they must be enabled to understand the need for, and the means of acquiring, specific *cultural competence* which will be contingent upon the particularities of their work. And, *intercultural media competence* is a necessary reflexive sensitivity to the tools of their trade which will enable media professionals to begin to comply with the demands of their professional codes in a viable and responsible manner.

Conclusions

This chapter has sought to provide through the concept of communities of practice, an insight into the specific contexts in which media content is produced. It is intended to provide an understanding of the institutional and subjective forces at play in shaping the routines of professional practice. From this basis coherent strategies for change may be planned. And, equally importantly, realistic expectations about the rate and nature of the change process should be in place.

The brief discussion above of the range of programs for change currently in place is indicative that there is now a movement to challenge the routine bias and discrimination, in both representation and employment, that has been so typical of media systems. The nature of the institutional axis of communities of practice provides grounds for a realistic pessimism about the likely rate of change that will be experienced. And the challenge to personal-professional development that is present in aspiring to responsible media practice strongly suggests that professional training will require significant modification. But, a sense of history, even over the last three decades, holds out reasonable grounds for optimism for the future.

Note

1 This systems approach draws upon the analysis of K. Chouhan and D. Weaver (2004) 'Race Equality Management', in C. Husband & B. Torry (eds.) *Transcultural Health Care Practice: an Educational Resource for Nurse and Health Care Practitioners*. London. Royal College of Nursing (accessible free to user at: www:rcn.org.uk/resources/transcultural/index.php).

9 The Multi-Ethnic Public Sphere and Differentiated Citizenship

As the arguments in successive chapters of this book have accumulated so then the complexity of the dynamic relationship between the media and ethnic identity has been revealed. Ethnic diversity has been a core agenda throughout these arguments, and a recurrent theme has been the necessary task of recognizing and respecting such diversity. The review of the literature on the representation of minority ethnic communities and indigenous peoples has been at pains to reveal the many ways in which the media may be partisan and act as vehicles of the majority ethnic communities' self-interested hegemonic program. In a complementary manner there has been an exploration of the role of the media as a necessary element in enabling all ethnic communities to reproduce their own culture and cohesiveness. What has been implicit in all of this has been an assumption that such concerns enjoy a degree of widespread normative support. However, this is an assumption which *cannot* be left unchallenged. Indeed there is a real need to interrogate the basis on which a concern for ethnic representation and minority media rights may be legitimately sustained. For the reality is that there is no widespread consensus on the necessity of respecting diversity. And, where there is a political willingness to recognize the rights of minority ethnic communities, there is no common framework of political theory, or practice, which underpins it.[1] Thus, this chapter has the aim of demanding that all who would engage with the debate on ethnicity, racisms and the media can make explicit the foundational basis for their political framing of this issue.

As with other issues discussed above, this is an area where critical questions are much more readily available than off-the-peg solutions. The argument that follows therefore presents our perspective as a provocation to the readers to reflexively examine their own position.

Diversity – Multiculturalism – The Politics of Difference

The racist and voluble bigot has no difficulty in responding to ethnic diversity. They are sensitive to ethnic diversity in their life-world; even hyper-sensitive to it. They are confident in their categorization (racist labeling) of difference, and clear about their feelings and beliefs about members of these categories (stereotypes and negative affective dispositions). They are unambiguous in the clarity of their behavioral intentions toward minority ethnic persons (exclusion/discrimination). And, they have a certitude about the reasonableness of all of the above which is provided by their strongly held racist ideology. There is a coherence about their beliefs, values and actions which provides a stable and gratifyingly self-fulfiling relationship to their world which is defined by perceived threat, conflict and exaggerated cultural pride.

For very many 'progressive', 'liberal' and 'nice' people in the contemporary world this degree of personal coherence in negotiating ethnic diversity in their life is elusive. Generic notions of neighborliness, tolerance or religious charity frequently inform individual responses to ethnic diversity. But in being the taken-for-granted moral substrata of their actions, they have not necessarily been articulated at a level of consciousness that provides an ontological certitude that can withstand moral panics about immigration and asylum seekers, or the real transformation of neighborhoods and societies that follow upon significant demographic change. And, indeed, as we have noted repeatedly above, given the complexity and contradictions in individual hegemonically shaped consciousness, other values and beliefs may be both more coherent and more salient. Nationalism and class interest come to mind as two such ideological constructions. Thus, at the individual level it is reasonable to anticipate degrees of ambiguity in personal responses to ethnic diversity in the contemporary world.

At the level of the state, we have every reason *NOT* to expect uniformity across states in their formal policy response to ethnic diversity within their population. As each nation state has developed, in producing their own fabric of political institutions they have also simultaneously forged their own unique political settlement in which key elements of political philosophy have been melded together as *their* national model of democracy, or authoritarianism. In Europe alone this potent heavy hand of history has produced widely divergent political models and practice, that has in consequence generated very different means of responding to ethnic diversity (Koopmans and Statham, 2000; Heckman and Bosswick, 1995). For example, France, following the Jacobin principles of its revolution, has through the concept of *laicite* been highly resistant to formally recognizing diversity within its citizenry. To make allowance for gender, religion *or* ethnicity would be to undermine the fundamental unity of citizenship (Hargreaves, 1995). In the UK on the other hand, with hundreds of years of experience of 'managing diversity' in the Empire and Commonwealth, the new developments in ethnic diversity from the 1950s to the 1980s were met with a ready willingness to legislate in order to manage 'race relations' (Solomos and Back, 1995). And, currently in the new era of nation-building in the Baltic States freed from Soviet control, a sensitive consciousness of recent occupation and domination not surprisingly impacts upon their political practice (Brubaker, 1996; Lauristin and Vihalemm, 1997). Thus, any attempt to discuss the media rights of minority ethnic communities within the economic and social fabric of a specific nation state necessarily becomes framed by the dominant political model for managing diversity that is operative within that state. Therefore, generic arguments about *the rights* of minority ethnic populations, such as the indigenous peoples discussed in Chapter 5, are de facto expressed politically within a national agenda that has a distinctive historical basis, and particular current discourse.

Each state has its own dominant paradigm for negotiating the demands of pluralism within their political practice. Recognition of ethnic diversity cannot be neatly separated off from recognition of gender, sexual orientation, age, disability or other social markers. But, as we have seen above, the constructions of ethnicity and 'race', places ethnic diversity in a unique relation to each of these in every society. 'Multiculturalism', as a generic concept that encapsulates a state's willingness to recognize ethnic diversity through its policy and practice, is a highly contested phenomenon. The term itself has no certain meaning, and its expression in practice has been proven to be potentially ambiguous and problematic (Goldberg, 1994; Jewson and Mason, 1986). Indeed, the definition and practice of multiculturalism have become highly contested political issues.

However, before engaging with the implications of the current politics of multiculturalism it is appropriate, and necessary, to first of all explicitly address some aspects of political theory that will sharpen our understanding of why this issue is so frequently deeply contested. We will briefly explore some relevant aspects of how managing ethnic diversity may in fundamental ways be framed by foundational political agendas.

Recognizing Diversity

A prior condition to any policy response to ethnic diversity is a recognition of difference. Much of the discussion in the previous chapters has focused upon the manner in which difference has been categorized: specifically how labels have been historically constructed and attributed to self and others. But here our concern focuses upon how the management of the relation between different categories of *homo sapiens* defined in ethnic and national terms is normalized and legitimated. Clearly, race theory and racist practice manages these relations coherently through an ordering of the world into hierarchies of superiority: 'us' superior, 'them' inferior. However, in post-Enlightenment liberal theory there is a countervailing dynamic, particularly expressed through the essential unity implicit in the notion of citizenship. There is perhaps a common deep-seated sentiment that links many Western European social democracies and it is their commitment to liberalism and what Charles Taylor has called the politics of recognition. He argues that: 'The importance of recognition is now universally acknowledged in one form or another; on an intimate plane, we are all aware of how identity can be formed or malformed through the course of our contact with significant others. On the social plane, we have a continuing politics of equal recognition' (1992: 36).

At the heart of this politics of *equal recognition* there lies an assumed common humanity in which we share common universal needs: in essence, you respect me and I respect you, and we treat each other equally. This foundational universalism has been central to many national multicultural policies, in which showing respect for others has essentially meant treating all people the same.

However, as we have seen throughout this text, majority populations routinely have difficulties in *feeling* and believing that a wide range of minority populations are truly equal and worthy of equal respect. Particularly, as we have seen, the historical construction of ethnic differences makes spontaneous equal recognition problematic. An ideological construction that has proved a highly successful tool for bridging the gap between the principles of equal recognition and the practice of ethnic interaction has been the notion of *tolerance*. Tolerance is widely seen as an unambiguous personal virtue and a valuable political lubricant. In both social science writing and political thinking, tolerance has been routinely seen as the polar opposite of prejudice.

However, tolerance is far from the benign entity such thinking might suggest. As we have previously argued:

> For tolerance to be necessary, there must be a prior belief that the person to be tolerated has an intrinsically undesirable characteristic, or that they are not fundamentally entitled to the benefits which are to be allowed them. Those to be tolerated, by definition, possess some such social stigma.
>
> Tolerance is the exercise of largesse by the powerful, ultimately on behalf of the powerful. It is the generous extension of forbearance toward someone who is intrinsically objectionable or not deserving of the privilege being allowed. (Husband, 1994b: 65)

If a response to recognizing the media needs and rights of minority ethnic communities within the state is founded on a belief in the essential tolerance of the majority population then the minority communities are implicitly expected to be grateful for what they get. For, since tolerance is a *discretionary power* exercised by the majority, it inevitably denies the legitimacy of minority community claims that *they have a right* to the resources they need and seek.[2]

Additionally, nation states appear to be complacently comfortable with the notion that there is a natural limit to their tolerance; that they should not be pushed too far in the spirit of equal recognition. In their analysis of the Belgian response to ethnic diversity, Blommaert and Verschueren (1998) talk of the construction of an idea of 'the threshold of tolerance'. In essence, this asserts that there is a natural limit beyond which it is not reasonable to expect majority populations to sustain their 'normal' level of tolerance. They argue that:

> The threshold of tolerance is an objectifying socio-mathematical concept that defines the conditions under which the all-European tolerance and openness may be cancelled without affecting the basic self-image. The European does not become intolerant, until this threshold is crossed. Just let him or her step back over the same threshold, i.e. just reduce the number of foreigners again, and the good old tolerance will return. In other words, even in moments of intolerance the European is still tolerant at heart, and the observed behaviour is completely due to the factual circumstances which render it impossible to exercise this essential openness. Needless to say, the threshold of tolerance is not an exclusively Belgian notion. It is commonly used in other European countries. (1998: 78)

The awesome political utility of this notion of the threshold of tolerance lies in its capacity to defend the assertion that tolerance is a defining capacity of the virtuous majority, whilst simultaneously allowing for conditions where it has a natural breaking point due to unreasonable external pressures. It follows from this that a proper state politics of diversity lies in creating the environment in which tolerance may be guaranteed. This, of course, may mean draconian border policies, institutional mechanisms to contain the 'unreasonable' demands of minority-ethnic communities and a creative cultural massage of the majority identity. In the chapters above, all of these strategies may be discerned in the state's (majority-ethnic) response to minority-ethnic communities' demands. The containment implicit in the tokenistic powers of the Sami Parliaments, or the Australian, Aboriginal and Torre Strait Islander Commission (ATSIC), and the 'partial' commitment of media industry equal opportunity strategies is symptomatic of this tolerant politics of equal recognition.

However, it has not only been the self-interested lubricant of tolerance that has been revealed as a problematic element in the politics of equal recognition. Of equal force and relevance has been a fundamental critique of the universalism that lies at the core of this paradigm. In a radical challenge to liberal universalism Young (1989) has persuasively argued that in the context of universalist provision for diverse populations it is the interests and the priorities of the majority that define what are the normative needs and cultural practices that should be addressed through *equal* provision. In this context, universalism is a close cousin of paternalism.

In the last decade an alternative conception of structuring a response to managing diversity has been developed through what Taylor has called the *'politics of difference'*. He has argued that:

> the development of the modern notion of identity, has given rise to a politics of difference. There is of course a universalist basis to this as well, making for the overlap and confusion between the two. Everyone should be recognised for his or her unique identity. But recognition here means something else. With the politics of equal dignity, what is established is meant to be universally the same, an identical basket of rights and immunities; with the politics of difference, what we are asked to recognise is the unique identity of this individual or group, their distinctiveness from everyone else. The idea is that it is precisely this distinctness that has been ignored, glossed over, assimilated to a dominant or majority identity. (1992: 38)

As Taylor eloquently makes clear, the flaw in the universalist politics of recognition lies precisely in the assumption, indeed insistence, that people be treated, quite literally, equally. This pre-empts any meaningful acknowledgement of individual and communities' quite different needs and priorities. Instead of reducing equality to identical resources and provision, the politics of difference retains the fundamental acknowledgement of individual worth, whilst tenaciously retaining an awareness of unique individual needs. In other words, the politics of difference in effect insists that if you want to treat me equally, you may have to treat me differently. It requires that a raft of equal rights be expressed in an appropriate range of particularistic responses. (This, for example, is exactly the issue at the heart of adequate transcultural health care practice. See for example, Holland and Hogg, 2001; Henley and Schott, 1999; Husband and Torry, 2004.)

The quiet decencies of a liberal politics of recognition have very adequately served a state policy pivoted around a benign universalism. Both have been capable of seamless articulation with the humanistic principles of equivalence built into a wide range of theisms, and in political paradigms including liberalism and socialism. It has been a political philosophy and practice that has simultaneously nurtured the self-regard of the privileged and powerful, and the dependence and compliance of the powerless. The fundamental challenge of the politics of difference has radically destabilized this hegemonic package.

This has not only resulted from the inherent arguments of the politics of difference, but also because the emergence of this paradigm has been paralleled by a powerful mobilization of identity politics *per se*. With the dislocation, though not demise, of class politics, and the fragmentation of gender politics, nation states across continents have witnessed a powerful surge of identity politics expressed within, and outside, established political structures. It is arguable that such identity politics have come to supply an anchor in the turbulent waters of globalization and social change.

For minority ethnic populations the intersection of identity politics and the philosophy of the politics of difference has liberated and amplified a pre-existing rejection of the paternalism and tokenistic universalist equality offered by majority groups. They do not require the tolerance of the majority, *but assert their rights.*[3]

Minority ethnic communities who have learnt to reject the homogenizing logics of majority liberal universalism are everywhere rejecting assimilation into the national norm. From a rights perspective citizenship requires of them loyalty to the state, not uncritical investment in a national identity which assigns them a marginal, and/or inferior status. Postmodern hybridity is not confined to nuancing ethnicity with gender and generation: it is also a practice which opens up the possibility, and viability, of new hyphenated national affiliations (Werbner and Modood, 1997; Werbner, 2002). Explicitly discernible in the dynamics of diasporic communities, and equally apparent in the identity politics of national minorities and indigenous peoples, the politics of difference argues for the essential compatibility of a common obligation to participate in civil society as equals, and a commitment to negotiating cultural co-existence.

The clarity and assertiveness with which the logics of the politics of difference are often expressed by minority ethnic politics easily create a reaction in which the majority community feel that the *reasonableness* of their privileged status is challenged and threatened. For the convinced xenophobe and racist nationalist this challenge is experienced as an outrageous expression of minority-ethnic arrogance and rapacious greed. (In media terms frequently expressed as an intolerable threat to the economic and cultural resources of the majority.) Equally, progressive liberals within the majority-ethnic populations may feel confused and angry when what they see as their tolerant niceness is reflected back as tokenistic, paternalistic and self-interested. Sometimes, referred to as 'the victimisation of the majority' (Wodak and Matouscheck, 1993), this defensive response leads to renewed attempts to reassert the 'limits of tolerance' as natural and reasonable and necessary for the continued cohesion of the nation state.

Given these conflicting political dynamics it is hardly surprising that across the world the definition and practice of multiculturalism has been highly contested, and very varied. Multiculturalism has been critiqued as leftist demagogary. It has been challenged for its generalizations and essentializing of identities and it has been denounced as devisive of national cohesion. The sub-titles of just some of the recent books on the topic reveal something of these agendas: for example, Robert Hughes (1994) *Culture of Complaint: the Fraying of America*; Gertrude Himmelfarb (2001) *One Nation, Two Cultures: a Searching Examination of American Society in the Aftermath of Our Cultural Revolution*; and Brian Barry (2001) *Culture and Equality: an Egalitarian Critique of Multiculturalism*. On the other hand, particular policy initiatives framed by a 'multicultural' rationale have been critiqued by minority ethnic communities, members of national minorities and indigenous peoples for having been conceived and driven by interests that are ignorant of their culture, political priorities and modes of mobilization (Gilroy, 2001).

In the Canadian context, Juteau provides a helpful note on the varied nature and impact of multiculturalism. She argues that:

> In hindsight one can also see that multiculturalism served as a mobiliz-
> ing ideology for a heightened participation in public institutions. It
> allowed for the definition of a more inclusive discourse on the participa-
> tion of minoritized groups within the political community ... and fostered
> the erosion of the myth of national homogeneity founded on nature or on
> culture. Former conceptions of Canada have been altered and its Waspish
> core challenged. The acceptance of ethnic pluralism opens up a space for
> public debate, as exemplified in the critique of the folklorizing and essen-
> tializing aspects of multiculturalism, and the growing emphasis on mate-
> rial as well as on ideational interests. (1997: 108)

An acceptance of ethnic pluralism is not a position that can be taken for granted in the governmental or popular politics of our time. It has been a perspective that has observably grown in visibility and salience across a wide range of states over the last five decades. However, it remains a value position and a political practice that is far from consensual and is highly resisted in some quarters.[4] The significance of this for our analysis of ethnicity and the media is double-edged. It means that there is no normative package of theory and practice that can be invoked to inform our aspirations for media policy. And, as a corollary of this, it means that we must each be prepared to make explicit the emotional and intellectual bases of our own position on the management of diversity. The purpose of this discussion of 'recognizing diversity' is to engender a reflexive anxiety. Within any national context it is all too easy to absorb a taken-for-granted national paradigm on citizenship and identity. In rapidly moving to a righteous moral critique of particular instances of the (mis)represen-tation of minority-ethnic persons and communities we are very seldom challenged to explicitly reveal the macro-model of 'multiculturalism', and the contingent politics of difference, that implicitly frame this judgement. But, as anti-racist struggles in the past have revealed, unexpressed and unacknowledged differences in foundational belief structures all too

easily undermine attempts at collaboration to eradicate inequality
(Husband, 1991). Where media professionals, members of majority communities and members of minority communities aspire to change media
systems for the better, it is necessary to recognize potentially profound
differences in 'where you are coming from'.

A Multi-Ethnic Public Sphere?

In the last section we asked why is ethnic difference an issue, and in particular, are we clear about the basis for our predisposition to support some,
rather than other, models of managing diversity? In this section we invite
another area of speculation. Media researchers, media professionals and
the population at large have proved themselves to have an almost inexhaustible capacity to critique mass media content. Whether it is about the
neglect of 'high culture' and 'dumbing down'; or about moral laxity; or
about too much sport or not the right sport; or why that fool attains
celebrity status or why my favorite actor has vanished: criticism of the
media is one of *the* expressive indulgences of our time. But, criticizing *what
is* has not been matched by a complementary commitment of energy to
conceptualizing *what should be*. The exponential growth of critical literature
exposing the flawed representation of ethnicity in the media has certainly
not been matched by an equivalent effort to explicitly define what the ideal
multi-ethnic media environment should look like. As a modest attempt to
provoke more of that type of analysis we will briefly visit here one attempt
to pursue this trajectory (Husband, 1996, 1998, 2000).

In essence this section confronts the question: Why should we be wor-
ried about the media's representation of ethnicity and diversity? And, in
order to answer that question we may reasonably be expected to know
what we expect the media to do. In the context of this book this question
becomes focused toward asking what is the role of the media in multi-
ethnic societies? We can usefully start with the media's own claim for
their social and political relevance: namely, that they are the 'fourth estate
of the realm'. The media have been extensively discussed in terms of their
central role in facilitating deliberative democracy (Keane, 1991; Dahlgren
and Sparks, 1991). In this perspective the strength and vitality of the
media rests with their ability to guarantee a flow of information amongst
a population, and to do so in a way which facilitates a critical reflexivity.
Hence, the primordial cry of unimpeachable authority that underpins the
claims of 'the freedom of the press'. The development of modern media
have been inextricably interwoven with the structures and imagined
properties of modern democracy (Anderson, 1991).

The media are perceived to be essential to a dynamic *civil society* in
which citizens, and others, engage in defining their model of the good life;

and through associational activity restrain the powers of the state. Now, of course, as with other key concepts discussed in this context, the concept of civil society is far from being unproblematic (Kaldor, 2003). For one thing, the multi-ethnic demography of contemporary states raises the questions we have addressed above about how the state recognizes diversity, and (Keane, 2003) through its actions shapes civil society. Pluralism is a challenge to the state, and to our understanding of the operation of civil society (Baghramian and Ingram, 2000). Additionally, it is arguable that the notion of civil society is in itself specific to liberal democracies. As we develop our argument it is sufficient that we register the liberal democratic permeation of the concept of civil society and its contested status within political philosophy (see for example, Chambers and Kymlicka, 2002). Keane defines civil society as:

> ... an ideal-typical category ... that both describes and envisages a complex and dynamic ensemble of legally protected non-governmental institutions that tend to be non-violent, self-organizing, self-reflexive, and permanently in tension with each other and with the state institutions that 'frame', construct and enable their activities. (1998: 6)

This definition points to the reality that whilst civil society is seen as the cumulative activity of individuals and collectivities in pursuing their interests to, amongst other things, direct and constrain the activities of the state, it cannot be entirely independent of the state. At a minimum level the state must fulfil its obligation in relation to civil and political rights where it in effect must at least abstain from preventing individuals exercizing these rights. The particular form a civil society takes must reflect the diversity of interests present in society and the political and economic structures it must engage with. Importantly, Keane (*ibid*: 26) notes that 'a weak civil society is not a logical correlate of a strong state, and (inversely) that a strong, "over-developed" state does not produce a docile and quiescent society'. The interests of individuals within society tend to coalesce around particular issues and the formation, transformation and collapse of coalitions to pursue these interests are recurrent features of all societies. Much of political theory has addressed the forces that shape these processes and the resources employed in pursuing group interests (see for example, Keane, 1998; Putnam, 1993). Members of the working class may ally themselves with the right-wing bourgeoisie in anti-immigrant politics and tribal interests may radicalize the expression of economic competition. Civil society is a crucible for political activity, but not necessarily a vehicle for harmony. Particularly where there is oppression and racial exclusion it is reasonable to expect the conflicting interest groups to have quite different purposes in operating through civil society. The discourse of tolerance as employed by a majority tends to seek to obscure the fact that there are fundamental conflicts of interest between the oppressor and the oppressed. In such a society harmony, as a characteristic liberal democratic aspiration, can only be achieved by a hegemonic manipulation of civil society. Conversely, an active and vital civil society in such an oppressive context must be expected to be a vehicle of contestation and discomfiture.

For our purposes here it is fruitful to pursue the links between the media and civil society through the concept of the public sphere. In the contemporary world where the democratic deficit between the principles of deliberative democracy and the practice of democratic institutions is the subject not only of anguished academic analysis, but also of outraged popular polemic (Monbiot, 2000; Moore, 2001), the concept of the public sphere has about it an aspirational quality. It sketches a relation between people, information and the state that can best be seen as an ideal type model. Curran has provided a concise expression of these dynamics:

> According to classical theory: the public sphere (or in more traditional terminology: 'public forum') is the space between Government and society in which private individuals exercise formal and informal control over the state: formal control through the election of governments and informal control through the pressure of public opinion. The media are central to this process. They distribute the information necessary for citizens to make an informed choice at election time: they facilitate the formation of public opinion by providing an independent forum of debate; and they enable the people to shape the conduct of government by articulating their views. The media are thus the principal institutions of the public sphere or, in the rhetoric of nineteenth century liberalism, 'the fourth estate of the realm'. (1991: 2)

It is not difficult to see the potential linkages between this definition of the role of the media and the critical concerns expressed about media performance in the previous chapters. If modern nation states are ideally assumed to operate 'according to a distinctive logic of undistorted communication grounded in the value of deliberative democracy' (Chambers and Kymlicka, 2002: 5), then a diverse and vigorous media environment is essential to their successful operation. Yet, the cumulative message of the literature reviewed above is that the political economy of media operations typically is disadvantageous to the viability of minority ethnic media. If ethnically diverse societies are to have a range of media which reflect and represent the many identities and interests present within them then the routine logics of contemporary media production must be challenged. This challenge must go beyond an impassioned critique to a substantive policy shift which releases resources and supports innovation.

A political basis for such policy innovation can be found in the contemporary debates around minority-ethnic rights. As a complement to the discussion of the politics of difference above, we can look to the current debates around 'differentiated citizenship' which seeks to recognize the rights of groups rather than solely individuals, for protection under the law (Kymlicka, 1995, 2001; Fredman, 2001).

Differentiated Citizenship

As a necessary complement to Young's (1989) critique of the universalist application of a basket of rights within a multi-ethnic society, Kymlicka (1995) has developed a rights basis for 'multicultural citizenship'. A significant, and key element in his model is the recognition of the distinctive nature of groups and of the consequent necessity of recognizing group rights. It is through acknowledging the integrity of groups, and the indivisibility of their joint enjoyment and expression of a right, that this perspective moves beyond the individualism of classic liberal theory (see Petrova, 2001). Such an approach recognizes the nature of xenophobia and racism where individuals are victimised and disadvantaged not as individuals but because they are members of a group. As Van Dyke (1995: 50) argued:

> It would facilitate affirmative action if ethnic communities were accepted as right-and-duty-bearing units. After all, the discrimination for which affirmative action is compensatory was directed against individuals because of their membership in certain communities, and through them against the community as such. The discrimination was in a sense impersonal; it was not that a given person was to be denied certain opportunities and thus be excluded or kept down; it was rather that the whole community was to be kept in its place. The reciprocal of this is to take compensatory action for the whole community and to let individual members benefit even if they have not personally suffered discrimination. (Quoted in Fredman, 2001: 67)

Kymlicka (1995) distinguishes between *multinational states* and *polyethnic states*. Multinational states have developed as the consequence of the incorporation of previously self-governing territorially bounded cultures into a larger state. This would typically occur through federation or conquest, and would include countries like Spain, the UK and Switzerland, and indigenous peoples such as the Sami or Inuit. Polyethnic states on the other hand have a cultural diversity that has arisen from individual and family migration.

Echoing our discussion above, Kymlicka argues that the different historical circumstances underlying this ethnic diversity have significant implications for the political construction of the distinctions within differentiated citizenship. He argues that the distinct historical experiences of national minorities allows for their having rights to self-government which would not be available to minority-ethnic groups in polyethnic societies. In this way his model is entirely consistent with the claims of indigenous peoples discussed above: particularly as Kymlicka's model anticipates that these *self-government rights* would typically be attached to jurisdiction over a particular territory which is accepted as being historically associated with the national minority. Different forms of expression of such self-government can be seen in relation to the media environment of Australian Aborigines in remote designated areas or more substantially in the Canadian ceding of rights to the Inuit in Nunavut.

In addition to self-government rights Kymlicka proposes the existence of two other forms of group-differentiated rights (1995: 6–7; 26–33) *Special representation rights* arise from a recognition of the fact that in diverse societies the simple majority principle of decision making must always marginalize minority constituencies. Thus, it follows from a principled recognition of the rights of minority-ethnic communities, that they must be guaranteed seats within the deliberative bodies of the state. These special representation rights place the particular interests of national minorities and minority-ethnic groups within the power-broking institutions of society. This representation is essential in allowing the voice of minorities to be present at the site of struggle over the definition of priorities and the allocation of resources. Thus, in the study of the Sami media environment discussed above, (Markelin, 2003a), the location of the head of the Norwegian Sami radio and television on the board of the parent public service broadcaster, NRK, was seen to give him a distinct advantage over his peers in Finland and Sweden. Arguing your case from the inside is usually much more effective than pleading from the outside of the community of decision making. Access to knowledge about information flows and insights into the partisan alliances of interest are always more readily available from participation within the structures of power.

The third element in Kymlicka's model of group-differentiated rights are *polyethnic rights* which he defines in terms of financial support and legal protection for certain practices associated with particular ethnic or religious groups. These rights are clearly compatible with the principle of treating people equally by treating them differently. They start from a recognition of difference and operate on a principle of facilitating groups in sustaining their difference. Thus, polyethnic rights stand in opposition to the politics of assimilation. Polyethnic rights allow for the political recognition of the relatively disadvantaged position of minorities, and consequently support state funding for initiatives which may not be sustainable through simple market forces. Polyethnic rights are already enshrined in international and national legislation where the cultural and identity concerns of minority-ethnic groups are recognized and protected.

These rights go beyond protecting minorities from discrimination and victimization; they include a proactive agenda of positive intervention. Special state support for sustaining minority languages is a good example of such a policy. And, state support for minority media as in Nordic press subsidies, or funding for BRACS (Broadcasting in Aboriginal Communities Scheme) in Australia, or British funding of Welsh language television are instances of such polyethnic rights being recognized within media provision. One of the ironies of the domain of ethnicity and the media is the fact that polyethnic rights are often more extensively expressed *in practice*, than the principle of differentiated rights is formally, and popularly, accepted *in principle*.

Clearly the three elements of group-differentiated rights interact dynamically in practice. In many instances special representation rights are critical in getting the concerns of national minorities and minority-ethnic communities onto the political agenda. Perhaps even it is only through the operation of these rights that the legitimacy and potential of polyethnic rights and self-government rights can be asserted and pursued within the majority system. And self-government rights, when expressed in practice, in effect potentially place the minority community in a position to determine its own polyethnic priorities. Of course in many instances the political and economic situation of the national minority within the larger state may still leave it dependent upon the state for essential funding. The very different circumstances of indigenous peoples around the world attest strongly to this fact.

Differentiated Citizenship and the Multi-Ethnic Public Sphere

Kymlicka's development of the concept of differentiated citizenship points directly to the role of the state in establishing the framework of possibilities in which a diverse public sphere can operate. For there to be a viable multi-ethnic public sphere there must, ideally, be an institutional expression of human rights supported by the state. This includes complementary negative and positive human rights policies whereby the state abstains from inhibiting the individual's expression of their rights, and makes necessary strategic interventions to enable individuals, and groups, to express these rights in practice. Mbaye has spelt out this dynamic thus:

> civil and political rights are based on the principle of liberty, whereas economic, social and cultural rights derive from the principle of equality. In the case of the former rights, an abstention is required of the state: in effect the state must avoid preventing the exercise by individuals of the rights and liberties that are recognised as theirs ... Conversely, for the

enjoyment of the second category of rights the state must make provision for their achievement.

Such rights could be categorised by saying that civil and political rights are 'rights of', while economic, social and cultural rights are 'rights to'. These first and second generation rights are now completed by third generation rights, the achievement of which can no longer be obtained merely by abstention or provision on the part of the state, but requires solidarity between people and states. These rights of solidarity are basically the right of peace, the right to the environment and the right to development. There are however, other such rights. (1986: 28–9)

These first and second generation human rights can very clearly be applied to developing our understanding of the necessary characteristics of a multi-ethnic public sphere. Where a state apparatus operates as a vehicle for the interests of a specific fragment of the population, whether defined through 'race', ethnicity, tribe, nation or religion, then it almost certainly will deny the rights of those excluded by that political focus. The concept of citizenship, for example, is an ideological means of legitimizing the privileging of some, and the exclusion of others, from equal participation in the state's resources. In other words, state policies in multi-ethnic societies do not equitably address their first generation human rights obligations to all those dwelling within their territorial ambit. Equally, such states very typically develop policies which enable the access of some to the practical fulfilment of their rights (second generation rights), whilst neglecting or denying the equivalent claims of the marginalized.

The significance of this for our argument here can be made more explicit by addressing the centrality of communication in the practice of a public sphere. Keane has defined a public sphere as:

... a particular type of spatial relationship between two or more people, usually connected by a certain means of communication (television, radio, satellite, fax, telephone, email, etc.), in which non-violent controversies erupt, for a brief or more extended period of time, concerning the power relations operating within their given milieu of interaction and/or within the wider milieu of social and political structures within which the disputants are situated. A public sphere has the effect of de-sacralizing power relationships. It is the vital medium of naming the unnameable, pointing at frauds, taking sides, starting argument, inducing diffidenza (Eco), shaking the world, stopping it from falling asleep. (1998: 169–70)

This definition points to both the will to communicate and the essential role of the means to communicate as central to the operation of the public sphere. Indeed, there exists a body of argumentation and policy which specifically speaks of 'a right to communicate'. In the debates around media democratization an equitable basis for freedom of communication and access to the means of communication have been central. The controversy following upon the publication of the MacBride Report *Many Voices One World* (1980), and the bitter politics within Unesco around the New World Information and Communication Order (NWICO) demonstrated just how sensitive the powerful are to challenges to their disproportionate control of the means of communication (see Hancock, 1992). The issues around the right to communicate have a long history (Hujanen, 1988, 1989) and continue to be developed in a range of academic and policy domains (Roach, 1990, 1993; Keane, 1991, 1998; Hamelink, 1993).

For our purposes here the link between state responsibilities for the development of differentiated citizenship rights and the construction of a viable multi-ethnic public sphere may be initially determined in relation to their fulfilment of first and second generation obligations. The state must abstain from impeding an individual's expression of their communicative rights and thus create the space for the expression of individual, and collective, communicative freedoms. Thus, for example, legal prohibitions against the use of minority languages must not exist, nor can political constraints on the expression of opinion be assumed to be legitimate. However, the implications of 'tolerating the intolerable' through guaranteeing the communicative rights of racist and neo-fascist movements remains a fraught issue (Ricoeur, 1996; Kymlicka, 1995; Galeotti, 2001).

In essence, first generation rights serve to guarantee the legal/political framework that will guarantee the rights of communication to all.

However, the lack of state interference with communication does not guarantee an equitable capacity to communicate. As we have seen recurrently in the chapters above, in societies shaped by hierarchies of power and status, access to the means of production and distribution is far from equitable. Groups, who through past and/or current discrimination and marginalization have limited economic resources, cannot easily compete with the rich and powerful. Small communities may lack the demographic basis to constitute a sustainable commercial audience for print or broadcast media. It is precisely because the political economy of media systems is so central to the determination of any communities' media environment that second generation human rights policies are so central to the construction of a multi-ethnic public sphere. Through the application of the principles of group differentiated rights, the state must fulfil its second generation human rights functions by enabling the emergence, and continued vitality, of a media infrastructure that reflects the ethnic diversity present in the society. Thus, through state subsides for minority media, through the regulation of commercial media, through the policies of public service broadcasters, and through programs of education and training, amongst other things, the state may positively intervene in facilitating and sustaining a dynamic multi-ethnic public sphere. The cumulative evidence drawn from the chapters above is that when a state complacently limits its role to guaranteeing first generation rights it inexorably colludes in the effective disenfranchisement of specific communities from meaningful participation in a mediated public sphere. The concept of differentiated citizenship necessarily leads to an expectation of group identities being respected in state policy, and consequently it follows that in multi-ethnic societies we should anticipate a richly diversified media environment facilitating a dynamic and complex public sphere. Enabling minority ethnic communities to have a media infrastructure which can adequately give voice to their concerns, and appropriately represent the diversity within their community is one aspiration of the model proposed here. It is a necessary corrective to the silencing and misrepresentation reported above. However, it is not without its ambiguity.

The Multi-Ethnic Public Sphere – Dialogue or Fragmentation?

One of the realities of the contemporary media world is the extensive range of technological options available for the facilitation of communities. From mass circulation to local print media, global cinema and television production to community radio and television, fax and email, there is an extensive possibility of communication. Within the mass media these innovations and the expanded options of digitalization have created the technological capacity for extensive audience fragmentation. In the area of television we have seen the dominance of public service broadcasters and a few dominant networks being challenged by a plethora of new thematically specific media. Increasingly, individuals can navigate through a media environment in which they can actively select media which specifically reflect their own class, political and aesthetic interests. Whilst this is certainly true of the affluent middle classes in many societies; it may also be true of specific ethnic minority communities (Husband, 1994a; 2002; ter Wal, 2002). Thus, consumer choice is the motor of audience fragmentation where increasingly media address the narrow agendas of very specific target audiences. This reality has implications for the model of the multi-ethnic public sphere discussed above.

Indeed, in one pessimistic view this trajectory of events may well have undermined the very possibility of a public sphere as traditionally understood. Gitlin has suggested that what may in fact be emerging are numerous *sphericules*: 'does it not look as though the public sphere, in falling, has shattered into a scatter of globules, like mercury?' (Gitlin, 1998: 173).

It is certainly an implication of the development of a rich and diverse minority ethnic media environment that they will constitute the basis for semi-autonomous, parallel public spheres, defined by the identities of their audiences. Looked at from the perspective of the traditional public sphere, located within the territorial bounds of a nation state, this is a possibility that must be taken seriously. Given the exclusion and marginalization of many minority-ethnic groups from the media and other fora of the national public sphere, it is hardly surprising that minority media have a distinct significance for minority communities.

Echoing the discussion in previous chapters, it is also important to recognize that many of the communities of identity represented within the minority media fora are not themselves contained by the territorial boundaries of the state. Cunningham and Sinclair provide a persuasive and positive perspective on the nature of 'sphericules' when seen in the context of diasporic communities. They argue that:

> Thinking of global sphericules as constituted beyond the singular nation state, as global narrowcasting of polity and culture, assists in restoring them to a place – not necessarily counter-hegemonic but certainly culturally plural and dynamically contending with western forms of recognition – of undeniable importance for contemporary, culturally plural societies. (2001: 179)

In relating the media fragmentation of audiences to the global diasporic reality of contemporary ethnic identities, an important link is made with the transnational political economy of minority-ethnic media (Husband, 2000; Cunningham and Sinclair, 2000). Minority-ethnic media are not merely a reflection of shared identity politics, they are also necessarily an expression of a community's capacity to realize economic and political resources. In some instances where the diasporic history links a dispersed population to a highly developed and well resourced 'home country', then this mediated public sphere can be heavily subsidized by the parent media. The film production of Bollywood and the newspaper conglomerates of the Indian sub-continent effectively heavily subsidize the media of diasporic 'Asian' communities. Where small communities have no such natural source of support, such as the Sami in the Nordic states and the Aboriginal communities of Australia, then state support may be crucial. And for exile communities the media product of their 'home countries' may provide a necessary diet of politically distressing content that informs their oppositional communication strategies through largely extra-national media.

In the multi-ethnic societies of our contemporary world, internal diversity and trans-national diasporic connectedness, linked to technological capacity, have made the probability of communicative 'sphericules' a reality. Whether this is seen as a political threat to the effective promotion of civility and the good order of society, or whether it is viewed as a necessary consequence of pursuing an open and democratic society will be partially based on the position taken when defining the nature of the politics of diversity discussed above.

If the coercive powers of the majority-ethnic group are to be restrained from operating a hegemonic public sphere, in which the majority define the communication rights and opportunities of minorities, then the state must exercise its powers to *regulate* the media environment so as to sustain diversity. This will mean both *restraining* the powers of large conglomerates to narrow choice, and facilitate the emergence and sustained operation of media that expressly give a voice to minority-ethnic cultural and political priorities. An idealised 'ideal-type' definition of such a public sphere was given in Keane's utopian model.

> A fundamentally revised public service model should aim to facilitate a genuine commonwealth of forms of life, tastes and opinions, to empower a plurality of citizens who are governed neither by despotic states nor by market forces. It should circulate to them a wide variety of opinions. It should enable them to live democratically within the framework of multi-layered constitutional states which are held accountable to their citizens, who work and consume, live and love, quarrel and compromise within independent, self-organizing civil societies which underpin and transcend the narrow boundaries of state institutions. (1991: 126)

In his more recent (1998) work he has acknowledged the impacts of the continuing transformation of the powers of the state in response to the advancing processes of globalization in the last decade. In particular, the de-territorialization of media has meant that audiences can no longer be assumed to be members of a shared common territory managed by a sovereign nation state. In an attempt to relate the differing size and territorial reach of particular modes of communication he refers to 'micro-public spheres', 'meso-public spheres' and 'macro-public spheres'. Micro-public spheres he sees as operating in a range of tens to thousands of participants and they might include the use of such technologies as telephones, faxes, photocopiers, videos, camcorders and personal computers. It could equally well include community radio and press, or theatre and agit-prop. Micro-spheres remind us that difference is capable of sub-division. This level of communicative behavior can powerfully address the interface of particular identities with particular locales.

Meso-public spheres for Keane may encompass millions of people 'watching, listening or reading across vast distances' (*ibid*: 174). The territorial reach of such public spheres is typically coterminous with the territorial state, but may extend beyond its boundaries. We can think here of national broadcast media and large circulation newspapers. At the level of the state or region the media facilitating these meso-public spheres can be seen as constituting a particular subset of Sinclair et al.'s (1996) geo-linguistic regions in which language and a level of 'cultural proximity' constitute a bounded audience. Such audiences could be ethnic communities transcending national borders, such as the Sami, or national minorities within a nation state, such as the Basques or the Quebecois, or to take a class example, affluent Republicans in the USA. Class, wealth and political predisposition can provide powerful interactive forces in defining media audiences and 'sphericules'.

For Keane the macro-public spheres are constituted of hundreds of millions of persons and are the 'consequences of the international concentration of mass media firms previously owned and operated at the territorial nation-state level' (1998: 176). The global reach of such media provide a means of generating the space-time compression that is regarded as symptomatic of the *glocalized* world where events are experienced simultaneously, though differently, around the world. We can think of reportage of major wars, such as the recent second Gulf War; or of ecological (Green) issues; or of the branding of fashion, Nike and Coca-Cola. The reach of these media provide a connectedness which is existentially far removed from much of the personal solidary sensibilities of micro-public spheres.

The typology of public spheres suggested by Keane helps to clarify a number of points about the multi-ethnic public sphere. First of all, it helps to underline the relationship between media technologies and communicative styles and possibilities. It makes very evident the powerful determining impact of the political economy of all media operations. *Samizdat* could be achieved with a hand-powered printer and/or video camera. National broadcast media and global networks have their own distinct logics. And, importantly, this typology makes it clear that such mediated public spheres are not mutually exclusive. Each citizen may participate in many spheres, or 'sphericules' and no mediated public sphere is necessarily capable of being an irresistible dominant force. There is, however, a tension between the communicative needs and aspirations of specific ethnic communities and the media environment they find themselves located within. The cumulative evidence revealed in the chapters above, strongly supports the view that in the absence of differentiated citizenship rights expressed in media policy, the media environment of a minority ethnic community is a direct reflection of their political and economic marginalization, or power. Put another way, market forces within an inequitable and ethnically diverse society will not of themselves generate an equitable multi-ethnic public sphere.

Sustaining Difference and Guaranteeing Connectedness

In concluding this chapter, it is appropriate to critically draw together the themes that have run through it. In proactively theorizing a multi-ethnic public sphere it has been necessary to make explicit the willingness of a society to sustain difference. The assimilationist propensity of nineteenth-century nationalisms (Bauman, 1990) has no place in this scheme of things. In recognizing the de facto multi-ethnic demography of contemporary states, and the diasporic connectedness of many communities, a credible multi-ethnic public sphere can only be built upon a politics committed to pluralism. The model developed here has invoked the language and ethos of Taylor's politics of difference. And it has specifically suggested the absolute centrality of a political and personal preparedness to respond to ethnic diversity through a willingness to follow the credo – *'If you want to treat me equally be prepared to treat me differently'*.

In order to flesh out the route to pursuing such a political agenda the relevance of the contemporary widespread debate about human rights and its relation to the operation of the state has been examined through Kymlicka's development of the concept of differentiated citizenship. This points to the different ways in which the state may be expected to act in order to guarantee equitable communication rights for all, and a dynamic multi-ethnic public sphere. The argument here is that to begin with the state must fulfil its first generation human rights obligations, and not interfere with, or restrict, minority-ethnic communities' ability to exercise their communicative freedoms. Kymlicka's 'special representation rights' have a role to play here in allowing the voice of ethnic minorities to be heard within the seats of power, where at least discrimination and exclusion based on the ignorance and thoughtlessness of the majority may be challenged.

Where a state recognizes the distinct status of a national minority or indigenous people, and grants them 'self-government rights', then clearly a major degree of autonomy has been handed to these groups. However, the extent and terms of these rights often leaves a significant degree of power in the hands of the state, and its dominant ethnic interests. Additionally, self-government within relatively autonomous territories is not without its own problems. We have seen that the complex nature of ethnic identity formation and internal distinctions within such communities may be the basis of a different range of struggles. For example, the privileged access to shared resources that may be available to indigenous people granted control of their traditional homelands may generate essentialist politics about who is a 'real' member of the community. This may express itself in divisive struggles over who may speak on behalf of the community (Langton, 1993).

The 'polyethnic rights' outlined by Kymlicka fit comfortably with the state fulfiling its second generation human rights obligations. We have seen that the demographic characteristics of a minority-ethnic community or indigenous people may be such as to make them a non-viable audience for commercially financed media. Small minority populations present an economic challenge to the ideal of an equitable multi-ethnic public sphere and it is reasonable to expect the state to step in and by appropriate means subsidize the viability of minority media. There has been a long history in which public service broadcasters have been seen as having the institutional capacity and popular legitimacy to carry a major responsibility for this activity. However, as Keane (1998) and others have pointed out, public service broadcasting has suffered a major financial crisis in the past decade or more and the divorcing of audiences from national territories has undermined some of its legitimacy for fulfiling its traditional 'national' role. Thus, not surprisingly he warns against 'the perilous strategy of attempting to tie the fortunes of the public sphere ideal to an ailing institution' (1998: 163). However, if national public service broadcasters are embattled and under-resourced they also remain key players in providing a platform for pursuing the aims of a multi-ethnic public sphere.

At the same time, it is neither accurate nor sensible to write-off commercial media enterprises as in some way a natural enemy to the model being developed here. Both in terms of the massive scale of some transnational media audiences (Cunningham and Sinclair, 2000; Sinclair, 1999) and the viable demography of localized high density ethnically specific audiences the range of options for fitting ethnic audiences to media production is varied and very often effective. State media policy can, however, make the viability of these enterprises more, or less, difficult. In the current era of the rhetoric of the 'axis of evil' and the ubiquitous threat of terrorism it is possible to imagine an increase in neurotic state restraint and intervention in some proportion of minority-ethnic broadcasting. And, it is important to recognize the very real continuing presence of state censorship and media control in societies across the world. As we have seen above, state policy on ethnic diversity and political pluralism very directly impacts upon media freedoms.

However, it is equally important to note that the state is only one element of the determination of the public sphere. The autonomous mobilization of individuals and communities in pursuing their political and cultural interests is also a recurrent theme in the analysis of the media (Downing, 2001; Couldry, 2000). Focusing upon national and transnational media can lead to a failure to recognize the importance of the micro-public sphere and its capacity to subsequently impact on wider agendas. Cultural innovation may be 'marketed' and commodified in the mass media, but its genesis is not to be found their. The class, gendered and generational fragmentation of minority ethnic communities, linked to the unique historicity of any minority community's location within society, guarantees a diversity of experience and contemporary priorities *within* any ethnic community. The macro-public sphere cannot be expected to adequately address this reality.

In looking at the fragmentation of audiences and the emergence of relatively autonomous 'sphericules' we have touched upon this contemporary reality. The extensive diversity of minority-ethnic media reflects the reality of the complex construction of contemporary identities. This is exactly the deconstruction of collective social spaces that postmodern social theory has explored with persistent, and occasionally neurotic, fascination. It, therefore, follows that one consequence of the model presented here must be a consolidation and possible expansion of audience fragmentation. Parallel 'sphericules' serviced by their own distinctive range of media are a likely component of the anticipated multi-ethnic public sphere.

This certainly cuts against the grain of a traditional view of a relatively homogeneous public sphere binding a citizenry bounded by a common national affiliation and culture. Certainly in a multi-ethnic society scarred by racism and discrimination it should be anticipated that if you enfranchise the oppressed they will bite the oppressor. The vibrant and diverse public sphere proposed here is not a vehicle for Socratic dialogues sustained in an atmosphere of tolerant restraint. Ideally, giving a voice to the oppressed cannot be accompanied by constraints on what they should say. However, there are reasons to anticipate forms of constraint.

Communication implies mutual comprehension and within civil society dialogues across the boundaries of specific interest groups require that a medium for mutual intelligibility will be found. Indeed, one much expanded stratum of activity within contemporary society is occupied by a cacophony of social commentators who 'interpret' the behavior and utterances of 'others' to their own audience. Academics, novelists, and journalists are but a visible fragment of this activity: mullahs, rabbis and priests offer a religious perspective to micro-public spheres. And, at that level they are complemented by barbers, taxi-drivers, café acquaintances and relatives. At the meso-level the media offer partisan accounts of the past and present through news and entertainment. Perhaps what some call 'dumbing down' might regretfully be called 'linguistic tuning for an under-educated citizenry'.

Restraints on the freedoms of ethnic community expression may additionally be anticipated as a necessary guarantee of individual freedoms and dignity. We have already noted that ethnicity may be the motor of vehement invective and incitement to violence. There is ample evidence of ethnic communities, majority and minority, having racist and stereotypical views of out-groups and of seeking to restrict the individual freedoms of members of their own in-group. For such groups the media can be deployed as powerful tools of their oppressive politics. Faced with the question of 'how shall we tolerate intolerant minorities?' the answer must surely be, 'As would we intolerant majorities: we would not' (see for example, Kymlicka, 1995). State regulation of all media may necessarily include restraints on the abuse of communicative freedoms, including incitement to racial hatred.

If the multi-ethnic public sphere proposed here anticipates and indeed celebrates a complex and varied public sphere in which a wide range of 'sphericules' may co-exist, this does not imply a resigned acceptance of a virtually atomized civil society. First, participation in a 'sphericule' does not signify personal atomisation. As Cunningham and Sinclair (2001) pointed out the internal dynamics of any particular 'sphericule' may represent a focused connecting of people over wide territorial distances who find common cause in a specific diasporic or hybrid ethnic identity. Additionally, there is no reason to assume that the substantive discourse within a 'sphericule' is centripetal and myopic. On the contrary, in engaging with the contemporaneous agendas of a shared identity it may necessarily force communication outwards to engagement with other groups, to form alliances with similar others, or to contest the powers of competitors. And, no one person is contained or defined by the agendas of one 'sphericule'. Multi-faceted identities are likely to be expressed through participation in a range of relevant public spheres: for example, ethnic, gendered, professional. The networks of connectedness experienced in these various public spheres will themselves provide unique interconnections of experience and interest. In simple terms, the existence of multiple public spheres is not a necessary guarantee of an isolated and alienated public.

However, taken even half-way seriously, it seems reasonable to continue to find some sympathy for Todd Gitlin's pessimism. The triumph of identity politics expressed through the multi-ethnic public sphere envisioned here certainly seems capable of failing to optimize a sense of shared civility and common purpose amongst the total population. Audience fragmentation and the multiple 'sphericules' of this multi-ethnic sphere could certainly benefit from a range of meso-public spheres that purposefully underline the shared democratic co-existence of the population. If like can speak to like with ease, surely there is a need for a medium to bring difference together. The political purpose and communicative ethos of the traditional public service broadcaster has a continuing relevance. And, even though public service broadcasting institutions may have lost a great deal of their vitality and legitimacy, they are still significant elements in a multi-ethnic public sphere. Nor is the ethos of public service broadcasting uniquely confined to national public service broadcasting institutions. Its aspirations and production values can be identified and successfully translated into niches within commercial enterprises. In fulfiling its second generation human rights functions the state may reasonably be expected to support media that promote civility and dialogue in a multi-ethnic society.

Sustaining difference and guaranteeing a solidary connectedness amongst all people in a society is never going to be an easy task. In developing an admittedly utopian model of what a multi-ethnic public sphere might look like we have revealed something of the challenge to political thinking and practice that would be required. The ambitious program of differentiated citizenship, if nothing else, reveals the inadequacy of much contemporary policy and practice. Going beyond the distressing critiquing of the status quo reveals the greater challenge of addressing what should be.

Notes

1 As noted elsewhere in this text the concept of 'multiculturalism' is open to widely differing definitions and the values that frame particular states' response to the politics of diversity may vary significantly. Thus, for example, despite the variation in practice within the European Union the Copenhagen criteria adopted in 1993 included 'respect for and protection of minority rights' and the Laeken Declaration (http://europa.eu.int/documents/offtext/doc151201 en.htm) contains the statement: 'The European Union's one boundary is democracy and human rights. The Union is open only to countries which uphold basic values such as free elections, respect for minorities and respect for the rule of law'. The European Union thus provides in itself an interesting case study in how declared common core values may take on very different expressions in political rhetoric and in practical policy. The report on 'Minority Protection' in the accession states and five member states provides a valuable insight into this variation. (Open Society Institute, 2002).

2 The problematic nature and role of tolerance in contemporary life has remained a focus for contemporary political philosophy. See, for example, Walzer, 1997; Ricoeur, 1996; Galeotti, 2001.

3 As we have seen above in the case of indigenous peoples, the contemporary primacy of rights-based discourses in framing inter-group relations provides a further salient variable in shaping the particular dynamics of contemporary debates on the management of diversity.

4 Skrentny (2002) provides an illuminating account of 'The Minority Rights Revolution' in the United States which reveals the complex historical juxtaposition of interests and players that shaped American minority rights policy and provided the foundations for its continued divisiveness.

References

1990 Trust/Liberty (2000) *Joint Submission by NGOs to the UN Committee for the Elimination of all forms of Racial Discrimination (CERD)*. London: The 1990 Trust/Liberty.

Abel, B. (1988) *The British Legal Profession*. Oxford: Blackwell.

Abley, M. (2003) 'Hunters of Australia', *Times Literary Supplement No 5212*, 21 February, pp. 6–7.

Abrams, D. and Hogg, M.A. (1990) *Social Identity Theory: Constructive and Critical Advances*. London: Harvester Wheatsheaf.

Abrams, D. and Hogg, M.A. (eds) (1999) *Social Identity and Social Cognition*. Oxford: Blackwell.

Adorno, T.W., Frenkel-Brunswick, E., Levinson, D.J. and Sandford, R.N. (1950) *The Authoritarian Personality*. New York: Harper.

Ahmad, W.I.U. (1992) 'The maligned healer: the "hakim" and western medicine', *New Community*, 18 (3): 521–36.

Ahmad, W.I.U. (1993a) 'Making black people sick: "race", ideology and health research'. Chapter 2 in W.I.U. Ahmad, (ed.), *'Race' and Health in Contemporary Britain*. Buckingham: Open University Press.

Ahmad, W.I.U. (ed.) (1993b) *'Race' and Health in Contemporary Britain*. Buckingham: Open University Press.

Ahmad, W.I.U. (ed.) (2000) *Ethnicity, Disability and Chronic Illness*. Buckingham: Open University Press.

Aikio, P. and Scheinin, M. (eds) (2000) *Operationalizing the Right of Indigenous Peoples to Self-determination*. Åbo Akademi University: Institute for Human Rights.

Alfredsson, G. (1998) 'Indigenous peoples and autonomy', in M. Suksi (ed.), *Autonomy: Applications and Implications*. The Hague: Kluwer Law International. pp. 125–37.

Alibhai-Brown, Y. (1999): *True Colours: Public Attitudes to Multiculturalism and the Role of Government*. London: Institute for Public Policy Research.

Allport, G.W. (1954) *The Nature of Prejudice*. Reading, MA: Addison-Wesley.

Alterman, E. (2003) *What Liberal Media? The Truth about BIAS and the News*. New York: Basic.

Althusser, L. (1971) 'Ideology and ideological state apparatuses (notes toward an investigation)', in L. Althusser (ed.), *Lenin and Philosophy*. London: New Left. pp. 123–73.

Amit-Talai, V. and Knowles, C. (1996) *Re-situating Identities*. Peterborough, Ontario: Broadview.

Anaya, S.J. (1996) *Indigenous Peoples in International Law*. New York: Oxford University Press.

Anaya, S.J. (2000) 'Self-determination as a collective human right under contemporary international law', in P. Aikio and M. Scheinin (eds), *op.cit*. pp. 3–18.

Anderson, P. (1983) *Imagined Communities: Reflections on the Origins and Spread of Nationalism*. London: NLB and Verso.

Andrews, M.M. and Boyle, J.S. (1999) *Transcultural Concepts in Nursing Care*. Philadelphia, PA: Lippincott.

Ang, I. (1991) *Desperately Seeking the Audience*. London: Routledge.

Appadurai, A. (1996) *Modernity at Large: Cultural Dimensions of Globalization*. Minneapolis: University of Minnesota Press.

Appleyard, R. (1988) *International Migration Today*. Paris: UNESCO.

Araújo, J.Z. (2001) *A Negação do Brasil: o negro na telenovela brasileira*. São Paulo: Editora SENAC.

Argyle, M. (1994) *The Psychology of Interpersonal Behaviour*. London: Penguin.

Atkin, K. (1996) 'The production of health and social care'. Unpublished PhD thesis, University of York.

Attwood, B. and Arnold, J. (eds) (1992) 'Power, knowledge and Aborigines', Special Edition – *Journal of Australian Studies*. Bundoora: La Trobe University Press.

Austin, J.L. (1965) *How to do Things with Words*. New York: Oxford University Press.

Australian Human Rights and Equal Opportunity Commission (1997) *Bringing them Home: Report of the National Inquiry into the Separation of Aboriginal and Torres Strait Island Children from their Families*. Sydney: Human Rights and Equal Opportunity Commission.

Bachollet, R., Debost, J.-B., Lelieur, A.-C., and Peyrière, M.-C. (1992) *Négripub: l'image des noirs dans la publicité*. Paris: Éditions Somogy.

Back, L. and Solomos, J. (2000) *Theories of Race and Racism*. London: Routledge.

Baghramian, M. and Ingram, A. (2000) *Pluralism: The Philosophy and Politics of Diversity*. London: Routledge.

Baker, H.A. (1993) 'Scene ... not heard', in R. Gooding-Williams (ed.), *Reading Rodney King, Reading Urban Uprisings*. New York: Routledge, pp. 38–48.

Bakhtin, M.M. (1986) 'The problem of speech genres', in M.M. Bakhtin (ed.), *Speech Genres and other late essays*. Austin, TX: University of Texas Press. pp. 60–102.

Balakrishnan, G. (1996) *Mapping the Nation*. London: Verso.

Banton, M. and Harwood, J. (1975) *The Race Concept*. London: David and Charles.

Barker, J. (1981) *The New Racism*. London: Junction.

Barnett, M. (2003) *Eyewitness to a Genocide: the United Nations and Rwanda*. Ithaca, NY: Cornell University Press.

Barry, B. (2001) *Culture and Equality*. Cambridge: Polity.

Barth, F. (1969) *Ethnic Groups and Boundaries*. London: Allen and Unwin.

Barthes, R. (1988) 'Myth today', in R. Barthes (ed.), *Mythologies*. New York: Noonday.

Baregay, A. and Boubeker, A. (1993) *Les images publiques de l'immigration*. Paris: Harmattan.

Barzun, J. (1965 [1937]) *Race: a Study in Superstition*. New York: Harper and Row.

Batty, P. (1993) 'Singing the electric: aboriginal television in Australia', in T. Dowmunt (ed.), *Channels of Resistance*. London: British Film Institute. pp. 106–25.

Bauman, Z. (1990) 'Modernity and ambivalence', in M. Featherstone (ed.), *Global Culture*. London: Sage.

Bauman, Z. (1993) *Postmodern Ethics*. Oxford: Blackwell.

Bauman, Z. (1998) *Globalization: the Human Consequences*. New York: Columbia University Press.

Bean, P. (1986) *Mental Disorder and Legal Control*. Cambridge: Cambridge University Press.

Beishon, S., Virdee, S. and Hagell, A. (1995) *Nursing in a Multi-ethnic NHS*. London: Policy Studies Institute.

Bell, P. (1993) *Multicultural Australia in the Media*. Canberra: Office of Multicultural Affairs.

Belsey, A. and Chadwick, R. (1992) *Ethical Issues in Journalism and the Media*. London: Routledge.

Benner, P. (1984) *From Novice to Expert*. Menlo Park, CA: Addison-Wesley.

Bennett, T., Buckridge, P., Carter, D. and Mercer, C. (1992) *Celebrating the Nation*. St Leonard's NSW: Allen–Unwin.

Berelson, B. (1971) *Content Analysis in Communication Research*. New York: Hafner.

Berg, B.A. (2001) *Holdninger til samer og samiske forhold 1996–2000. En undersøkelse av avisene Aftenposten, Nordlys, Finnmark Dagblad, Altaposten og Finnmarken for perioden 1.1.1996–31.12.1999*, report for the Ministry of Local Government and Regional Development commissioned by the Centre for Sámi Studies, Tromsø: University of Tromsø.

Berkhofer, R.F. Jr (1988) 'White conception of Indians', in W.E. Washburn (ed.), *History of Indian-White Relations*, pp. 522–47, Volume 4 of W.C. Sturevant (ed.), *Handbook of North American Indians*. Washington: Smithsonian Institution.

Berkowitz, D. (ed.) (1997) *Social Meanings of News: a Text-Reader*. Thousand Oaks, CA: Sage Publications Inc.

Berlet, C. (1998) 'Who is mediating the storm? Right-wing alternative information networks', in L. Kintz and J. Lesage (eds), *Media, Culture and the Religious Right*. Minneapolis: University of Minnesota Press. pp. 249–73.

Bernstein, M. and Studlar, G. (1997) *Visions of the East: Orientalism in Film*. London: I.B. Tauris.

Berthoud, R. and Beishon, S. (1997) 'People, families and households', Chapter 2 in T. Modood, R. Berthoud, J. Lakey, J. Nazroo, P. Smith, S. Virdee and S. Beishon. *Ethnic Minorities in Britain*. London: PSI.

Betz, H. (1994). *Radical Right-wing Populism in Western Europe*. New York: St Martin's.

Betz, H. and Immerfall, S. (1998). *The New Politics of the Right: Neo-populist Parties and Movements in Established Democracies*. New York: St Martin's.

Bhabha, H.K. (1994) *The Location of Culture*. London: Routledge.

Bhavnani, K.K. and Phoenix, A. (1994) *Shifting Identities Shifting Racisms*. London: Sage.

Biorcio, R. (2003) 'The Lega Nord and the Italian media system', in G. Mazzoleni et al. (eds), *The Media and Neo-populism*. New York: Praeger. pp. 71–94.

Bird, S.E. (2001) ' "Indians are like that": negotiating identity in a media world', in K. Ross and P. Playdon (eds), *Black Marks: Minority Ethnic Audiences and Media*. Idershot: Ashgate. pp. 105–22.

Birenbaum, G. and Villa, M. (2003) 'Media and neo-populism in France', in G. Mazzoleni et al. (eds), *The Media and Neo-populism*. New York: Praeger. pp. 45–70.

Bizeul, D. (2003) *Avec ceux du FN: un sociologue au Front National*. Paris: Editions La Découverte.

Black, I. (2000) 'Europe "should accept" 75m new migrants' The *Guardian* – Friday, 28th July.

Blommaert, J. and Verschueren, J. (1998) *Debating Diversity – Analysing the Discourse of Tolerance*. Routledge: London.

Bobo, J. (1995) *Black Women as Cultural Readers*. New York: Columbia University Press.

Bonnett, A. (2000) *Anti-Racism*. London: Routledge.

Boorstin, D.J. (1963) *The Image: or What Happened to the American Dream?* Harmondsworth: Penguin.

Bottomley, G. and de Lepervanche, M. (eds) (1984) *Ethnicity, Class and Gender in Australia*. Sydney: George, Allen and Unwin.

Bottomore, T. (1992) 'Citizenship and social class, forty years on', in T.H. Marshall and T. Bottomore (eds), *Citizenship and Social Class*. London: Pluto Press. pp. 55–93.

Beishon, S., Virdee, S. and Hagell, A. (1995) *Citizenship and Social Class*. London: Pluto.

Bouillaud, C. (2003) 'La Lega Nord ou comment ne pas réussir a être populiste (1989–2002)', in O. Ihl, J. Chêne, E. Vial and G. Waterlot (eds), *La tentation populiste au cœur de l'Europe*. Paris: Editions La Découverte. pp. 130–45.

Bourdieu, P. (1988) *Homo Academicus*. Cambridge: Polity.

Braeckman, C. (1996) *Terreur Africaine: Burundi, Rwanda, Zaïre – les racines de la violence*. Paris: Fayard.

Braeckman, C. (2003) *Les nouveaux prédateurs: politique des puissances en Afrique centrale*. Paris: Fayard.

Brodkin, K. (1998) *How Jews Became White Folks and What that Says about Race in America*. Brunswick, NJ: Rutgers University Press.

Brown, D.R., Firestone, C.M. and Mickiewicz, E. (1994) *Television/Radio News and Minorities*. Queenstown, MD: The Aspen Institute.

Brown, R. (1995) *Prejudice*. Oxford: Blackwell.

Browne, D.R. (1996) *Electronic Media and Indigenous Peoples: a Voice of Our Own?* Ames: Iowa State University Press.

Brubaker, W.R. (1996) *Nationalism Reframed*. Cambridge: Cambridge University Press.

Burkitt, I. (1999) *Bodies of Thought: Embodiment, Identity and Modernity*. London: Sage.

Burkitt, I., Husband, C., Mackenzie, J. and Torn, A. (2001) *Nurse Education and Communities of Practice*. London: ENB.

Burr, V. (1995) *An Introduction to Social Constructionism*. London: Routledge.

Buscombe, E. (ed.) (1988) *The Hollywood Western*. London: BFI Publications.

Butler, D. (1991) 'Ulster unionism and British broadcasting journalism', in B. Rolston (ed.), *The Media and Northern Ireland: Covering the Troubles*. Basingstoke: Macmillan. pp. 99–121.

Caldiron, G. (2001) *La destra plurale: dalla preferenza nazionale alla tolleranza zero*. Rome: Manifestolibri.

Calhoun, C. (ed.) (1993) *Habermas and the Public Sphere*. Cambridge, MA: MIT Press.

Campbell, C.P. (1995) *Race, Myth and the News*. Thousand Oaks, CA: Sage.

Camus, J.-Y. (2002) 'Métamorphoses de l'extrême droite en Europe', in *Le monde diplomatique*, 578 (May), p. 3.

Cannadine, D. (2001) *Ornamentalism*. London: Penguin Books.

Capozza, D. and Brown, R. (2000) *Social Identity Processes*. London: Sage.

Carr, S. (2001) *Hollywood and Anti-semitism: a Cultural History up to World War II*. New York: Cambridge University Press.

Casasus, G. (2003) 'La nouvelle droite en Allemagne et en Suisse: entre droite classique et extrême droite' in O. Ihl, J. Chêne, E. Vial and G. Waterlot (eds), *La tentation populiste au cœur de l'Europe*. Paris: Editions La Découverte. pp. 198–212.

Castles, S. (1993) 'Migration and minorities in Europe', Chapter 2 in J. Wrench and J. Solomos (eds), *Racism and Migration in Western Europe*. Oxford: Berg.

Castles, S. (2000) *Ethnicity and Globalization*. London: Sage.

Castles, S. and Miller, M.J. (1993) *The Age of Migration*. London: Macmillan.

Centre for Contemporary Cultural Studies (1982) *The Empire Strikes Back*. London: Hutchinson.

Chaliand, G. and Rageau, J.P. (1991) *Atlas des diasporas*. Paris: Editions Odile Jacob.

Chaliand, G. and Rageau, J.P. (1997) *The Penguin Atlas of Diaspora*. London: Penguin.

Chambers, S. and Kymlicka, W. (2002) *Alternative Conceptions of Civil Society*. Princeton: Princeton University Press.

Charaudeau, P., Lochard, G., Soulages, J.-C., Fernandez, M. and Croll, A. (2001) *La Télévision et la guerre: déformation ou construction de la réalité? Le conflit en Bosnie (1990–1994)*. Brussels: De Boeck.

Chibnall, S. (1977) *Law-and-Order News: an Analysis of Crime Reporting in the British Press*. London: Tavistock.

Chomsky, N. (1965) *Aspects of the Theory of Syntax*. Cambridge, MA: MIT Press.

Chrétien, J-P., Duparquier, J.-F., Kabanda, M. and Ngarambe, J. (2002) *Rwanda: les médias du génocide*, 2nd edn. Paris: Editions Karthala.

Christians, C.G., Fackler, M., Rotzoll, K.B. and McKee, K.B. (2001) *Media Ethics: Cases and Moral Reasoning*. New York: Longman.

Clifford, James (1994) 'Diasporas', *Cultural Anthropology*, 9 (3): 302–38.

Cochrange, R. and Sashidharan, S.P. (1996) 'Mental health and ethnic minorities: a review of literature and implications for services', in *CRD – Ethnicity and Health: Review of Literature and Guidance for Purchasers in the Areas of Cardiovascular Disease, Mental Health and Haemoglobinopathies*. NHS Centre for Reviews and Dissemination. University of York.

Colley, L. (1992) *Britons: Forging the Nation*. New Haven, CT: Yale University Press.

Collin, M. (2001) *Guerrilla Radio: Rock 'n' Roll Radio and Serbia's Underground Resistance*. New York: Thunder's Mouth Press/Nation Books.

Collinson, D.L., Knights, D. and Collinson, M. (1990) *Managing to Discriminate*. London: Routledge.

Commission for Racial Equality (1995) *Racial Equality means Quality – a Standard for Racial Equality for Local Government in England and Wales*. CRE: London.

Cottle, S. (1997) *Television and Ethnic Minorities – Producers' Perspectives*. Aldershot: Avebury.

Cottle, S. (2000) *Ethnic Minorities and the Media*. Buckingham: Open University Press.

Couldry, N. (2000) *The Place of Media Power*. London: Routledge.

Covington, S. (1997) *Moving a Public Policy Agenda: the Strategic Philanthropy of Conservative Foundations*. Washington, DC: National Committee For Responsive Philanthropy.

Cunningham, S. and Sinclair, J. (2000) *Floating Lives: the Media and Asian Diasporas*. St Lucia, Queensland: University of Queensland Press.

Cunningham, S and Sinclair, J. (eds) (2001) *Floating Lives: the Media and Asian Diasporas*. Lanham, MD: Rowman and Littlefield.

Curran, J. (1991) 'Rethinking the media as a public sphere', in P. Dahlgren and C. Sparks (eds), *op. cit.* pp. 27–57.

Curtis, L. (1984) *Ireland: the Propaganda War*. London: Pluto.

Curtis, L.P. Jr (1968) *Anglo-Saxons and Celts*. New York: New York University Press.

Dabydeen, D. (1987) *Hogarth's Blacks: Images of Blacks in 18th Century English Art*. Athens, GA: University of Georgia Press.

Daes, E.-I.A. (1997) 'Preliminary working paper on indigenous peoples and their relationship to the land', contained in UN document: E/CN.4/Sub2/1997/17, cited in Henricksen (2001) *op. cit.*

Daes, E.-I.A. (2000) 'The spirit and letter of the right to self-determination of indigenous peoples: reflections on the making of the United Nations draft declaration', in P. Aikio and M. Scheinin (eds), *op. cit.* pp. 67–84.

Dahlgren, P. and Sparks, C. (eds) (1991) *Communication and Citizenship: Journalism and the Public Sphere in the New Media Age*. London: Routledge.

Dallaire, R. (2003) *Shake Hands with the Devil: the Failure of Humanity in Rwanda*. Toronto: Random House Canada.

Danky, J. and Cherney, J. (1996) 'Beyond Limbaugh: the Far Right's publishing spectrum'. *Reference Services Review*, 24 (Spring), 43–56.

Danziger, K. (1976) 'The dual aspect of human communication', Chapter 2 in *Interpersonal Communication*. Oxford: Pergamon.

Danziger, K. (1976) *Interpersonal Communication*. Oxford: Pergamon.

Davies, J. and Smith, C.R. (1997) *Gender, Ethnicity and Sexuality in Contemporary American Film*. Edinburgh: Keele University Press.

Davis, A.Y. (1998) 'Masked racism: reflections on the prison industrial complex'. *ColorLines* 1.2.

Decker, F. (2003) 'Les impasses du populisme de droite en Allemagne', in O. Ihl, J. Chêne, É. Vial and G. Waterlot (eds), *La Tentation Populiste au Cœur de l'Europe*. Paris: Editions La Découverte. pp. 213–27.

Dennis, E. and Pease, E.C. (1997) *The Media in Black and White*. New Brunswick: Transaction.

Denzin, N.K. (2002) *Reading 'Race'*. London: Sage.

Department of Health (2000) *The Vital Connection*. London: Department of Health.

Des Forges, A. (1999) *'Leave None To Tell The Story': Genocide in Rwanda*. New York: Human Rights Watch/Fédération Internationale des Ligues des Droits de l'Homme.

DeSwaan, A. (1990) *The Management of Normality*. London: Routledge.

Dewey, A.E. (1987) 'Address to the Sixteenth Colloquy on European Law' in Council of Europe (1987) *The Law of Asylum and Refugees: Present Tendencies and Future Perspectives*. Proceedings of the Sixteenth Colloquy on European Law, Lund, 15–17 September 1986, Strasbourg. Council of Europe, Strasbourg: Publications Section.

Dickinson, R., Harindranath, R. and Linné, O. (eds) (1998) *Approaches to Audiences: a Reader*. London: Edward Arnold.

Dixson, M. (1999) *The Imaginery Australian*. Sydney: University of New South Wales Press.

Dobson, S.M. (1991) *Transcultural Nursing*. London: Scutari.

Donia, R.J. and Fine, J.V.A. Jr (1994) *Bosnia and Hercegovina: a Tradition Betrayed*. London: Hurst and Co.

Dower, J. (1986) *War Without Mercy: 'Race' and Power in the Pacific War*. New York: Pantheon.

Downing, J. (1975) 'The (balanced) white view', in C.H. Husband (ed.), *White Media, Black Britain*. London: Hutchinson Arrow. pp. 90–137.

Downing, J. (1988) 'Alternative public realm: the organization of the 1980s anti-nuclear press in West Germany and Britain'. *Media, Culture and Society*, 10 (2): 165–83.

Downing, J. (1990) 'US media discourse on South Africa: the development of a situation model', *Discourse and Society*, 1 (1): 39–60.

Downing, J. (1996) *Internationalizing Media Theory: Transition, Power, Culture; Reflections on Media in Russia, Poland and Hungary, 1980–95*. London: Sage.

Downing, J. (1999a) 'Global networks toward new communities', in The Institute for Information Studies, *The Promise of Global Networks*. Queenstown, MD: The Aspen Institute. pp. 137–159.

Downing, J. (1999b) '"Hate speech" and "First Amendment absolutism" discourses in the US', *Discourse and Society*, 10 (2): 175–89.

Downing, J. (2001) *Radical Media: Rebellious Communication and Social Movements*. Thousand Oaks, CA: Sage.

Downing, J. (2003a) 'Audiences and readers of alternative media', *Media, Culture* and *Society*, 25 (5): 625–45.

Downing, J. (2003b) 'Hemispheric cultural unity and the denial of white racism', in G. Tremblay, (ed.), *Panam: industries culturelles et dialogue des civilizations dans les Amériques*. Montréal, Canada: Les Presses de l'Université Laval. pp. 123–37.

Downing, J.D.H. and Husband, C. (1999) 'Media, ethnicity and the construction of difference: monitoring the impact of the media in a multi-ethnic world', in K. Nordenstreng and M. Griffin (eds), *International Media Monitoring*. Cresskill, NJ: Hampton Press. pp. 277–306.

Dummett, M. (2001) *On Immigration and Refugees*. London: Routledge.

Dunn, T. (1996) *The Militarization of the US-Mexico Border 1978–1992: Low-intensity Conflict Doctrine comes Home*. Austin, TX: University of Texas Press.

Durkheim, E. (1995) *The Elementary Forms of Religious Life*. New York: Free Press.

Dyer, R. (1997) *White*. New York: Routledge.

Ekman, P. and Friesen, W.V. (1969) 'The repertoire of nonverbal behaviour: Categories, Origin, Usage and Coding', *Semiotica*, 1, 49–98.

Elliot, J., Walker, R., Balson, G., Choudheri, S. and Husband, C. (2002) *Getting on Against the Odds: How Black and Ethnic Minority Nurses can Progress into Leadership*. London: NHS Leadership Centre, Department of Health.

Elliott, P. (1972) *The Framework of Television Production*. London: Constable.

Elliott, P. (1977) 'Reporting Northern Ireland: a study of news in Great Britain, Northern Ireland, and the Republic of Ireland', in *Ethnicity and the Media*. Paris: UNESCO. pp. 263–376.

Entman, R. and Rojecki, A. (2000) *The Black Image in the White Mind*. Chicago: Chicago University Press.

Ericson, R.V., Baranek, P.M. and Chan, J.B.L. (1991) *Representing Order: Crime, Law and Justice in the News Media*. Toronto: University of Toronto Press.

Eriksen, T.H. (1995) *Small Places, Large Issues*. London: Pluto.

Eriksen, T.H. (1995) 'Ethnicity', Chapter 16 in T.H. Eriksen (ed.), *Small Places, Large Issues – an Introduction to Social and Cultural Anthropology*. London: Pluto.

Essed, P. (1991) *Understanding Everyday Racism*. London: Sage.

EU Accession Monitoring Program (2002) *Monitoring the EU Accession Process: Minority Protection*. Budapest: Open Society Institute.

EUMC (2002) European Monitoring Centre on Racism and Xenophobia. *Annual Report*. Vienna, Austria: EUMC.

European Monitoring Centre on Racism and Xenophobia (1999) *Cultural Diversity Against Racism*. Cologne: Westdeutscher Rundfunk.

Eysenck, H.J. (1971) '*Race*', *Intelligence and Education*. London: Temple Smith.

Fair, J. (1993) 'War, famine and poverty: 'race' in the construction of Africa's media image', *Journal of Communication Inquiry* 17 (2): 5–23.

Fairchild, H.N. (1928) *The Noble Savage: a Study in Romantic Naturalism*. New York: Columbia University Press.

Femia, J. (1981) *Gramsci's Political Thought: Hegemony, Consciousness, and the Revolutionary Process*. Oxford: Clarendon.

Ferguson, R. (1999) *Representing 'Race'*. London: Arnold.

Fernández, C. and Paxman, A. (2000) *Ei Tigre: Emilio Azcárraga y sa imperio televisa*. Mexico City: Editorial Grijalbo.

Fernando, S. (1991) *Mental Health, 'Race', Culture*. London: Macmillan/MIND.

Fernando, S. (ed.) (1995) *Mental Health in a Multi-ethnic Society*. London: Routledge.

Fernhout, R. (1993) 'Europe 1993 and its Refugees', *Ethnic and Racial Studies*, 16 (3): 492–506.

Fisk, J., Hodge, B. and Turner, G. (1987) *Myths of Oz: Reading Australian Popular Culture*. Sydney: Allen and Unwin.

Foot, P. (1965) *Immigration and 'Race' in British Politics*. Harmondsworth: Penguin.

Fox, D.T. (1993) 'Honouring the treaty', in T. Dowmunt (ed.), *Channels of Resistance: Global Television and Local Empowerment*. London: British Film Institute.

Fox, R.L. and Van Sickel, R.W. (2001) *Tabloid Justice: Criminal Justice in an Age of Media Frenzy*. Boulder, CO: Lynne Rienner.

Frachon, C. and Vargaftig, M. (1993) *Télévision d'Europe et immigration*. Paris: INA/Association Dialogue Entre les Cultures.

Francis, E. (1989) 'Black people, dangerousness and psychiatric compulsion', in A. Bracks and C. Grimshaw (eds), *Mental Health Care in Crisis*. London: Pluto.

François, B. and Neveu, E. (eds) (1999) *Espaces publics mosaïques: acteurs, arènes et rhétoriques des débats publics contemporains*. Rennes: Presses Universitaires de Rennes.

Frankl, R. (1998) 'Transformation of televangelism: repacking Christian family values', in L. Kintz and J. Lesage (eds), *Media, Culture and the Religious Right*. Minneapolis: University of Minnesota Press. pp. 163–89.

Franklin, B. and Murphy, D. (1998) *Making the Local News*. London: Routledge.

Fraser, C. (1978) 'Communication in interaction', in H. Tajfel and C. Fraser (eds), *Introducing Social Psychology*. Harmondsworth: Penguin Books.

Fraser, S. (ed.) (1995) *The Bell Curve Wars*. New York: Basic Books.

Fredman, S. (ed.) (2001) *Discrimination and Human Rights: the Case of Racism*. Oxford: Oxford University Press.

Fredrickson, G.M. (1971) *The Black Image in the White Mind: the Debate on Afro-American Character and Destiny, 1817–1914*. New York: Harper and Row.

Freud, S. (1930) *Civilisation and its Discontent*. Harmondsworth: Penguin.

Furuly, J.G. (1994) 'Samer – mer enn Norge Rundt?', *Samora*, 4, 7–9.

Galeotti, A.E. (2001) *Toleration as Recognition*. Cambridge: Cambridge University Press.

Gandy, O.H. (1998) *Communication and 'Race': a Structural Perspective*. London: Edward Arnold.

Gans, H.J. (1979) *Deciding What's News*. New York: Vintage.

García Canclini, N. (2001) *Consumers and Citizens: Globalization and Multi-cultural Conflicts*. Minneapolis, MN: University of Minnesota Press.

Garnham, N. (2000) *Emancipation, the Media and Modernity*. Oxford: Oxford University Press.

Gasana, J. (2002) 'Remember Rwanda?', *World Watch* 15.2, 23–33.

Geipel, J. (1969) *The Europeans: an Ethnohistorical Survey*. London: Longman.

Gerbner, G., Morris, M. and Signorielli, N. (1999) 'Profiling television violence', in K. Nordenstreng and M. Griffin (eds), *International Media Monitoring*. Presskill, NJ: Hampton Press. pp. 335–65.

Gerrish, K., Husband, C. and Mackenzie, J. (1996) *Nursing for a Multi-Ethnic Society*. Buckingham: Open University Press.

Giddens, A. (1979) *Central Problems in Social Theory*. London: Macmillan.

Giddens, A. (1984) *The Constitution of Society*. Cambridge: Polity Press.

Giger, J.C. and Davidhizar, R.E. (1999) *Transcultural Nursing*. St. Louis: Mosby.

Gilens, M. (1999) *Why Americans Hate Welfare: 'Race', Media and the Politics of Antipoverty Policy*. Chicago: University of Chicago Press.

Gillespie, M. (1995) *Television, Ethnicity and Cultural Change*. London: Routledge.

Gillespie, M. (2000) 'Transnational Communications and Diaspora Communities', in S. Cottle, *op.cit.*, 164–78.

Gilmore, R.W. (1998) 'Globalisation and US prison growth: From military Keynesianism to post-Keynesian militarism', *'Race' and Class*, 40 (2–3): 171–88.

Gilmore, R.W. (1999–2000) 'Behind the power of 41 bullets: what is domestic militarization and how did it come about?', *ColorLines*, 2 (4): 16–20.

Gilroy, P. (1993) *The Black Atlantic: Modernity and Double Consciousness*. London: Verso.

Gilroy, P. (2000) *Between Camps*. London: Penguin.

Gilroy, P. (2001) *Between Camps: 'Race', Identity and Nationalism at the End of the Colour Line*. London: Penguin.

Gitlin, T. (1994) *Inside Prime Time*, 2nd edn. Berkeley, CA: University of California Press.

Gitlin, T. (1998) 'Public Sphere or Public Sphericules?', in T. Liebes and J. Curran (eds), *Media, Ritual and Identity*. London: Routledge. pp. 175–202.

Gitlin, T. (2000) *Inside Prime Time*, 2nd edn. Berkeley, CA: University of California Press.

Glendinning, C., Lewis, J. and Meredith, B. (1988) *National Primary Care Research and Development Centre – Daughters who Care: Daughters Caring for Mothers at Home*. London: Routledge and Kegan Paul.

Glenny, M. (1999) *The Balkans, 1804–1999: Nationalism, War and the Great Powers*. London: Granta.

Goffman, E. (1959) *The Presentation of Self in Everyday Life*. New York: Doubleday Anchor.

Goffman, E. (1967) *Interaction Ritual*. New York: Doubleday Anchor.

Goldberg, D.T. (1994) *Multiculturalism*. Oxford: Blackwell.

Gordon, P. and Klug, F. (1986) *New Right New Racism*. London: Searching Publications.

Gossiaux, J.F. (2002) *Pouvoirs ethniques dans les Balkans*. Paris: Presses Universitaires de France.

Gouteux, J.P. (2002) *La nuit rwandaise: l'implication française dans le dernier génocide du siècle*. Paris: L'Esprit Frappeur/Dagorno.

Govaert, S. (1998) 'Bruxelles convoitée par l'extrême droite', *Le Monde Diplomatique* (January), 7.

Gow, J., Paterson, R. and Preston, A. (eds) (1996) *Bosnia by Television*. London: BFI Publishing.

Gramsci, A. (1971) *Selections from the Prison Notebooks*. London: Lawrence and Wishart.

Gray, G. and Winter, C. (eds) (1997) *The Resurgence of Racism: Howard, Hanson and the 'Race' Debate*. Clayton: Monash Publications in History.

Gray, H. (1995) *Watching 'Race': Television and the Struggle for 'Blackness'*. Minneaplis: University of Minnesota Press.

Greenberg, B.S. (1972) *Non-whites on British Television*. London: BBC Research Department.

Grewal, I. (1996) *Home and Harem*. London: Leicester University Press.

Grewal, S., Kay, J., Landor, L., Lewis, G. and Parmar, P. (1988) *Charting the Journey*. London: Sheba Feminist Publishers.

Gitlin, T. (2000) *Inside Prime Time*. Berkeley, CA: University of California Press.

Guerrero, E. (1993) *Framing Blackness: the African American Image in Film*. Philadelphia, PA: Temple University Press.

Guichaoua, A. (ed.) (1995) *Les crises politiques au Burundi et au Rwanda (1993–1994)*. Lille and Paris: Université des Sciences et Technologies de Lille/Editions Karthala.

Guillaumin, C. (1995) *Racism, Sexism, Power and Ideology*. London: Routledge.

Gurnah, A. (1989) 'The politics of racism awareness training', *Critical Social Policy, 10, Winter*, 6–20.

Haack, S. (1998) *Evidence and Inquiry*. Oxford: Blackwell.

Hackett, R.H. and Zhao, Y. (1998) *Sustaining Democracy? Journalism and the Politics of Objectivity*. Toronto: Garamond.

Hafez, K. (ed.) (2003) *Media Ethics in the Dialogue of Cultures*. Hamburg: Deutsches Orient-Institut.

Hage, G. (1998) *White Nation: Fantasies of White Supremacy in a Multicultural Society*. Annandale, NSW: Pluto Press, Australia.

Hall, S. (1990) 'The whites of their eyes' (revised), in M. Alvarado and J.O. Thompson (eds), *The Media Reader*. London: BFI Publications. pp. 7–23.

Hall, S. (1996a) 'The problem of ideology: Marxism without guarantees', in D. Morley and K.-H. Chen (eds), *Stuart Hall: Critical Dialogues in Cultural Studies*. London: Routledge. pp. 25–46.

Hall, S. (1996b) 'Gramsci's relevance for the study of 'race' and ethnicity', in D. Morley and K.-H. Chen (eds), *Stuart Hall: Critical Dialogues in Cultural Studies*. London: Routledge. pp. 411–40.

Hall, S., Critcher, C., Jefferson, T., Clarke, J. and Roberts, B. (1978) *Policing the Crisis: 'Mugging', the State and Law and Order*. London: Macmillan.

Haller, J.S. (1995) *Outcasts from Evolution: Scientific Attitudes of Racial Inferiority, 1859–1900*. Carbondale, IL: University of Southern Illinois Press.

Hamelink, C.J. (1993) 'Europe and democratic deficit', *Media Development*, 140 (4): 8–11.

Hammond, P. and Herman, E.S. (eds) (2000) *Degraded Capability: the Media and the Kosovo Crisis*. London: Pluto.

Hancock, A. (1992) *Communication Planning Revisited*. Paris: UNESCO.

Hannum, H. (1996) *Autonomy, Sovereignty, and Self-Determination: the Accommodation of Conflicting Rights*, 2nd revised edition. Philadelphia: University of Pennsylvania Press.

Harasym, S. (ed.) (1990) *The Post-Colonial Critic*. London: Routledge.

Hardisty, J. (1999) *Mobilizing Resentment: Conservative Resurgence from the John Birch Society to the Promise Keepers*. Boston: Beacon.

Hargreaves, A.G. (1995) *Immigration, 'Race', and Ethnicity in Contemporary France*. London: Routledge.

Hartley, J. and McKee, A. (2000) *The Indigenous Public Sphere*. Oxford: Oxford University Press.

Hartley, P. (1993) *Interpersonal Communication*. London: Routledge.

Hartmann, P. and Husband, C. (1974) *Racism and the Mass Media*. London: Davis-Poynter.

Hartmann, P., Husband, C. and Clark, J. (1974) 'Race as news: a study of the handling of "race" in the British press from 1963 to 1970', *'Race' as News*. Paris: The UNESCO Press. pp. 91–173.

Hechter, M. (1975) *Internal Colonialism*. London: Routledge and Kegan Paul.

Heckman, F. (1995) 'Is there a migration policy in Germany?' in F. Heckmann and W. Bosswick (eds), *Migration Policies: a Comparative Perspective*. Stuttgart: Ferdinand Enke Verlag.

Heckmann, F. and Bosswick, W. (eds) (1995) *Migration Policies: a Comparative Perspective*. Stuttgart: Enke Verlag.

Heider, D. (2000) *White News*. Mahwah, NJ: Lawrence Erlbaum.

Heintze, H.J. (1998) 'On the legal understanding of autonomy', in M. Suksi (ed.), *Autonomy: Applications and Implications*. The Hague: Kluwer Law International. pp. 7–32.

Hemming, S. (1992) 'Changing History: New Images of Aboriginal History', in E. Bourke and B. Edwards (eds), *op.cit.* pp. 16–37.

Henley, A. and Schott, J. (1999) *Culture, Religion and Patient Care in a Multi-ethnic Society: a Handbook for Professionals*. London: Age Concern.

Hencke, D. (2000) 'Skills shortage prompts immigration rethink', The *Guardian*, 4 September.

Henneman, E.A., Lee, J.L. and Cohen, J.I. (1995) 'Collaboration: a concept analysis', in *Journal of Advanced Nursing*, 21: 103–9.

Henricksen, J.B. (2001) 'Implementation of the Right of Self-determination of Indigenous Peoples'. *Indigenous Affairs*, No. 3: p. 6–21.

Herman, E. and Chomsky, N. (1988) *Manufacturing Consent: the Political Economy of the Mass Media*. New York: Pantheon.

Herman, E. and McChesney, R. (1997) *Global Media: Missionaries of International Capitalism*. London: Cassell.

Hill, M. (ed.) (1997) *Whiteness: a Critical Reader*. New York: New York University Press.

Hill, M.J. and Issacharoff, R.M. (1971) *Community Action and 'Race' Relations*. London: Oxford University Press.

Hilliard, R.L., and Keith, M.C. (1999). *Waves of Rancor: Tuning in the Radical Right*. Armonk, NY: M.E. Sharpe.

Himmelfarb, G. (2001) *One Nation, Two Cultures: a Searching Examination of American Society in the Aftermath of Our Cultural Revolution*. New York: Vintage.

Himmelman, A. (1994) 'Collaboration for change: definitions, models and roles – with a user-friendly guide to collaborative processes from the authors: Communities working collaboratively for change', in M. Hermanm (ed.), *Resolving Conflict: Strategies for Local Government*. Washington, DC: International City/County Management Association.

Himmelstein, J.L. (1990) *To the Right: the Transformation of American Conservatism.* Berkeley, CA: University of California Press.

Hinton, P. (1993) *The Psychology of Interpersonal Perception.* London: Routledge.

Hobsbawm, E.J. (1983) 'Introduction: inventing traditions', Chapter 1 in E.J. Hobsbawn and T. Ranger (eds), *The Invention of Tradition.* Cambridge: Cambridge University Press.

Hobsbawn, E.J. and Ranger, T. (1983) *The Invention of Tradition.* Cambridge: Cambridge University Press.

Hogg, M.A. and Abrams, D. (1988) *Social Identification: a Social Psychology of Intergroup Relations and Group Processes.* London: Routledge.

Hogg, P.W. (1992) *Constitutional Law of Canada,* Vol. 2. Scarborough, Ontario: Carswell.

Holland, K. and Hogg, C. (2001) *Cultural Awareness in Nursing and Health Care: an Introductory Text.* London: Arnold.

Holland, J. (1996) 'Covering the northern crisis: the US Press and Northern Ireland', in W. Rolston and D. Miller (eds), *War and Words: the Northern Ireland Media Reader.* Belfast: Beyond the Pale Publications. pp. 377–402.

Home Office (2000) *Race Equality in Public Services.* London: HMSO.

hooks, b. (1981) *Ain't I A Woman?* Boston: South End Press.

hooks, b. (1991) *Yearning: Race, Gender and Cultural Politics.* London: Turnaround.

hooks, b. (1992) *Black Looks: Race and Representation.* Boston, MA: South End Press.

Horgan, J. (2001) *Irish Media: a Critical History since 1922.* London: Routledge.

Horn, F. (1999) 'Sami and greenlandic media' – special issue of *Juridica Lapponica*, No. 22. Rovaniemi: The Northern Institute for Environmental and Minority Law.

Horsfield, G. and Stewart, J. (2003) 'One Nation and Australian media', in G. Mazzoleni et al. (eds), *The Media and Neo-Populism.* New York: Praeger. pp. 121–47.

HoSang, D. (1999–2000) 'The economics of the new brutality', *ColorLines*, 2 (4): 21–26.

Hughes, R. (1987) *The Fatal Shore.* London: Collins Harvill.

Hughes, R. (1994) *The Culture of Complaint.* London: Harvill.

Hujanen, T. (1988) *The Role of Information in the Realization of the Human Rights of Migrant Workers.* Tampere: Department of Journalism and Mass Communication. University of Tampere.

Hujanen, T. (1989) *Information, Communication and the Human Rights of Migrants.* Lausanne: Bureau Lausannois pour les Immigrés.

Hunt, D. (1997) *Screening the Los Angeles 'Riots': Race, Seeing and Resistance.* New York: Cambridge University Press.

Hunt, D. (1999) *O.J. Simpson Facts and Fictions: News Rituals in the Construction of Reality.* New York: Cambridge University Press.

Hunter, M. (1998a) 'Militer au *Front*', *Le monde diplomatique*, (May), 16.

Hunter, M. (1998b) 'Les réseaux européens du *Front National*', *Le monde diplomatique* (December), 3.

Huntington, S.P. (1993) 'The clash of the civilizations?', *Foreign Affairs*, 72 (3): 22–50.

Husband, C. (ed.) (1975) *White Media and Black Britain.* London: Arrow Books.

Husband, C. (1982) 'Introduction: "Race", the Continuity of a Concept', in C. Husband (ed.), *Race in Britain: Continuity and Change.* London: Hutchinson.

Husband, C. (ed.) (1987) *Race in Britain: Continuity and Change,* 2nd edition. London: Hutchinson Education.

Husband, C. (1991) ' "Race", conflictual politics and anti-racist social work: lessons from the past for action in the '90s', in *Setting the Context for Change.* London: Central Council For Education and Training in Social Work.

Husband, C. (ed.) (1994a) *A Richer Vision: the Development of Ethnic Minority Media in Western Democracies.* Unesco: John Libbey.

Husband, C. (1994b) *'Race' and Nation: the British Experience.* Perth, Australia: Paradigm.

Husband, C. (1995) 'The morally active practitioner and the ethics of anti-racist social work', in R. Hugman and D. Smith (eds), *Ethical Issues in Social Work.* London: Routledge. pp. 84–103.

Husband, C. (1996) 'The right to be understood: conceiving the multi-ethnic public sphere', *Innovation*, 9 (2): 205–15.

Husband, C. (ed.) (1996) *A Richer Vision*. Unesco: John Libbey.

Husband, C. (1998) 'Differentiated citizenship and the multi-ethnic public sphere', *Journal of International Communication*, 5 (1 and 2): 134–148.

Husband, C. (1999) 'Negotiating identities in a diasporic context', in D. Turton and J. Gonzalez (eds), *Cultural Identities and Ethnic Minorities in Europe*. Bilbao: University of Deusto. pp. 87–101.

Husband, C. (2000) 'media and the public sphere in multi-ethnic societies', in S. Cottle (ed.), *Ethnic Minorities and the Media*. Buckingham: Open University Press.

Husband, C. (2001) 'Über den Kampf gegen Rassismus hinaus: Entwurf einer polyetnischen Medienlandschaft', in B. Busch, B. Hipfl and K. Robins (eds), *Bewegte Identitäten. Medien in transkulturellen Kontexten*. Klagenfurt: Drava-Verlag.

Husband, C. (2002) 'Diasporic identities and diasporic economics: the case of minority ethnic media', in M. Martiniello and B. Picquard (eds), *Diversity in the City*. Bilbao: University of Deusto Press.

Husband, C. (2004a) 'The politics of diversity', in C. Husband and B. Torry (eds), *op. cit.*

Husband, C. (2004b) 'Transcultural communication', in C. Husband and B. Torry (eds), *op. cit.*

Husband, C. and Alam, Y. (2001) 'Beyond the rhetoric of codes of practice: ethnicity and media monitoring reviewed', *Nord-Süd Aktuell*, XV, No. 4, 680–691.

Husband, C. and Alam, Y. (2002) 'Codes of practice and media performance: a systems report', in *Tuning in to Diversity*. Utrecht: OnLine More Colour in the Media/Mira Media. Available at. http://www.multicultural.net.

Husband, C. and Torry, B. (eds) (2004) *Transcultural Health Care Practice: au Educational Resource for Nurses and Health Care Practitioners*. London: Royal College of Nursing. Www.rcn.org.uk/resources/transcultural/index.php

Idivuoma, M. (1999) 'Samer på pränt. En studie av fem svenska tidningars rapportering om samer', unpublished research essay in journalism for Mitthögskolan i Sundsvall, Sweden.

Ignatiev, N. (1995) *How the Irish Became White*. New York: Routledge.

Ihl, O., Chêne, J., Vial, E. and Waterlot, G. (eds) (2003) *La tentation populiste au coeur de l'Europe*. Paris: Editions La Découverte.

Iley, K. and Nazroo, J. (2001) 'Ethnic inequalities in mental health', in L. Culley and S. Dyson (eds), *Ethnicity and Nursing Practice*. Basingstoke: Palgrave.

Iordanova, D. (2001) *Cinema of Flames: Balkan Film, Culture and the Media*. London: BFI Publishing.

Isaksson, P. (1996) 'Kun koko kylä piiloutui: saamelaiset Yrjö Kajavan.

Jackson, P. and Penrose, J. (1993) *Constructions of 'Race', Place and Nation*. London: UCL Press.

Jakubowicz, A., Goodall, H. and Martin, J. (1994) *Racism, Ethnicity and the Media*. St Leonards, New South Wales: Allen and Unwin.

James. A., Hockey, J. and Dawson, A. (1997) *After Writing Culture: Epistemology and Praxis in Contemporary Anthropology*. London: Routledge.

James, C.L.R. (1984) *Beyond a Boundary*. London: Serpents Tail (reprint of the 1963 edition published by Duke University Press).

Jayasuriya, L., Walker, D. and Gothard, J. (2003) *Legacies of White Australia*. Crawley, W.A: University of Western Australia Press.

Jeffrey, B. (1999) *Hard Right Turn: the New Face of Neo-Conservatism in Canada*. New York: HarperCollins.

Jewson, N. and Mason, D. (1986) 'The Theory and Practice of Equal Opportunities Policies', *Sociological Review* 34 (2): 307–34.

Jhally, S. and Lewis, J. (1992) *Enlightened Racism: The Cosby Show, Audiences and the Myth of the American Dream*. Boulder, CO: Westview.

Johnson, E. (1998) 'The emergence of Christian video and the cultivation of videoevangelism', in L. Kintz and J. Lesage (eds), *Media, Culture and the Religious Right*. Minneapolis: University of Minnesota Press. pp. 191–210.

Johnstone, D. (2002) *Fools' Crusade: Yugoslavia, NATO and Western Delusions*. New York: Monthly Review.

Jordan, W.D. (1968) *White over Black: American Attitudes toward the Negro, 1550–1812*. Chapel Hill, NC: University of North Carolina Press.

Jordan, W.D. (1969) *White Over Black*. Harmondsworth: Penguin.

Juteau, D. (1997) 'Multicultural citizenship: the challenge of pluralism in Canada', in V. Bader (ed.), *Citizenship and Exclusion*. Basingstoke: Macmillan. pp. 96–112.

Kabbani, R. (1994) *Imperial Fictions: Europe's Myths of Orient*. London: Pandora.

Kahn, J. (2000) 'The parade of sovereignties: establishing the vocabulary of the new Russian Federalism', *Post-Soviet Affairs* 16 (1): 58–89.

Kaldor, M. (2003) *Global Civil Society*. Oxford: Polity.

Kareem, J. and Littlewood, R. (1992) *Intercultural Therapy*. Oxford: Blackwell.

Karim, K.H. (2000) *Islamic Peril: Media and Global Violence*. Montreal: Black Rose.

Katznelson, I. (1973) *Black Men, White Cities*. London: Oxford University Press.

Kayimahe, V. (2001) *France-Rwanda: les coulisses du génocide*. Paris: L'EspritFrappeur/Dagorno.

Keane, J. (1991) *The Media and Democracy*. Cambridge: Polity.

Keane, J. (1998) *Civil Society: Old Images, New Visions*. Oxford: Polity.

Keane, J. (2003) *Global Civil Society*. Cambridge: Cambridge University Press.

Keith, M. and Pile, S. (1993) *Place and the Politics of Identity*. London: Routledge.

Kelleher, D. and Hillier, S. (1996) *Researching Cultural Differences in Health*. London: Routledge.

Kellner, D. (1995) 'Advertising and consumer culture,' in J. Downing, A. Mohammadi and A. Sreberny-Mohammadi (eds), *Questioning the Media: A Critical Introduction*. 2nd edn. Thousand Oaks, CA: Sage Publications Inc. pp. 329–45.

Kellow, C.L. and Steeves, H.L. (1998) 'The role of radio in the Rwandan genocide', *Journal of Communication* 48 (3): 107–28.

Kiernan, M. (1998) *Media Ethics*. London: Routledge.

Kiernan, V.G. (1969) *The Lords of Human Kind*. London: Weidenfeld and Nicholson.

Kilpatrick, J. (1999) *Celluloid Indians: Native Americans and Film*. Lincoln, NE: University of Nebraska Press.

Kim, Y.Y. (1992) 'Intercultural communication competence: a systems theoretic view', in W.B. Gudykunst and Y.Y. Kim (eds), *Readings on Communication with Strangers*. New York: McGraw-Hill.

Kintz, L. and Lesage, J. (eds) (1998) *Media, Culture and the Religious Right*. Minneapolis: University of Minnesota Press.

Klare, M. and Kornbluh, P. (eds) (1987) *Low Intensity Warfare: how the USA Fights Wars without Declaring them*. New York: Pantheon.

Klier, J.D. and Lambroza, S. (eds) (1992) *Pogroms: Anti-Jewish Violence in Modern Russian History*. Cambridge: Cambridge University Press.

Kolar-Panov, D. (1997) *Video, War and the Diasporic Imagination*. London: Routledge.

Koopmans, R. and Statham, P. (2000) *Challenging Immigration and Ethnic Relations Politics*. Oxford: Oxford University Press.

Kotkin, J. (1992) *Tribes: How 'Race', Religion and Identity Determine Success in the New Global Economy*. New York: Random House.

Kreps, G.L. and Kunimoto, E.N. (1994) *Effective Communication in Multicultural Health Care Settings*. London: Sage.

Krieg, A. (1999) 'Vacance argumentative: l'usage du *(sic)* dans la presse d'extrême droite contemporaine', *Mots/Les Langages du Politique* 58 (March), 11–34.

Krieg-Planque, A. (2003) '*Purification ethnique*': *une formule et son histoire*. Paris: CNRS Editions.

Krippendorff, K. (1980) *Content Analysis*. Thousand Oaks, CA: Sage.

Kung, Wen-chi (1997) *Indigenous Peoples and the Press: a Study of Taiwan*. Unpublished PhD thesis. Loughborough University.

Kurspahić, K. (2003) *Prime Time Crime: Balkan Media in War and Peace*. Washington DC: United States Institute of Peace Press.

Kymlicka, W. (1995) *Multicultural Citizenship*. Oxford: Oxford University Press.

Kymlicka, W. (2001) *Politics in the Vernacular*. Oxford: Oxford University Press.

Kymlicka, W. and Norman, W. (2000) *Citizenship in Diverse Societies*. Oxford: Oxford University Press.

Land, J. (1998) 'Sitting in Limbaugh: bombast in broadcasting', in L. Kintz and J. Lesage (eds), *Media, Culture and the Religious Right*. Minneapolis: University of Minnesota Press. pp. 227–43.

Langton, M. (1993) 'Well, I Heard It on the Radio and I Saw it on the Television'. Sydney: Australian Film Commission.

Laqueur, W. (1993). *Black Hundred: the Rise of the Extremist Right in Russia*. New York: HarperCollins.

Larrain, J. (1979) *The Concept of Ideology*. Athens, GA: University of Georgia Press.

Lauristin, M. and Vihalemm, P. (1997) *Return to the Western World*. Tartu: Tartu University Press.

Lave, J. and Wenger, E. (1991) *Situated Learning*. Cambridge: Cambridge University Press.

Law, I. (2000) *Race in the News*. Basingstoke: Palgrave.

Lears, T.J.J. (1985) 'The concept of cultural hegemony: problems and possibilities', *The American Historical Review*, 90 (3): (June), 567–93.

Ledwith, F. and Husband, C. (1999) 'Social analysis: policy and managerial issues', in K. Bhui and D. Olafide (eds), *Mental Health Service Provision for a Multi-cultural Society*. London: W.B. Saunders. pp. 197–210.

Lehtola, V.P. (1995) 'Alempi kulttuuri, katoava kansa? Saamelaiset ja sosiaalidarwinismi 1920–ja 1930–luvun kirjallisuudessa', *Faravid* (Pohjoissuomen historiallisan yhdistyksen vuosikirja), No. 17/1993, pp. 233–58.

Lehtola, V.P. (1997) *Rajamaan identiteetti: lappilaisuuden rakentaminen 1920–ja 1930 luvun kirjallisuudessa*. Helsinki: Suomen Kirjallisuuden Seura.

Lehtola, V.P. (1999) 'Aito lappalainen ei syó haarukalla ja veitsellä. Stereotypiat ja saamelainen kulttuuritutkimus', in M. Tuominen, S. Tuulentie, V-P. Lehtola and M. Autti (eds), *Pohjoiset identiteetit ja mentaliteetit, osa I: Outamaalta tunturiin*. Jyväskylä: Gummerus Kirjapaino Oy. pp. 15–32.

Lehtola, Jorma (2000) *Lailasta Lailaan: tarinoita elokuvan sitkeistä lappalaisista*. tnarce kustannus-puntsi.

Lesage, J. (1998) 'Christian coalition leadership training', in L. Kintz and J. Lesage (eds), *Media, Culture and the Religious Right*. Minneapolis: University of Minnesota Press. pp. 295–325.

Lesser, E.L., Fontaine, M.A. and Slusher, J.A. (2000) *Knowledge and Communities*. Boston: Butterworth-Heinemann.

Lippman, L. (1981) *Generations of Resistance*. Melbourne: Longman Cheshire.

Lippman, W. (1922) *Public Opinion*. New York: Free.

Lipsitz, G. (1998) *Possessive Investment in Whiteness: how White People Benefit from Identity Politics*. Philadelphia, PA: Temple University Press.

Littlewood, R. and Lipsedge, M. (1982) *Aliens and Alienists*. Harmondsworth: Penguin.

Lock, D.C. (1992) *Increasing Multicultural Understanding*. London: Sage.

Luckman, J. (1999) *Transcultural Communication in Nursing*. Albany, NY: Delmar.

Lustgarten, L. (1989) 'Racial inequality and the limits of the law', in R. Jenkins and J. Solomos (eds), *Racism and Equal Opportunity Policies in the 1980s*. 2nd edn. Cambridge: Cambridge University Press.

Lyman, R. (2002) 'Black actors: still keeping their eyes on the prize', *The New York Times*, 27 February, E1.

MacBride, S. (1980) *Many Voices, One World: Towards a New More Just and More Efficient World Information and Communication Order*. Paris: Unesco and WACC.

MacDonald, D.B. (2003) *Balkan Holocausts? Serbian and Croatian Victim-centred Propaganda and the War in Yugoslavia*. Manchester: Manchester University Press.

Macpherson, Sir William (1999) *The Stephen Lawrence Inquiry: Report of an Inquiry*. London: Home Office. (This report can be accessed online through Black Information Network: www.blink.org.uk)

Malik, S. (2002) *Representing Black Britain: Black and Asian Images on Television*. London: Sage.

Mansbridge, J. (2000) 'What does a representative do? Descriptive representation in communicative settings of distrust, uncrystallized interests and historically denigrated status', in W. Kymlicka and W. Norman *op. cit.* pp. 99–123.

Markelin, L. (2003a) 'Media, ethnicity and power: A comparative analysis of the nordic Sámi media environment in relation to state policies'. PhD thesis, University of Bradford, England.

Markelin, L. (2003b) 'En gemensam samisk offentlighet? Om en nordisk samisk medieinfrastruktur', in B. Bjerkli and P. Selle (eds), *Samer, makt og demokrati. Sametinget og den nye samiske offentligheten*. Oslo: Gyldendal Akademisk. pp. 398–424.

Martiniello, M. (1993) *L'ethnicité dans les sciences sociales contemporaines. Coll. Que-sais-je?* Paris: Presses Universitaires de France.

Martinez Cobo, J.R. (1986) *Study of the Problem of Discrimination Against Indigenous Populations.* U.N. document E/CN.4/Sub4/1986/7.

Maschino, M. (2003) 'Vers une police black-blanc-beur?', *Le monde diplomatique* (October), p. 10.

Mason, D. (1986) 'Controversies and continuities in 'race' and ethnic relations theory', in J. Rex and D. Mason (eds), *Theories of 'Race' and Ethnic Relations.* Cambridge: Cambridge University Press. pp. 1–19.

Mason, D. and Jewson, N. (1992) 'Race', equal opportunities policies and employment practice: Reflections on the 1980s, prospects for the 1990s', in *New Community*, 19 (1): 99–112.

Massing, P.W. (1949) *Rehearsal for Destruction: a Study of Political Anti-Semitism in Imperial Germany.* New York: Harper and Bros.

Mazzoleni, G., Stewart, J. and Horsfield, B. (eds) (2003) *The Media and Neo-populism.* New York: Praeger.

Mbaye, K. (1986) 'Introduction to the African Charter on human and peoples' rights', in International Commission on Jurists (ed.), *Human and Peoples' Rights in Africa and the African Charter.* Geneva: International Commission of Jurists.

McChesney, R. (1997) *Corporate Media and the Threat to Democracy.* New York: Seven Stories.

McConahay, J.B. (1986) 'Modern racism, ambivalence and the modern racism scale', in S.L. Gaertner and J.F. Dovidio (eds), *Prejudice, Discrimination and Racism.* Orlando: Academic. pp. 91–125.

McGuire, J. and Reeves, G. (2003) 'The rise of populist politics in India', in G. Mazzoleni et al. (eds), *The Media and Neo-populism.* New York: Praeger. pp. 95–119.

McLaren, P. (1994) 'White terror and oppositional agency: towards a critical multiculturalism', Chapter 1 in D.T. Goldberg, (ed.), *Multiculturalism: a Critical Reader.* Oxford: Blackwell.

McQuail, D. (1992) *Media Performance.* London: Sage.

Mead, G.H. (1934) *Mind, Self and Society.* Chicago: University of Chicago Press.

Means Coleman, R. (1998) *African American Viewers and the Black Situation Comedy: Situating Racial Humor.* New York: Garland.

Meekosha, H. (1993) 'The bodies politic: equality, difference and community practice', in H. Butcher, A. Glen, P. Henderson and J. Smith (eds), *Community and Public Policy.* London: Pluto.

Melilli, M. (2003) *Europa in fondo a destra: vecchi e nuovi fascismi.* Rome: Derivi Approdi.

Melvern, L. (2004) *Conspiracy To Murder: the Rwandan genocide.* London: Verso.

Mickler, S. (1998) *The Myth of Privilege.* South Fremantle: Fremantle Arts Centre Press.

Miles, R. (1989) *Racism.* London: Routledge.

Miller, D. (1994) *Don't Mention The War: Northern Ireland, Propaganda and the Media.* London: Pluto.

Miller, J. (1985) *Koori: a Will to Win.* North Ryde NSW: Angus and Robertson.

Miller, P. and Rose, N. (1988) 'The Tavistock programme: the government of subjectivity and social life', *Sociology.* 22 (2): 171–92.

Modood, T. et al. (1997) *Ethnic Minorities in Britain: Diversity and Disadvantage.* London: Policy Studies Institute.

Mohanty, C.T., Russo, A. and Torres, L. (1991) *Third World Women and the Politics of Feminism.* Bloomington: Indiana University Press.

Molnar, H. and Meadows, M. (2001) *Songlines to Satellites: Indigenous Communication in Australia, the South Pacific and Canada.* Annandale, NSW: Pluto Press, Australia.

Monbiot, G. (2000) *Captive State.* London: Pan Macmillan.

Moore, M. (2002) *Stupid White Men.* London: Penguin.

Morley, D. and Robins, K. (1995) *Spaces of Identity: Global Media, Electronic Landscapes and Cultural Boundaries.* London: Routledge.

Morris, C. (1955) *Signs, Language and Behavior.* New York: Braziller.

Morris, N. and Waisbord, S. (eds) (2001) *Media and Globalization: Why the State Matters.* Lanham: Rowman and Littlefield.

Mosco, V. (1996) *The Political Economy of Communication.* London: Sage.

Myntti, K. (2000) 'The right of indigenous peoples to self-determination and effective participation', in P. Aikio and M. Scheinin (eds), *op. cit.*

Naficy, H. (1993) *The Making of Exile Cultures: Iranian Television in Los Angeles*. Minneapolis: University of Minnesota Press.

Naimark, N. (2001) *Fires of Hatred: Ethnic Cleansing in Twentieth-Century Europe*. Cambridge, MA: Harvard University Press.

Nazroo, J.Y. (1997) *The Health of Britain's Ethnic Minorities*. London: Policy Studies Institute.

Negrouche, N. (2001) 'Alibi terroriste pour racisme antimaghrebin', *Le Monde Diplomatique* (November), p. 20.

Niemi, E. (1997) 'Sami history and the frontier myth: a perspective on the northern Sami spatial and rights history', in H. Gaski (ed.), *Sami Culture in a New Era: the Norwegian Sami Experience*. Karasjok: Davvi Girji. pp. 62–85.

Nord-Süd Aktuell (2001) 'Media and migration: ethnicity and transculturality in the media age', *Nord-Süd Aktuell* XV, 4, pp. 567–767.

Nordenstreng, K. (ed.) (1995) *Reports on Media Ethics in Europe*. Tampere: Department of Journalism and Mass Communication. University of Tampere. Series B41.

Nordenstreng, K. (1999) 'European landscape of media self-regulation', in *Freedom and Responsibility: Yearbook 1998/99*. Vienna: OSCE Representative on Freedom of the Media. pp. 169–85.

Nordenstreng, K. (2000) 'The structural context of media ethics: how media are regulated in democratic society', in B. Pattyn (ed.), *Media Ethics: Opening Social Dialogue*. Leuven: Peters. pp. 69–86.

Nordenstreng, K. (2003) 'Something to be done: transnational media monitoring', in K. Hafez (ed.), *op.cit.* pp. 215–27.

Nordenstreng, K. and Griffin, M. (1999) *International Media Monitoring*. Cresskill, N.J: Hampton.

Noriega, C. and López, A. (eds) (1996) *The Ethnic Eye: Latino Media Arts*. Minneapolis: University of Minnesota Press.

Noriega, C. (ed.) (1992) *Chicanos and Film: Representation and Resistance*. Minneapolis: University of Minnesota Press.

Noriega, C.A. (2000) *Shot in America: Television, the State, and the Rise of Independent Chicano Cinema*. Minneapolis: Minnesota University Press.

Norris, D.A. (1999) *In the Wake of the Balkan Myth: Questions of Identity and Modernity*. New York: St Martin's.

Omi, M. and Winant, H. (1986) *Racial Formation in the United States*. New York: Routledge.

On Line/More Colour in the Media: extensive website found at: http://www.multi-cultural.net

Orfali, B. (1990) *L'adhésion au Front National: de la minorité active au mouvement social*. Paris: Editions Kimé.

Parekh, B. (2000a) *Rethinking Multiculturalism: Cultural Diversity and Political Theory*. London: Macmillan Press.

Parekh, B. (2000b) *The Future of Multi-ethnic Britain*. London: Profile.

Parenti, C. (1999) *Lockdown America: Police and Prisons in the Age of Crisis*. London, Verso.

Park, R.E. (1970[1922]) *The Immigrant Press and its Control*. Westport, CT: Greenwood Press.

Parkinson, A. (1998) *Ulster Loyalism and the British Media*. Dublin: Four Courts.

Parry, R. (1995) 'The right-wing media machine', *Extra!*, 8 (2)(March-April), 6–10.

Paxman, J. (1999) *The English – A Portrait of a People*. London: Penguin.

Pedelty, M. (1995) *War Stories: the Culture of Foreign Correspondents*. New York: Routledge.

Pedersen, Ø.L. (1997) 'Mediemyter om det samiske', in *Hovedfagsårsboken 1997–8*. Oslo: Department of Sociology, Oslo University.

Pedon, É. and Walter, J. (1999) 'Photographes et argumentation dans les documents électoraux du *Front National*', *Mots/Les Langages du Politique*, 58 (March), 35–56.

Perea, J.F. (ed.) (1997) *Immigrants Out! The New Nativism and the Anti-Immigrant Impulse in the United States*. Albany, NY: New York University Press.

Pérez, R. (1985) 'The campaign against Fort Apache, the Bronx', in D. Kahn and D. Neumaier (eds), *Cultures in Contention*. Seattle, WA: Real Comet.

Pergnier, M. (2002) *Mots en guerre: discours médiatique et conflits balkaniques*. Lausanne: Editions L'Age d'Homme.

Perica, V. (2002) *Balkan Idols: Religion and Nationalism in Yugoslav States*. New York: Oxford University Press.

Petrova, D. (2001) *Racial Discrimination and the Rights of Minority Cultures, op. cit.* in S. Fredman, pp. 45–76.

Pettman, J. (1992) *Living in the Margins*. Sydney: Allen and Unwin.

Pfefferkorn, R. (1997) 'Fascinations autrichiennes pour M. Haider', *Le Monde Diplomatique*, (February), 13.

Philo, G. and Beattie, L. (1999) 'Race, migration and the media', Chapter II in G. Philo and L. Beattie (eds), *Message Received*. Harlow: Longman.

Pietikäinen, S. (2000) *Discourses of Differentiation: Ethnic Representations in Newspaper Texts, Jyväskylä Studies of Communication 12*. Jyväskylä: Jyväskylä University Printing House.

Pilgrim, D. and Rogers, A. (1993) *A Sociology of Mental Health and Illness*. Buckingham: Open University Press.

Pilgrim, D. and Treacher, A. (1992) *Clinical Psychology Observed*. London: Routledge.

Pintado-Vertner, R. and Chang, J. (1999–2000) 'The war on youth'. *ColorLines*, 2 (4): 9–15.

Pitcavage, M. (1996) 'Welcome to a new world (disorder): a visit to a gun show', *The Militia Watchdog* [Online]. Available at: www.militia-watchdog.org/gunshow.htm.

Plasser, F. and Ulram, P.A. (2003) 'Striking a responsive chord: mass media and right-wing populism in Austria', in G. Mazzoleni et al. (eds), *The Media and Neo-populism*. New York: Praeger. pp. 21–43.

Portelli, H. (1974) *Gramsci et la Question Religieuse*. Paris: Éditions Anthropos.

Pottier, J. (2002) *Re-Imagining Rwanda: Conflict, Survival and Disinformation in the Late Twentieth Century*. Cambridge: Cambridge University Press.

Putnam, R. (1993) *Making Democracy Work*. Princeton: Princeton University Press.

Rabah, S. (1998) *L'Islam dans le discours médiatique: comment les médias se représentent l'Islam en France?* Beirut: Les Editions Al-Bouraq.

Radhakrishnan, R. (1996) *Diasporic Mediations: Between Home and Location*. Minneapolis: University of Minnesota Press.

Rajagopal, A. (2001) *Politics After Television: Religious Nationalism and the Reshaping of the Indian Public*. New York: Cambridge University Press.

Ramírez-Berg, C. (1993), *Cinema of Solitude: a Critical Analysis of Mexican Film 1967–1983*. Austin, TX: University of Texas Press.

Ramírez-Berg, C. (2002) *Latino Images in Film: Stereotypes, Subversion, Resistance*. Austin TX: University of Texas Press.

Rattansi, A. and Westwood, S. (1994) *Racism, Modernity and Identity*. Oxford: Blackwell.

Ray, M. (2000) 'Bollywood down under: Fiji Indian cultural history and popular assertion', in S. Cunningham and J. Sinclair (eds), *op. cit.*, 136–84.

Read, J. and Coppin, P. (1999) *The Life of Nyamal Lawman: Peter Coppin*. Canberra: Aboriginal Studies Press.

Reese, S., Gandy, O. and Grant, A. (eds) (2001) *Framing Public Life: Perspectives on Media and our Understanding of the Social World*. Mahwah, NJ: Lawrence Erlbaum.

Reeves, F. (1983) *British Racial Discourse*. Cambridge: Cambridge University Press.

Reeves, J.L. and Campbell, R. (1994) *Cracked Coverage: Television News, the Anti-Cocaine Crusade, and the Reagan Legacy*. Durham, NC: Duke University Press.

Reid, J.J. (1992) 'Total war, the annihilation ethic, and the Armenian genocide, 1870–1918', in R. Hovannisian (ed.), *The Armenian Genocide: History, Politics, Ethics*. New York: St Martin's. pp. 21–52.

Reynolds, H. (1999) *Why Weren't We Told?* Camberwell, Victoria: Penguin.

Richards, D.A.J. (1999) *Italian American: the Racializing of an Ethnic Identity*. New York: New York University Press.

Ricœur, P. (1996) *Tolerance Between Intolerance and the Tolerable*. Providence, RI: Berghahn.

Riggins, S.H. (1992) *Ethnic Minority Media*. Newbury Park, CA: Sage.

Roach, C. (1990) 'The movement for a new world information and communication order: a second wave?', *Media, Culture and Society*, 12 (3): 283–307.

Roach, C. (1993) 'The MacBride round table as a non-governmental organization?' Paper delivered at the fifth MacBride Round Table, Dublin City University, Dublin, June 1993.

Robinson, L. (1995) *Psychology for Social Workers*. London: Routledge.

Robinson, L. (1998) *'Race', Communication and the Caring Professions*. Buckingham: Open University Press.

Rodríguez, A. (2000) *Making Latino News: 'Race', Language, Class*. Thousand Oaks, CA: Sage Publications Inc.

Rogers, A. (1990) 'Policing mental disorder: controversies, myths and realities', *Social Policy and Administration*, 23 (3): 226–37.

Rolston, B. (ed.) (1991a) *The Media and Northern Ireland: Covering the Troubles*. London: Macmillan.

Rolston, B. (1991b) 'News fit to print: Belfast's daily newspapers', in Rolston (1991a), *Op. cit.* pp. 152–86.

Rolston, B. (1991c) *Politics and Painting: Murals and Conflict in Northern Ireland*. Rutherford, NJ: Fairleigh Dickenson University Press.

Rolston, B. and Miller, D. (eds) (1996) *War and Words: the Northern Ireland Media Reader*. Belfast: Beyond the Pale.

Rose, E.J.B., et al. (1968) *Colour and Citizenship*. London: Oxford University Press.

Ross, K. and Playdon, P. (eds) (2001) *Black Marks: Minority Ethnic Audiences and Media*. Aldershot: Ashgate.

Rowse, T. (1993) *After Mabo*. Carlton: Melbourne University Press.

Ruesch, J. and Bateson, G. (1951) *Communication: the Social Matrix of Psychiatry*. New York: Norton.

Said, E. (1985) *Orientalism*. Harmondsworth: Penguin.

Sandlund, T. (2000) *Racism och etnicitet; den finlandssvenska tidningspressen*. Helsingfors: CEREN, Helsingfors Universitet.

Santa Ana, O. (2002) *Brown Tide Rising: Metaphors of Latinos in Contemporary American Public Discourse*. Austin, TX: University of Texas Press.

Sartre, J.P. (1956) *Being and Nothingness*. New York: Philosophical Library.

Schlesinger, P. (1987) *Putting 'Reality' Together: BBC News*, 2nd edn. London: Routledge.

Schlesinger, P. (1991) 'On the shape and scope of counter-insurgency thought', in P. Schlesinger (ed.), *Media, State, Nation*. London: Sage. pp. 66–91.

Schlesinger, P., Murdock, G. and Elliott, P. (1983) *Televising 'Terrorism': Political Violence in Popular Culture*. London: Comedia.

Schlesinger, P., Dobash, R.E. and Weaver, C.K. (1992) *Women Viewing Violence*. London: BFI Publications.

Schlesinger, P. and Tumber, H. (1994) *Reporting Crime: the Media Politics of Criminal Justice*. Oxford: Blackwell.

Seidel, G. (1986) 'Culture, nation and 'race' in the British and French New Right', in R. Levitas (ed.), *The Ideology of the New Right*. Oxford: Polity.

Shaheen, J. (2001) *Reel Bad Arabs: How Hollywood Vilifies a People*. New York: Olive Branch.

Shapiro, I. and Kymlicka, W. (1997) *Ethnicity and Group Rights*. New York: New York University Press.

Shaw, J.W., Nordlie, P.G. and Shapiro, R.M. (eds) (1987) *Strategies for Improving 'Race' Relations*. Manchester: Manchester University Press.

Shohat, E. and Stam, R. (1994) *Unthinking Eurocentrism: Multiculturalism and the Media*. London: Routledge.

Showstack Sassoon, A. (1987) *Gramsci's Politics*, 2nd edn. Minneapolis: University of Minnesota Press.

Showstack Sassoon, A. (2000) *Gramsci and Contemporary Politics*. London: Routledge.

Silber, L. and Little, A. (1996) *Yugoslavia: Death of a Nation*. New York: TV Books Inc/Penguin USA.

Sinclair, J. (1999) *Latin American Television: a Global View*. Oxford: Oxford University Press.

Sinclair, J., Jacka, E. and Cunningham, S. (1996) *New Patterns in Global Television: Peripheral Vision.* Oxford: Oxford University Press.

Sivanandan, A. (1981) 'RAT and the degradation of black struggle', *'Race' and Class*, 25 (2): 1–33.

Skogerbø, Eli (2000) 'Konflikt eller kuriosa? Om representasjon av den samiske minoriteten i majoritetsmediene i Norge', *Nordicom Information*, 3–4: 65–76.

Skrentny, J.D. (2002) *The Minority Right Revolution.* Cambridge, MA: Belknap.

Smith, A.M. (1994) *New Right Discourse on 'Race' and Sexuality: Britain, 1968–1990.* Cambridge: Cambridge University Press.

Smith-Shomade, B. (2002) *Shaded Lives: African-American Women and Television.* Brunswick, NJ: Rutgess University Press.

Solomos, J. (1993) *'Race' and Racism in Britain.* Basingstoke: Macmillan.

Solomos, J. and Back, L. (1995) *'Race', Politics and Social Change.* London: Routledge.

Souchard, M., Wahnich, S. Cuminal, I. and Wathier, V. (1997) *Le Pen, Les Mots: Analyse d'un discours d'extrême droite.* Paris: La Découverte.

Spivak, G.C. and Harasym, S. (1990) *The Post Colonial Critic.* London: Routledge.

Sreberny-Mohammadi, A. and Mohammadi, A. (1994) *Small Media, Big Revolution: Communication, Culture, and the Iranian Revolution.* Minneapolis: University of Minnesota Press.

Stanner, W.E.H. (1968) *After the Dreaming: the 1968 Boyer Lectures.* Sydney: Australian Broadcasting Commission.

Steet, L. (2000) *Veils and Daggers: A Century of National Geographic's Representation of the Arab World.* Philadelphia, PA: Temple University Press.

Stephenson, M.A. and Ratnapala, S. (eds) (1993) *Mabo: a Judicial Revolution.* St Lucia: University of Queensland Press.

Stockwell, S. and Scott, P. (2000) *All-Media Guide to Fair and Cross-cultural Reporting.* Australian Key Centre for Cultural and Media Policy. Brisbane: Griffith University.

Stoler, A.L. (1997) *'Race' and the Education of Desire.* Durham: Duke University Press.

Stratton, J. (1998) *'Race' Daze: Australia in Identity Crisis.* Annandale, NSW: Pluto.

Taguieff, P.-A. (2002) *L'illusion populiste.* Paris: Berg International.

Tajfel, H. (1982) *Social Identity and Intergroup Relations.* Cambridge: Cambridge University Press.

Tajfel, H. and Fraser, C. (eds) (1978) *Introducing Social Psychology.* Harmondsworth: Penguin.

Taylor, C. (1991) *The Ethics of Authenticity.* Cambridge, MA.: Harvard University Press.

Taylor, C. (1992) *Multiculturalism and 'the Politics of Recognition'.* Princeton, NJ: Princeton University Press.

Tebbit, N. (1990) *The Field.* London: IPC Country and Leisure Media Ltd.

ter Wal, J. (ed.) (2002) *Racism and Cultural Diversity in the Mass Media.* Vienna: European Monitoring Centre on Racism and Xenophobia.

Tévanian, P. (2001) *Le racisme républicain: réflexions sur le modèle français de discrimination.* Paris: L'EspritFrappeur.

Tharp, M. (2001) *Marketing and Consumer Identity in Multicultural America.* Thousand Oaks, CA: Sage.

Thomas, J. (1991) 'Toeing the line: why the American press fails', in Rolston (1991a), *op. cit.* 122–35.

Thompson, M. (1999) *Forging War: The Media in Serbia, Croatia, Bosnia and Hercegovina.* Luton: Luton University Press.

Top, B. and Doppert, M. (1993) *Balance or Blunder.* Amsterdam: Working Group Migrants and the Media of the Netherlands Association of Journalists.

Torres, R., Miron, D., Louis, F. and Inda, J.X. (1999) *'Race', Identity and Citizenship.* Oxford: Blackwell.

Traynor, M. (1999) *Managerialism and Nursing.* London: Routledge.

Trench, B. (1991) 'In search of hope: coverage of the Northern conflict in the Dublin daily papers', in Rolston (1991a), *op. cit.*, pp. 136–51.

Trower, P., Bryant, B., Argyle, M. and Mazillier, J. (1978) *Social Skills and Mental Health.* London: Methuen.

Troyna, B. (1981) *Public Awareness and the Media.* London: Commission for Racial Equality.

Tuchman, G. (1978) *Making News: a Study in the Construction of Reality.* New York: Free Press.

Tudor Hart, J. (1971) 'The inverse care law', *The Lancet*, I: 405–12.

Turner, J.C. (1987) *Rediscovering the Social Group*. Oxford: Basil Blackwell.

Turner, J.C. (1987) 'A Self-Categorization Theory', in J.C. Turner, *op. cit.*, pp. 42–67

Turton, D. and Gonzalez, J. (1999) *Cultural Identities and Ethnic Minorities in Europe*. Bilbao: University of Deusto.

Turton, D. and Gonzalez, J. (2000) *Ethnic Diversity in Europe: Challenges to the Nation State*. Bilbao: University of Deusto.

UKCC (May: 2000) *Requirements for Pre-registration Nursing Programmes*. London: United Kingdom Central Council for Nursing, Midwifery and Health Visiting.

UKCC (September: 2000) *Requirements for Pre-Registration Midwifery*. London: United Kingdom Central Council for Nursing, Midwifery and Health Visiting.

Unesco (1974) *Race As News*. Paris: Unesco.

Unesco (1977) *Ethnicity and the Media*. Paris: Unesco.

Unesco (1986) *Mass Media and the Minorities*. Bangkok: Unesco.

United Nations (1993) *Draft Declaration on the Rights of Indigenous Peoples*. Working Group on Indigenous Populations. UNdoc E/CN.4/Sub.2/1993.29.

Valdivia, A. (2000) *A Latina in the Land of Hollywood and Other Essays on Media Culture*. Tucson, AR: University of Arizona Press.

Valentine, C. (1968) *Culture and Poverty*. Chicago: Chicago University Press.

Van den Berghe, P.L. (1981) *The Ethnic Phenomenon*. New York: Elsevier.

Van den Berghe, P.L. (1986) 'Ethnicity and the socio-biology debate', in J. Rex and D. Mason (eds), *Theories of 'Race' and Ethnic Relations*. Cambridge: Cambridge University Press.

van Dijk, T.A. (1991) *Racism and the Press*. London: Routledge.

van Dijk, T.A. (1993) *Elite Discourse and Racism*. Newbury Park: Sage.

van Dijk, T.A. and Smitherman-Donaldson, G. (eds) (1988) *Discourse and Discrimination*. Detroit, MI: Wayne State University Press.

Van Dyke, V. (1995) 'The individual, the state and ethnic communities in political theory', in W. Kymlicka (ed.), *The Rights of Minority Cultures*. Oxford: Oxford University Press.

Vilby, K. (1987) 'Media and refugees: The role the media could play in solving the problems of the refugees', in Council of Europe (1987) *The Law of Asylum and Refugees: Present Tendencies and Future Perspectives*. Proceedings of the Sixteenth Colloquy on European Law, Lund, 15–17 September 1986, Strasbourg. Council of Europe, Strasbourg: Publications Section.

Vincent, R., Nordenstreng, K. and Traber, M. (1999) *Towards Equity in Global Communication: MacBride Update*. Cresskill, N.J: Hampton Press.

Vulliamy, E. (1994) *Seasons in Hell: Understanding Bosnia's War*. London: Simon and Schuster.

Wacquant, L. (2000) *Les prisons de la misère*. Paris: Liber.

Wall, M. (1997a) 'The Rwanda crisis: an analysis of news magazine coverage', *Gazette*, 59 (2): 121–34.

Wall, M. (1997b) 'A "pernicious new strain of the old Nazi virus" and an "orgy of tribal slaughter": a comparison of US news magazine coverage of the crises in Bosnia and Rwanda', *Gazette*, 59 (6) 411–28.

Wallman, S. (1986) 'Ethnicity and the boundary process in context', in J. Rex and D. Mason (eds), *Theories of 'Race' and Ethnic Relations*. Cambridge: Cambridge University Press.

Walsh, M. (1992) *Opus Dei: An Investigation into the Secret Society Struggling for Power Within the Roman Catholic Church*. New York: HarperCollins.

Walvin, J. (1971) *The Black Presence*. London: Orback and Chambers.

Walzer, M. (1997) *On Toleration*. New Haven, CT: Yale University Press.

Watkins, C. (1998) *Representing: Hip Hop Culture and the Production of Black Cinema*. Chicago: University of Chicago Press.

Waxler-Morrison, N., Anderson, J. and Richardson, E. (1990) *Cross Cultural Caring*. Vancouver: KBC.

Webb, J. and Enstice, A. (1998) *Aliens and Savages: Fiction, Politics and Prejudice in Australia*. Sydney: HarperCollins.

Weh, L. (1987) 'Recent tendencies in the evolution of national law and practice in the field of asylum and refugees', in Council of Europe (1987) *The Law of Asylum and Refugees: Present*

Tendencies and Future Perspectives. Proceedings of the Sixteenth Colloquy on European Law, Lund, 15–17 September 1986, Strasbourg. Council of Europe, Strasbourg: Publications Section.

Weimer, M. (1996) *Japan, 'Race' and Identity.* London: Routledge.

Werbner, P. (2002) *Imagined Diasporas Among Manchester Muslims.* Oxford: James Currey.

Werbner, P. and Modood, T. (1997) *Debating Cultural Hybridity.* London: Zed.

Westdeutcher Rundfuk (1999) *Cultural Diversity – Against Racism.* Koln: Westdeutcher Rundfuk.

Weston, M.A. (1996) *Native Americans in the News. Images of Indians in the Twentieth Century Press.* Westpoint, CT: Greenwood Press.

Wetherell, M. and Potter, J. (1992) *Mapping the Language of Racism,* New York: Harvester/ Wheatsheaf.

Whine, M. (1997). 'The Far Right on the Internet', in B.D. Loader (ed.), *The Governance of Cyberspace.* New York: Routledge. pp. 209–27.

Williams, A. (1998) 'Conservative media activism: the Free Congress Foundation and National Empowerment Television', in L. Kintz and J. Lesage (eds), *Media, Culture and the Religious Right.* Minneapolis: University of Minnesota Press. pp. 275–94.

Williams, J. (1985) 'Redefining institutional racism', *Ethnic and Racial Studies,* 8 (3): 323–48.

Williams, M.S. (2000) 'The uneasy alliance of group representation and deliberative democracy', in W. Kymlicka and W. Norman, *op. cit.* pp. 123–54.

Williams, R. (1977) *Marxism and Literature.* New York: Oxford University Press.

Wilmer, F. (1993) *The Indigenous Voice in World Politics.* Newbury Park: Sage.

Winant, H. (1994) *Racial Conditions.* Minneapolis: University of Minnesota Press.

Winterton, G. (1986) *Monarchy to Republic.* Oxford: Oxford University Press.

Wodak, R. and Matouschek, B. (1993) ' "We are dealing with people whose origins one can clearly tell just by looking": critical discourse analysis and the study of neo-racism in contemporary Austria', *Discourse and Society,* 4 (2): 225–48.

Wrench, J. and Solomos, J. (1993) *Racism and Migration in Western Europe.* Oxford: Berg.

Wright, P. (1985) *On Living in an Old Country.* London: Verso.

Young, I.M. (1989) 'Polity and group difference: a critique of the ideal of universal citizenship', *Ethics Vol.* 99 (2) pp. 250–274.

Young, I.M. (1997) *Intersecting Voices.* Princeton NJ: Princeton University Press.

Young, L. (1996) *Fear of the Dark: 'Race', Gender and Sexuality in the Cinema.* London: Routledge.

Young, R. (1990) *White Mythologies: Writing, History and the West.* London: Routledge.

Young, R.J. (1995) *Colonial Desire: Hybridity in Theory, Culture and Race.* London: Routledge.

Young, R.J.C. (1996) *Colonial Desire: Hybridity in Theory, Culture and 'Race'.* London: Routledge.

Young-Bruehl, E. (1996) *The Anatomy of Prejudices.* Cambridge: Harvard University Press.

Zickmund, S. (1997) 'Approaching the radical other: the discursive culture of cyberhate', in S.G. Jones (ed.), *Virtual Culture: Identity and Communication in Cybersociety.* London: Sage. pp. 185–205.

Zook, K.B. (1999) *Color By Fox: the Fox Network and the Revolution in Black Television.* New York: Oxford University Press.

Zuberi, N. (2001) *Sounds English: Transnational Popular Music.* Urbana, IL: University of Illinois Press.

Index

Alam, Yunis viii, 159 n.1
Allport, Gordon, on social psychology
of prejudice 9–10
Alternative media 68–70
Appadurai, Arjun 56–57
Audiences and media users 51–55, 68–70, 164

Barthes, Roland 39–40
Barzun, Jacques 3–4
Burkitt, Ian 175, 176

Children Now 172, 173, 174 n.3; *see also*
Media advocacy groups
'Civil society' concept, critiqued 65–66
Codes of practice *see* Communities of
Practice; Professional media codes
Communities of practice 175–179; *see also*
Professional media codes
Content analysis method, critiqued 27–29
Cultural markers 88–89, 116–118
Nationality 96–98
'Race,' ethnicity, and comparable
markers 86–88, 117–118
Religion 89–91, 98–99, 106–107
Tribe 86, 105, 109–112
See also Eriksen; Stereotypes
Culture ministry, US unusual in not
having 161
Cunningham and Sinclair, 'sphericules'
16, 19, 57, 123, 211, 216–217
Cybercommunity concept, critiqued 67

Dallaire, Roméo, UN general during
Rwandan genocide 111–112, 115
Diaspora 55–57
Concept critiqued 18–20
Difference, concept 1–4, ch. 9 *passim*
Differentiated citizenship 127, 128, 143,
ch. 9 *passim*
Discourse analysis, method 43–45
Discursive de-racialization 7–8, 76–77
Discursive and practical
consciousness 175–176
'Diversity' policies 164–170, 178–179,
183–184, 194–202
Durkheim, Émile 41–42

Elliott, Philip 49
Eriksen, T.H., ethnicity as relational and
processual 15–17
Essentialism 21–22
Ethnicity
Concept, critiqued 12–22
Hybridity 18–19
Infrastructural dimensions 19–20
Extreme Right 60–85
Definitions 60–63
Extreme Right and mainstream Right
61, 62, 72–74
Links to law enforcement bodies 79–82
and 'neo-populist' movements 74–79

Framing concept, critiqued 36–37
Free speech and hate speech 70–71
Front National, France 61, 69–70, 73

Genocide 87–88, 96–97, 101, 105–106,
109–116, 122, 124, 129
Globalization concept, critiqued 67–68
Gray, Herman 43, 46–47

Hall, Stuart 40, 42–43
Hegemony concept, critiqued 38–41
Hollywood TV industry 160–174
Hollywood professional Guilds 166,
171, 172, 173

Identity and inter-group dynamics 1–2,
12–19, ch. 4 *passim*
Ideology concept, critiqued 38–41
Image concept, critiqued 29–32
Immigration ix–x
British media definition 7, 8, 44, 54
'Economic' migrants and 'political'
refugees 26
French politics of 77–78
Policies 72–73, 75, 79
US media coverage 81
IMRAX (International Federation of
Journalists) 147, 184
Indigeneity
Aboriginal Australians 129–133, 137–139
And media representation 133–139

Indigeneity *cont.*
  And media political economy 139–142
  Central Australian Aboriginal Media
    Assn. 141
  Distinctiveness within ethnicity
    debates 122–123
  International law, the State, and
    indigeneity 123–128
  Native Americans 136–137
  Pauline Hanson and One Nation
    party 132
  Sámi peoples in Nordic nations 130,
    136, 137, 142
  Self-determination issues 123–128
  See also Whiteness, studies of/Australia
Iordanova, Dina, on Balkans in the global
  imaginary 100, 105

Jeffery, Brooke, on contemporary slide
  to the political right 74
Johnstone, Diana, on Bosnia and Kosovo
  105–106, 121 n. 18 and n. 19

Keane, John, on public sphere concept
  203, 208, 212–213
Kingsley, Charles, on Ireland 3
Kymlicka, Will, on multinational and
  polyethnic states 205–207, 214

Markelin, Lia, on Sami media 136, 140–141,
  142, 143 n.1
Mass media 7–12, ch. 2 and *passim*
  Minority-ethnic media 16, 19, 55–57
  Monitoring by media organizations
    145–153
  Monitoring as a political intervention
    154–158, 168–169
  See also Children Now; IMRAX; media
    advocacy groups; On Line/More
    Colour in the Media; Vienna
    Monitoring Centre
Massing, Paul, on long genesis of the
  Nazi Holocaust 87–88
Media advocacy groups 147, 154–158,
  160–174
  Brown-out tactics 168
  Divisions among U.S. Latino
    organizations 167–168
  Four US TV networks' initiatives
    compared 169–170
  Limitations and potential for change
    151–158, 161–162, 170, 173, 183–184
  Multi-Ethnic Coalition 169, 170, 172, 173
  Timeline of activities in Hollywood
    1992–2002 170–173
  See also Mass media/Media monitoring

Media monitoring *see* Mass media
Multiculturalism 1–2, 194–202

NAACP (National Association for
  the Advancement of Colored
  People), USA 160, 167, 169,
  170, 172, 173
  Hollywood Chapter as maverick
    170–171
National Council of La Raza (NCLR),
  USA 167, 171
'Nationalities' *see* Yugoslavia
Northern Ireland civil war 88–95
  Media roles in 91–95
    Within Northern Ireland 92, 93
    Internationally 92–95
  See also Cultural markers/religion

On Line/More Colour in the Media 184
Organizational dimensions of media
  production 162–164, 176–179

Panov, Mitko, documentary on Yugoslav
  civil war 119, n.12
Pogrom, ongoing low-intensity 60, 79–82,
  chs 3–4 *passim*
Political economy and media
  production 49–51, 139–142,
  162–164, 176–179
Postmodernist perspective 28–29
Practicalities of pursuing media change
  from within 160–161, 173–174,
  179–184; *see also* Responsible
  media practice
Professional media codes, critiqued
  146–153
  Objectivity notion, critiqued 154
  Potential as vehicles for constructive
    change 153
  Professional nursing codes,
    comparison 175–179
Public sphere concept, critiqued 66–67
  Multi-ethnic public sphere
    202–205, 207–218

'Race', concept 1–12
  Postmodernist analysis of 'race' 20–21
  'Race awareness training', Britain 180
  'Racialization' 4–6
  See also discourse; racism
Racism, Concept
  Culturalist versions 6–8
  Defined as psychological prejudice,
    critique 9–12
Racism, importance of psychological
  dimension

Racism, Concept *cont.*
   Institutional 10–12, 150–151, 178
   and social class 89
   and gender 89
Ramírez-Berg, Charles 28, 34
Red River and John Wayne 47
Representation, concept critiqued 41–43
   Quantitative vs qualitative criteria
      164–165, 169, 173
Research on media and 'race'
   Action research, various discussions
      chs. 6–8
   Ethical and political criteria x–xi, 10–12
   Methodological complexity
      ch.1 *passim*; 34–35
   Sociological context ix–x
Return of Navajo Boy 48
Representation, concept critiqued 41–43
Responsible media practice, competence in
   Cultural communicative 188–190
   Intercultural communicative 185–188
   Intercultural media 190–192
   'Pipeline' role of colleges and
      universities 165–166
Rwandan genocide 86, 105, 109–116
   Domestic media roles in 112–114
   International media roles in 114–116
   Problematic use of 'moderate Hutu'
      terminology 121, n.27
   US-French rivalries in neighboring
      Congo 110, 116
   See also Cultural markers

Said, Edward 44–45
State policies on media, 'race'
   and 'ethnicity'
   Constructive options ch. 9 *passim*
   Destructive practices chs 3–4 *passim*
Stekler, Paul, documentary on
      George Wallace and the rightward
      drift of US politics since the
      1970s 84 n.29

Stereotypes 32–36, 88, 90–91, 105–106,
   112–115; *see also* Cultural markers
Symptomatic reading methodology,
   critiqued 28–29
Systems approach to countering media
   racism 179–182
   Review phase 182–183

Taylor, Charles, the 'politics of
   difference' 199
Text, concept critiqued 45–48
Thompson, John, on media in Yugoslav
   crises 100–103, 118
Tolerance, critiqued 197–200
'Tribes' *see* Rwanda

Van Dijk, Teun A. 43–44
Vienna Monitoring Center on Racism
   and Xenophobia 147

Wall, Melissa 105, 115
Wallman, Sandra 16–18
Watkins, S. Craig 28, 35
Whiteness, studies of 32–33
   In Australia 129–133

Yugoslavia, former, civil war in 95–109
   Genocide claims about 96–97,
      101, 105–106
   'Nationalities' in 96–100
   Religious and language factors
      in 97–99
   Roles of media 100–109
      In Bosnia-Hercegovina 103–104
      In Croatia 102–103
      Internationally 105–109
      In Kosovo crisis, Serb civilians
         bombed 107–109
      Serbia 100–102, 104
   See also Cultural markers/nationality

Zuberi, Nabeel 57